Joyce's Kaleidoscope

JOYCE'S KALEIDOSCOPE

An Invitation to *Finnegans Wake*

Philip Kitcher

OXFORD
UNIVERSITY PRESS
2007

OXFORD
UNIVERSITY PRESS

Oxford University Press, Inc., publishes works that further
Oxford University's objective of excellence
in research, scholarship, and education.

Oxford New York
Auckland Cape Town Dar es Salaam Hong Kong Karachi
Kuala Lumpur Madrid Melbourne Mexico City Nairobi
New Delhi Shanghai Taipei Toronto

With offices in
Argentina Austria Brazil Chile Czech Republic France Greece
Guatemala Hungary Italy Japan Poland Portugal Singapore
South Korea Switzerland Thailand Turkey Ukraine Vietnam

Published by Oxford University Press, Inc.
198 Madison Avenue, New York, New York 10016

www.oup.com

Oxford is a registered trademark of Oxford University Press

Library of Congress Cataloging-in-Publication Data
Kitcher, Philip, 1947–
Joyce's kaleidoscope : an invitation to Finnegans wake / Philip Kitcher.
p. cm.
Includes index.
ISBN 13: 978-0-19-532103-6
1. Joyce, James, 1882–1941. Finnegans wake. I. Title.
PR6019.O9F593555 2007
823'.912—dc22 2006031551

To Christ's Hospital
with gratitude for the opportunities it offered
to me and to countless others.

May they prosper who love it.

Thou hast nor youth, nor age,
But as it were an after-dinner's sleep
Dreaming on both . . .

ACKNOWLEDGMENTS

I am extremely grateful to five generous friends who read an earlier draft and who provided me with excellent advice: the suggestions of Regenia Gagnier, Dick Kuhns, Cynthia Rettig, Bruce Robbins, and Jim Shapiro have led to many improvements (and it was helpful that these sensitive readers often recommended the same things). Two thoughtful anonymous readers responded with a firm sense of what I was trying to do and, rather than trying to persuade me to write a different book, made constructive proposals for improving the one I had envisaged; I appreciate both their good advice and their patience with someone outside the academic Joycean community who wanted to attempt a different approach to *Finnegans Wake*. My editor at Oxford University Press, Shannon McLachlan, has been extremely supportive and has offered excellent counsel both on general issues and on points of detail. I would also like to thank Christina Gibson of Oxford University Press for helping with many facets of the book's production, and Keith Faivre for his exceptional care in overseeing the final editing and printing.

David Albert was in at the beginning, as we started to read *Finnegans Wake* together. His keen intellect and his abundant generosity have been expressed in numerous conversations, from which I have learned enormously. His responses to my ideas, both in inchoate form and in drafts of this book, have greatly improved the final version.

I have also been extraordinarily lucky to have, as colleague and friend at Columbia, Michael Seidel. Michael has offered support, encouragement, and his own expertise as a leading Joyce scholar. In his unfailingly constructive comments on my drafts, he has led me to see some large matters in a new light and has guided me on any number of smaller issues. Without his help, this book might well not have existed, and it certainly would be far more flawed than it is.

It is a joy to record my thanks and appreciation and to reflect that I have benefited so much from people who exemplify the Joycean virtues.

CONTENTS

A NOTE ON CITATIONS

I give references to the *Wake* by page and line (hence "331: 15" refers to page 331 line 15). *Almost* all editions have a common pagination and layout, and I have used the standard, and widely available, Viking/Penguin. Giving line numbers is intended to help readers locate the passages I quote, and, in cases where I refer without quoting, it seems indispensable. Occasionally, there are small disagreements between the Penguin edition (edited by John Bishop, 1999) and the Viking edition (ninth printing, 1960); the Viking edition agrees with the Faber and Faber edition (third edition, 1964). Where there are discrepancies, I have preferred the Viking (Faber) versions, partly because these editions "embody all author's corrections" and because they clarify the structure and sense of the relevant passages.

References to *Ulysses* are to the Viking/Penguin edition. Some other editions (notably the Modern Library) have a slightly different pagination (generally with somewhat lower numbers). In the case of *Portrait of the Artist as a Young Man* and *Dubliners*, I have also used the Viking/Penguin editions.

In referring to the divisions of the *Wake*, I cite Part and Chapter (thus "II-3" refers to Chapter 3 of Part II). Some contemporary Joyce scholars prefer to regard the *Wake* as divided into *episodes* rather than *chapters*. I have opted for an older usage, in part because I do not see that the concept of chapters entails any conception of the *Wake* as a "conventional novel" (which it most evidently is not!), and in part because I sometimes want to talk about episodes *within* a chapter. It is very hard to think of I-3, I-4, III-4, or IV as single episodes.

Extracts from *Finnegans Wake* are reproduced with the permission of the estate. © Copyright the Estate of James Joyce. My sincere thanks also to Shannon McLachlan and Christina Gibson for their hard work in overseeing my request for permission, and to several generous Joyce scholars who gave their time to support that request.

Because the music of Joyce's prose is so important to *Finnegans Wake*, I prepared a recording of selected passages to serve as further elaboration and defense of the interpretation I offer in the present book, hoping that this recording could accompany the printed text. Unfortunately, permission to distribute the recording in this way has not been granted.

AWAKENING

I probably acquired my first copy of *Finnegans Wake* because those who gave it to me counted on its famous obscurity. In 1965, I was to be awarded a school prize. Prizes were always books, and I was asked to draw up a list. I included *Ulysses* among my choices.

Several years before, I had discovered James Joyce, first through reading *A Portrait of the Artist as a Young Man*. Eager to read more by this extraordinary writer, I had been disappointed that the corpus was so small. *Dubliners*, Joyce's collection of stories, struck my schoolboy taste as less remarkable than *Portrait*, an understandable adolescent judgment that adulthood would reverse. From my teachers, and from older schoolboys, I had learned that there was another novel, a masterpiece, notoriously difficult and, equally notoriously, obscene, all characteristics bound to appeal to an ambitious teenager. The school library contained a copy, and I began to read it.

My informants had it two-thirds right, I thought, not obscene but challenging, and, above all, a masterpiece. During my mid-teens I read it twice, slowly, missing an enormous amount but also recognizing how much was there to be missed. So I asked for *Ulysses* as a prize.

Shortly after submitting my list I was informed that this selection was not acceptable and that I should propose something else. The response puzzled me. Worries about the obscenity of *Ulysses* seemed quaint residues of old prejudices, quite incompatible with the conversations I had had with my teachers about the book or with the approach to literature I had absorbed from them; and, after all, it was in the *school library*, available for even thirteen-year-olds to pull from the shelf. Today I am less puzzled. I envisage the committee of masters who supervised prizes anticipating the arrival of some of the school's governors at the ceremony, gentlemen florid of face and portly of build; I imagine the masters prefiguring the outrage expressed in a wagging finger—"Some boy, some boy, has asked for, has been allowed to choose, this, this *filth!*"—and even worrying about a possible apoplectic event.

My perplexity was beside the point; I had to make a substitution. Choosing a different author seemed incompatible with my reverence for Joyce, but I already owned paperback copies of *Dubliners* and *Portrait*. I knew, however, that there was a last Joycean novel, one even more famously difficult than *Ulysses*, one from which I had looked at short extracts (which I optimistically thought might prove more comprehensible in context). My amended list asked for *Finnegans Wake*.

It was approved without demur. Perhaps nobody on the committee knew that the bawdy count of the *Wake* is an order of magnitude higher than that of *Ulysses*. Or perhaps everyone assumed that none of the potentially apoplectic governors would know that. Or maybe they judged that any boy seeking titillation would have paid for it dearly if he ransacked the *Wake* for dirty bits. In any event, I marched off the dais with a copy, inscribed to me as a prize for Debating.

At the Christmas holidays in 1965, I started to read it. Whether my pace was fast or slow, it made no difference—I felt lost in the bush; not a single solitary syllable made sense. I persevered, reminding myself that, three years before, a concentrated reading had opened up for me the apparently inexhaustible riches of *Ulysses*. Surely there must be treasures here too, treasures deposited by Joyce over the seventeen-year period he devoted to his last work, and I should study patience (appreciating that the only thing is patience). I staggered on until page 40, or thereabouts, before deciding against further hours of sitting in blank incomprehension. I vowed that I would return, perhaps after reading some of the critical discussions of the book.

During my undergraduate years I kept my vow—twice. These readings took me further into the *Wake* and occasionally offered a good joke. The prevalent sense, however, was always of confusion and puzzlement that the brilliance I so admired in Joyce's other prose works was hidden from me. Eventually, frustration led me to stop and to turn to some more rewarding book. The guides I consulted had enabled me to pick out something resembling "characters" and "plot," but my interpretative ability seemed limited by what they explicitly explained, and, to compound my disappointment with them, the reconstructions they offered impressed me as scattered and trivial. Joyce's great secrets seemed no more disclosed to the commentators than they were to me.

In my late thirties I made one last attempt, plunging onward, despite incomprehension, almost to page 400. I stopped because I realized that my goal had gradually shifted—instead of reading to understand, I was trying to force my way through to the end—and that it was silly to treat the *Wake*, or any book, as a challenge to *Sitzfleisch*. My copy went back to the shelf, and, as my eyes passed over the books, I would sometimes feel its reproach, its sad reminder that I would never read the final work of the author whose penultimate book I had come to regard as the greatest novel in our language.

So it would have been but for a chance conversation. In the spring of 2000, as I left my office at Columbia to attend a showing of a film version of the final volume (*Le Temps Retrouvé*) of Proust's masterpiece, I encountered my friend and colleague, David Albert, who asked me where I was rushing off to. The conversation revealed our common love of Proust, and I proposed that we might read the huge novel together. David rejected the idea and proposed

Finnegans Wake instead. It quickly transpired that our experiences were similar, that each of us had found Joyce early, that each had read and reread *Ulysses,* and that both of us had undertaken several expeditions against *Finnegans Wake* and had been turned back.

By the fall of 2000, the *Finnegans Wake* support group of the Columbia Philosophy Department had expanded to a membership of five. We would meet on alternate Tuesday evenings in my apartment, armed with secondary volumes galore, assigning ourselves the book in thirty-page installments. Combining our individual reactions, reading to one another, and lubricating the sessions with glasses of John Jameson and Son's finest whiskey, we began to find the *Wake* a delight rather than a chore. At the Christmas recess, we had moved into Part II, and, although there were plenty of pages that still lay in shadow, we had found enough light to keep us going.

Yet I was still dissatisfied. How could a work of fiction, *any* work of fiction, justify such enormous effort merely to penetrate it? Why did we need all these volumes, this pooling of pieces of relatively arcane learning? The music and magic of individual passages in the *Wake* were now apparent to us, and, drawing on the experiences of our reading aloud to one another, I had begun to experiment with ways of reading out loud, as if I were trying out different approaches to a song. My discontent lay in recognizing that the individual notes, the vocal phrases, were not integrated into any whole: I could not see how these snatches of melody contributed to a broader music. Beyond that recognition lay another, the appreciation that the guides we read were not helping, that, at best, they taught me to burnish a single tone, not to produce, or hear, a longer line, an aria, an opera.

In January 2001, I left New York for a conference in Arizona. Although it was not really in the spirit of our cooperative enterprise, I had been reading ahead in the *Wake,* and I decided to take my copy with me. Carry-on luggage couldn't accommodate the piles of secondary works that routinely surrounded me as I read the Great Text, so Joyce and I were again alone together.

The cabin of an airplane doesn't present itself as an ideal place for reading *Finnegans Wake,* but, for the first time, on the long trip to Tucson, I felt I was *reading* the *Wake,* that individual notes were composing into broader patterns, that I could hear a larger fragment of the whole music. Next day, as I sat in the Arizona sunshine, the impression was deepened: I could read the pages at the same pace, a slow pace to be sure, that I had once brought to my first reading of *Ulysses,* and, like my fifteen-year-old self, I was appreciating what I recognized was a tiny part of what was there. By the time the return journey was over, I had read to the end, not with frustration, not with determination and gritted teeth, but with enormous pleasure.

That pleasure increased as I went round and round, again and again. Under the pressure of professional demands, our reading group collapsed (as such enterprises tend to do when busy people are involved), but David and I continued to talk together. For us, the instigators, the group succeeded, and we achieved our official goal of reading *Finnegans Wake*. Along the way, though, that goal had become almost irrelevant in the great joy of discovering in Joyce's last novel even greater riches than those we had long admired in his earlier work.

As I read and reread, finding ever more in each chapter and on each page, a project began to define itself. I proposed to David that we each try to write essays about our perspectives on the *Wake*—and it was clear from our conversations that there would be interesting kinship and interesting differences between them—and that, if these essays turned out well, we could juxtapose them in a short volume. During the course of my graduate education, I had discovered Stanley Cavell's pioneering essay on *King Lear* and been inspired by it. The *Wake*, once obscure but now endlessly fascinating, seemed to call for just that kind of philosophical writing. Moreover, in the interim, other philosophers had recognized the possibilities Cavell had so brilliantly discerned: Alexander Nehamas, Martha Nussbaum, and Robert Pippin had written insightfully about a variety of authors—Thomas Mann, Henry James, Proust, Dickens, and even Joyce (although about *Ulysses*, not the *Wake*).

For any philosopher who ventures into new territory, however, there are always proper doubts: Do I have any real expertise? Often the right response to those doubts is to learn the things the practitioners know, to steep oneself in evolutionary biology, or cognitive science, or musicology, or international law. On other occasions, however, it's appropriate to function as an outsider, to try to bring a perspective different from those already available. I had read (and I knew that David had read) a significant sample of work about Joyce and about *Finnegans Wake*, and I knew that if I (or we) had anything to contribute, it would not be by refining the ideas of those who explore matters of individual detail: I could not contribute to standard Joycean scholarship or to the discussions scholars trained in literature would naturally provide, but could only bring some philosophical skills of close analysis and a different range of reading. Perhaps this different background might enable me to find, and to expose, broad structures, themes, and issues in the *Wake*.

So I silenced my doubts. David and I agreed that we should give it a try. In the summer of 2004, I sat down to write a longish essay . . .

Joyce began work on *Finnegans Wake* in 1922, the year that Shakespeare & Company published *Ulysses*, and the book finally appeared on his birthday, February 2, in 1939. During the intervening years, parts of the text were published as "Work in Progress"—the eventual title being a closely guarded secret, finally guessed by one of his close friends. *Ulysses* had made him a celebrity, but even those who had long appreciated his genius were disconcerted by the new work. Some of his friends rallied to its defense, publishing a symposium on "Work in Progress," and Joyce wrote lengthy letters identifying some of the sources of his elaborate allusions. For all that, *Finnegans Wake* has never attracted the large number of readers who take on the "difficulties" of *Ulysses,* and even the plaudits publicly offered on its behalf invite the charge that they are vague puffery. (The back of my Penguin copy contains an extract from Harold Bloom's *The Western Canon* declaring the *Wake* to be "Joyce's masterpiece," and suggesting that "If aesthetic merit were ever again to center the canon, *Finnegans Wake* would be as close as our chaos could come to the heights of Shakespeare and Dante"; strong words, but, as he half admits, Bloom's full discussion, principally focused on Joyce's witty engagement with Shakespeare, does little to explain why they are warranted.)

There is a prevalent sense, shared by those too intimidated to try to read it, those who have tried and failed, and most of those who write about it, that *Finnegans Wake* can only be read by deciphering the new language Joyce devised for it from the word—or even syllable—up, and that Joyce's letters, or the dictionaries and sources he consulted, collectively add up to a Rosetta Stone, diligent attention to which will eventually reveal the significance of the whole. The composition of the *Wake* is often perceived as a process in which the author deliberately compressed his text and disguised his meaning—it is easy to cite the increasing density of the drafts or to rehearse the famous anecdotes in which Joyce asks his most devoted admirers whether it is obscure enough yet. Viewed in that light, the book is an enormous riddle, a colossal puzzle that challenges the ingenuity of those who would "solve" it, and it is hardly surprising that many people decide not to devote the vast amount of time it demands, that others give up in frustration, and that those who have unriddled a small portion delight in displaying what they have accomplished.

My awakening, and my interest in writing about the *Wake,* begins with the conviction that this is all wrong, that it is hopeless to build up, piece by piece, and to try to find some significant larger whole. As the Caterpillar once told Alice, you can't ask for directions until you know where you want to go; nor can you interrogate the myriad possibilities Joyce's neologisms allow unless you have some guiding sense of what the point of writing in this way might be. To reduce a great author to a compositor of puzzles, however individually witty, is to invite the charge that this is the work of a show-off, of someone who wants to baffle readers for as long as they are willing to take the pun-ishment. But there is an alternative: to start with a view of the predicament this novel addresses and with a tentative explanation of why the linguistic novelties are needed.

How is any entering reader to find an appropriate perspective? As I'll suggest in the first chapter, reading the *Wake* by starting at the end and taking the chapters in reverse order provides helpful clues. For the moment, however, I want to motivate my own perspective in a different way, by understanding this last novel as continuous with its predecessors. I begin with a banality: in his fiction after *Dubliners* (and even there in its closing story), Joyce's focus was always on himself, on his role as writer and as family man, and on his struggles with his religion and his native country. *Portrait* reveals his protagonist's youthful quest for an identity, a vocation, recording the struggle to answer the ancient question "How to live?" when the life is in prospect. *Ulysses* returns to the same question at two later stages, at a time when decisions have been made but when the "straight way" seems to have been lost.[1] Both of Joyce's main surrogates, Stephen Dedalus the aspiring artist and Leopold Bloom the paterfamilias and outsider, are wanderers, men of different ages whose lives have gone astray and who need to reopen the question of their chosen direction. *Finnegans Wake*, I suggest, returns to the same issue, the question of evaluating a life, from the perspective of age. It is no longer a matter of deciding what to do, for the doing is done, but of coming to terms with what has been, of hoping to vindicate the long years that are now running out.

Portrait is a young man's book, one that can stir countless adolescent readers who feel the uncertainties of the lives they imagine for themselves. Although I first read it as an adolescent, *Ulysses* is a book for the middle years, one whose full impact depends on a sense of reversals and on understanding the loss of direction: the particular problems Bloom faces can be appreciated by those who do not share them—it is not necessary to have lost a son or to belong to a marginalized race. Similarly with the *Wake*. It is, I suggest, a book that speaks forcefully to those at the age of its author, those in late middle age, those who must recognize that the contours of their lives have been well defined and who wonder how those lives will end and whether they will have amounted to anything. The specific shocks and lapses suffered by the protagonists in the *Wake*'s swirl of stories are as contingent as Stephen's struggles with Catholicism or Bloom's encounters with anti-Semitism. The theme that grips is a question that arises for people of a certain age—but, as I hope to show, Joyce's deep response to that question has import for others, for a much broader range of men and women.

Famously, the *Wake* is a dream book, and that is no accident. For when there is no real chance of steering your life in a new direction, the question "How to live?" carries the threat that the trajectory you have pursued has been all wrong—and that threat is hard to face directly. *Ulysses* takes its readers deep into the thoughts of Stephen, Molly, and, above all, Bloom, but there are moments where consciousness has to reorient its gaze, most prominently when Bloom refuses to think about Boylan's assignation with Molly. As the end of life approaches, there is a pressure both to make sense of it, with luck to reassure yourself that it has been worthwhile, and to back away from the faults, the flaws, the unfulfilled aspirations, the weaknesses, the lapses, and the reversals. How can the accounting be done if the contemplation of some of the entries is unbearable? Joyce offers an answer: dream work.

The line of interpretation I've just sketched is extremely crude and simple, reducing intricate novels to struggles with a single philosophical question (albeit the oldest and most central issue of philosophy). I offer it only as *one* way of addressing the problem I posed earlier, the problem of discovering a general perspective from which to approach the *Wake*. In the chapters that follow, I'll elaborate that perspective in much more detail, with the aim of showing how it can illuminate the novel. I shall try to show how it is the continuation, and the most profound conclusion, of Joyce's lifelong interrogation of himself and his life, his *Portrait of the Artist as an Aging Man*.

Before beginning my reading in earnest, there are further aspects of my approach I want to make explicit, since they may prove helpful by way of orientation. Joyce was a musician, whose life had always been pervaded by song, and the music of the *Wake* offers a way into the text. A well-known ballad gave him his title, and fragments of song, the old songs sung in the parlor and the pub, appear in every chapter. Far more important, however, are the musical resonances of the neologisms. Reading the book *with* others, as I eventually did, involves reading the book *to* others, translating the letters into sound, and, if all goes well, allowing the text to sing. To hear a recording of Joyce's own reading (and there is a famous, easily available recording of the very last pages of Part I) is to hear a musician making music.

The last story of *Dubliners*, "The Dead," opens with a long scene at the Morkans' annual epiphany party, a party at which the guests make music, at which the old songs are sung around the household piano. That activity of music-making, centered on the familiar songs to which the *Wake* alludes, again and again, was a large part of the culture Joyce knew (and the culture of my own youth, my generation probably being the last to enjoy it)—virtually everyone would join in. Considered as a musical work, a gigantic songbook, the *Wake* issues the same invitation. Joyce may have a fine voice, one that lilts beautifully over affecting cadences—although his tongue does occasionally trip—but he should inspire us to sing with him and not merely to listen admiringly. Readers of the *Wake* can join in, even if they feel like party guests who don't know all the words and are sometimes hazy about where the tune goes.

For the sounding out of this new language almost invariably conveys a mood, an emotional tone, out of which more precise understanding can grow. Just as the amateur singer may be unaware of the clever progression the composer has deployed, while appreciating the effect that progression produces, so, too, the reciter of the *Wake* can be entirely oblivious of the intricate welding of Albanian and Tagalog in a portmanteau word but still catch the resonance. Sound provides clues for interrogating sense.

There is yet another facet of Joyce's musicianship in the *Wake*, one that has guided the reading strategy I shall pursue. Traditional commentary emphasizes a debt to Vico in the structure of the novel: Joyce drew on Vico's conception of history as cyclic and as divided into ages in which similar patterns unfold. Yet those inclined to turn to Vico for Deep Clues about The Structure of the *Wake* will be disappointed—Joyce was a casual borrower, a magpie. Far more useful, I think, is the *musical* structure of the book, evident in the different musical languages employed in different chapters (Joyce doesn't develop a single "new language" but makes the individual chapters of his last work as stylistically distinct as those of *Ulysses*) and in what I see as the most fundamental division of his material.

Effectively, the opening chapter is an orchestral prelude, an introduction, or an overture. Major themes are sounded but not developed. The second chapter begins a far more elaborate presentation of those themes that will run through the rest of Part I (approximately two hundred pages). Finally, we are given their development on an even larger scale, a huge symphony that occupies the last four hundred pages of the book. Its ending leads back to the beginning, and, if we choose, we can return to the overture, to Part I, hearing it now as a coda, a distillation of the sonic complexities of Parts II–IV.[2]

At all three levels, there is the same affective movement, an initial descent and confrontation with the flaws and blots on a life, an increasing sense of failure and worthlessness as the imperfections and contradictions are recognized, and then an understanding of the possibilities of tolerance, acceptance, and forgiveness. An aging man, a dreamer, reflects on what has been, anxious about the course his life has taken. Out of those reflections swirl doubts, captured in dream stories that initially offer veils and protections only to snatch them away. Doubt deepens into despair and defeat; all the possibilities for a valuable identity seem to have been tried. Yet, in probing the mundane, even squalid, details of an apparently botched and inconsequential existence, Joyce's dreamer, and his readers, can develop a new complex of attitudes toward the assessment of lives, one that understands their value in terms of ordinary, partial achievements, and that celebrates specifically Joycean virtues: kindness, generosity, patience, tolerance, forgiveness.

Finnegans Wake, as I read it and hear it, is a great symphonic presentation. Its exuberant comedy prefigures a final acceptance of ourselves and our lives, a rejection of exalted, transcendent measures, and a delight in the ordinary. The delight, however, is hard won, and so, too, are the Joycean virtues. The dreamer cannot simply turn away from the blots and blemishes, in the way that Bloom closes his mind to particular thoughts. Instead, this examination must be thorough, the failures must be faced, and forgiveness, when it comes, must be charged with a full recognition of what is to be accepted. So the chapters return, again and again, to the same worries, seeking reassurance that the vindication achieved earlier did not come too easily.

My bald, undefended assertions are intended to prepare the way for readers of different types, those intimidated by the *Wake*, those who have struggled with it, and those who already know it and love it—for, perhaps with misguided ambition, I hope to offer something for all of these. I have tried to write a book for would-be readers who, like me on my earlier attempts, begin and give up in confusion; but I also want to offer a systematic view of this extraordinary novel, one that will make manifest themes that those who delight in it have implicitly felt. My attempt to write for disparate audiences informs the organization of my discussion.

I start with four chapters intended to *show* more fully the perspective I've bluntly outlined here. Working back from the end of the *Wake*, I offer impressionistic studies of passages I take to be crucial. Quoting freely, I try to provide a surround within which Joyce's words can be read—and heard—not with any intention to exhaust their significance but to convey tone and mood. Newcomers to the *Wake* will probably feel that many of the Joycean neologisms remain puzzling, but I hope they will hear the music beyond the strange rhythms and harmonies (or, to switch artistic medium, see the impressionistic forms beyond the brushstrokes).

The impressionistic treatment is intended to make more vivid, more substantial, Joyce's questioning of life in retrospect. On that basis, I proceed to elaborate more carefully and systematically how I approach the *Wake* and how my approach differs from that of other readers. Chapters 5–7 attempt to articulate the ideas and principles that guide my reading.

The remainder of the book, Chapters 8–20 (with the exception of the concluding chapter in which I summarize the principal ideas that have emerged), is a chapter-by-chapter reading of the *Wake*. I hope it will serve both as a helpful guide for those who are approaching Joyce's last novel for the first time (or those who are resolved to give it another try) and as a detailed elaboration and defense of my interpretation. Even more, I hope it will inspire others to undertake their own large-scale readings—for I think we have Joyce's word that there are many.

A "longish essay" has grown. Its growth has been directed by the joy of discovering ever more in a text that, for so long, baffled and frustrated me. In his fiction, Joyce constructs an imaginative world in which the deepest questions about human life are explored with atypical honesty, generosity, and courage. Instead of a "disappointingly small" corpus, I've come to see a sequence of works for the progressive stages of our lives, a sequence that leads to *Finnegans Wake* as summation and conclusion. If the working out of *one* approach to his final novel can help others to explore their own ways in Joyce's *Wake*, then I hope that this extraordinary work will no longer appear dark and impenetrable, a playground only for the most erudite scholars, but will take its proper place among the masterpieces of world literature, a luminous and delightful gift to passionate readers everywhere.

Joyce's Kaleidoscope

1

SO SOFT THIS MORNING, OURS

For every type of action we perform, every scene we witness, every person with whom we engage, there will come a last occasion of doing, seeing, or meeting. Often we are only aware in retrospect that something that has figured in our lives has happened for the last time, that a particular chapter is over. At other times, however, we know at the moment that we shall not see this face or this place again, that this form of activity is over for us: we stand in the house in which we have grown up, or in the home we have made for our children, and recognize that we shall never be back. The sadness or nostalgia that sweeps over us under these circumstances may be tempered by our realization that a new mode of life is opening for us, one that will bring its own experiences and rewards, that the elements in the kaleidoscope of our lives are falling into different patterns.

Yet the finitude of human life makes it likely that some of these final occasions will be bereft of any such consolation. There are forms of activity we take for granted, simple things that underlie much that we do and most of what we delight in, elements of the kaleidoscope whose removal would leave so little that any reconfiguration of them would be impoverished and dreary. Someone whose life has been lived in a particular place may have walked beside the river, watching the trees come into bud, shade the stream, the leaves fall and be carried away by the current, the trees stand bare in the wind, and may know that this walk is the final one, that soon there will be no more walking, that the cycle that starts with the indistinct blur around the denuded branches will not be seen again. That knowledge can provoke disappointment and dissatisfaction with the experience itself—however beautifully the light glints from the trees or catches the eddies, it is only one angle, one perspective, one version of the scene, and it cannot sum up the many occasions that culminate in this one. Even while one is realizing that this part of life is going, it is already gone.

A wake is an occasion for looking back on a life, both in mourning and in celebration. Joyce chose his title well. For, although there's lots of fun at Finnegan's Wake (and in *Finnegans Wake*), there's also another mood, an autumnal tone, retrospective, questioning, aware of limitations and of possibilities unrealized. Under the laughter, however boisterous it may often be, I hear the voice of a reflective, aging man, not so much hoping and planning for the future as wondering about the significance of what has been. There is a concern with the final stages of life and how the whole looks from the standpoint of its closing.

In the chapter he set in the form of a quiz show, Joyce gives us a general answer to the question of how our lives will look:

> Now, to be on anew and basking again in the panaroma of all flores of speech, if a human being duly fatigued by his dayety in the sooty, having plenxty off time on his gouty hands and vacants of space at his sleepish feet and as hapless behind the dreams of accuracy as any camelot prince of dinmurk, were at this auctual futule preteriting unstant, in the states of suspensive exanimation, accorded, throughout the eye of a noodle, with an ear-sighted view of old hopeinhavin with all the ingredient and egregiunt whights and ways to which in the curse of his persistence the course of his tory will had been having recourses, . . . then *what* would that fargazer seem to seemself to seem seeming of, dimm it all?
>
>   Answer: A collideorscape! (143: 3–12, 26–8)

There is plenty to tease out in this rich passage.[1] One of its intimations, the one that especially concerns me, is the delineation of an old man (one who might "curse the gout, serpigo, and the rheum / For ending [him] no sooner" [*Measure for Measure*, III.i.31–2]), looking mistily back on *his* life, *his* past (as well as the human past), and seeing it as a kaleidoscope, a device in which the same elements constantly rearrange themselves in new patterns. Not only that, however—but also elements with which people collide or scrape, that leave them bruised and wounded, elements from which we might try to escape, although our curse is that escape is futile, about as likely as passing through the eye of a needle.

The circularity of the *Wake* might be taken as an invitation to start anywhere—it is, famously, "the book of Doublends Jined" (20: 15–16)—and so why not here? Although I want to borrow Joyce's image of the collideorscape, I shall begin in a different place, with the very end. If the *Wake* is famously obscure because it is a book of the night, then we might expect to find maximal clarity at the moment of waking, perhaps seeing in the retrospective view what the swirls of "the dreams of accuracy" have meant. (The idea that the perspective from the wake is especially clear can be sustained whichever sense we give to "wake"—the obscurities are dissolved in the morning and on the occasion of mourning.) In the very last pages, as at the end of *Ulysses*, we hear the voice of a woman, a wife. She is older than Molly Bloom, and she talks of the possibility of a walk, hoping to rouse her husband to revisit a scene that has meant much to both of them. As her invitation flows on, it becomes an occasion for reviewing the course of her life, for putting into her words what that tired "fargazer" might see. The envisaged walk might be their last return to a cherished spot, their last walk together, the last walk for each of them. Their lives are ending. She has to discover what they have meant.

The single chapter that closes the *Wake* opens with the sounds of morning and with the promise of the new. "[S]eeds of light" are brought to the "cowld owld sowls" (593: 20). The first parts of the chapter renew many of the familiar themes that have coursed through the earlier parts, often with a distinctive energy and a softening of the darker tones. Then, at 619: 20, the prose attains a new clarity as the female voice begins an eight-page coda:

Soft morning, city! Lsp! I am leafy speafing.

Who is she?

Lewis Carroll's Alice famously objected to a book "without pictures or conversations," and, although Alice might have been flattered to find her name and her escapades in the *Wake,* she might have been even more baffled by a book without plot or characters. If Alice were as astute as her creator, she would have realized that the difficulty arises from the absence of *stable* characters, for it seems that the voices we hear belong to people who can fuse or divide with kaleidoscopic rapidity. There will be much more to say later about the various individuals and conglomerates who flicker through Joyce's pages, but, for the moment, it will be enough to pick out two personae who are especially prominent: a male figure, known to readers and critics as HCE (and signaled by the occurrence of these letters in closely juxtaposed words), and a female figure, ALP (whose presence is highlighted in similar fashion), to whom HCE is married. HCE is almost certainly not named "Here Comes Everybody" or "Haveth Childers Everywhere" or "Humphrey Chimpden Earwicker," nor does it matter much if his true surname is "Porter"; he is everyman, great or humble, sometimes showing up as Jesus or the Buddha or Finn MacCool, sometimes as the proprietor of an Inn in Chapelizod, and sometimes identified with the Head of Howth (at the North End of Dublin Bay). By the same token, ALP is probably not "Anna Livia Plurabella," but she is identified with women young and old and with the river Liffey itself. It is best to think of them by their three-letter acronyms, as HCE and ALP.

The voice that announces the soft morning is that of ALP, lying drowsily beside her sleeping husband. It is a morning, late in their marriage and late in their lives. She closes the *Wake* by delivering a prose poem on her vision of her life.

5

Many commentators have remarked that Joyce was a great poet who wrote mediocre verse. From "The Dead" (the closing story of *Dubliners*) through *A Portrait of the Artist as a Young Man* and *Ulysses* to *Finnegans Wake*, his poetic genius reaches its height in magnificent prose passages. None is superior to ALP's final monologue, and that, perhaps, is one reason to begin either reading the *Wake* or a reading of the *Wake* with its final eight pages. Even more important, to my mind, is the perspective the monologue offers us, the perspective of the retrospective appraisal, the woman who sees the end and looks backward, seeking to come to terms with the course of her life. All the *Wake* leads us to this, and we find an interesting way of unraveling the book's mysteries if we see it as headed here.

The morning announced at the beginning of Part IV seems to be full of springtime hope, but, by the time ALP speaks, the leaves are long out and summer is gone. It is a "soft morning," the air is moist and the leaves are falling—"I am leafy, your goolden" (619: 29)—by the end, only one will be left to be carried by the Liffey's current (628: 6–7). Earlier passages have foreshadowed this. ALP stands for all of us:

> Countlessness of livestories have netherfallen by this plage, flick as flowflakes, litters from aloft, like a waast wizzard all of whirlworlds. Now all are tombed to the mound, isges to isges, erde from erde. (17: 26–30)

The same speaker, who *may* be identifiable as one of ALP's sons, anticipates her language in extending the theme: "But speak it allsosiftly, moulder!" (18: 8). Another image, from the dark center of the *Wake*, evokes even more clearly the mood of its closing:

> Of this Mr A (tillalaric) and these wasch woman (dapplehued), fhronehflord and feeofeeds, who had insue keen and able and a spindlesong aside, nothing more is told until now, his awebrume hour, her sere Sahara of sad oakleaves. And then. Be old. (336: 12–16)

We start with the family structure (rivalrous sons and a daughter) that is associated with HCE and ALP, with the grand (but self-undermining) references to authority that often mark HCE's presence, and then we are given an evocative description of what their lives come to: an "awebrume hour," one of smoke and mist, autumnally brown, filled with fear and concern, a dry, sad ending, with fallen, golden leaves. Juxtaposing these passages, we may think of ALP's "leafy" speech as set in the twilight of their lives, as the memories, parts of their life story, the leaves with which she is left and with which she leaves, flicker down and drift to the banks of the river, so that her vision of her past dissolves behind her.

Yet, on this autumn morning, in the autumnal years of her life and of her marriage, ALP does not begin with a backward look but with an attempt at renewal. The "sere Sahara of sad oakleaves" passage does not end with the old (and the "old"), but:

> The next thing is. We are once amore as babes awondering in a wold made fresh where with the hen in the storyaboot we start from scratch. (336: 16–18)

So, too, ALP looks for the possibility of a return for herself and HCE:

> The woods are fond always. As were we their babes in. And robins in crews so. It is for me goolden wending. Unless? Away! Rise up, man of the hooths, you have slept so long! (619: 23–6)

Even for the old, the morning is full of promise, as if their lives can be made over, starting "from scratch," in an innocent pastoral world, with birds chirping. (The sentence about the robins might seem, at first glance, one of Joyce's less successful puns, but, as we shall discover, there is method here.)

ALP urges her husband, the dormant lump that makes a hill under the sheet, to rise up. He does not respond, and, if we recall a passage from the beginning of this chapter, we may wonder whether he can respond. There it was suggested that HCE is not needed for this bright new day.

> So let him slap, the sap! Till they take down his shatter from his shap. He canease. Fill stap. (595: 31–2)

That doubt, the possibility that HCE's day—and life—is done may lie behind that interpolated question, "Unless?" presaging doubts and sad judgments that will become more prominent as ALP proceeds. But she tries to set any such concerns aside, imagining how he may look in the clothes, recently returned from the laundry:

> And stand up tall! Straight. I want to see you looking fine for me. (620: 1–2)

He should wear his suit[2]—and she names the price, which included something for "the bulge" (620: 5). HCE may have a misshapen shoulder or a slight hump, something that may make him an object of mockery or derision, something that may set him apart and outside. Yet she is proud of him, still devoted, still wanting to be his companion on an early walk:

> Come and let us! We always said we'd. And go abroad. Rathgreany way perhaps. (620: 10–11)

Late in a marriage, late in a life, there remain projects postponed, things that have served to bind two wills together, symbols of their joint existence—and these, ALP suggests, can still be realized. They have, this morning, a special opportunity.

7

But how late in life can it be? If they are really celebrating a golden wedding, then ALP cannot surely have school-age sons and an even younger daughter, as her next lines seem to imply. In the dream stories and dream voices of the *Wake*, different times are superimposed—ALP has "nor youth, nor age," but dreams of both. She dreams from the perspective of a life nearing its conclusion, when almost all the fragmentary patterns have sprung into place on the kaleidoscope, and momentarily recalls her children as young, when their care constrained certain kinds of parental activities or even made them impossible. In the main line of this early morning reverie, the children are absent; the focus is on renewal with her elderly husband. There is still time for that.

> It is the softest morning that ever I can ever remember me. But she won't rain showerly, our Ilma. Yet. Until it's the time. And me and you have made our. (621: 8–10)

Again, there are hints of concern here. Will there be time for them to carry out this walk, this last joint activity on which she sets so much store?

A meditation on HCE's peculiarities of appearance leads to a more accented version of the doubt.

> Maybe that's why you hold your hodd as if. And people thinks you missed the scaffold. Of fell design. I'll close me eyes. So not to see. Or see only a youth in his florizel, a boy in innocence, peeling a twig, a child beside a weenywhite steed. The child we all love to place our hope in for ever. All men has done something. Be the time they've come to the weight of old fletch. We'll lave it. So. We will take our walk before in the timpul they ring the earthly bells. In the church by the hearse-yard. (621: 27–35)

ALP has come to accept her husband's failings. Like her own children, HCE—and their marriage—began in innocence, full of promise, but the hopes were disappointed. That is the way of things. A fall is inevitable. Those who look on and are hurt by it can only, if they love, leave it or lave it, wash it away either from memory or by purging the emotional reaction; they can only forgive or forget. (It's telling that ALP can't finish the sentence, for to do so would explicitly recognize what is left undone in their joint life, and that would be to raise possibilities of failure. She is not yet ready to do that.) They can try to go forward with the real person they love, not grieving for the lost ideal but finding value in their life together, making use of time before they are pulled back, before the bells toll, before the hearse carries them to the churchyard. Birds may announce the coming death, kicking up their "treestirm shindy" (621: 36). HCE's have flown. ALP tries (vainly, I think) to see them as kind auguries.

She hopes they can walk together, adjusting their stride to one another. A walk would be healthy for them. And it would bring them together, for it seems to her, momentarily, that they have become distanced from one another, "[a]s if you had been long far away" (622: 14). Perhaps it is the world that has driven them apart, with its prying, gossip, and mischief-making. ALP wants to return to a special place, one that he should remember, a place in which they were once young, innocent, and unbruised. Most important, they should be alone—"Not a soul but ourselves"; the renewal of innocence, like Crusoe's island, must be a place from which others are excluded. The approval of others is unnecessary; aspirations to cut a dash in society are silly—"Plain fancies. It's in the castles air" (623: 18–19).

Their task, at this late stage, is to decipher their life together, understand the "scrips of nutsnolleges" (623: 32) they have. Like squirrels, they have hoarded against the wintry days of life's ending, and their hoard consists of tattered texts, bits and pieces of incomplete records of their shared experiences. Such fragments have they shored against their ruins, and, for ALP to find consolation, they must now be deciphered. She is torn between the hope that HCE will reaffirm his youthful promise, that, like Ibsen's master builder, he will, even now, climb to the heights, and a starker assessment of his accomplishments: "All your graundplotting and the little it brought!" (624: 12–13). The optimism of her initial invitation is eroding, but she continues her description of the walk as she imagines it. In her mind's eye, she conjures the city on which he hoped to leave his mark, the same city she—Liffey—has run through so long.

The Eblanamagna you behazyheld loomening up out of the dumblynass.
But the still sama sitta. I've lapped so long. (625: 26–7)[3]

Her vision of the failure of their hopes to improve, to transform, produces a bitter reflection on the past: "Why I'm all these years within years in soffran, allbeleaved" (625: 29–30). Yet one last dream inspires her, that they walk together, in the open, seen by all, like bride and groom again, affirming their dedication to one another for the world to see.

My selection of passages from the initial two-thirds of this extraordinary monologue suggests themes that dominate a reflective retrospective view of a life centered on a marriage. The initial delight, the sense of a world made fresh, is now seen as a prelude to inevitable failures and compromises. There are suggestions that a hostile world can break in and disrupt the private sphere. Outsiders, people who are different, people who have large bold dreams, may be mocked, derided, even humiliated. Individuals are opaque, hard to decipher by those who know them, and love them, best. The course of the marriage between HCE and ALP has found all of these things, again and again, and it has consisted in a sequence of gallant attempts to learn from them, to correct, and to do better. No doubt there have been many successes, moments of joy, for not everything goes badly, but, in the "awebrume hour," as the contours of life are seen more generally, and perhaps more accurately, the failures loom largest. Because there are now few—if any— chances for renewal, the call to begin again is more urgent and less confident.

Finally, however, the call itself becomes impossible, and there is only the retrospective vision. As ALP completes her thought of the triumphant procession with HCE, her persona shifts. No longer the wife in bed, she becomes the river, racing now toward the sea. She is faint, calling on HCE for support. As the river passes through Dublin, she revisits places she knew as a child—and she comes to know that there is now only memory; there are no more episodes of her tale with "To be continued"; "There'll be others but non so for me" (626: 19–20). Identities blur; memories of her life with HCE are confounded with her childhood with her father. Surging into this is the central memory of HCE's courtship of her (626: 22–32)—hardly surprising if we recall that that is "the height of his life from a bride's eye stammpunct" (309: 3–4). He promised her, she recalls, the keys of her heart (626: 30–1).[4]

Now, however, there is confusion. Something is changing, and they are separating. She cannot understand. Her brief benedictions for the young hold out the hope for HCE of renewal with a younger version of herself.[5] As she wishes them happiness, she adds, ominously, the hope that she may be wrong—for ALP knows better than to believe in happiness. The thought of a fresh start, with none for her, yields a pang of regret for a past state of innocence, for her childhood. But that was never possible:

It's something fails us. First we feel. Then we fall. (627: 11)

Now, with the firm acceptance that her "time is come" (627: 14), ALP offers a simpler, more caustic version of her life. She has done what she could, but it has been full of cares and troubles. Nobody has understood her. The tone turns bitter:

All me life I have been lived among them but now they are becoming lothed to me. And I am lothing their little warm tricks. And lothing their mean cosy turns. And all the greedy gushes out through their small souls. And all the lazy leaks down over their brash bodies. How small it's all! (627: 16–20)

Even HCE is repudiated.

I thought you were all glittering with the noblest of carriage. You're only a bumpkin. I thought you the great in all things, in guilt and in glory. You're but a puny. (627: 21–4)

She turns to home, to the sea, to death.

Yet this is not ALP's last word. After she has lamented the bitterness of her ending, we hear again the voice of the wife. She will slip away before the family is up. River and wife intermingle, and the sight, sound, and smell of the sea call her on, half in yearning, half in fear. She ends:

My leaves have drifted from me. All. But one clings still. I'll bear it on me. To remind me of. Lff! So soft this morning, ours. Yes. Carry me along, taddy, like you done through the toy fair! If I seen him bearing

down on me now under whitespread wings like he'd come from Arkan-
gels, I sink I'd die down over his feet, humbly dumbly, only to washup.
Yes, tid. There's where. First. We pass through grass behush the bush
to. Whish! A gull. Gulls. Far calls. Coming, far! End here. Us then.
Finn, again! Take. Bussoftlhee, mememormee! Till thousandsthee. Lps.
The keys to. Given! A way a lone a last a loved a long the (628: 6–16)

Her sentence continues, of course, with the opening word of the *Wake*—
"riverrun"—pitching us back into the cycle of dreams.

I want, however, to ponder the end and the meaning of these evocative
words. The renunciation of HCE and their joint life is only temporary. In accepting her father, and rushing into his arms, she finds herself again in the
embrace of her husband. All the memories of their marriage have drifted away,
all except one. That recollection, one that "clings" to her, is to remind her of
"Lff!"—life, perhaps, or love. In the softness of the morning, the morning that
is theirs, she speaks Molly Bloom's word of affirmation, as she imagines father/
husband bearing her along in delight. If that were real, she would fall at his feet,
humbly and devotedly, at the feet of this strange man who is often compared to
Humpty Dumpty and who seems to have had so many great falls. But she would
only "washup," cleanse him, soothe him, worship him, perhaps. Once again, she
affirms their love and visualizes the place of their first lovemaking, perhaps like
Molly and Bloom on Howth head, treading quietly through the grass to a quiet
place, all their own, away from eyes and ears. To the sound of the gulls' cries
(which, if we recall II-4, accompany the ship on which Tristan and Isolde con-
summate their love), she imagines this as an ending for them in the ecstatic moment of first union. But life continued for them and will continue for others. As
it ends for her, she can only repeat and fulfill HCE's promise. Kiss (buss) gently;
remember; or perhaps "me me more me," a last expression of desire for more
of life, this life, love, this love; perhaps that it should be thousandfold repeated,
until there is no more of either of them. The lips press. The keys to her heart, to
his heart, have been given. With eleven ordinary monosyllables, ALP sums up.

A way—for her life is only one way, with its individual directions and con-
volutions. A lone—for, despite all intimacy, all moments of union, she lives
and dies alone, at best partly understood. A last—because this moment is her
ending, just as the walk she envisaged was to be a final recapturing of their life
together. A loved—because love is at the center of her life, her love for HCE and
for the people, places, and things touched by their love. A long—because the
way has been hard, and the bitter moments of repudiation, although overcome,
cannot be denied; and also because her way is along the path she imagined
walking with her husband, along the riverrun.

I have tried to use ALP's closing monologue to evoke a mood and thereby to
introduce ideas that can offer *one* approach to the *Wake*. In the chapters that

follow, I shall attempt a reading based on the thought that a central preoccupation of this work is with the assessment and vindication of a human life, a vindication to be achieved, if at all, only in retrospect, from the perspective of age, ideally perhaps from the judgment of a wake. Joyce, I suggest, thought long about his life and its value, sometimes bitterly but often with acquiescence. Like Bloom, and like HCE, his role as husband and father was an important part of his conception of himself—but of course it was not the whole. In the *Wake*, as in *Ulysses*, he was prepared to look at marital love with an unsparing eye, taking it warts and blemishes, failures and infidelities, and all. Just as Molly has the closing word on her own marriage, so, too, ALP, in her "sere Sahara of sad oakleaves," provides a last assessment. We shall return to that assessment later, and I shall try to correct some of the partiality of the perspective with which I have begun. For now, however, I want to trace this story of a waning life and its self-understanding back, looking first at the chapter that precedes the finale.

2

HIS REIGNBOLT'S SHOT

Important though ALP is to the *Wake*—and her significance is underscored by assigning her the closing words—the dominant figure throughout is her husband, HCE. His guilt, his shortcomings, his failures pervade the entire book. Since for both husband and wife the value of their lives is bound up with the success of their life together, either can speak for both, and ALP's bitter reflections, just before the sweep of her final generous endorsement of their love, recognize the deficiencies of their union. We are prepared for both the bitterness and the generosity by the closing chapter of Part III, where we attend, as in a cinema, a theater, or even more exactly the amphitheater of an anatomy demonstration, the dissection of their aging marriage. We look down on them "in their bed of trial, on the bolster of hardship, by the glimmer of memory, under coverlets of cowardice" (558: 26–7).

This chapter presents a kaleidoscope of scenes, sometimes with abrupt shifts.[1] The *Wake* as a whole is a sequence of dream episodes, and here we take up again a dream story that has been suspended—or interrupted—for four chapters (or about 170 pages). At the end of II-3, we left HCE, as publican, in the bar of his inn, vilified and defeated, drunk on the lees left by his resentful, accusatory, even spiteful, clientele, and, finally, slumped on a box in the corner. We are offered a dream account of how he finds his way to bed.

The aged maid-of-all-work at the Inn, sometimes known as Kate, here dubbed "Kothereen the Slop" (556: 32) apparently hears a banging at the door. Descending the stairs, she discovers the collapsed HCE. It is not an attractive sight:

> in his honeymoon trim, holding up his fingerhals, with the clookey in his fisstball, tocher of davy's, tocher of ivileagh, for her to whisht, you sowbelly, and the whites of his pious eyebulbs swering her to silence and coort; (557: 9–12)

In fact, this is the second visit of Kate to HCE in the bar, for, earlier in the evening, before the customers left, she apparently came with a message from

ALP, urging HCE to shut up shop and join her in bed (333-4). The import of that invitation was not hard to fathom, since "the missus" was undressing—she "had her agony stays outsize her sari chemise" (333: 20)—and there's a whispered interpolation "pierce me, hunky, I'm full of meunders!" (333: 22–3). But HCE does not go up. Instead he keeps the bar open, perhaps because he is so concerned with social acceptance, with the camaraderie of his customers, with fitting in—just that complex of impulses ALP identifies and criticizes in her closing monologue (622–3), chiding his vanity in failing to recognize that they can be enough for each other.

Now, however, he holds up his fingers to Kate to silence her exclamation, or her reproach perhaps, and they exchange a glance, his eyes (I think) pleading for mercy and forgiveness. One hand holds something, the key of the clock (as if like Tristram Shandy's father, he followed the ritual of winding the clock before the weekly regimen of marital sex) or possibly his penis. We do not see how he ascends the stair and finds his way to bed, but that must happen, for he is in bed when the story continues.

It is worth pausing briefly to ask about Kate, about the original summons and the later retrieval of HCE. Is she, perhaps, the older ALP who descends first to urge him to come to bed and later to rescue him from his tipsy despair? To see her in that role is already to set the scene of III-4 in a tone of marital disillusion. Once again, in a small way, HCE has pursued a vain dream, been disappointed, failed his wife, and she has, as she so often seems to do, picked up the pieces, forgiven him, and guided him to rest. She has shown here, then, the generosity and magnanimity that pervades her closing monologue.

And so to bed. We are given a description of the married couple.[2] It is not flattering.

> Man looking round, beastly expression, fishy eyes, paralleliped homo-platts, ghazometron pondus, exhibits rage. Business. Ruddy blond, Armenian bole, black patch, beer wig, gross build, episcopalian, any age. Woman, sitting, looks at ceiling, haggish expression, peaky nose, trekant mouth, fithery wight, exhibits fear. Welshrabbit teint, Nubian shine, nasal fossette, turfy tuft, undersized, free kirk, no age.
> (559: 22–9)

An aging husband with a gross build and a beastly expression lies behind his worn, haggish wife, with her sharp nose and cheesy skin. They have been awakened by the cry of a child. As before, in the dream montage of the *Wake*, youth and age are fluid, and the decaying bodies we see respond to a voice from the child of years before. They go upstairs, ALP leading (560: 24–7), the lumbering HCE in the rear, and the description changes to a kindlier mode, as euphemisms displace the harsh language of the scene setting.

They visit the two rooms in which their children sleep, and the language now oozes a sickly sweetness in descanting on the beauty and innocence of the young daughter.[3] Turning to the room of the twin sons, we are offered a contrast between the beauty and promise of the one and the black biliousness of the other. The latter, the froward son, has been crying in his sleep, and he needs ALP's reassurance that it was only a dream. The figures of this dream within a dream are unreal.

> Hear are no phanthares in the room at all, avikkeen. No bad bold faathern, dear one. (565: 19–20)

Like Haines, the English interloper in the tower Stephen Dedalus shared with Buck Mulligan, the little boy has nightmares of panthers; or perhaps of wicked, cruel fathers.

The real father does not speak. But he has had two visions, one of the budding beauty of his daughter, the other of his wife as she precedes him up the stair: "we are commanding from fullback, woman permitting, a profusely fine birdseyeview from beauhind this park" (564: 6–8). The references to the "cheeks," the surrounding "boskage," and "daddies housings" (14, 16, 18) leave little doubt about what HCE sees.[4] And when we hear him again, after ALP has soothed the child, he voices, whether aloud or not we need not decide, a desire for intercourse with his wife. ALP whispers

> He is quieter now

and HCE replies, more drowsily (or tipsily)

> Legalentitled. Accesstopartnuzz. Notwildebeestsch. Byrightofoaptz. Twainbeonerflsh. Haveandholdpp. (571: 27–9)

As they were awakened, he may have looked bestial. But, he claims, they are human, and, for them, the act of intercourse will be surrounded with the distinctive features of human lovemaking, with a grace and dignity that distinguish it from the instinctual and grotesque coupling of the beasts. Love, their love for one another, is central to their lives, and, even in their age, they will give physical expression to that love, a physical expression that will embody part of what makes their lives, as human lives, valuable and significant. Unlike the animals, they have entered into a covenant.

Yet there are already suggestions that this may be an illusory romanticization of reality. There was no grace or beauty in the descriptions of the waking couple, and, although the language is gentler, it continues to underscore HCE's ungainliness and the fading of ALP's charms. The landscape that corresponds to her body invites a coarse description: it is "shagsome all and beastful" (566: 33). He stands before her with "a such unfettered belly" and a condom comically perched (567: 5–7).[5] More mildly, HCE is recognized as "lot stoutlier than of formerly" (570: 17–18). Furthermore, there is considerable ambiguity about what has inspired his surge of desire for ALP. Much earlier, in the initial identification of the "bed of trial," we were told about

his mace of might mortified, her beautifell hung up on a nail...
(558: 28–9)

Her sexual charms have faded, they are cast off, and must be donned artificially; they do not stir her husband, especially not in his alcohol-assisted stupor. But now, after the trip upstairs, he is stirred. By the vision of his daughter, sleeping beauty?[6] Or by that view revealed by ALP's flimsy garments, as she scampers up the stairs ahead of him? We do not know. And nor does HCE.

There follows a beautiful passage as they turn from the boys' room and slowly descend the stair, a passage that does transcend the bestial qualities into which their marriage, their love, their lives have threatened to dissolve, a passage that prepares us for the acceptance that ALP will achieve with her closing lines (576: 17–580: 36). It is both a review of their life together and the perils of their marriage, and one of Joyce's great secular prayers. Beginning with a many-sided description of them, recognizing them as lovers and parents (576: 26–8), it asks that they may be guided:

> Big Measter Finnykin with Phenicia Parkes, lame of his ear and gape of her leg, most correctingly, we beseach of you, down their ladder-case of nightwatch service and bring them at suntime flush with the nethermost gangrung of their stepchildren, guide them through the labyrinth of their samilikes and the alteregoases of their pseudoselves, hedge them bothways from all roamers whose names are ligious, from loss of bearings deliver them; . . . (576: 28–35)

This descent of the stair, then, is also the course of the rest of their married lives, and it is easy for either, or both, to miss a step and fall.

The danger would come from a loss of bearings, a confusion of what HCE (or ALP) is with a flawed self-conception, a pseudoself, an alias, a misleading alter ego. They can be led to roam and rove into ventures, projects, or relations that are not for them, that betray what they are. By the same token, the world can break in on their marriage, directing their attention away from what is most important—as indeed it did earlier in the dream story, when HCE remained in the bar. But in their journey, the walk they take together, they have been mostly successful, avoiding the reefs and shoals on which marriages can be wrecked:

> down the scales, the way they went up, under talls and threading tor-mentors, shunning the startraps and slipping in sliders . . . (579: 2–4)

So, although they have long been wed, envisaging their "diamond wedding tour" (578: 31–2), they have held to simple maxims, and there is hope for their future: "Oil's wells in our lands" (579: 24).

At this point, however, the voice of the prayer checks itself and moderates the optimistic mood that has been emerging. ALP and HCE continue to need help and guidance:

> Now their laws assist them and ease their fall! (579: 26)

16

Those simple laws—and Joyce's catalog is one of his many successful riffs on proverbs and conventional moral advice—are sensible and often generous, not only enjoining thrift, industry, and prudence, but also recommending a spirit both realist and generous ("Commit no miracles," "Hatenot havenots" [579: 13–14, 16]). However sensible, no list of maxims can guard against the vicissitudes of life, and the picture of this marriage is genuinely mixed: sometimes they have "feathered foes' nests and fouled their own" (579: 36–580: 1). The earlier triumphal account of their marriage gives way to a sterner tale of obstacles overcome—but overcome they are, and after the disappointments the prayer can wish them a quiet ending: "Pharaoh with fairy, two lie, let them!" (580: 12–13). They should be eased in their descent, in their fall, in their decline, as they descend to sleep and to death ("till their hour with their scene be struck for ever" [580: 15–16]).

They are close to the bottom, approaching their bedroom.

> They near the base of the chill stair, that large incorporate licensed vintner, such as he is, from former times, nine hosts in himself, in his hydrocomic establishment and his ambling limfy peepingpartner, the slave of the ring that worries the hand that sways the lamp that shadows the walk that . . . (580: 23–7)

We are off on one of Joyce's versions of the house that Jack built, used here to connect the secular prayer and the review of the marriage with one of those disturbing intrusions against which the praying voice has warned. At the beginning is the couple who have survived, who have emerged from the struggles and disappointments of former times, bruised but united, such as they are. ALP is still bound by the wedding ring, although it may chafe at her hand, the hand that holds the lamp, a lamp that casts a shadow. Where will this chain end? With a ballad, a carnival song, crude in its way and cruel, intended to humiliate HCE, a ballad originally sung early in the *Wake* (44–7) and revived in a new form in the vilification expressed by the customers in the bar (371–3). The connection brings home the power of the outside world to intrude on this pair, to mock and destroy. The ring encircles the finger and symbolically binds both partners together; the hand holds the lamp; the lamp will cast a shadow on the bedroom blind; and the blind is visible from the street. On the street there walks a sinister figure—"Wachtman Havelook seequeerscenes" (556: 23–4)—easily identifiable as "Sackerson," a figure sometimes playing the role of policeman, sometimes (as here, it seems) a squalid derelict, and most frequently the odd-job man of HCE's inn, Kate's male counterpart, who can ambiguously indicate an older version of HCE.[7] (As ALP says in her negative verdict on this decrepit pair, "He's for thee what she's for me" [620: 33].) This onlooker, glancing up at the bedroom window, may soon see a "queer scene," as the shadow cast by the lamp heaves and shudders across the blind, a sight that can start a rumor that will eventually find its way into a spiteful song.

What is to be seen will be a fumbling and messy reprise of what was once graceful and beautiful, an act that could be viewed as central to human life (and love), not something grotesque and bestial. To subject this aging copulation to the gaze of outsiders is a violation; it is to be regretted—"I'm sorry! I saw. I'm sorry! I'm sorry to say I saw!" (581: 24–5). Indeed, we[8] should be grateful to HCE and ALP ("our forced payrents" [576: 27]), and we should wish "him with his famblings no end of slow poison" (582: 4–5); here the wish is both for HCE and his family, and an acceptance of his fumblings—the "slow poison," I suggest, is simply life. For the next passage takes up the thoughts of the significance of lives lived together and of the retrospective assessment of them that will loom large in ALP's closing monologue.

> Scant hope theirs or ours to escape life's high carnage of semperidentity by subsisting peasemeal upon variables. Bloody certainly have we got to see to it ere smellful demise surprends us on this concrete that down the gullies of the eras we may catch ourselves looking forward to what will in no time be staring you larrikins on the postface in that multimirror megaron of returningties, whirled without end to end. (582: 14–21)

The immediate response to this grim evaluation is a halting effort to drown out the judgment in song.

The challenge, for ALP and HCE, indeed for all of us, is to find a human identity to which we can adhere during the course of life, one that can withstand the forces that wound and destroy it, the bloody carnage of embodied ideals. To be human is to think of oneself in particular terms and to live in accordance with that conception, and the maiming or mutilation of our individuality can occur when we fall away and fail to be true to it—when we fall from what we have reflectively decided to be because we are lured aside ("by the roamers whose names are ligious" [576: 34]), when we trade our commitments for a mess of pottage. If we fail, then we shall see in advance, as we look toward the vision of our lives that will be available from their ending, that it shows a variable and disordered patchwork. And beyond that ending there is nothing for us, no further life to which this is simply a preparatory stage, but only the same for others, on and on, others who face the same challenge of finding and being themselves.

For HCE and ALP, the dominant conception of their lives is one of union in love. When we juxtapose that conception with the chill thought of those two stark sentences (582: 14–21), two questions immediately arise: first, can they hold to this conception in their lives? Second, is the conception itself enough, enough, that is, to answer a doubt that life lived by it is not worth living? The two questions are, of course, connected, for the eruption of doubt about the value of a life lived by a particular human identity can, whether sound or not, undermine the will to persevere with that identity. In the dream story, those questions are focused in a particular way, as we observe the coupling of the aging pair and ask if this is any more than the momentary physical satisfaction of the beasts.

HCE and ALP sweat and strain like farm animals; his face is red; her teeth chatter (582: 30; 583: 3–4; 583: 12). It is hard work, and ALP has a sense of the absurdity of the scene, watching her "old stick-in-the-block," "slogging his paunch about" (583: 26, 27). That choice of description for HCE's shuddering belly serves Joyce as pivot for a switch in imagery. Quite suddenly, the account of the intercourse is stuffed with the jargon of cricket—there are stumps and wickets, googlies and yorkers, and much more (583–4). Cricket is the most graceful of games, elegant and beautiful, played on golden afternoons, with long vistas. Great batsmen, stroke-makers, rely on timing and finesse, effort-lessly parrying and driving the ball. But it is not always like that. A match can be ugly and inelegant—batsmen may slog rather than stroke the ball, bowlers may labor all day in the field for scant returns. At the end of the day, despite all their efforts, they may have failed to bowl out the other side, trying every trick they know on a wicket that gives them no help and watching as the batsmen amass huge totals. Despite all ALP's encouragements, this copulation shows signs of enormous strain—ending with a colossal score "nine hundred and dirty too not out" (584: 24). Is this success?

If HCE is the bowler, then it is an utter failure—and he has had a "Noball" (a foul) called on him by the umpire (584: 23). A neighboring hen laughs, and HCE is described as "at all times long past conquering cock of the morgans" (584: 25)—easily read as a reference to a past that is no longer present. There is a question of blame (584: 26), suggesting that intercourse has failed in some way, that it has been incomplete, that HCE never reached orgasm (one obvious reading of "You never wet the tea!" [585: 31]).

Yet that is not the only reading. Maybe, although a slogger, he is one of the triumphant batsmen, building up an extraordinary number of runs. Maybe he is still the conquering cock of the morning, in tune with the rooster who crows (584: 27) not just to announce the dawn. Maybe the failure to wet the tea results from HCE's homage to Malthus (585: 11), patron saint of birth control, present in this bedroom in the form of the condom (the "buntingcap" [567: 7], or "man's gummy article, pink" [559: 15–16]). Maybe we should con-nect the crier's call to adjournment—"O yes! O yes!" (585: 26)—with Molly's affirmation.

There is no need to resolve the matter—we can leave it to the protagonists themselves. For whatever fluids have emerged or failed to emerge, it is plain that much sweat has been exuded. These aging bodies have thrust against one another strenuously and clumsily, and if they have found satisfaction it is hard to see it as a beautiful expression of love or to rely on it for the future. An on-looker within the dream story might easily find it grotesque and be moved to mocking laughter.

We have already appreciated the possibility of a prurient watcher who might be excited and amused by the antics he sees shadowed on the window. And the light that ALP held is now shining in the bedroom:

> O, O, her fairy setalite. Casting such shadows to Persia's blind! The man in the street can see the coming event. Photoflashing it far too wide. It will be known through all Urania soon. (583: 14–16)

Moreover, as we shall shortly learn, "pollysigh patrolman Seekersenn" (586: 28) has been wandering in the neighborhood and will have seen the light "turkling eitheranny of thuncles windopes" (586: 30–1). The eyes of the world have penetrated the union of this pair, and what is seen and reported, "far too wide," can inspire derisive laughter. That laughter, representing a detached verdict, might blow away any romantic illusions, enhancing the doubts that ALP and HCE themselves have felt. They may come to wonder whether a life centered on the kind of love they have is any more than a surface gloss on brutish instinct, whether it could survive the hard look from the end of their lives.

Post-copulatory depression sets in. They have to concede that their desires for one another have waned.

> Others are as tired of themselves as you are. Let each one learn to bore himself. (585: 35–6)

Perhaps the world is right to laugh at those who hold on to the myth that a loving union between husband and wife can endure throughout a lifetime, and that that suffices to make a valuable life for both. Perhaps we are right to leave open the question whether what moved HCE to sexual desire was love for his wife or the sight of the lovely young girl who sleeps upstairs.

So, as the chapter winds to its end, the insidious voices murmur in the pubs. Rumor, familiar rumor that we know from the earlier parts of the *Wake*,[9] swirls around HCE. The dissolving of his life takes on a more global character, until we reach a verdict that I take to bear directly on the central dream story of this chapter.

> That's his last tryon to march through the grand tryomphal arch. His reignbolt's shot. Never again! How you do that like, Mista Chimepiece? (590: 9–11)

The voice of the myth-debunker exults over HCE. His reign, the establishing of order over his life, is over. The rainbow, symbol of peace, is dissolved, leaving the elements of his life in disorder. He has believed in marriage and family, enduring union and lasting love, and he has believed in the possibility of the continued expression of that love. But all he has produced here is a gasping caricature of romantic love, one that shows that the entire ideal was a myth, a self-deception. We fool ourselves in thinking that there are ways of living that make our lives genuinely human, genuinely worthwhile. In the end, age will disclose what youth clothes with deceptive grace, that our lovemaking is the impulsive action of animals in rut. As his sexual life ends, HCE can ponder these things. His bolt is shot.

Yet we do not end quite here. There is a further view of HCE and ALP, as they lie asleep. Small wonder—"After having drummed all he dun. Hun! Worked out to an inch of his core" (590: 26–7). Before we "ring down" the curtain, however, there is a consoling thought, ALP's contented thanks:

> While the queenbee he staggerhorned blesses her bliss for to feel her funnyman's functions. Tag. Rumbling. (590: 27–9)

Fumbling it may have been. Even, as the malicious voice suggests, the last act of their lovemaking (day, a new day, is, after all, rumbling). Nonetheless, she can delight in it, accepting it as something more than the brutish behavior described in the hostile descriptions. Perhaps we should not endorse too quickly the negative verdict on love and marriage as ideals to live by.

And, of course, as ALP knows, and HCE should know, there is more to their union, more to their love, than sexual expression. Age may bring sexual failure without invalidating the love or forestalling its full elaboration in other ways. This couple may defend their lives by taking a more multifaceted view of them. Indeed, HCE has already spoken in his defense, issued his apologia. He has already taken that wider perspective. In the next chapter, I shall explore what he has had to say.

Before that, however, we need to register our judgment of the performance we have witnessed. As I suggested, we have sat in an amphitheater, watching an anatomical demonstration, looking on at the dissection of a union. The spectacle has enough of the theater about it that we should express overtly how we want to respond. Joyce's apparently enigmatic close offers us some possibilities.

> Tiers, tiers and tiers. Rounds. (590: 30)

"Rounds," you might think, because, in the architecture of the *Wake* that Joyce drew from Vico, the next and last part will be the return—day, remember, is breaking. "Tiers" and "Rounds" together suggest the amphitheater in which we have been looking on. But one response to this drama would be to shed tears for the decline and passing of HCE and ALP, tears of compassion for their efforts and failures, tears, perhaps, for their misconception of their lives. Or, moved by ALP's stalwart delight in her "funnyman," we might offer rounds of applause. Perhaps, despite all, they have come through.

Should we applaud or weep? Joyce wrote both. I think he meant both.

3

RESPECTABLE

The dream story in which HCE collapses in the bar and is assisted to bed is interrupted by a sequence of dream episodes ostensibly focused on his son Shaun, the son whom we will see asleep upstairs in the inn, the favored one, like a "blissed angel" (562: 25), who, in his earlier appearance as Chuff, figured as the "fine frank fairhaired fellow of the fairytales" (220: 12–13). Part III of the *Wake* follows the unraveling of Shaun, from his confident stance as defender of civic virtue and bourgeois order to a cacophony of contradictory voices, roused from within him under the seemingly unsystematic probings of a "star-chamber quiry" (475: 18). Among these voices, we hear ALP and Shaun's sister, Issy, and, as the questions dig deeper, the oracular mumbling of Sackerson and the rattling gossip of Kate (530: 23–4; 530: 36–531: 26). The last to emerge, deepest within Shaun, is HCE, whose presence has dominated the *Wake*, whose words have sometimes been reported, but whose unedited speech we have never before heard at any length.[1]

HCE is hauled from the depths, apparently to answer the charges against him, charges that have to do with his alleged improprieties in Phoenix Park, where, so runs the tale, he observed two young women urinating and was himself observed by three soldiers.[2] Initially, he makes some feeble efforts to respond to these allegations, asserting his purity "as a cleanliving man" (532: 14) and emphasizing his dedication—especially his sexual dedication—to his wife (532: 30–533: 6). Their household is dutifully religious, and any doubts can be settled by the testimony of reverend clergymen (533: 8–14, 27–33). Having offered these reassurances, HCE feels that he has done enough and is evidently keen to disappear back into the depths (533: 36–534: 2).

Unfortunately the stammering dismissals tend to undercut themselves, trailing off into language that too closely alludes to the circumstances of the charges (as, for example, in the odd reference to "serial dreams of faire women, Mannequins Passe," with its obvious link to the Brussels statue of the urinating boy [532: 33]); HCE protests too much, and in unfortunate ways to boot. So, after enigmatic comments from the questioners—the four evangelists serve as the inquisitors of the "star chamber"—HCE begins again. He will be unruffled: "Calm has entered. Big big Calm, announcer" (534: 7). But the resolution quickly evaporates, and he launches into a diatribe against those who have accused him, attacking their conduct and their characters. Once again, the language suggests that HCE is more concerned with the substance of the charge than he is allowing (as, for example, in the links to female genitalia and urination [534: 20–1]). He concludes with a blustering sequence of epithets (535: 13–21).

The interrogators seem unconvinced—perhaps they do not hear clearly what HCE is saying, or perhaps they understand all too clearly some of the uncomfortable allusions of his words. At any event, he is moved to try another tack, a maudlin appeal for compassion.

> Old Whitehowth he is speaking again. Ope Eustace tube! Pity poor whiteoath! Dear gone mummeries, goby! Tell the woyld I have lived true thousand hells. Pity, please, lady, for poor O.W. in this profundust snobbing I have caught. . . . Pity poor Haveth Childers Everywhere with Mudder! (535: 26–9, 34–5)

"Whitehead," or "Whitehowth," is an apt name for the aging HCE, who pleads for pity, who has endured the torments of damnation, who has been snubbed, mobbed, and jobbed (possibly, if we accept ALP's later verdict, brought on by his urge for social acceptance, his willingness to cultivate the leading figures of the community [622: 24–33]). The initials he gives himself are equally appropriate, recalling Oscar Wilde and Wilde's plea *De Profundis*. Although "Whitehowth" seems to respond to the complaints that his official questioners cannot hear him, it is significant that the plea is directed to a lady—surely to his lady, for it is the forgiveness of ALP that he most urgently needs (just as Wilde, convicted and derided, needed the forgiveness of his wife).

The moment of anguished self-exposure is relatively brief. HCE assumes a different tone and distances himself from the groveling supplicant. The "Communicator," who has just spoken, is out of sorts and needs cheering up; perhaps he is suffering from a touch of indigestion (535: 36; 536: 3–4; 536: 7–8).[3] HCE speaks with sympathy for this tortured persona, eventually dismissing what has been said:

> Mood! Mood! It looks like someone other bearing my burdens. I cannot let it. (536: 26–7)

The attempt at airy dismissal is, of course, a wonderfully revealing inversion— the right exculpatory story should not be that another is taking on HCE's guilt, but that this apparent communication from HCE has accepted a burden of guilt improperly, perhaps the burden of someone else.

We are off again on a new series of inept attempts to respond to the charges. HCE declares his candor, boasts that an appropriate sentence for what is alleged would be minor, and declares that he would protest even that (28–34). Once again he tries to take on the marks of propriety, conform to the standards of the community, and vow that he will give up "all practices" (537: 16). Once again, he pours scorn on the credibility of those who have told stories against him. It is, he suggests, absurd, completely laughable (538: 18–19). Yet, as before, the declarations are marked by oddities and irrelevances that undercut the jaunty dismissal (see, for example, 538: 21–6).

Then there is a change, as if HCE realizes that he must do what he claims to have done, to bare himself, to present his own vision of who he is and what he has made of his life. It begins, I think, with his attempt to say a little more about the ways in which he meets the standards of propriety. First, he presents himself as a man who appreciates finer things.

> I should tell you that honestly, on my honour of a Nearwicked, I always think in a wordworth's of that primed favourite continental poet, Daunty, Gouty and Shopkeeper, A.G., whom the generality admoyers in this that is and that this is to come. (539: 4–8)[4]

Like Bloom, HCE may be bent on self-improvement, making up in adulthood for the deficiencies of his education. His acceptance of cultural canons accompanies a sober dedication to business:

> I am doing my dids bits and have made of my prudentials good. I have been told I own stolemines or something of that sorth in the sooth of Spainien. (539: 13–14)

From these preparatory suggestions he sweeps into a much more elaborate account of his life story and its accomplishments.

He came from overseas, from abroad. An outsider, he found a haven in an unpromising place:

> in Poplinstown, alore Fort Dunlip, then-on-sea, hole of Serbonian bog, now city of magnificent distances . . . (539: 24–5)

HCE has founded a city, effecting a wonderful transformation of what had previously been dismal and squalid. The language is expansive, overblown, in the style of gigantism at which Joyce is so adept (as, for example, in the "Cyclops" episode of *Ulysses*).

> This seat of our city it is of all sides pleasant, comfortable and wholesome. If you would traverse hills, they are not far off. If champain land, it lieth of all parts. If you would be delited with fresh water, the famous river, called of Ptolemy the Libnia Labia, runneth fast by. If you will take the view of the sea, it is at hand. Give heed! (540: 3–8)

The four inquisitors are moved to voice travelogue slogans singing the praises of HCE's city.

We have heard hints of this before. In the first question of the quiz show chapter, HCE is linked to a city:

> he stands in a lovely park, sea is not far, importunate towns of X, Y, and Z are easily over reached. (138: 4–6)

Later, as they begin their evening studies, the children start geography with local knowledge:

> In these places sojournemus, where Eblinn water, leased of carr and fen, leaving amont her shoals and salmen browses, whom inshore breezes woo with freshets, windeth to her broads. . . . Orchards here are lodged; sainted lawrels evremberried. (264: 15–19, 25–6)

Yet even the most enthusiastic travel agent would blush at offering these descriptions. HCE's sweeping claim is enormously incredible, both because of the distance between the wonderful city he describes and the reality of Dublin and because, as we know, he neither founded the city nor transformed it. Even the kind and indulgent voice of ALP recognizes the grandiosity of his schemes (624: 12–13). Indeed, she is inclined to laugh "at that wheeze of old windbag, Blusterboss, blowharding about all he didn't do" (273: 22–3). Perhaps, then, we should join her in dismissive laughter at HCE's latest attempt to explain himself?

I think not. In this dream episode we are offered a serious exposition of what HCE takes his life to be about, made vivid by projecting his story on an enormous screen. He has founded no city, but we can start to understand those aspects of his actions he takes to be important by looking at the elements of the fantasy he inflates for us.

He has created order, peace, and tranquility (540: 29–33). He has built great and beautiful structures (541: 4–7). He has defended the city against threats from without (541: 14–24). Sometimes the protection has been quite intimate and domestic:

> For sleeking beauties I spinned their nightinveils, to slumbred beast I tummed the thief air. (541: 30–1)

Reading this in light of the concerns of the coming chapter—HCE's visit to the sleeping children, the eruption of sexual desire, the panther of the dreams, and the difference between human and beast—it is not hard to spot a core of genuine achievement behind the pompous catalog of civic accomplishments; within the family, HCE has provided security and protection, surrounding and cultivating the innocent daughter, quieting—or turning a deaf ear to—the bestial voices within.

Like Plato, HCE uses his vision of the city to show on a large canvas the principal features of something smaller; unlike Plato, his concern is not with the lineaments of the individual soul but with the achievements of the husband and paterfamilias, the successful structures of family life. Before I draw out the connections and examine their significance, however, we should gain a more complete picture of the amenities provided for the city. HCE claims to have cultivated the environs (541: 36–542: 2), to have set up a reliable and extensive water supply (542: 4–12), encouraging temperance and sobriety, to have provided food (542: 29–30), and, perhaps more doubtfully, to have sent out "heyweywomen to refresh the ballwearied" (542: 36; 543: 1). The rhetoric soars into a vision of empire—"with a slog to square leg I sent my boundary to Botany Bay" (543: 3–4; again HCE appears in cricketing mode)—and culminates in an evocation of Solomon in his glory.

The next phase of HCE's apologia starts with a census of his citizens, beginning appropriately with his family. I shall return to this interesting passage shortly, but it will be useful first to understand where he is heading. From the enumeration of the population, he emerges as ruler and lawgiver, recognized and honored with his own heraldic crest (545–6). Then comes a new theme, the announcement of "faithful Fulvia," wife and river (546: 30). The introduction is unexpectedly fraught with worry—if she had been faithless, wandering uphill "upon search of louvers" (546: 32)—the anxiety is incomplete, but I read the consequence as rendering everything else, however splendid, quite worthless. HCE quickly suppresses it (perhaps too quickly)—"Yet know it was vastly otherwise which I have heard it by mmummy goods waif" (547: 3–4); rivers, after all, do not flow uphill. He was, he claims, her first complete lover, one who "waged love on her: and spoiled her undines" (547: 7–8).

He domesticated her, brought her in regular and magnificent courses. Moved by his love for her, he did great things:

> and I bade those polyfizzyboisterous seas to retire with hemselves from os (rookwards, thou seaesea stamoror!) and I abridged with domfine norsemanship till I had done abate her maidan race, my baresark bride, and knew her fleshly when with all my bawdy did I her whorship, min bryllupswibe: Heaven, he hallthundered; Heydays, he flung blissforhers. And I cast my tenspan joys on her, arsched overtupped, from bank of call to echobank . . . (547: 24–31)

It is clear, I think, that all the creative effort of which he has boasted in the previous pages has this for its very specific end: it is a great marriage gift to ALP. (It is also clear, from the numerous double entendres in this passage—"bawdy," "whorship," "arsched"—that, for all the attempt at magisterial rhetoric, there are serious questions about the nature and value of this union.)

He poured tributes of all kinds upon her, clothes to adorn her body and jewelery (548: 17–29, 32–3). The city was caught up in festival—"there was no night for nights were days" (549: 6). He voyaged far and wide for her, but there were also moments of domestic quiet: "I sate me and settled with the little crither of my hearth" (549: 29–30). Food, articles of toilet, entertainments were showered on her (550). He made for her a place in a community, with friends whose smiles and respect are worth having (550: 27–33).[5] The city was transformed with facilities for her, institutions of learning and religion, walks and parks, vineyards and gardens and roads (550–2). All this, he proclaims, to bring joy to ALP, who goes riding (and we should surely connect this to the "galloping" lovemaking of the next chapter [583: 3–13]):

> for her pleashadure: and she lalaughed in her diddydid domino to the switcheries of the whip. Down with them! Kick! Playup! (554: 7–9)

There is, then, a short version of HCE's apologia: he came, an outsider, fell in love, wooed and won; and he worked for his wife to transform, to create, and to build, with her sustenance, comfort, and pleasure always in mind.

We need only take seriously the projecting of this story on a giant screen insofar as that serves the purpose of illuminating what HCE has striven for on a domestic scale. If, as I believe, this wonderfully overblown and brilliantly entertaining sequence of speeches is his appropriate response to the denigrating stories that swirl about him, if it is an explanation of who he is and what he takes his life to be all about, then at the center is his marriage to ALP and the efforts he has undertaken in support of that marriage. The conception of marriage offered here is, however, significantly different from that developed in ALP's closing monologue or in the private ecstasies to which the efforts of the aging couple on their "bed of trial" aspire—and, perhaps, grotesquely caricature. HCE's vision has no dearth of sexual celebration, as is plain from the passionate evocation of his early life with ALP, but it is conjoined with the integration of the loving relationship into many areas of life. Work, conceived in terms of providing necessary food, clothing, and shelter, acquires a new meaning in sustaining their joint existence. There is a home to be built, adjusted to joint tastes; entertainments are to be enjoyed together; the couple share walks and excursions, quiet moments at the hearth or in the garden. Perhaps there are joint religious devotions or a mutual expansion of intellectual horizons. All this can be traced in the lines of HCE's grandiose picture.

There are two further elements, one which has already surfaced and one which sharply differentiates HCE's conception from that of ALP's closing words. They surely have in common the vision of the home as a place in which children are born, are protected and nurtured. Where they differ—and here ALP's yearning for a private ("Robinson Crusoe") life may embody an embittered sense of the world's hostility—is in HCE's emphasis on community. This emerges not only in his obvious interest in the respect and admiration of others, but also in the vision of himself as presiding over a society in which tolerance reigns and all kinds of people are welcome.

Back, then, to the census. It begins, as it should given the conception of his life that HCE has chosen, with the children—"This missy, my taughters, and these man, my son" (543: 15–16). We then spread outward, beginning with "the quality" and descending the social scale:

> from my fief of the villa of the Ostmanorum to Thorstan's, *recte* Thomars Sraid, and from Huggin Pleaze to William Inglis his house, that man de Loundres, in all their barony of Saltus, bonders and foeburghers, helots and zelots, strutting oges and swaggering macks, the darsy jeamses, the drury joneses, redmaids and bleucotts, in hommage all and felony, all who have received tickets . . . (543: 16–21)

This is a wonderfully rich Pepysian catalog—and Pepys, like HCE, had a clear eye for the niceties of social distinction—and if it stopped with the "foeburghers," we might hear the voice of a climbing snob. It doesn't, however, end there but continues into the masses—the workers, the fanatics, the dandies, and the raffish pretenders, perhaps the "ladies" who haunt the theater district, kitchen girls with reddened skin, or maybe scarlet women, charity school boys, even, perhaps, criminals, although the "hommage all and felony" may simply embrace all men and boys, all women and girls. That catholic inclusiveness is underscored by what HCE says next.

The enormous sentence that begins with the family ("This missy") will extend over two pages (from 543: 15–545: 14). Most of the words are expended on telling us who will figure on a very long list. Only in the last two lines do we learn what is being said of the people so enumerated. HCE concludes with his arms wide open:

> all, let them all come, they are my villeins, with chartularies I have talledged them . . . (545: 13–14)

His home, his protection, his affection, it seems, will be open to all—like a feudal lord or the mayor of a town (*ville*) he throws wide the portals. At least to "all who have received tickets."

What exactly does it take to have a ticket? The refrain of the intervening pages supplies the answer. In this, one of the funniest passages of an extraordinarily funny book, Joyce offers, deadpan, a series of newspaper advertisements for the kinds of tenancies (and tenants) no sane person would want. (The list is constructed, in part, by using phrases from a book on urban poverty.[6])

The beginning is not too bad:

> fair home overcrowded, tidy but very little furniture, respectable, whole family attends daily mass and is dead sick of bread and butter, sometime in the militia, mentally strained from reading work on German physics, shares closet with eight other dwellings, more than respectable . . . (543: 22–6)

Quite quickly, though, the situations become more desperate

> house lost in dirt and blocked with refuse, getting on like Roe's distill-
> ery on fire, slovenly wife active with the jug, in business for himself, has
> a tenth illegitimate coming, partly respectable . . . (543: 32–5)

and worse

> resting after colonial service, labours at plant, the despair of his many
> benefactresses, calories exclusively from rowntrees and dumplings, one
> bar of sunlight does them all january and half february, the V. de V's
> (animal diet) live in five-storied semidetached but rarely pay trades-
> men, went security for friend who absconded, shares same closet with
> fourteen similar cottages and an illfamed lodginghouse, more respect-
> able than some . . . (544: 33–545: 4)

and even worse

> head of domestic economy never mentioned, queery how they live,
> reputed to procure, last four occupants carried out, mental compan-
> ionship with mates only, respectability unsuccessfully aimed at . . .
> (545: 5–8)

The descriptions are sharply at odds with HCE's characterization of the city as he has transformed it, conjuring the squalor of life in cities in general and Dublin in particular, but these people and places are not to be rejected but embraced within the envisaged community. For they are respectable—worthy of respect and of fellow-feeling. Or if not respectable, at least they aim at respectability.

Like ALP, generous in her forgiveness and forbearance in the closing pages, HCE has his own style of generosity, and it is on display here. He comes before us, tolerant and large-hearted, ready to include those who make some sort of effort, dismally unsuccessful though it may be. If we suppose, at this point in our analysis of him, that his marriage and his love for ALP are central to his conception of what his life is and means, then the love and marriage he envisages are themselves shaped by his sense of how they relate to others. Although love and marriage have their intense private joys, they also have a public face; they are in the world, not withdrawn from it; they are embodied in actions and activities that involve other people, a community of friends and neighbors, bound together by reciprocal services, sometimes by mutual liking, always by respect and toleration. Love and marriage, as well as those who love and are married, are respectable—or aim at respectability. If they fail to win the respect of a surrounding community, then that is a loss, a genuine loss that cannot be waved away with the thought that the lovers can find their own private place, for it truncates or eliminates all sorts of modes of expression of the love. An outsider, perhaps, may be particularly drawn to this conception of marriage, so that the charge that he is not respectable, that he has no place in the community, can prove especially devastating.

Like Leopold Bloom, HCE is an outsider—not only in his own account of the wooing of ALP but also in those we are given elsewhere in the *Wake*, he comes overseas to settle in Dublin. Like Bloom, he wants to be part of the community that he has chosen (or, in Bloom's case, the community his father chose). Confronting the xenophobic Citizen, Bloom declares that his country is Ireland (*Ulysses,* 325) and eventually nearly suffers physical assault from those who mark him as foreign (*Ulysses,* 335–9); throughout the book, there is plenty of evidence that people most integrated within the Dublin community are aloof toward Bloom (see, for example, the "Hades" and "Aeolus" episodes).[7] HCE encounters the same kind of antipathy and rejection, and his life is diminished by it.

Joyce, like Bloom and like HCE, was a man whose family was central to his life. Quite evidently, however, Bloom is only one of his alter egos within the pages of *Ulysses*—there is also Stephen, prepared to break with community and convention, willing to stand outside. The *Wake,* like *Ulysses,* contains a representative of this aspect of its author. It is not willing to limit itself to dream stories that explore, and question, the value of lives founded on marriage and family. In fact, as we shall see more clearly later, HCE's own conception of himself is less single-minded than I have so far taken it to be. As the passages that extol the glorious city might hint, part of his vindication of his life consists in pointing to the products of his creative energy.[8] Before any further attempt to analyze the strands in HCE's complex identity—or complex of identities—I now want to consider a character who embodies a quite different vision of human life, the frightened dreamer of the upstairs bedroom, the "teething wretch" (563: 4), the "bold bad bleak boy of the storybooks" (219: 24), Shem the Penman.

4

NAYMAN OF NOLAND

To adapt oneself to a community, integrating married life within it, can easily demand a willingness to conform that, in the light of the "awebrume hour," will make it seem as though one has forfeited one's self, abandoned individuality for the sake of comfortable acceptance. HCE's great vision of marriage embedded within and reaching out to a broader society effectively sidesteps the problem by supposing that he has the power to work his creative will, to raise up the institutions and to set the rules—those who have the tickets for admission are to be his "villeins." In her bitter retrospective on the life she has lived, ALP sees matters differently—she has "lothed" the smallness of those among whom they have dwelt. Surrounded by the herd, the small-minded, prurient, resentful people whose evil-smelling judgments have poisoned the air around them, they and their marriage have been infected. To command—especially to command nobly, wisely, tolerantly, and generously—is one thing; to serve quite another.

Throughout the *Wake* two strong voices contend with one another, one accepting the need to conform oneself to norms adopted by others, the other rebelling against what it views as an identity-dissolving servitude. Both voices sound within HCE (and, I think, within ALP, too), and one of the problems that lie behind his distinctive stammer is the problem of responding to both of them. As we shall see, the figure of HCE's son Shaun often gives expression to the value of conformity—although it would be quite wrong to think that his voice is "pure" (as it is sometimes described as being [407: 14–16; the full characterization makes the irony clear]) or that the choices for human lives are confined to the simplest and purest expressions of these voices. The portrait of the rebel is typically provided for us by the descriptions, often vituperative, given by the conformist voice (or conformist voices), and the rebel himself often turns out to be Shaun's twin brother Shem.

HCE, as we know, is constantly subject to murky accusations that he has engaged in unseemly, even seamy, activities. The indictment of Shem is both clearer and fiercer. Shem emerges, along with other principal characters and scenes of the dream stories, in Joyce's quiz show (I-6), whose answers are given by Shaun (although there are dim suggestions that some of them might not be his or might not accurately address the question [126: 7–9]). Question 11 inquires whether the respondent would care to join a character, described in the most unflattering terms:

> If you met on the binge a poor acheseyeld from Ailing, when the tune
> of his tremble shook shimmy on shin, while his countrary raged in the
> weak of his wailing, . . . (148: 33–5)

and so on, in a pastiche of a song—"Exile of Erin" by Thomas Campbell—that is stuffed with negative nouns and adjectives. It takes very little reflection to recognize "acheseyeld from Ailing" as a pithy characterization of Joyce, constantly ailing with aching eyes, committed to his self-imposed exile from Erin. The question concludes by posing the invitation as an offer no one could accept, and the respondent's lengthy, professorial answer begins with firm rejection. As it proceeds, however, matters become more complicated, and, almost in spite of itself, the voice cannot avoid a more nuanced presentation. Established authority starts to look less uncontroversially acceptable; rebellion may have a point.[1]

Question 12, the last one in the quiz, will connect the unsavory figure of Question 11 with Shem. Both question and answer are brilliantly ambiguous:

> 12. Sacer esto?
> Answer: *Semus sumus!* (168: 13–14)

Is he sacred? / Is he accursed? / I am Shem / We are the same. Shem, the rebel, may be accursed, beyond the pale, an exile; or he may be sacred, the exposer of corruption, the advocate of a new order, the true individual who cuts himself free of the past and creates himself afresh. Shem offers a potential answer to the complex of questions I have seen at the heart of the *Wake*, an answer that elaborates the fierce determination for self-fashioning with which we leave Stephen Dedalus at the end of *Portrait*—we might even think of it as the view from *Portrait*. The attack on Shem can thus be seen both as a repudiation of the answer and as a reminder of what makes it attractive. We cannot avoid taking Shem (or Stephen) seriously as a possibility for ourselves; the question of his status is one for each of us.

The last questions of the quiz show prepare the bill of indictment leveled against Shem in the next chapter. The voice that gives us the biography of Shem is firm and prosecutorial; no quarter is given. We start with a physical description of the accused as a patchwork, made of bits and pieces, none of which fulfill their proper functions:

> the wrong shoulder higher than the right, all ears, an artificial tongue
> with a natural curl, not a foot to stand on, a handful of thumbs, a blind
> stomach, a deaf heart, a loose liver, . . . (169: 14–17)

This portrait of the artist already contains, in embryo, some of the themes that the prosecutor will amplify. Shem listens attentively, perhaps even when it is improper, stooping at keyholes to overhear. His language (like that of *Ulysses*, and even more that of the *Wake*) is unnatural, but it is used to sneer (the curl of the tongue is, I suggest, sufficiently close to the curl of the lip). His heart is deaf, devoid of any natural sympathy or understanding. His liver may be affected by alcoholic overindulgence, and that would be typical of his general moral condition. Cold-blooded, lecherous, hypersensitive to slights: the catalogue continues. An ungenerous acquaintance of the Stephen Dedalus whom we meet in *Ulysses* (or even at the end of *Portrait*) might apply all these descriptions.

Yet Shem is clever. He is a riddler, a questioner, one who can subvert the more staid and respectable visions of his young playmates. The accuser offers us a story of children at play, when Shem

> dictited to of all his little brothron and sweestureens the first riddle of the universe: asking, when is a man not a man?: telling them take their time, yungfries, and wait till the tide stops . . . (170: 3–6)

Already, we know that there is a catch, that Shem is imposing on the other children (he "dictated"), that he is setting them up for a fall and wants them to consider carefully so that they can appreciate their own failures of imagination when they go wrong (as he is confident they will). The answers consider the obvious ways in which one can be unmanned—obvious, at least, within the compass of everyday thoughts about human life, human susceptibility, and human virtue: by the sound of thunder (of which Joyce was notoriously frightened), by infidelity, by lapse of religious faith, by death, by wine, by age, by bad manners, by wild speculation, and so on. All are wrong. So Shem, "the doctator" (teacher and dictator [170: 22]) wins, by telling them that it is

> when he is a—yours till the rending of the rocks,—Sham. (170: 24)

What does this answer mean? And why the odd interpolation? The apocalyptic perspective, I believe, signals the context of judgment from the end of a life, the retrospective view of ALP's last monologue. Shem is teaching—and teasing—his conformist contemporaries that they should imagine looking back on their lives from the end and ask themselves if their lives have been human, whether they have amounted to anything. The devastating possibility is that, in that context, they will see themselves as having failed because they have been shams—they have not lived lives of their own but have conformed, gone along with the ideas and ideals of others. Their answers suggest that that is precisely what they are and how they are. Their conventional imaginings survey the conventional ways of going wrong and do not consider that the essential failure to be human consists in not having forged one's own identity. Shem's riddle and its solution counter the answer to the *Wake*'s central question offered by

HCE in his great apologia, disputing the value of a life centered on a marriage embedded in, and subject to the norms of, a community.

Shem's *Credo* (and even Iago can have a *Credo*) is that expressed by Stephen Dedalus at the end of *Portrait:*

> I go to encounter for the millionth time the reality of experience and to forge in the smithy of my soul the uncreated conscience of my race. (*Portrait*, 252–3)

Conscience and consciousness are not to be borrowed, but forged—forged, but not a forgery. Shem is dedicated to the work of self-forging. He is resolved not to be a sham.

The prosecutorial voice understands nothing of this. To be a sham, according to the accuser, is to fail to accord with established tastes, to deviate from the norms of society. The charge starts with apparent triviality: Shem's tastes in food and drink are "low" (170–1). Of course, the demand for uniformity even in matters gustatory reveals just how far the pressures to conform can penetrate. Unlike the properly brought up who prefer their fish fresh, Shem has a taste for "salmon tinned" (170: 27). Further, he is averse to good old-fashioned hearty food:

> None of your inchthick blueblooded Balaclava fried-at-belief-stakes or juicejelly legs of the Grex's molten mutton or greasilygristly grunters' goupons or slice upon slab of luscious goosebosom with lump after load of plumpudding stuffing all aswim in a swamp of bogoakgravy for that greekenhearted yude! (170: 32–171: 1)

Perhaps this prosecutor moonlights as an apostle for vegetarianism.[2]

There is more going on here than the trivial topic would suggest. The pun on "stakes" indicates that Shem's reluctance to dine on traditional food is part and parcel of his rejection of an ethos, of his abandonment of the tenets of a culture, principles for which his predecessors have suffered and died. Shem, like Stephen, wants to escape from history, a history the prosecutor sees as constitutive of what he is and ought to want to be, but which the rebel regards as a nightmare, tending perhaps toward a shout in the street,[3] the voice of a baying coercive mob. The same connection is made in a less direct fashion in the reference to tinned salmon. Part of the fun at Finnegan's Wake is that the guests eat and drink, and, it appears, some of the nourishment is to be supplied by the corpse (7: 8–15). Unfortunately, something is rotten in the state of the dead: although almost "rubicund Salmosalar," "he is smolten in our mist, woebecanned and packt away"—in short, turned into tinned salmon, and that, as the narrator tells us, means that the "meal's dead off" (7: 16–19). Shem's preference, then, is not for what we ought to imbibe from the past, from tradition, from the history of his community, but a rotten version of it. To change the metaphor, in forging his conscience he must rely on conceptions and categories that have been handed down to him—he cannot stand completely outside history—but he uses them in novel ways, giving priority to things that tradition has scorned, questioned, and rejected. If Shem (or Stephen) supposes that he can begin completely afresh, fashioning his own identity from some point completely outside history and tradition, then he is deeply deceived. There is no such point to be found.

The review of Shem's tastes in drink initially appears as a simple repetition of these points: no good, healthy (traditionally approved), manly beverages for him, but "some sort of a rhubarbarous maundarin yellagreen funkleblue windigut diodying applejack squeezed from sour grapefruice" (171: 16–18; Joyce's favorite tipple was a Swiss white wine). The choice of adjectives prepares us for later accusations that Shem is a coward, duplicitous as well as envious and resentful. Yet the characterization continues with a new charge. Shem drinks too much, and when he does, he can turn vulgarly obscene (171: 23–8). Despite the prosecutor's scorn, we might sympathize with Shem, the avoider of red meat—the bullockbefriending bard, perhaps[4]; it is less easy to warm to the lascivious drunk with his scatalogical snigger. Indeed, as we proceed, the charges will carry more sting.

For Shem is prepared to use his acquaintances, to cadge and to scrounge. He extricates himself from difficult situations by leaving, running away, keeping out of sight and slinking into whatever cover he can find. Dishonest and manipulative, he adjusts his account of matters to suit the audience, even when the subject concerns his family. In the interest of impressing others, or simply making ends meet, he will offer a version of

> the whole lifelong swrine story of his entire low cornaille existence, abusing his deceased ancestors wherever the sods were and one moment tarabooming great blunderguns (poh!) about his farfamed fine Poppamore, Mr Humhum, whom history, climate and entertainment made the first of his sept and always up to debt, though Eavens ears ow many fines he faces, and another moment visanvrerssas, cruaching three jeers (pah!) for his rotten little ghost of a Peppybeg, Mr Himmyshimmy, a blighty, a reeky, a lighty, a scrapy, a babbly, a ninny, dirty seventh among thieves and always bottom sawyer . . . (173: 19–29)

The more flattering story is connected to HCE, indicated by the usual device of words introduced by those letters, but the antisemitic slur suggests that the negative picture features Bloom, one of Stephen's father figures in *Ulysses*. The other, Simon Dedalus, is also present, as is clear from the echo of Stephen's enumeration of the attributes of his father:

> A medical student, an oarsman, a tenor, an amateur actor, a shouting politician, a small landlord, a small investor, a drinker, a good fellow, a storyteller, somebody's secretary, something in a distillery,

a taxgatherer, a bankrupt and at present a praiser of his own past.
(*Portrait*, 241)

The prosecutor's charge is that nothing is sacred to Shem—in the interests of preserving his miserable existence, he will betray anything and anyone; "*sacer*" means "accursed."

The duplicity shows up in Shem's willingness to agree with anyone, and to ingratiate himself with everyone, when it can suit his purposes (174). If difficulties arise for causes to which one might think him devoted, he will cut and run. No ideal of home, of community, of country, or of freedom has any hold on him. Everything is to be subordinated to his self-preservation, to the continuation of his life. And for what?

For his art, of course. Shem is a Penman, and the prosecutor is well aware of the form the defense will take. The defense is forestalled in two ways, by driving home to us, again and again, how treacherous and repulsive Shem's conduct is and by denigrating the value of the cause to which he is devoted. "Maistre Sheames de la Plume," it is claimed, thinks of himself in high terms—he is

> aware of no other shaggspick, other Shakhisbeard, either prexactly un-
> like his polar andthisishis or procisely the seem as woops (parn!) as what
> he fancied or guessed the sames as he was himself . . . (177: 31–5)

Shakespeare is frequently a looming figure in the consciousness of Joyce's protagonists (and in the *Wake*), a standard against which to measure the value of what the artist has made: Stephen's lecture on *Hamlet* excites the comment—"After God Shakespeare has created most"[5]; the thought is echoed in the *Wake* ("[a]s Great Shapessphere puns it" [295: 3–4]). The bard is Joyce's summit of human creative endeavor (and, one feels, he hopes that some future commentator might add a coda to Dumas's line: "After Shakespeare, Joyce has created most"—a not completely implausible assessment).

If this is Shem's vision of himself, then he is woefully deluded. For what he produces in "the inspissated grime of his glaucous den" is his "usylessly unreadable Blue Book of Eccles" (179: 25–7). Although he imagines a wonderful reception for this, it is a slow struggle to write because of his hideous physical condition (180: 17–30). The prosecutor intimates that Shem's artistic impulses can only be released in the presence of squalid titillations—perhaps he needs used female undergarments "to start city life together," for "[h]is jymes is out of job, would sit and write" (181: 29–30).[6] The environment in which he labors to compose contains a vast assembly of detritus, some of it mundane, much disgusting, and including garters from an impressive range of women (183: 8–184: 2). Out of it, he writes a work that rejects the learning of his masters and is turned down because the publication of it would violate law (184: 33–185: 5). To discuss this work, without giving offense to the devout, requires the prosecutor to continue in Latin (185: 8–26)—but, to make sure we get the point, he translates just those parts that would excite anger or disgust.

Shem's art, we are told, proceeds by making ink out of his own feces and urine and using for "foolscap" his entire body (185: 14–36). What this yields is the *Wake* itself, a vision of "cyclewheeling history" (186: 2). Yet here, perhaps, the prosecutor makes a tactical mistake, allowing Shem, for one moment, to characterize what he is about:

> (thereby, he said, reflecting from his own individual person life unliv-
> able, transaccidentated through the slow fires of consciousness into
> a dividual chaos, perilous, potent, common to allflesh, human only,
> mortal) but with each word that would not pass away the squidself
> which he had squirtscreened from the crystalline world waned cha-
> greenold and doriangrayer in its dudhud. (186: 2–8)

As I read it, this passage contains two important clues to understanding the *Wake* and its surrogate author, Shem.

First, the *Wake* is not so much a vision of human history as the way in which individual lives are structured so as to respond to the challenge of rendering them livable. That challenge arises because no structure is given to us, nothing from outside humanity can provide point or meaning to what we do—life is "human only, mortal." The challenge arises for each of us, for "allflesh," and is, strictly speaking, irresoluble ("life unlivable"). Even those who try to forge something in the smithy of their souls ("the slow fires of consciousness") will only manage to impose a partial order and structure on the haphazard business of human existence ("a dividual chaos"), and even that will always be on the verge of dissolving, important though it is to us ("perilous, potent"). This is the problem, I have suggested, to which HCE and ALP are responding with their variant conceptions of marriage and of love.

The second clue comes from the characterization of Shem's very different response to the challenge. Unlike those devoted to family, who preserve and maintain themselves in and for one another, the artist deliberately consumes himself, sacrificing every other part of his existence, so that it may be trans-formed into the work of art.[7] The physical human being decays so that the work of art may endure, an inversion of Wilde's tale of the portrait of Dorian Gray.[8] Shem may be in his "dudhud," but the word of the *Wake* survives; and this, he might claim in defense, is one way to respond to the challenge, one way to "beat time" (419: 8).[9] Moreover, this remains true even if the work is con-demned, misunderstood, banned, or vilified, even if the "parochial watch," represented by "Petty constable Sistersen of the Kruis-Kroon-Kraal" regards it as an obscene effusion of ink (186: 17, 19, 20).

Late nineteenth-century thought provides plenty of sources for Shem's interpolated defense. Nietzsche's account of the life-affirming individual, prepared to dare all and sacrifice all in the cause of self creation is one. Ibsen, probably more influential on Joyce,[10] is another, and Ibsen, more than Nietzsche, reveals to us the human costs of daring self-creation. This is the second horn of the prosecutor's charge against Shem: not only is the art worse than worthless, but the creation of it requires terrible sacrifices.

For Shem, like Stephen, will not serve (*Portrait*, 239). The prosecutor makes dark references to mother and murder (187: 13, 15),[11] reminding us of Stephen's refusal to honor his mother's wish to take part in religious ritual and of Buck Mulligan's accusation: "You could have knelt down, damn it, Kinch, when your dying mother asked you, . . . " (*Ulysses*, 7). Perhaps satirizing Shem's willingness to transform life into art, the prosecutor invites us to imagine the death of the mother as high comedy (187: 15–23).[12] Moved by this to his summation, the prosecutor—now "JUSTIUS"—addresses Shem directly and immediately offers a more explicit charge of betrayal:

> Where have you been in the uterim, enjoying yourself all the morning since your last wetbed confession? I advise you to conceal yourself, my little friend, as I have said a moment ago and put your hands in my hands and have a nightslong homely little confiteor about things. (187: 36–188: 4)

Shem has put his own concerns, the squalid satisfactions of his life and art, before the devotion he owed to his mother, the woman whose uterus carried him, for whom he would not confess. He must make amends, return, do absolution, accept again the wisdom of the tradition in which he was reared, like the adolescent boy, reminded by a priest who offers a lurid picture of hell to his "dear little brothers in Christ" of his fall from grace, the boy who once gave a painful recitation of his sins (*Portrait*, III).

Justius even hints at a second betrayal, implicating Shem in the spread of the rumor about HCE. As his summation proceeds, there is a glancing reference to a father figure (191: 34–6), followed quickly by allusions to the contents of the malicious stories that swirl around him. Then, in conclusion, he offers "a little judas tonic" (193: 9), inviting Shem to peer in the "rockingglass," where he sees a "secret," something that proceeds from one person to another, in just the manner of the original scandal about HCE (193: 17–23; compare 36–43). Perhaps, then, Shem's "art" consists in the act of betrayal that brings about the father's humiliation. Justius has only one possible verdict: "You are mad!" (193: 28).

Justius originally speaks to "himother," addressing Shem by a telling name: "Stand forth, Nayman of Noland" (187: 24, 28). Shem, he claims, is a denier, one who abandons, mutilates, desecrates, and destroys his past, his traditions, his country, and his family. But Justius does not have the last word. He is followed by "MERCIUS" who talks "of hisself" (193: 31)—as if finally the prosecutor were admitting kinship with the accused or the accused responding to the prosecutor, as if they were one flesh (or "all-flesh"). Mercius begins with an admission of fault—"I who oathily forswore the womb that bore you and the paps I sometimes sucked" (193: 32–4).[13] He is not insensitive to the past, and, indeed, looking back "ere the compline hour of being alone athands itself and a puff or so before we yield our spiritus to the wind" (194: 4–6), his heart is "attrite" (194: 3). We should recall, perhaps, that the problem of giving structure to our lives is insoluble—"life unlivable"—that chaos can only partially be ordered. So, at the end of Shem's day, there will be parts of his life that he must deeply regret, parts that will not fit, even though he has forged his own identity, even though he is not a sham.

And, indeed, the strange voice of Mercius is double, switching mid-sentence from the contrite fraternal tone of Shem-Shaun to the comforting reassurance of ALP, "little wonderful mummy" (194: 33), who brings the forgiveness she might have given them as naughty children. Instead of the "deathbone," wielded by Justius, Mercius

> lifts the lifewand and the dumb speak.
> —Quoiquoiquoiquoiquoiquoiquoiquoiq! (195: 5–6)

The content of what the previously dumb utter may not matter much—it may be trivial or absurd, a record of the mundane sequence of intrinsically unimportant events in a city that is in no way extraordinary or even "Ibscenest nansence" (535: 19). The significance is that they have spoken with their own voice, that from the chaos of "life unlivable" some individual response has come.

I read this closing speech as introducing three important ideas. First, our vision of Shem the rebel should encompass the possibility that he is not the narcissist, unmindful of others and bent only on selfish satisfactions, that the prosecutor envisages. The "squirtscreening" of the "squidself" may be extraordinarily painful, even though the artist has dedicated himself completely to it. Second, however valuable the creative rejection of stale tradition turns out to be—even if it should be "sphere-shaping"—the creative life will still be untidy, messy, incomplete. Elements in it will fail to fit the whole; the chaos will only be partially ordered. That will be clear in the sacrifices made, and felt, by the heart that is committed to making them but remains regretful; "attrite" suggests both contrition and the consciousness that what one has done is the best approximation to the right.[14] Third, there is a way of responding to this predicament, one that makes forgiveness and acceptance—even joy—possible. That attitude, associated here with the coming of ALP, returns us to the wonderfully generous acquiescence of the last pages.

Shem, I have suggested, offers a vision of how a human life might be lived, one that contrasts with those I have traced in ALP's monologue and in

HCE's attempt at self-vindication. There are many ways of questioning that vision, and it is important for anyone drawn to realizing it to confront those questions—if the prosecutor did not exist, Shem would have to invent him. The prosecutor lives within Shem—as Shem and ALP live within HCE—or, better, as all these voices live within the dreamer at the *Wake*. The problem for the dreamer is to understand and to assess their competing claims.

5

CROSSMESS PARZEL

It is time to proceed more slowly and more systematically. I have been attempting to use four different parts of the *Wake* to introduce, rather impressionistically, some questions I take to be at the heart of this fascinating—but perplexing—work. My strategy has been to provide a frame of some very general issues about human life and embed within it a selection of passages, hoping that, within that frame and given that juxtaposition, Joyce's obscure words would be easier to interpret. I have not tried to parse each word, to trace down all the allusions, to follow out the clues given to us by Joyce and his friends, but simply to connect parts of the book with a mood and with some broad themes. One might well protest that this approach is far too cavalier to yield any insight—or even that it only obtains what successes it does because I have browsed in the "easier" parts of the *Wake.* Yet I hope that my four introductory discussions have made it seem useful to provide a more finished version of the framework I have sketched, that they will offer a new perspective to those already familiar with the book, that they will help readers who struggle with it, and that they will provide a point of entry for people who have previously been daunted by it. In this chapter and the next two, I want to be more explicit and precise about the perspective I am recommending and about the status I am claiming for it. I shall begin by contrasting my approach with other strategies for reading the *Wake.*

Joyce described his book in many ways, including some of what we can reasonably take to be his favorite characterizations within the book itself. One that occurs relatively late suggests that it is a gift, a "beautiful crossmess parzel" (619: 4–5). Overtly hostile (or cross) readers might focus on the "mess," but a more benign reaction would take Joyce simply to have set us a gigantic puzzle, a lifetime's worth of the most ingenious, taxing, and witty cryptic crosswords. Many people who become enamored of the *Wake* effectively treat it in this way, concentrating on this passage or that, exploring the many possible puns, finding a touch of Sanskrit here or Kigali there, uncovering an allusion to Irish legend or Egyptian burial rituals, tracing a connection to a popular song of the 1890s or a sign in the window of a Dublin merchant. This activity can be enormous fun, and it is, of course, perfectly harmless. Yet if this is all that can be made of the *Wake*, then the admirers of *Ulysses* who worried that Joyce was wasting seventeen years of his life were right; the great setters of crossword puzzles have done as much (and with less sacrifice).[1] The man whom Nora overheard at night in the next room, laughing as he wrote, also struggled with failing eyesight, with criticism from friends that was bound to provoke doubt. If all he produced was a trove of puzzles, however rich, it was not worth the effort.[2]

There is an obvious way to think of the *Wake* that gives it more credit. By solving these individual puzzles, we build up a large mosaic within which significant patterns and insights will emerge. I want to question this conception: I do not believe that the value of this masterpiece—for masterpiece it is—can be gleaned from dedicated campaigns of puzzle solution. Quite the reverse. Until we have some general conception of how we think the book is to be conceived, there is little hope that individual passages can be puzzled out in ways that allow for integration.[3]

Should we assume, however, that integration is a proper goal? Perhaps instead of seeking coherence, we ought to take the *Wake* as expressing the human predicament after Babel? I suggest that the construction of a cacophany of voices is no more obviously worthy of the seventeen years of Joyce's labors than the provision of a compendium of brainteasers. Moreover the voices of the *Wake* do not merely talk; they are linked together by shared references and common motifs, engaged in something that looks like conversation. The demand for coherence, as I shall understand it, isn't a denial of the strangeness of the conversation, a wrong-headed desire to "normalize" this novel or to take it realistically, but rather a search for ways in which constant reworking of the same materials serves a genuine point.

One of Joyce's other characterizations of the *Wake* is helpful in orienting the reader. It is, he suggested, a "nonday diary," an "allnights newseryreel" (489: 35). The references to the night are plainly important—a familiar, perhaps hackneyed, way of contrasting *Ulysses* and the *Wake* is to dub the former "the book of the day" and the latter "the book of the night." There are limits to the illumination provided by this contrast (as we shall see later), but it is perfectly good as far as it goes. For now, I want to focus on the other elements in the description, since they also seem revealing.

Diaries are places in which individuals record the events of their lives, often events they recognize as having little significance for others. Sometimes a diary can serve as a place for working out who one is, a smithy in which one's identity is forged, and that may occur selfconsciously (as with people who think of their diary as a place for finding themselves) or in the process of creating an individual organization of the daily round (as, for example, it does with Pepys). A diary can be a forum within which the inner voices that clamor for attention can put their claims on the record.

A newsreel—or, more exactly, the sort of newsreel Joyce saw in the cinemas he visited—provides a jumpy sequence of pictures of detached events, the events that seem important at the time. There is little difficulty in recognizing what is supposed to be occurring—newsreels are not hard to understand—but the selection of events and the commentary can easily be adjusted to the interests, and prejudices, of the intended audience. "Newseryreel" does not only suggest "newsreel," however, but also "nursery rhyme." Nursery rhymes are apparently simple, often vehicles for presenting particular ideas or ideals for children, sometimes telling trivial stories, sometimes nonsensical. The *Wake* not only uses nursery rhymes, but it also seems full of trivial stories (often repeated, or repeated with variations) and appears to contain passages that are nonsensical. I shall try to show that it is also a vehicle for presenting ideas and ideals, although perhaps not for children.

But if that is the case, why does it have to be so hard? Why do we need to puzzle it all out? Couldn't it be like a diary or a newsreel, relatively transparent?[4] The obvious response to these questions is to emphasize the idea that the *Wake* is the book of the night. That response is, I think, inadequate. For if we take seriously the thought of presenting to the reader some equivalent to the diary we keep in our sleep, some counterpart of the newsreels we dream through or of the nursery rhymes that run through our sleeping heads, then that presentation must come to terms with the fact that the reader is awake, is thinking in our everyday waking terms, and needs some device or instrument to conjure up these supposedly different presentations. Without any such device, readers are likely to go blank—as many do, and have done, on plunging into *Finnegans Wake*. Freud, we should recall, worked quite hard to provide access to our night thoughts by writing *The Interpretation of Dreams* in plain language.

I think we should take quite seriously Molly Bloom's exasperated exclamation to her husband: "O, rocks! . . . Tell us in plain words" (*Ulysses*, 64). One reason for doing so is that her demand is echoed by one of the *Wake*'s washerwomen:

Honddu jarkon! Tell us in franca langua. And call a spate a spate.
(198: 18–19)

Another is that Joyce seems to take great delight in the challenges he is setting for the reader. As one nears the end of a long book, it is disconcerting to read that "Not a salutary sellable sound is since" (598: 4). Much earlier, the author seems to gloat over the difficulties he is setting:

You is feeling like you was lost in the bush, boy? You says: It is a puling sample jungle of woods. You most shouts out: Bethicket me for a stump of a beech if I have the poultriest notions what the farest he all means.
(112: 3–6)

(Interestingly, this passage is not only quite transparent, but also occurs in one of the chapters of the *Wake* where the meanings of individual words are easiest to pin down.) Those who read with the background knowledge of differences among successive drafts and appreciate how Joyce made the words and sentences denser, thicker, and more opaque, or who have heard the famous story of his discussions with Stuart Gilbert about how to make the book more complex and impenetrable, can easily view the whole thing as a tease, an exercise in intellectual one-upmanship, a puzzle composed by a setter—Shem the riddler?—who chuckles as he anticipates the hard time his would-be solvers will have.[5]

I believe that Molly Bloom raises an important question: Why was it impossible for Joyce to write his book in plain English? I shall try to offer an answer, an answer that makes him more than a willful composer of puzzles. First, however, I want to develop a strategy that rejects many of the presuppositions of conventional approaches.

The *Wake* comes to its potential readers enmeshed in a very unusual secondary literature. There are reader's guides and plot summaries, censuses of Joyce's sources and annotations to every page. The suggestion is that, without all of this, one won't have a chance—that with respect to the *Wake* we are all in the position of the dim student who needs to understand some classic text, for whom helpful notes with condensations of the story are written. Now it is certainly true that annotated versions are helpful even for sophisticated readers: Eliot provided valuable notes for *The Waste Land*, and for anyone who is not a medieval historian, Dante's annotators offer illuminating background on the people he discusses. Yet it is worth reflecting on how ordinary readers use this ancillary material, for it is definitely not a matter of proceeding laboriously, line by line, earnestly flipping backward and forward between text and notes. That is no way to read a poem, whether the poet is Dante, Eliot, or Joyce.

Tacitly, the guidebooks and their users take for granted the idea that there is something Joyce meant, something that he carefully and cunningly concealed, and that, by consulting dictionaries in seventy-odd languages, handbooks of Celtic mythology, the central texts of many world religions, and so forth, one can arrive at the meaning of the individual passages, connect them together, and so—the Everest moment—finally achieve a complete summary of the plot. Or, since dedicated scholars have already done that for us, we can piggy-back on their efforts—we shall need several of them, since the synthesizers sometimes disagree—and, armed with our various Baedekers, we can begin our tour of the *Wake*. This seems to me all wrong. The scholars are indeed sometimes useful, but, where they are, they are useful in just the ways the annotators to Dante are useful. We need to learn to read the *Wake* as we do the *Inferno* (in whatever is our native language).

Here, then, is an interpretive suggestion. Instead of thinking that there are individual puzzles, each with a solution that can be ascertained by peeling back the layers of Joyce's learning, our task is to find a set of readings for his words, sentences, paragraphs, and chapters that produce an illuminating pattern on the kaleidoscope—where the reader sets the standard for what counts as illuminating. Knowing something about the linguistic roots of one of his portmanteau words or learning about a myth to which he alluded *might* be helpful in each case—and there are bound to be *some* places in the 628 pages where this kind of information is valuable—but we cannot, nor should we, aspire to carry this out in *every* case: it is up to us where we consult the notes. Our reading should be active, starting from a gestalt on the work, and proceeding to try to adopt it as broadly as we can. The units with which we start should be relatively big ones—chapters rather than words—and our concern should be to identify large structures and themes, moods and tones, and let the detailed readings of individual words fall into place in light of these patterns. This, of course, is the "impressionistic" strategy pursued in the four sections above, but I do not wish to claim that my specific articulations of the strategy in those chapters are uniquely favored.

If we take seriously Joyce's suggestion that "every word will be bound over to carry three score and ten toptypsical readings throughout the book of Doublends Jined" (20: 14–16), then the consequence would be a combinatorial explosion of interpretations—seventy raised to whatever power we take to measure the number of words that require reading. Perhaps there are constraints that limit the number of combinations, requirements of coherence and consistency—but why exactly should this be if the *Wake* is indeed the book of the night? Yet, as every reader knows, the challenge is not to select our favorite from among some huge array of possible readings that are laid before us—as in those stories that allow the reader particular options at branch points—but to come up with even one reading that makes sense of the whole. For that, we should not demand of our perspective or gestalt that it maximize the number of individual words to which we can give some meaning; if it speaks to us, even while leading us to downplay, or avoid, certain sections of the text, that is good; if we find that we can constantly deepen and elaborate it as we explore more and more parts of the *Wake,* that is even better.[6]

I anticipate a natural rejoinder: how does the neophyte construct this gestalt? Perhaps with a look at one of the available guides, not by way of dogged pursuit, but in the manner of initial orientation.[7] After that, it is, I think, a matter of responding to mood and tone, often conveyed by the sonic associations of Joyce's musical prose. I would apply to the *Wake* the wise advice given to me by the gifted teacher who introduced me to *Paradise Lost:* "Read it aloud," she said, "and listen to the cadences; when you go back and puzzle out the syntax, you will usually find that Milton is saying what you thought he said."[8] The sheer sound of passages of the *Wake* can frequently generate a sense of what may be going on, and, when this is applied to the details of the words and sentences, one begins to elaborate one of those many readings.

My recommended strategy can easily appear irresponsible and unscholarly. Can we really afford to ignore Joyce's vast learning and his intentions, sometimes laid out in letters to his bemused friends? Can we turn our backs on the official—Viconian—structure of the *Wake?* My pragmatic response is to be grateful for these where they advance our work of active construction and ignore them where they do not. Consider the reliance on Vico. That might loom large if we saw the *Wake* as a global approach to human history, an elaboration of Vico's famous cyclic vision. I do not see how to do that; Joyce's selection of episodes from the history of our species is idiosyncratic and unrepresentative; they are used to mirror the predicaments of the individual characters of the dream stories; "cyclewheeling history," as we have already seen, plays a part, at least according to Shem, in the individual's quest for self-understanding (186: 2–6). As I read him, Joyce borrowed two main thoughts from Vico: he elaborated the idea that human beings face a particular set of predicaments that arise again and again; and he was intrigued by the idea of thunder as a creative force, not only frightening human beings, but also driving them into community. These do not arise from a particularly profound reading of *La Scienza Nuova*—and that fact is typical of Joyce, a man with a mind of almost unsurpassed breadth but one that was relatively shallow. Joyce engaged with a wide range of texts and traditions, but he was far more concerned with their large central themes than with the details.[9]

Nor do I think that Joyce's explicit accounts of how pieces of the *Wake* are supposed to work need play a guiding role in our attempts to read it. Quite understandably, he was concerned to explain what he was about to Harriet Shaw Weaver, who had supported him so staunchly, and, in a letter of 1924, he gave her a characterization of the first two chapters of Part III as

> a description of a postman traveling backwards in the night through the events already narrated. It is written in the form of a *via crucis* of 14 stations but in reality it is only a barrel rolling down the river Liffey.[10]

As we read these chapters, it is not hard to identify affinities with the passion story. But we hardly need to know the details of the theology on which Joyce is drawing. It is enough if we can capture the tone and mood that the idea of the stations of the cross is meant to evoke—and if Joyce was right to use this idea as an organizing principle, it will be because he can use it to set that tone. Effectively, he is co-opting the skills of the theologians and liturgists, and we ought to be able to respond to him in parallel to the ways the faithful responded (or respond) to them, without knowing how the trick is pulled off.

Stuart Gilbert, working in close association with Joyce, produced a wonderfully illuminating guide to *Ulysses*.[11] A small part of what Gilbert offers us concerns the architectural details of Joyce's construction, and, at the beginning of his discussion of each chapter, he places a list of the associated art, color, organ of the body, and so forth. I confess that there are many parts of *Ulysses* for which this kind of information does not advance my appreciation at all, and, for the rest, the enhancement is quite minor. Much of the contextual material, both in Joyce's letters and in the expositions of his friends, strikes me in similar fashion. To the extent that these are supposed to be our guides to the *Wake*, it is as if we had only the trivia of the architectural details from Gilbert's book and none of the insightful substantive discussions.

Yet Joyce himself, in his brilliantly funny chapter on the interpretation of documents (I-5), emphasizes the importance of context in reading. To neglect "the enveloping facts" (109: 14) is, he suggests,

> just as hurtful to sound sense . . . as were some fellow in the act of perhaps getting an intro from another fellow turning out to be a friend in need of his, say, to a lady of the latter's acquaintance, engaged in performing the elaborative antecistral ceremony of upstheres, straightaway to run off and vision her plump and plain in her natural altogether, preferring to close his blinkhard's eyes to the ethiquethical fact that she was, after all, wearing for the space of the time being some definite articles of evolutionary clothing . . . (109: 15–23)

and we are plunged into one of the *Wake*'s many celebrations of female costume (typically undergarments, for which, like "Jymes" of the advertisement [181], the author seems to have particular fondness). The passage is surely tongue-in-cheek—it begins, after all, with the thought that in interpreting a letter, one needs to take a hard look at the envelope. In any event, what counts as the "enveloping facts" is a matter to be determined, and one that should be determined by the interests of the interpreter. Echoing the spirit of HCE's grand invitation to his "villeins," we might suggest that *"chacun à son goût"* is an appropriate slogan—or, to extend Joyce's simile, if some "fellows" want to contemplate this or that aspect of "feminine clothiering" (109: 31), even to envision the lady "plump and plain in her natural altogether," this is a matter for individual tastes.

The *Wake* includes hints that Joyce envisages the kind of active, constructive reading I am advocating. In the only instances of a clichéd form of address to the reader, he invokes not a "gentle reader" but a "gentlewriter" (63: 10) and a "drear writer" (476: 21). I take the designation seriously; each of us must, in effect, write our version of the *Wake* from the materials Joyce has given us. Yet if that is so, why did he labor so hard to pack into it so much esoteric learning, so many languages? Not, I suggest, because we were set the very specific task of retrieving his own patterns of association and response, but because he needed to ensure that the materials he was providing were sufficiently rich to serve as a rewarding basis for our creative efforts. We can give a more benign interpretation to the celebrated conversation with Gilbert: Joyce needed to know if the text was complicated enough yet, not because he wanted to reveal his wisdom only to the persevering faithful, but because he hoped to write a book that would inspire idiosyncratic, creative readings from a large number of reader/writers, each of whom would find within it sufficient resources to reward sustained imaginative effort.[12]

If this is correct, then we have a genuine alternative to Joyce the show-off, composer of intractable riddles. We also have a partial answer to Molly Bloom's exasperation. On that score, however, significantly more can be said.

Those of Joyce's friends who served as early champions of "Work in Progress" emphasized his rejuvenation of language. A fascination with words is clear from the first page of the first story of *Dubliners*, and in *Portrait* and *Ulysses*, Joyce had stretched the limits of English vocabulary.[13] Yet a conception of Joyce as exploring the possibilities of language, soaring into new verbal spheres, comes dangerously close to the unsatisfactory portrait of the clever riddler. While some of his defenders are inclined to exult in the linguistic novelties for their own sake, others take Joyce to have been moved to his innovations by the nature of his topic and themes.[14]

What topic? What themes? Here we should return to what I suggested earlier was a sound, but limited, characterization: the *Wake* is the book of the night as *Ulysses* is the book of the day; the waking scenes at the beginning of Part IV offer plenty of support for this conception (see, for example, 597: 1–2; 598: 6–9). Perhaps the most sustained, imaginative, scholarly account of the *Wake* as a whole—John Bishop's *James Joyce's Book of the Dark* [15]—takes the characterization very seriously, exploring, often insightfully and brilliantly, the presentation of a sleeping figure, whose eyes are shut and ears are open.[16] Yet if this were all, the content and significance of the *Wake* would be quite puzzling. Why do these dim and fluid characters float through the dream stories? Why this choice of apparently trivial stories, told again and again, often with variations? Why should anyone care to read a reconstruction, however ingenious, of our lives when we sleep? Why does Joyce have any basis for, or expertise in, offering that sort of reconstruction? Why not read Freud instead—or a learned article from the neuroscientists who study sleep?

To focus my doubts, it is valuable to think about the other part of the characterization: *Ulysses* as the "book of the day." As vast numbers of people who have not read it know, *Ulysses* describes the events of a single day in Dublin—June 16 1904, the day young James Joyce first walked out with Nora Barnacle. Not all the events, of course. A tiny selection from the panoply of Dublin life. We follow the actions of a number of ordinary Dubliners as they go about their very ordinary business—and we follow the thoughts of three, most completely those of Leopold Bloom, advertisement canvasser. Now there are plainly millions of potential novels to be written that focus on a single day, that survey mundane actions, and that trace the thoughts of three characters, emphasizing one of them in particular, novels that would be unbearably tedious and unprofitable. What makes *Ulysses* one of the greatest novels in the English language—the second greatest, I would say[17]—is that the reconstructed thoughts of Bloom, of Stephen, and of Molly are *worth* following, showing us what it is to struggle, to aspire, to fail, to fall, to betray and be betrayed, to befriend, to forgive, showing us some of what human life is, how it is limited and confused, how it can be triumphant and worthwhile. There is a recipe for making "the book of the day"; there is no recipe for writing *Ulysses*.

The *Wake*, I believe, surpasses any characterization as "the book of the night" in exactly parallel fashion. It is not an academic attempt to reconstruct the experience of being asleep—whatever that project might turn out to be—but, like its predecessor, an attempt to explore our humanity by probing even deeper into our minds. It is, as Joyce continued to believe in the face of others' doubts, an even more ambitious attempt to pursue the themes that had occupied him throughout his career. The exposure of night thoughts is to deepen and elaborate his vision of human life.

Ulysses provides us with a plot, a sequence of events, around which to anchor the thoughts and emotions of the protagonists. It might seem that we need the same for the *Wake*, that a first step will be to understand the action, to reconstruct the plot. There have been many attempts to do just that, and I take them to be far less interesting or illuminating than Bishop's decision to sacrifice plot and concentrate on nocturnal experience. Any serious attempt to trace a plot through the *Wake* will have to sweat and strain to find out just whose voice is speaking and exactly what actions are being reported, when these matters are, quite deliberately, swathed in darkness. Sometimes, one simply has to guess, and it should come as no surprise when thoughtful and informed commentators cannot make up their minds whether a particular attribution should be made to Shem or to Shaun, or just how the story of the Captain and the tailor (II-3) is supposed to go. But if we are to have revealing exploration of night thoughts without a sequence of actions to which to relate them, what is the alternative?

With the exception of Bishop's imaginative study, most of the secondary literature on the *Wake* is obsessed with the details of plot—and this strikes me as a serious limitation. Literary critics often spend little time on establishing the plot; they take it for granted and get on with the more interesting work of exploring its significance; where matters of plot have to be settled, that is typically a preliminary to pondering broader issues, not the *summum bonum*, what I earlier called the "Everest event." In the case of the *Wake*, after the plot has been worked out, there seems little more to do—perhaps because the plots that can be retrieved are so silly, trivial, and worthless. Why should we care what HCE was accused of and who accused him? Or why should we worry whether the intercourse of III-4 was complete?

The active reader should go for the significance, the questions that are being posed, and let whatever plot can be discovered take care of itself. It is, at last, time to absolve Joyce from the charge of having reconstructed a mere "crossmess parzel" and to explain to Molly why the *Wake* cannot be written in standard English. This is a sequence of dream stories—*vignettes* as I shall henceforth call them—that serve as foci for the dreamer's concerns. Behind them are all sorts of thoughts, desires, and fears that cannot readily be expressed in ordinary language, that cannot be faced in waking life. We do not need to add these vignettes up to form a whole. They can be allowed to glide into one another, to fuse, to mutate. They are a forum in which the dreamer can worry his deepest questions. Our task, as active readers, is to isolate those deepest questions—questions that may prove real for us, possibly different questions for different people—and to let the vignettes serve as vehicles for trying out a variety of answers. We do not need to decide on the identities of the characters in the vignettes or take a stand on the "real" outcome of the story.

In effect, aspiring readers have been offered two choices: some of the guides to the *Wake* struggle to transform it into a standard novel, one with characters and a plot; other studies (typically more academic, less generally accessible, and more sophisticated) understand Joyce to be doing something else, something quite disconnected from traditional novelistic aspirations— presenting the voices of Dublin,[18] perhaps, or conjuring nocturnal experience. The search-for-the-plot approach faces the formidable objection that any recoverable "story" appears breathtakingly silly. The plot-repudiating alternatives are vulnerable to the charge that they reduce the *Wake* to a set of arbitrary fragments—ignoring the continuities of the conversation, the recurrence of motifs, they find, at best, some disjointed, bravura performances of the sorts in which scholars may delight.

I am proposing a third possibility. The dreamwork of the *Wake* consists of a set of fluid stories for the probing and exploration of questions that are hard—unbearably hard—to face directly. The structure is not to be found in some painstakingly reconstructed "plot" but in the investigations and excavations of the dreamer. The details of these stories need concern the reader only insofar as they bear on the uncomfortable issues that are being posed. We are invited to follow an inquiry—one that matters profoundly to all of us. That is a generic approach to the *Wake*. In the first four sections, I was more specific, proposing that the questions with which the dreamer is concerned center around the problem of making sense of a human life. The next chapter will elaborate this proposal.

6

LIFE'S ROBULOUS REBUS

Reading the *Wake*, as we begin to feel that not a single syllable makes sense, or that we are lost in the bush, a natural first question is to ask what is going on. Derivatively, we may wonder who is speaking, how the characters mentioned relate to one another or to figures who have floated through previous passages. I recommend starting with a different query: *Why* is this material occurring here? *What purpose* is being served for the dreamer by the elaboration of a vignette of this particular form? If we suppose that there is an enduring collection of urges, desires, and hopes, anxieties, fears, and uncertainties, which are constitutive of the subject to whom this kaleidoscope is presented—that the vignettes bring to the fore scenes and predicaments with which he must collide or scrape, or from which he must escape—then our principal interpretive project will consist in trying to discover the nature of this underlying psychological condition. Perhaps we shall suppose that attributing certain kinds of aspirations or fears would make sense of some of the vignettes, that, viewed from our tentative interpretation, those vignettes would provide ways for expressing or working out the dreamer's deepest concerns. Suggested by some passages, a line of reading can be elaborated, refined—or overthrown—by attempting to apply it more broadly. In doing so, we may come to a view of the "plot" (insofar as there is such a thing), answering the question of what is happening or who is speaking; or, feeling that we understand the significance for the dreamer, we may simply decide that reconstructing any "plot" is irrelevant, that these specific details don't need to be settled.

Who is this dreamer? Because HCE is so dominating a presence in the vignettes, it is tempting to apply his name to the dreamer as well; this, however, might blind us to the ways in which the dreamer's response to the vignettes can depend on identification with figures distinct from, even opposed to, HCE. Or perhaps the dreamer is Joyce himself, writing, once again, the story of his life. There is much to be said for this idea, for Joyce plainly uses the incidents of his life, his exile from Dublin, his requests for money, even the individual titles of sections of his earlier works, in the vignettes.[1] Yet, I think we should beware of too tight a connection between the dreamer and Joyce, just as we should keep a distance between Bloom or Stephen and their creator. Instead, I propose that the dreamer is any man of a certain sort, a "usual sort of ornery josser" (109: 3)—but of a certain age.

It would be hard to leave the dreamer's sex indeterminate. The sexual urges and anxieties that permeate the dreamer's night experiences cannot be worked through without introducing scenes and events that are viewed from some definite perspective—and Joyce chose a male perspective.[2] That does not mean that female experience is absent from the vignettes, for there are female voices that speak to the dreamer, sometimes figuring as independent characters and sometimes as parts of his own identification. Moreover, as I suggested earlier and will explore further below, many of the problems and predicaments that whirl through the dream center on the value of mutual love and marriage, and, correspondingly, a large number of vignettes might serve a purpose for a dreamer of either sex.

More important, I think, is the fact that the dreamer is an *aging* man. Although there are times when the character in a vignette with whom he identifies is young and vigorous, when it is natural to speak of the dream as centered on a younger self, it is crucial to the *Wake* that all stages of life, through middle-age and beyond, are accessible as perspectives for identification. In a sense, the dreamer has "nor youth nor age," but because he spends this night "dreaming of both"—and dreaming from the perspective of long experience—we must see him as conscious of the fact that the large majority of his life is spent.

One significant part of that life is a marriage and a family. Like the dominant figure of *Ulysses*, Joyce, both author and family man, gives us a dreamer whose life has been centered on an enduring cluster of intimate relationships. Indeed, we might well start by thinking of him as a version of Bloom, thirty or so years on, whose dreams interrogate a life that we can easily project from that one day in June 1904. There are plenty of suggestions that the dreamer's central locus of identification, HCE, is connected with Bloom. One of the clues in the first question of the quiz chapter reads:

> Dear Hewitt Castello, Equerry, were daylighted with our outing and are looking backwards to unearly summers, from Rhoda Dundrums; . . .
> (135: 29–31)

Recalling that HCE is frequently identified with Howth, a passage from Molly's long monologue explains the significance of outing, summer, and rhododendrons:

> the sun shines for you he said the day we were lying among the rhododendrons on Howth head . . . the day I got him to propose to me yes
> (*Ulysses*, 782)

HCE's humiliation in the bar of the inn is permeated by allusions to the Citizen's attack on Bloom, starting with the first line of the chapter, "It may not or maybe a no concern of the Guinnesses but" (309: 1), which contains an acrostic of Ulysses' self-designation for the Cyclops: "I'm no-man." ALP, it seems, once heard a piano tuner and leaned out from "her droemer window" (327: 22)—and we recall that Molly Bloom did something very similar as the blind piano tuner was tapping his way back to pick up a tuning fork (*Ulysses,* 225–6, 289).[3]

Just as another side of Joyce is present in *Ulysses* in the person of Stephen, so, too, as I-7 makes clear, another character of the dreams, Shem (or Glugg, or Jerry) serves as a focus for aspects of the dreamer that are played down in HCE. Indeed, the dreamer is a man of many parts, and the difficulty of the language of the *Wake* is a response to this fact. Identities blur and fuse because of the dreamer's attempt to take on characteristics that cannot be reconciled. Connections have to be made where there is a war of contraries. To say exactly who the dreamer is would be to resolve the problem centrally posed by this long stream of vignettes, the problem of forging a stable identity. Not HCE, not Joyce, not Bloom, not Stephen, the dreamer is a chorus of many partially conflicting *personae*—among whom all of these figure—an aging man who struggles to integrate the facets of himself and of his life.

As the night nears its end, there is a suggesting that the stream of vignettes has been a "disselving" (608: 5), which I interpret as a separation of the pieces out of which the dreamer's psyche is composed. The actors who have figured in the drama, HCE, ALP, Shem, Shaun, Issy, and a host of lesser characters, have sometimes been foci for the dreamer's identification, sometimes foils for his identification with another character. The dreamer, it appears, is "more mob than man" (261: 21–2), but his task is to turn a mob into a single man.[4] To do that is to find a genuine identity, one that can make sense—or as much sense as possible—of all the hopes, fears, desires, and anxieties that clamor within him, so that the life he has lived can be seen as an expression of who he really is. We use that phrase, "The real me," and kindred expressions— and so does Joyce: "We seem to us (the real Us!)" (62: 26)—but at the heart of the *Wake* is the thought that this is deeply problematic. The dreamer is hard at work trying to solve "life's robulous rebus" (12: 34).

The problem was formulated, with ardor and confidence, by the young Stephen Dedalus, at the end of *Portrait,* and it is confronted, with a waning of confidence, by the Stephen we meet at the beginning of *Ulysses.* The aspiration is to be oneself, to find or create who one truly would want to be, a person who has not simply taken over the stale patterns of the past, but one who escapes from the nightmare of history, one who will not serve, one who can anticipate that, from the vantage point of age, the choices made will be vindicated. The real self is one that is actively chosen, without unreflectively acquiescing in the plans of others, but that is not enough; a life lived according to that choice must be retrospectively approved—one must be able to say, "If I had it to do over again, that is how I would choose it."[5] People can fail if they suppress, distort, or mutilate some of their psychological propensities, and that will show up in a late judgment that voices within them have not been properly heard.

Stephen's ardent dedication of himself seems doomed. The destruction of youthful promise looks almost inevitable. As another of the quiz show clues for HCE suggests, he

> is not so pleased that heavy swearsome strongsmelling irregular-shaped men should blottout active handsome wellformed frankeyed boys; . . . (134: 24–6)

The sense of failure looks forward to the sad verdict of ALP in a passage I have already quoted. Commenting on what life has done to her aging husband, she says:

> I'll close me eyes. So not to see. Or see only a youth in his florizel, a boy in innocence, peeling a twig, a child beside a weenywhite steed. The child we all love to place our hope in for ever. All men has done something. Be the time they've come to the weight of old fletch. (621: 29–33)

Perhaps, then, Stephen's declaration is simply naïve; perhaps there is no way of achieving an identity that can guide a life that one will retrospectively judge to have been the one to have chosen, one that will seem worthwhile.

That bitter assessment is not ALP's last word; nor is it where Joyce leaves his dreamer (or us). Yet, there are plenty of moments in the *Wake* where the problems posed for reflective people who ponder how to live come to seem completely intractable. Here, for instance, is Shaun's stark valediction (more exactly one of his valedictions) to his sister and her companions.

> Ye can stop as ye are, little lay mothers, and wait in wish and wish in vain till the grame reaper draws nigh, with the sickle of the sickles, as a blessing in disguise. (457: 8–10)

The idea that aspirations will be vain and expectations unfulfilled is accompanied with the thought that any divinity that has shaped human lives for his own obscure purposes turns out to have very little concern with what matters to us.

> A tear or two in time is all there's toot. And then in a click of the clock, toot toot, and doff doff we pop with sinnerettes in silkettes lining longroutes for His Diligence Majesty, our longdistance laird that likes creation. To whoosh! (457: 21–4)

I find in this a mordant skepticism about any providential deity who "likes" the products of his creative activity, although there might be one that liked creat-*ing*, dabbling with this or that experiment, without concern to the bit players who figure in it, or one that liked "creation," in the sense of kicking up a fuss and making havoc.

By the end of *Portrait*, Stephen Dedalus had outgrown the terror a retreat sermon had once inspired in him. Human life is to obtain its significance from what *we* do, not from what is demanded of us by some "longdistance laird." All too frequently, what we do does not amount to much, even to anything. We can set against Stephen's aspirations the cramped and impoverished lives of the ordinary people who pass before us in *Dubliners:* the lapsed priest; Eveline, whose anxieties check what might have been a flight to freedom (but perhaps a leap into disaster); the servant girl gulled by the "gallant"; the landlady's daughter and her reluctant husband-to-be; the mother whose frustration and fury destroys what might have been a rare moment of fulfillment for her daughter. With the exception of the central characters of "The Dead," per-haps none is more poignant than Little Chandler, who has seen his dreams for a literary life gradually deflate, who feels stifled by the circumstances of his do-mestic life, and who, after a dispiriting meeting with his more successful friend Ignatius Gallaher, returns home to a crying child. The mounting frustrations lead to what we know is an uncharacteristic action for this mild, gentle man.

> It was useless. He couldn't read. He couldn't do anything. The wailing of the child pierced the drum of his ear. It was useless, useless! He was a prisoner for life. His arms trembled with anger and suddenly bending to the child's face he shouted:
> —Stop! (*Dubliners*, 84)

Despite his best efforts to soothe the frightened child, the sobbing becomes more intense. Chandler's wife returns, first accusing, then indifferent to her husband as she settles the infant.

> Little Chandler felt his cheeks suffused with shame and he stood back out of the lamplight. He listened while the paroxysm of the child's sobbing grew less and less; and tears of remorse started to his eyes. (*Dubliners*, 85)

So we leave him. But it is not hard to envisage how his life will go on. Maybe this will be a turning point, the moment at which he gives up his literary ambi-tions forever, closes off that part of himself, dedicating himself to the marriage about which he has begun to harbor doubts. Or perhaps this is a "little cloud" that portends a series of storms, so that Chandler's domestic life will be as unfruitful and unhappy as his work in the larger world. Either way, we know that the aging Chandler, looking back, will have plenty to regret—that "a tear or two in time" is all there will have been to it.

Quite early in the *Wake,* we are given a view around Dublin, inspecting the ways in which the citizens—the cast of *Dubliners,* the minor characters of *Ulysses*—get along from day to day.

> But all they are all there scraping along to sneeze out a likelihood that will solve and salve life's robulous rebus, hopping round his middle like kippers on a griddle, O, as he lays dormont from the macroborg of Holdhard to the microbirg of Pied de Poudre. Behove this sound of Irish sense. Really? Here English might be seen. Royally? One sovereign punned to petery pence. Regally? The silence speaks the scene. Fake!
>
> So This Is Dyoublong?
>
> Hush! Caution! Echoland! (12: 32–13: 5)

The predicament of these Dubliners is barely adequate at best ("scraping along"); if they squeeze out a livelihood—or a "likelihood," a chance of a livelihood—it is by activities that are like symptoms of illness or unintentional reflexes ("sneezes"); confronted by the challenge of what to do with their lives, these are bare efforts at solving—or possibly at "salving," assuaging the kinds of doubt that affected Little Chandler. You can do that by the kinds of activities that go on at Finnegan's Wake—drinking and energetic dancing ("like kippers on a griddle"). In the middle of all this is death—a dead giant, present in the geography of Dublin.

What do we find here? Joyce responds with a Swiftian pastiche. This, he suggests, is what the Dubliners, the Irish, take to make sense. They ape the aspirations, habits, behavior of their apparently more successful conquering neighbors. In effect they subsist on charity, the poor residues of diluted donations. Impoverished and colonized, they are ultimately silent. There is nothing real, noble, or authentic here, no life to which human beings should aspire. It is fake. Or, in Shem's answer, a sham. For any reflective person, there must arise a question: Do you belong? Can you make a human life, a worthwhile life, in this way? The answer is clearly—and sadly—"No," for this is a land of echoes, without any power to speak in its own voice.

For some of Joyce's characters, those on whom he lavishes most attention, there is hope. We leave Bloom and Stephen and Molly without knowing what we know about Little Chandler. It is not easy for any of the three, but they are not doomed; we can envisage that their lives might go on in ways that would lead them to say, when they know "What has gone" because they see "How it ends" (614: 19), that there has been a pattern to their lives, one that they have woven and that they do not regret; perhaps the same is true of others in Joyce's pages—of Gabriel Conroy, for example, or Martin Cunningham; it is a possibility for—and a central preoccupation of—the dreamer of the *Wake.*

Joyce's dreamer is an aging man whose deepest anxiety revolves around whether the life he has almost completed makes sense. Plainly he has not done what the young Stephen aspired to do: that, as ALP tells us so clearly, is impossible. But has he done enough to enable him to ratify the choices, to quieten the skeptical voices within him, to respond to his unsatisfied yearnings with the response that they have been given their due? The vignettes of the *Wake* are explorations of that question. To understand how such explorations go, we need to make the question more specific.

The dreamer is a man who is drawn to intimate relationships, above all those within the family, between parents and children, between husband and wife. He is also moved by the desire to create and by the thought that a life gains its individuality and its worth from the creative effort expended within it. He is also inclined to think of family relationships not simply as confined to some private sphere from which the rest of the world is excluded, but as nourished and enriched through being embedded in a broader society; in similar fashion, creative effort should have an effect on others. Yet the dreamer fears that the world is hostile, that it can easily damage or distort the life of a family; further, immersion in the world and concern for affecting it can all too easily corrupt the creative vision. The dreamer worries that the price of conformity is that one becomes a sham; the committed individualist, the rebel, by contrast, will become an outsider, confined perhaps to a life of bilious narcissism. Overarching all of these are genuine doubts about the possibility and value of enduring love. Can one avoid betraying and being betrayed? Is the commitment to a single love an expression of timid conformism, an inhibiting of human freedom and vitality by tired superstitions and prejudices? Does the waning of physical desire and the decline of the body reveal the ideology of love for what it is, a romantic myth, superimposed upon our brutish nature?

The dreamer is an aging man for whom there arises a cluster of overlapping issues about individuality and conformity, about public life and private life, about creativity and intimate relationships, and about the existence and value of enduring love. Some of the issues arise in quite obvious ways in the vignettes of the *Wake*. The cost of an extreme devotion to individuality and freedom at all costs is vividly portrayed in the indictment of Shem in I-7 and is seen from a different perspective in the children's game of II-1. The internal stresses of bourgeois conformism are apparent in the dissolving of Shaun in the first two chapters of Part III. Yet this is only to give the most simple (and simplistic) description of a much more complex fabric. Because the issues are so closely interwoven with one another, the vignettes often contain strands leading in different directions; often the linguistic density is a way of keeping many different affiliations before us.

Consider, for example, a question raised in one of the densest (and ultimately most rewarding) sections of the *Wake*, the scene of HCE's humiliation in the bar:

> how comes ever a body in our taylorised world to selve out thishis, whither it gives a primeum nobilees for our notomise or naught, the

farst wriggle from the ubivence, whereom is man, that old offender,
nother man, wheile he is asame. (356: 10–14)

We begin with issues about individuality, and we end with them. How does any
one of us—or all of us—come to dig out (delve) or solve the problem of making
a genuine self, one of which you could say, with conviction, "this is mine"? How
do we avoid the problems of routinization and uniformity, imposed by the "tay-
lorisation" of the world around us—the Taylor system of industrial standardiza-
tion, the artificial cutting of the suit whose design takes on all the redundant
leftovers of fashions old and recent? The first riddle of the universe is, as Shem
said it was, "When is a man not a man?"—or maybe "When is a man another (or
"another's"?) man?"; we have Shem's answer (when he's a sham) and a variant
(when he's the same—when he conforms). But this isn't just the first riddle—it
may be forced, or a piece of farce, the effort of a joking riddler who sees that an
appropriate response is to laugh at the whole show; or maybe it's a wriggle, an
evasion, where what is being evaded is the idea that we are not, inevitably, offenders. Here there surfaces the doubt about the possibility of constancy and
fidelity in any of our attempts to direct our lives—in particular in our commitment to those we love. In between comes a glancing reference to the *primum
mobile*—the providential creator whom Shaun will see as "longdistance laird,"
and who probably cares "naught" for our self-dissections (anatomies) or whether
we succeed or not ("not-to-miss-es"). Yet there are also filiations here to the possibility of public honors, the prize of nobility, on which, in his *apologia*, HCE
will eventually descant. There are thus all sorts of thoughts tangled up in this
question (and there are surely many more than I have mentioned): possibilities
of free self-creation might be important in a uniform world, or they might be
laughed off as an evasion; the fall might be inevitable or avoidable. In the context,
they are posed as a challenge—part of HCE's self-defense—to those who accuse
him. The effect is like that of an overloaded alibi, one that smears together all
sorts of potential lines of defense whether they are consistent or not.

The figure of Sackerson provides another place at which the various
concerns intersect. He is often the representation of the prying outsider who
either intrudes on the private life of the family (556: 23–30; 583: 14–16) or in-
terferes with the creativity of the artist (186: 19–22). We first meet Sackerson
as a subhuman figure, an ancestral hominid in an African landscape.

It is slaking nuncheon out of some thing's brain pan. Me seemeth a
dragon man. He is almonthst on the kiep fief by here, is Comestipple
Sacksoun . . . (15: 33–5)

The striking image recalls the introduction of Count Ugolino in Canto 32
of the *Inferno*, sating his hunger by biting into the brains of Archbishop
Ruggieri, who had betrayed him. Both Ugolino and Ruggieri are traitors,
found in almost the bottom circle in hell. Sackerson, too, is associated with

betrayal, for, in some of his guises, he is part of the extended household of the inn, the decrepit handyman, an unsavory and untrustworthy figure (see, for example, 141: 8–27). ALP is suspicious of the way in which he sneaks around after HCE: "[d]ogging you round cove and haven" (620: 33–4). She has good reason. At crucial moments of the humiliation in the bar, it seems that Sackerson is affecting the action: offering money to bribe the customers into hostility to HCE (312), plotting while HCE is temporarily absent (319), and precipitating anger at closing time (370–1).

Sackerson can serve as a pivot point for turning from the worry that a hostile outside world may intrude to the concern that the private sphere may be disrupted by betrayal. Indeed, if we take the initial connection with Ugolino and Ruggieri seriously, the worries become more tangled. The betrayed Ugolino was confined to a tower and starved—and, in Dante's version (Canto 33), his children offered themselves to their father as food. There are hints, then, of betrayal that gnaws at the intimate relations within the family and thus of a suspicion that those intimate relations are not all they seem, that they are not sufficiently strong or valuable to vindicate a life. We are back once again with the idea of the bestial within, with its veneer of romantic gloss—with Sacksoun on the savannah, a specimen of hominids evolving, not fully human.

I want to close this chapter with a somewhat more detailed account of an anxiety that, as we have seen, tends to generate this sense of a romantic veneer superimposed on our bestial nature, the worry that the waning of life reveals ourselves to ourselves more clearly. We weaken and become unable to think seriously about the new achievement that will transform the character of our life. What we shall have accomplished is a matter of what we have already done. HCE can only point to the past, to his vigorous wooing of ALP and the creative activity he dedicated to her. She is clear that his energies have run out, despite her wistful hope that he might still climb up, like Solness, Ibsen's master builder, and stand on the summit for her; we know, and she does too, that HCE is too dizzy, that if, like "Bygmester Finnegan" (4: 18) he were to try to ascend, his hand would stutter, his head would shake, he would fail and fall.

Although we have a more recurrent emphasis on HCE's decline, ALP is also past the days of her fulfillment. As the children learn their lessons, they are told of the larger possibilities for men and the laborious, ever narrowing lot of women:

> from the languors and weakness of limberlimbed lassihood till the head, back and heartaches of waxedup womanage . . . (270: 7–10)

The message is intensified later in the same passage:

> Though Wonderlawn's lost us for ever. Alis, alas, she broke the glass! Liddell lokker through the leafery, ours is mistery of pain. (270: 19–22)

To which Issy, wise beyond her years, adds one of her most straightforward (and apt) notes:

> Dear and I trust in all frivolity I may be pardoned for trespassing but I think I may add hell.[6] (270 n. 3)

She has learned from "gramma's grammar" (268: 17), and her ostensible grandmother, withered Kate, is a sobering reminder of what ALP is becoming.

She no longer corresponds to the fervent language in which HCE described his wooing of her; her "beautifell" (her wig and her "fell beauty") is "hung up on a nail," detached, no longer part of her (558: 28–9). The vision of ALP as no longer sexually attractive is juxtaposed with that of HCE's waning desire ("his mace of might mortified" [558: 29]); that may be reinforced by the drink, but we should also wonder whether he stayed to drink because he lacked desire. Can her body still arouse him? Or, if it can, is the arousal any more than an animal response to a suggestive swaying in the dim hallway? Does any sexual response in him now depend on the perceived charms of other—younger—women?[7]

These are, I believe, important questions for the dreamer, and they lie behind the sequence of vignettes that dominates Part I of the *Wake*. The dreamer worries about the extinction of his sexual desire, partly because it signals the closing of one important aspect of his life and, more broadly, his decline, partly because it raises doubts about the nature and meaning of his intimate relationship with his wife. Within him is an urge to keep this part of him alive, even to discover, at this late stage, a new freedom and fresh adventure. Yet that, he recognizes, would also be a betrayal, perhaps even unforgivable; seen from the outside, it might be absurd, grotesque, undignified, contemptible, and eminently deserving derisive laughter.

At a much earlier stage in their lives, Bloom's sexual relations with Molly have been disrupted by the death of their infant son, Rudy. On that June 16, Molly is physically unfaithful, taking Blazes Boylan into her bed. Bloom also wanders. He retrieves from the Post Office another installment of the clandestine correspondence he has been carrying out under an assumed name. Later in the day, by the sea shore, he will look on at a young girl, Gerty MacDowell, who, moved by her own romantic dreams, will lean back on the rocks and expose "all her graceful beautifully shaped legs to him" (*Ulysses*, 359)—and Bloom will reach sexual climax. At the very end, of course, there will be a reunion with Molly in the marriage bed, not taking the form of sexual intercourse, but a reunion nonetheless. Both betrayal and fidelity find places here, although, by concluding his book in the way he does, Joyce makes their mutual faithfulness the dominant form.

We have no grounds for believing that the dreamer or his spouse have wandered in the ways of Bloom and Molly; nor do we have any evidence that their sexual relationship has been distorted by some intrafamilial tragedy. They are simply aging people for whom something that matters is felt to be dying, and the dreamer (at least) resists. One expression of the resistance is in the thought of the stimulation produced by seeing exposed the bodies of younger women—the vignette recreates for HCE something of Bloom's experience at the shore. Yet the resistance is itself resisted, marked as a betrayal of ALP, as a disgraceful, even disgusting, action. So there come into the vignette three hostile watchers—it is almost as if the observers included Gerty's "grandpapa Giltrap" (*Ulysses*, 352) and his bosom friend, the Citizen.[8] This apparently simple, seamy incident and its various aftermaths serve, as we shall see, to elaborate and focus many of the dreamer's desires, fears, and anxieties and to embody their conflicts. The need for community, the costs of conformity, the desire to recapture youth, the urge to freedom, fears of a hostile world, and, above all, doubts about the quality and value of his love all surface in the complex of vignettes that grow from the incident in the Park.

Articulating these points will occupy us at much greater length in Chapter 8. For now, I want to underscore the importance to the dreamer of the waning of sexual desire and the mixed attraction of liaisons with younger women by looking briefly at what can easily seem one of the most distasteful aspects of the *Wake*. Ostensibly, HCE has a beautiful adolescent daughter Issy, and, as I have suggested in Chapter 2, she can excite his sexual desire: in the coupling on the "bed of trial," it is a serious possibility that the vision of the sleeping beauty has played a part in the reinvigoration of HCE. At several points in the *Wake*, we hear Issy's voice, and it is hardly the voice of innocent girlhood; rather it oozes sex and narcissism, it is calculated both to arouse and to tease, and it promises ecstatic delight in a world that is clearly marked as illicit and forbidden.

Issy speaks the "little language" of Swift's *Journal to Stella*, the work of an older, sexually conflicted man, torn between continence and desire, attracted to two much younger women. The twentieth-century version is far more suggestive:

> Now open, pet, your lips, pepette, like I used my sweet parted lipsabuss with Dan Holohan of facetious memory taught me after the flannel dance, with the proof of love, up Smock Alley, the first night he smelled pouder and I coloured beneath my fan, *pipetta mia*, when you learned me the linguo to melt. (147: 29–34)[9]

To whom does Issy issue her invitations? To HCE? To Shaun? To the dreamer? I take her to serve as the voice that says to the dreamer both, "Your sexual desires are not dead—they can find satisfaction, even bliss, with me" and "I am forbidden, and any liaison with me would be absurd." Her hyper-sweet sexuality is marked as utterly prohibited by her status as the daughter of the dreamer's principal locus of identification, HCE: she is tempting, but taboo. Moreover, even when the dreamer, striving to recapture youth, envisages himself as the young Shaun, the illicit status remains; Shaun and Issy are brother and sister.

One small example will serve to show how Issy can give voice to the dreamer's desires and anxieties. The Swiftian "little language" is interrupted by the thought of an old man, probably a priest, laying not-so-holy hands on Issy in church (146: 6–9). She is moved to a brilliant piece of Swiftian pastiche:

> How vain's that hope in cleric's heart Who still pursues th'adult' rous art, Cocksure that rusty gown of his Will make fair Sue forget his phiz! (146: 9–11)

The dreamer is suddenly brought vividly before us in the vignette. He is old and lecherous, his desires inflamed by the vision of "fair Sue." Yet his confidence—and his arousal—are both absurd. Whatever status he has counts for nothing. The lined and leering face is grotesque. He is in decline. Fresh love is not for him.[10] Issy's voice both lures him on and exposes why he should not listen. It provides a vivid expression of his conflict.

One final note. In supposing that the vignettes of the *Wake* are vehicles for the dreamer's expression and exploration of large concerns about the endurance and value of love, the place of creativity, the vindication of life, and the achievement of identity, I may seem to have slighted the extraordinary humor of the book. In fact, there is no direct connection between serious themes and gloomy tone. Like Shakespeare, Joyce was capable of presenting the most grave and profound issues with a light comic touch. He achieved that in *Ulysses* and went even further in the *Wake*. Nor is this accomplishment simply a matter of imposing a patina of laughter on tragic material. For, as we shall eventually see, there is no tragedy here. Joyce's vein of comedy runs deep, and it is an integral part of the *Wake*'s responses to the dreamer's worries—indeed to our human concerns.[11]

7

CHREE SCORE AND CEN
COPCYPSICAL READINGS

Three score and ten, according to one of Joyce's sources for the *Wake,* is the span allotted for a human life. If each word of the book is supposed to carry "three score and ten toptypsical readings" (20: 15), then surely the multiplicity affects the number of possible readings of a life. So indeed it does. Like Simon Dedalus, Stephen's father, each of us is capable of taking on many identities. One issue for us is to find one that makes life livable (186: 2–3). Or, to be able to offer a particular one of the answers to one of the questions posed in the course of the children's game:

Was liffe worth leaving? Nej! (230: 25)

Was it worth going into exile (leaving the Liffey)? Was life worth leaving? Was life worth living? With respect to the last question, we would like to be able to read the exclamation "Nej!" as the Greek "Ne" (Yes!) rather than the denial that more naturally comes to mind.

For the dreamer, as for us, the difficulty is to find an identity that will allow for that answer. But how exactly will the question be settled? I have suggested above that we can expect to find an answer in a retrospective vision of our lives, from the perspective of the "awebrume hour"—so that the challenge is to decide prospectively in a way we can later ratify. Yet, although we may know *more* from that later position, we may still not know *enough.* One of the great themes of the *Wake* is our opacity to ourselves, the problem of working out what we have done or who we have been. As we shall see, that problem involves some of the same sources of confusion that figure in our attempts to decide how to resolve the conflicts of the voices within us; as we shall also see, two difficulties are not necessarily worse than one.

Whether we think in terms of human history or of an individual life story, all that ever comes down to us is a set of fragments. We know so little of what has happened.

> Somewhere, parently, in the ginnandgo gap between antediluvious and
> annadominant the copyist must have fled with his scroll. The billy flood
> rose or an elk charged him or the sultrup worldwright from the excel-
> sissimost empyrean (bolt, in sum) earthspake or the Dannamen gallous
> banged pan the bliddy duran. (14: 16–21)[1]

None of us is simply a recording device, storing up information for the future;
we have to act, and action takes many other forms than writing down what we
notice. But, in any event, what we notice and choose to record is only a minis-
cule fragment of what is occurring at the time, singled out by the concerns of
the moment—and easily interrupted by contingent causes, either on the small
scale (threatening animals) or on the large (announcements from the heavens
or thunderbolts hurled by deities). After this comes the human work of retrospectively ordering what we have happened to collect and preserve.

> A bone, a pebble, a ramskin; chip them, chap them, cut them up all-
> ways; leave them to terracook in the muttheringpot: and Gutenmorg
> with his cromagnom charter, tintingfast and great primer must once
> for omniboss step rubrickredd out of the worldpress else is there no
> virtue more in alcohoran. For that (the rapt one warns) is what papyr is
> meed of, made of, hides and hints and misses in prints. (20: 5–11)

What we receive then, is selected, shaped, organized by human interpreters,
far from the ideal of divine speech, clear and authoritative, that is the supposed
source of the *Qur'an*. We know that the record we have will conceal various
things, that there will be clues to alternative possibilities within it, mistakes
and confusions that we might correct—and so, again and again, we can return
to what has come down to us, reshaping it, mixing it so that it becomes palat-
able, turning the old story into something different, achieving a new interpretation. Small wonder then that, as the culmination of this passage, the alleged
univocality of the sacred text of Islam gives way to the idea of the *Wake* itself
as a text of many voices—three score and ten toptypical readings.

    This applies, I have claimed, as much to an individual life as to the grand
events of history. Initially, we might think that there is no parallel here, since the
clues from history are assembled by many and eventually fashioned into a whole
by people with quite different perspectives. For a single person, concerned to
write and understand the story of his own life, matters can appear different: the
clues come as memories to a single consciousness, they are shaped by a single
self. That, however, is to ignore the problem at the core of the dreamer's concerns: how are the claims of the competing voices to be reconciled to constitute
a single self, the subject of a worthwhile life? Different voices will fasten on
different parts of a life, calling them by different names and telling different
stories. There can be many versions of what a life has been. Even at its end, one
will have to decide which of them tells the appropriate version.

It is not hard to see that the difficulty of reconstructing the narrative of a life is parallel to that of choosing how to balance the conflicting voices. Consider, for example, the issue of who is to tell, or write, the account of a life, who is to be the "biografiend" (55: 6; here the German "fiend"—"enemy"—points back to the battle for identity). A possible answer is that the authoritative version can only come from the outside, that it is only available, perhaps, to the celebrants at the wake. To acquiesce in that, or even in the more limited idea that the judgments of others have a bearing on what has been done and what it is worth, is to view the members of one's community as legitimately constraining claimants, to whom one's choices should respond. Another option is that we cannot accept the terms in which others would tell our own individual stories—our lives are our own and each of us is the legitimate judge of what is central. The choice of how to tell what has happened in a life is like the choice (or choices) that gives (give) rise to the life to be narrated.

Historical developments, including the lives of prominent individuals, can be told in many ways, giving rise to cheers or jeers. Joyce connects the many possibilities for history with the multiplicity of stories for a single person in one of the densest chapters of the *Wake* (I-3):

> Chee chee cheers for Upkingbilly and crow cru cramwells Downaboo! Hup boys and hat him! See! Oilbeam they're lost we've found remembrandtsers, their hours to date link these heirs to here but wowhere are those yours of Yesterdays? (53: 36–54: 3)

The historical figures are, of course, dead. We construct pictures of them—accomplished portraits that bring out what we take to be significant, what we view as the pieces of the past that have bequeathed something to us. Others who came before us did the same, and, because they had alternative conceptions of what mattered, their portraits were different and have themselves vanished. History is constantly being rewritten in light of our shifting concerns, and the cheers for King Billy today may be the jeers of tomorrow—or may be replaced by silence.

The chapter in which this passage is embedded is, as we shall see, largely devoted to the problems of achieving an appropriate account of history, with the ultimate goal of making sense of HCE and of the status of his conflicting impulses. Joyce continues by explicitly drawing the analogous conclusion for the life of an ordinary person.

> Any dog's life you list you may still hear them at it, like sixes and seventies as eversure as Halley's comet, ulemamen, sobranjewomen, storthingboys and dumagirls, as they pass its bleak and bronze portal of your Casaconcordia: Huru more Nee, minny frickans? Hwoorledes har Dee det? Losdoor onleft mladies, cue. Millecientotrigintadue scudi. (54: 7–12)

It turns out that, in passing through the doorway of the "House of concord," we have entered a public convenience, although the greetings and directions are interrupted by the question of the anguished Christ—"Why, Lord, why?" ("Tippoty, kyrie, tippoty" [54: 12]). The attempt to reach consensus about the character and value of a life—any old ordinary life—fails, as the representatives who debate in what is supposed to be a "house of concord" wrangle about—are at sixes and sevens[2] about—the same questions (presumably the sorts of questions that trouble the dreamer), returning to them again and again with the regularity of Halley's comet. Perhaps the bleak portal marks a "bleak house," and we are to think of the interminable discussions of the court of chancery. Yet entering, working it through, going round and round in frustrating uncertainty, is as necessary as evacuating our bladders or our bowels, even though we might cry out in pained incomprehension as to *why* we have to do this.

The connection between the multiplicity of historical narratives and the many versions of a single life provides a useful context for taking up an obvious feature of the *Wake* that I have so far underplayed. It is almost impossible to open the book without disclosing the names of great figures of history, myth, or literature. Wellington, Napoleon, and Caesar, Wilde, Swift, and Lewis Carroll, Jesus, the Prophet, and the Buddha, Finn MacCool and Parnell, Tristan and Isolde—these are only some of the more frequent visitors to the dreamer's vignettes. Part of the reason for their presence is obvious. They serve as large projections of aspects of the vignettes, as dramatically overblown and arresting as HCE's grand account of his transformation of Dublin. Sometimes they are also parts of the connective tissue between vignettes, serving to link one part of the dreamer's concerns with another.

One early example of the technique is especially obvious and prepares the reader for others to follow. Kate, or "the mistress Kathe," leads us into the Wellington museum (the "Willingdone Museyroom"), and she guides us around the exhibits.

> This is the crimealine of the alps hooping to sheltershock the three lipoleums. This is the jinnies with their legahorns feinting to read in their handmade's book of stralegy while making their war undisides the Willingdone. The jinnies is a cooin her hand and the jinnies is a ravin her hair and the Willingdone git the band up. This is big Willingdone mormorial tallowscoop Wounderworker obscides on the flanks of the jinnies. Sexcaliber hrosspower. (8: 29–36)

Not much interpretive effort is needed to connect this with Phoenix Park, site of the Wellington monument, and with the vignette that presents HCE as observing the two young women urinating while the three soldiers look on. (In this version, HCE seems to go beyond watching; moreover, the sheltering of the three "lipoleums" by the "crimealine of the alps" suggests that ALP may be covering three males with the hoops of her skirt; if so, then the three may be her two sons and her husband—in which case, HCE is self-accused.) So far, then, we have the allegations about HCE projected on to the theater of the Napoleonic wars, with the hint of connection to another military campaign, the Crimea.

As Kate's account continues, that hint develops with allusions to other forms of exposure; there is a reference to the French General Cambronne, who allegedly shouted "Merde!" at the battle of Waterloo (9: 27). Then the story deviates, as the "Willingdone" picks up a trophy, the "half of the threefoiled hat of lipoleums" (10: 8). A nearby exhibit shows "the Willingdone hanking the half of the hat of lipoleums up the tail on the buckside of his big white harse" (10: 10–11). Now it seems we are in another war and another story—the story of "Buckley and the Russian General" that will recur most prominently in II-3. One of Joyce's father's favorites, it features an ordinary Irish soldier who had a Russian general in his sights; as the general dropped his trousers to defecate, Buckley took pity on him and held fire; when, however, the general picked up a clod of turf to clean himself, Buckley lost his compunction, shot, and killed the general. We have migrated, then, from Waterloo to the Crimea, and Willingdone is now the Russian general, in the business of producing the substance that corresponds to Cambronne's shouted word.

> This is the dooforhim seeboy blow the whole of the half of the hat of lipoleums off of the top of the tail on the back of his big wide harse.
> (10: 19–21)

In effect, the dreamer's anxieties have moved, through this museum tour, from the initial concerns about waning sexual desire and the intrafamilial issues that raises: is his yearning for renewal itself a form of infidelity? That is where we start, with the enveloping "crimealine" that covers the family. But the watchers, the three "lipoleums," become outsiders, disclosing and deriding what is strictly private. They threaten humiliation, exposure of the individual in the performance of his grossest animal functions. By the end, I think, the dreamer is focused on the doubt that his life consists of a partial covering of an unseemly bestial nature, a covering that could easily be blown away.

Large-scale projection and connection are only part of the function of these historical and mythical figures. They also serve to remind us that there is no significant difference between life on a large scale and life in the small. Like the Russian general, HCE can be exposed and defeated; like Christ, he can endure his "three and a hellof hours' agony of silence, *ex profundis malorum*" (75: 18). It would be an error to believe that the larger lives are immune from the kinds of questions that arise for those that are humbler. In neither instance can we be sure of the worth or value of the choices that have been made. Whether those who come after, the "heirs," cheer, jeer, or simply forget will depend on the effects the lives have generated and the interests of those who may be affected. As those interests change, there will be different "remembrandtsers," alternative portraits of the past. This applies as much to the judgments of the mourners at the wake as to those of the historians who look back on the course of civilization.

Ulysses prepares the way for this oscillation between the quotidian world and the dramas of history in comparing the wandering of an advertisement canvasser to the exploits of Odysseus. The connections in the *Wake* are far more explicit and far more many sided, but they embody the same conviction that similar questions arise in the large and in the small. So, for example, HCE can be characterized on very different scales:

> towers, an eddistoon amid the lampless, casting swannbeams on the deep; threatens thunder upon malefactors and sends whispers up fraufrau's froufrous; . . . business, reading newspaper, smoking cigar, arranging tumblers on table, eating meals, pleasure, etcetera, etcetera, pleasure, eating meals, arranging tumblers on table, smoking cigar, reading newspaper, business; . . . those were the days and he was their hero. (127: 15–17, 20–23, 25)

The guide to the lost, the great beacon of the lighthouse, seems, like the authoritative judge, a large and powerful figure, one whose life will "tower" in the pages of history. The ordinary Dublin man, whose daily round goes round and round—and the direction seems to make no difference—is one of those likely to vanish without a trace; some there be who have no memorial and are perished as though they had never been. A life, it appears, cannot become more mundane than this. Yet both characterizations apply to the same person, both are different capsule descriptions of the same existence. Moreover, these are accompanied by other designations that mix the great and the small. The threatening judge may figure in some accounts as the ladies' man; the everyday life may appear, like Bloom's, the life of a hero.

As I have already confessed, I cannot see how to read the *Wake* as a vast allegory of human history. Like Plato in the *Republic*, Joyce goes to the large to illuminate the small, and his principal interest lies in understanding the predicaments of individual lives. Just as it would be absurd to think of Bloom as a source of illumination for Greek mythology, so, too, I reject the view that the *Wake* provides a new perspective on the great figures of human history or on the process in which they are embedded. In fact, heretical though it may sound, I do not believe that Joyce has any great interest in large theories of history or any ambitious theses to defend in this area.

Vico provides him with an image of history as cyclic, but all that this means for the structure of the *Wake* is that the giant figures of myth and epic can be seen as versions of HCE, and HCE himself can be discovered within his son, Shaun. More generally, there is a suggestion that the dreamer's anxieties are not idiosyncratic but widespread—I am not sure that Joyce would declare them to be universal—that large numbers of people will have to resolve questions about private and public, creative work and intimate relationships, the possibility and value of enduring love. It is enough for this book if there is a collection of issues, widely shared, that can be focused and explored in a thousand and one vignettes that interweave with one another.

Yet one might think there is more to it than that. Almost at the beginning there is a fall, sounded in the first of Joyce's Viconian hundred-letter thunder words, and the fall in the original garden is all over the text: again and again, we encounter the serpent and the temptation, the idea of the fortunate sin (*O felix culpa!*), and other associations of the Christian story of our origins. An obvious hypothesis is that Joyce thinks of this as a pattern for his episodes, that any acceptable narrative of a human life will have to come to terms with a fall from innocence and will be judged by the character of the actions that flow from that fall. In the last pages, ALP seems sometimes to yearn for a state of pastoral innocence and to see her life as a descent from that wonderful state.

> My great blue bedroom, the air so quiet, scarce a cloud. In peace and silence. I could have stayed up there for always only. It's something fails us. First we feel. Then we fall. (627: 9–11)

This is far from the only occasion on which we have a sense of innocence lost.[3] Much earlier, Alice's breaking of the glass was seen as the permanent loss of "Wonderlawn." That state of innocence, conceived as the primeval condition of history, is given near the beginning of the *Wake* in a "paisably eirenical" vision (14: 30; Joyce's formulation simultaneously conjures up peace and the pastoral, independent Ireland, irenic coexistence, and irony).

> Lean neath stone pine the pastor lies with his crook; young pricket by pricket's sister nibbleth on returned viridities; amaid her rocking grasses the herb trinity shams lowliness; skyup is of evergrey. Thus, too, for donkey's years. (14: 32–5)

After a while, of course, this idyllic condition is broken up. Strife and contention enter, civilization develops, and life becomes as we know it. Nor is it hard to understand what the cause of the lapse might be: Joyce's description of the primordial condition is loaded with vocabulary suggesting that sexual impulses are being redirected or held in check (even "the herb trinity," in the context of "viridities," may contain an allusion to the male genitalia).

Interestingly enough, this tale of the origins of human history is followed by something different, the appearance "on the kopje" of a figure with "mammamuscles most mousterious" (15: 29, 32–3). As we saw in Chapter 6, this is Sackerson—"Comestipple Sacksoun"—but the point for the present is that he belongs to a very different narrative of origins, one we would view as an orthodox account of hominid evolution ("mousterious" calls up an important period in human prehistory). Nor is this an isolated intrusion of the Darwinian account, which surfaces in many parts of the book. Issy is especially fond of it, rephrasing her interlocutor's question:

> Of I be leib in the immoralities? O, you mean the strangle for love and the sowiveall of the prettiest? Yep, we open hap coseries in the home. (145: 26–8)

Her gloss on the part of the children's text that explains the importance to women of "the It with an itch in it, . . . , the business each was bred to breed by" (268: 4, 6) is to make the Darwinian point explicit: "the law of the jungerl" (268: n.3). Finally, in the tortuous reconstruction of origins that marks the opening of the second part of the "star-chamber quiry" (501 ff.), the account of the garden with its huge central tree quickly becomes interleaved with suggestions of the evolutionary narrative: the tree is full of

> Erasmus Smith's burstall boys with their underhand leadpencils climbing to her crotch for the origin of spices and charlotte darlings with silk blue askmes chattering in dissent to them, gibbonses and gobbenses. (504: 26–9)

"Erasmus" is the name of Darwin's grandfather, author of a quasi-evolutionary poem centered on a garden, and William Smith is another of Darwin's precursors; we can also find here the titles of two of Darwin's most influential works (*The Descent of Man* as well as the *Origin*), together with a name that designates both a species of ape and a historian famously dedicated to the construction of a secular narrative. Joyce is prepared to mix the biblical story with quite different historical accounts.

Indeed, the idea of an innocent state from which we fall and from which we can be redeemed is consistently undermined. As I already suggested, the pastoral charm of the world inhabited by "pricket" and "pricket's sister" (14: 32–5) seems already to contain the (sexual) sources of its own transformation. Nor does Joyce think that our lapsed condition requires a savior. The fall is indeed fortunate—

> O foenix culprit! Ex nickylow malo comes mickelmassed bonum (23: 16–17)[4]

—but that is because of its perfectly ordinary consequences. If the stricken giant of the first chapter could read his own obituary, the "moaning pipers" (which provide *one* version of his life and its significance) would tell him that, but for him, and what he might anxiously take to be his lapses,

> there would not be a holey spier on the town nor a vestal flouting in the dock, nay to make plein avowals, nor a yew nor an eye to play cash cash in Novo Nilbud by swamplight . . . (23: 35–24: 1)

Lives are vindicated, when and to the extent that they are, by the ways in which those who are affected by them make sense of their legacies, and that, as this passage makes clear, is always open ended and ambiguous; a "spier" might be a steeple, a spear, or a spy, vessels might float in the dock or young women might be hauled up on charges of prostitution, business might go on or we might play childish games (hide and seek, "*cache-cache*")—and the value of all of these things, even of the existence of "you and I," or of plants and the possibility of vision, might prove matters of debate. Once again, Joyce allows for the possibility of a large number of narratives, but, significantly, none of them is a tale of transcendent redemption.

The *Wake* is full of celebrations of the ordinary, delight in everyday things and commonplace pleasures, and it is easy to confuse these expressions of joy with a supposed longing for a state of innocence. The children's game, for example, is interrupted with a twilight vision of the zoo in the Park, an evocation of great tranquility (244: 13–246: 4), easily read as the momentary attainment of an innocent world. Instead, I regard it as a child's vision of the peace that accompanies the sleepiness of the animals as dusk descends—and it is important to realize that the vision is available because the children are assured of the security of home. Similarly, a little later, we are offered a view of ALP at the stove, preparing the food that her children will eat.

> Ansighosa pokes in her potstill to souse at the sop be sodden enow and to hear all the bubbles besaying: the coming man, the future woman, the food that is to build, what he with fifteen years will do, the ring in her mouth of joyous guard, stars astir and stirabout. (246: 10–14)

This is no Eden, into which will shortly come innocents who have yet to fall. As we shall see below, a principal burden of this chapter and its successor is to deny the idea of childish innocence. That does not mean, however, that we should not delight in the ordinary task of making the supper or in ALP's dreams for her children's futures. For Joyce, there was no unspoilt Eden, but plenty of occasions for everyday joy.

I want to conclude this chapter with a preliminary look at that part of the *Wake* in which Joyce pays most attention to the issues of constructing an interpretation, or a narrative. In the discussion of ALP's "mamafesta," we start with the conception most antithetical to Joyce's own view, the idea of the complete univocity and authority of the *Qur'an* and (secondarily) the Bible.[5]

> In the name of Annah the Allmaziful, the Everliving, the Bringer of Plurabilities, haloed be her eve, her singtime sung, her rill be run, un-hemmed as it is uneven! (104: 1–3)

Yet the game has already been given away, for she brings "plurabilities," and the next paragraph is a very long list of possible titles for the "untitled mamafesta memorializing the Mosthighest," many of which are easily connected with the conceptions of the married life of HCE and ALP we have already explored. Ostensibly, the problem is to interpret a document that presents ALP's retrospective vision. From the start, however, we are plunged into ambiguities and difficulties.

For what is before us is not obviously what a single individual wrote. There are questions of authorship that can only be resolved by patiently assembling clues. Careful interpretation requires us to look at the "enveloping facts" (109: 14), which, since the document turns out to be a letter, requires us to contemplate the envelope itself. We can explore the circumstances under which the letter was recovered, the chain of transmission that has brought this particular copy into our hands. We can inquire into the special marks that appear on the copy and how they might have been produced. We can investigate the orthography and what it might reveal. Or we can apply to the text in front of us a general theory.

Joyce, I suggested, was not interested in substantive accounts of human history or in defending a general style of narrative for a human life. His lack of interest shows up in a bravura pastiche of some prominent general approaches. First, the psychoanalytic:

> but we grisly old Sykos who have done our unsmiling bit on 'alices, when they were yung and easily freudened, in the penumbra of the procuring room and what oracular comepression we have had apply to them! could (did we care to sell our feebought silence *in camera*) tell our very moistnostrilled one that *father* in such virgated contexts is not always that undemonstrative relative (often held up to our contumacy) who settles our hashbill for us and what an innocent allabroad's adverb such as Michaelly looks like can be suggestive of under the pudenda-scope . . . (115: 21–30)

Dialectical materialism fares no better:

> that Father Michael about this red time of the white terror equals the old regime and Margaret is the social revolution while cakes mean the party funds and dear thank you signifies national gratitude. (116: 7–10)

Joyce plainly thinks that these ways of finding repeated structures in history or in individual lives are no more adequate than the Christian structure of innocence, fall, and redemption. He is prepared to borrow as he sees fit, to use religious and Freudian concepts in particular, but he sees no reason to saddle himself with the rigid machinery in which those concepts were introduced. With respect to our psychological life in general, and our night thoughts in particular, he can agree with Freud on some global points, while supposing that his own explorations of the rich messiness of his characters are more revealing than the partial views obtained under the "pudendascope."

In the middle of the chapter, we eventually learn what the document under discussion say. Our copy consists in

> a goodishsized sheet of letterpaper originating by transhipt from-Boston (Mass.) of the last of the first to Dear whom it proceded to mention Maggy well & allathome's health well only the hate turned the mild on *the van* Houtens and the general's elections with a *lovely* face of some born gentleman with a beautiful present of wedding cakes for dear thankyou Chriesty and with grand funferall of poor Father Michael don't forget unto life's & Muggy well how are you Maggy & hopes soon to hear well & must now close it with fondest to the twoinns with four crosskisses for holy paul holey corner holipoli whollyisland pee ess from (locust may eat all but this sign shall they never) affectionate largelooking tache of tch. (111: 9–20)

The breathtaking triviality of this dream version of an ordinary letter can generate a natural reaction. By imagining so banal a text as being subjected to the pressure of all kinds of scholarly (and scholastic) devices, and perhaps especially by juxtaposing the interpretation of it with scholarly discussion of the *Tunc* page of the *Book of Kells*,[6] Joyce seems to be lampooning all efforts of academic interpretation. We can take the joke the other way, however. Christ's life and Christ's pain is no more important than that of ALP. Just as we reconstruct Christ's life from fragments, attempting to weave them into a story that makes sense, so we can do the same for her. The letter provides some scanty clues: a relative, possibly a sister, in exile far away; concern for children; celebration of marriage; involvement in religion. It may be a very ordinary life. But the narrative possibilities for saying what has happened in it, and whether and why it matters, are legion. As with Christ, so with ALP and HCE, we may never know—they may never know—if appropriate answers have been found.

In the last three chapters, I have tried to develop a more systematic view of the central themes and topics of the *Wake*. It is now time to start again, this time near the beginning, and trace these themes and topics through successive chapters.

8

THE HUBBUB CAUSED
IN EDENBOROUGH

To start *near* the beginning, but not *at* it. Like the opening pages of the "Sirens" section of *Ulysses* (although more accessible), the first chapter of the *Wake* assembles characters and material that will be developed throughout the book. Alternatively, it can be read as a summary of life from the perspective of the wake, a perspective temporally later than ALP's monologue. I shall use it in both ways, sometimes referring back to it to connect it with the vignettes of subsequent chapters, eventually viewing it as one of the book's several ways of concluding.

The chapter ends with an announcement of the central character of the vignettes to come, the one "ultimendly respunchable for the hubbub caused in Edenborough" (29: 35–6). HCE is responsible for the clamor in Eden (a place that will turn out to be very far from innocent); perhaps he will be punishable for it, possibly even physically beaten; and, as the anxious dreamer might hope, maybe he will eventually be vindicated as respectable. It is with respect and respectability that the story of HCE begins.

For we must start, it seems, by knowing who he is. That is a question also for the dreamer who identifies with him, for the dreamer is opaque to himself. We start with uncertainty, with doubts about what he should rightly be called, but "the best authenticated version, the Dumlat" (30: 10) provides a reassuring story. (As so often in the *Wake*, Joyce's inversion of a word—"Dumlat" for "Talmud"—leaves the reader to decide whether to take the attribution—"best authenticated"—at face-value or to reverse it.) It is a fairy tale account of how honor—the peak of respectability—was conferred on an upstanding citizen by the noblesse oblige of a visiting monarch. HCE is resting in his garden, when he learns that the sovereign is passing by. Hastening out, in an odd assortment of mismatched clothes, he pays his respects and earns what is supposed to be his name. In response to the king's question, "honest blunt Haromphreyld" (31: 8–9)—we have already been told that he is either Harold or Humphrey

Chimpden (30: 2)—replies: "Naw, yer maggers, aw war jist a cotchin on thon bluggy earwuggers" (31: 10–11). This inspires a feeble royal jest; the monarch is amused by the thought that he has "for surtrusty bailiwick a turnpiker who is by turns a pikebailer no seldomer than an earwigger" (31: 26–8). We have in this absurd dream distortion of a childish story a comforting account of how HCE came to be known as Humphrey (or Harold) Chimpden Earwicker, an account that harmonizes with the apogee of his apologia, when he explains how he came to acquire his heraldic crest (546: 2–8).

We were already alerted to the possibility of alternative versions, although they were brushed aside with the claim that this one is "the best authenticated." No sooner is the tale done, however, than the questions about accuracy begin to bubble up. They are dismissed with an indignant rebuke that suspicions are unworthy of so great a man—"this man is mountain" (32: 5). No credence should be given to

> the fallacy, as punical as finikin, that it was not the king kingself but his inseparable sisters, uncontrollable nighttalkers, Skertsiraizde with Donyahzade . . . (32: 6–8)

who quickly turn out to be actresses, or music-hall performers. But on what evidence can this rival story be dismissed? The storyteller blusters. From this time on, the records of "Haromphrey bear the sigla H.C.E." (32: 14). Moreover,

> it was equally certainly a pleasant turn of the populace which gave him as sense of those normative letters the nickname Here Comes Everybody. An imposing everybody he always indeed looked, constantly the same as and equal to himself and magnificently well worthy of any and all such universalisation, every time he continually surveyed . . . (32: 16–22)

the theater audience stretched out beneath his "viceregal booth" (32: 36). HCE reclines, with the neckerchief across his tuxedo-clad shoulders, and the audience seems as appreciative of his presence as they do of the action on the stage.[1] Where, it transpires, the piece being shown is—ominously enough—*A Royal Divorce* (32: 33).

The dreamer conjures up in this vignette a central figure whose standing is supposed to be attested by majesty itself, one who is "surtrusty"—super-trusty, but also, perhaps, absurd and rusty—a pillar of the community. Unfortunately, there are doubts that this is the right story. Possibly the name, the identity, is fixed to a different encounter, with two ladies of the night, who may talk—and walk—in public places, who are anything but respectable. Those doubts are not decisively settled—the alleged fallacy is "punical" or "finikin," punitive and picky, perhaps, but not labeled as outright false. The vignette changes scene, to the public acceptance of HCE as "folksforefather," surrounded by "the entirety of his house" (33: 4, 5). He is supposedly to be seen as model family man, widely liked and accepted in the community. Yet, even here, there are hints of a different story, for some of the "vociferatings" from the allegedly appreciative throng seem much more like threats or insults: *"Take off that white hat!"* *"Stop his Grog,"* and *"Loots in his Boots"* hardly sound like friendly acclamation (32: 22–4).[2]

Some of the dreamer's anxieties are already before us. There are worries about his status as an honored (respectable) member of the community, worries about his fidelity and the integrity of his marriage. Should the center of his life be seen as the authoritative recognition of his honest industry and civic virtue (the royal dubbing)? Should it be the appreciation by all of his calm protection of and devotion to his family (the admired viceregent in the theater)? Should it be the rejection and catcalls of his fellow citizens? Should it be the characterization given of him by the ladies who raised their skirts? Who is this man, and what exactly has he done and been?

The doubts cannot be suppressed. The vignette continues with the admission that "a baser meaning has been read into these characters the literal sense of which decency can safely scarcely hint" (33: 14–15). Even the most apparently positive versions of the stories the dreamer tells about himself allow for disturbing alternatives, indeed, for possibilities so threatening that they cannot be faced directly. We approach by way of metaphor: perhaps HCE suffers "a vile disease" (33: 17–18). Behind the imposing presentation of his respectability, he is corrupt. Once again, the voice blusters, but the charge is reformulated in slightly less euphemistic form. His accusers suggest that "he lay at one time under the ludicrous imputation of annoying Welsh fusiliers in the people's park" (33: 25–7).[3] The vignette tries to laugh this off:

> To anyone who knew and loved the christlikeness of the big cleanminded giant H.C. Earwicker throughout his excellency long vicefreegal existence the mere suggestion of him as a lustsleuth nosing for trouble in a boobytrap rings particularly preposterous. (33: 28–32)[4]

"Cleanminded," like HCE's protestation that he is "cleanliving" in his apologia (532: 16), starts to give the game away. There is an attempt to exonerate him by pointing to his established public persona; "viceregal" (32: 36) has now become "vicefreegal," as if the outward respectability should demonstrate that he is free from "vice girls"; but this is to miss the point of the accusatory whispers, for they insist that the outward show masks corruption within. The ineptness of the response is made completely evident by the start of the next sentence:

> Truth, beard on prophet, compels one to add that there is said to have been quondam (pfuit! pfuit!) some case of the kind implicating, it is interdum believed, a quidam (if he did not exist it would be necessary quoniam to invent him) . . . (33: 32–6)

The vignette is unraveling for the dreamer. Despite his wishes not to face the accusations directly, they cannot be silenced but emerge here, with legalisms and indefinite Latin pronouns masking what is being conceded. Even the attempt to maintain the habit of laughing them off (pfui! pfui!) is turned into an admission—fuit! fuit!: it was! it was!

Finally, denial turns to admission, with a desperate attempt to excuse or lighten the offense.

> Slander, let it lie its flattest, has never been able to convict our good and great and no ordinary Southron Earwicker, that homogenius man, as a pious author called him, of any graver impropriety than that, advanced by some woodwards or regarders, who did not dare deny, the shomers, that they had, chin Ted, chin Tam, chinchin Taffyd, that dayconsumed their soul of the corn, of having behaved with ongentilmensky immodus opposite a pair of dainty maidservants in the swoolth of the rushy hollow whither, or so the two gown and pinners pleaded, dame nature in all innocency had spontaneously and about the same hour of the eventide sent them both but whose published combinations of silkinlaine testimonies are, where not dubiously pure, visibly divergent, as wapt from wept, on minor points touching the nature of this, a first offence in vert or venison which was admittedly an incautious but, at its wildest, a partial exposure with such attenuating circumstances (garthen gaddeth green hwere sokeman brideth girling) as an abnormal Saint Swithin's summer and, (Jesses Rosasharon!) a ripe occasion to provoke it. (34: 12–29)

That, one assumes, is the best the defense counsel can do. We do not see the scene but only construct a number of reports about it—that of the onlookers who, it is claimed, had been drinking; that of the girls, whose motives, like their underwear, may not have been pure; that of HCE, who found himself in an unusual situation on a hot evening and responded to a part of himself that was normally under control. For, despite the pious author, HCE is not a homogeneous man—there may, as we shall see, be streaks of genius within him, but not all have been reconciled. That of course is the dreamer's predicament, and the sexual urge that HCE is reported as acting out is one that troubles the dreamer too. Is he, too, the subject of sexual cravings, at odds with his own conception of himself and with others' conceptions of him, that would burst out in overt action, under the right—or, more accurately, the wrong—circumstances? It is worth repeating an interpretive claim I made earlier: we do not need to suppose that the dreamer has done anything similar or has acted in any way that conflicts with his sense of what is proper for him. The doubt arises from the sensed possibility that, in his declining years, his interest might be aroused in ways that part of himself repudiates; that a side of him might see this as an expression of continued vigor and freedom, while another might regard it as a hideous betrayal, not only of those he loves but of himself.[5]

The focal story has struggled clear of many of the layers of euphemism in which the vignette originally wrapped it. There immediately arises a question of what the consequence will be for HCE's intimate relationships. Once again, the voice begins with reassurances: ALP rushes to the rescue. The dreamer hopes, perhaps, that there can be forgiveness. Whether this is so is, however, dark and unclear. She seems to berate the women involved, but her attitude to HCE is not certain.

> Guiltless of much laid to him he was clearly for once at least he clearly expressed himself as being with still a trace of his erstwhile burr and hence it has been received of us that it is true. (34: 34–35: 1)

To be guiltless of much is to be guilty of something. Nor is he *clearly* guiltless of much, for we can only say of him that he once told a clear story that might be accepted by those with a will to believe him. He told it with "a trace of his erstwhile burr," possibly his guilty stammer, or possibly the burr that sticks, a piece of incriminating evidence, a piece of the vegetation from the park, attached to his clothes.[6] What should we—what should ALP—make of him?

The anxious dreamer might wish to stop here, with a continuation of the vignette that would focus on the rescuing ALP and an agreeable reconciliation. Instead, the vignette presses relentlessly on, taking up the theme with which we began, HCE's status in the community. We are told of HCE, walking across the park and being accosted by "a cad with a pipe" (35: 11). Although the stranger is only reported as asking for the time, the encounter is plainly menacing; it may also embody a challenge to HCE's continued sexual vitality. HCE senses (correctly or incorrectly) the possibility of an attack: "unwishful as he felt of being hurled into eternity right then, plugged by a soft-nosed bullet from the sap" (35: 24–6). He tells the stranger the time but continues with far more than was requested, pouring out a stammering declaration of the falsity of the charges that have been leveled against him, and of the subhuman status of his accuser. It is all too much:

> that whereas the hakusay accusation againstm had been made, what was known in high quarters as was stood stated in Morganspost, by a creature in youman form who was quite beneath parr and several degrees lower than yore triplehydrad snake. (36: 3–7)

He tries to create a tone of camaraderie and ends by swearing a preposterous oath on the most exemplary representatives of respectability he can think of that "there is not one tittle of truth, allow me to tell you, in that purest of fibfib fabrications" (36: 33–4).

At this point this stranger is given a name, "Gaping Gill," appropriate enough for a fishy character who has just listened to so odd a recitation. Like

him, we may well wonder (gape) why a request for the time provokes so strenuous a denial of guilt. For the dreamer, however, this is all-too-comprehensible
a development. Like HCE, the dreamer knows that he is not a "homogenius"
man, and there is constant concern, exemplified in HCE's stammer and in
the construction by the dreamer of these vignettes, to come to terms with
the pieces that do not fit, to decide what is to be rejected and to excise it. The
encounter with the cad makes that felt need impossible to resist. The menacing stranger brings home to HCE the prospect of imminent death, and his
revealing protest is a desperate attempt to pull his life together, to present
a picture of it that he can endorse, an exercise in deathbed confession and
self-absolution.

From this point on, however, the vignette turns in a new direction, away
from HCE and toward what the world makes of him. We are plunged into the
mundane world of Dublin, often mean and squalid. Gill goes about his daily
business, returning home to eat, and, over supper, tells his wife of the odd
conversation. She has a sharp ear for gossip and is quick to pass on the news to
a priest—under the confidence of the confessional, of course. That confidence
is quickly broken in a conversation at a racetrack, where the priest and a colleague, a "layteacher of rural science" (38: 35), have gone for "a priestly flutter for safe and sane bets" (39: 1). They are overheard by two less salubrious
characters, and the tale begins to spread all over the city. Before we consider
the further diffusion and its consequences, it is worth pausing over these early
stages.

Gaping Gill entered the vignette as a stranger, but it is not so obvious that
he is retaining that identity. For when we meet his wife, she is introduced as
"[o]ur cad's bit of strife (knee Bareniece Maxwelton)," who, when she speaks
in the confessional, offers the story "among a hundred and eleven others" (38:
9, 13). One hundred and eleven is a number associated with ALP, often as the
number of her children (see, for example, [201: 28–9]; and, of course, three in
Roman notation looks like one hundred and eleven in Arabic). "Maxwelton"
is the first word of a well-known Scottish song, "Annie Laurie," and, sure
enough, the priest issues "annie lawrie promises" not to tell (38: 21).[7] Perhaps,
then, ALP is the cad's wife, and, in that case, Gill is HCE, and HCE stands
self-accused, self-exposed, and self-vilified.

There are other possibilities. "Bareniece" might remind us of another
niece, the niece-of-[the]-in-law of Jarl van Hoother who figures in a vignette
of the first chapter (21: 14–15). That niece, the Prankquean, disrupts the family of van Hoother, one of the many precursors of or surrogates for HCE who
emerge before his official entrance. What Gill's wife does in telling the story
to the priest is something of the same kind—she will play a role in the disruption of HCE's public and private life. If we make this identification, who, then,
is Gill? If she is related through marriage and belongs to a younger generation, then there is an obvious hypothesis: the cad is none other than one of

HCE's sons, and, as the link to "cadet" suggests, he would be the latter born of the twins, Shem. Returning to the strange encounter in the park, we might note that the cad was "carryin his overgoat under his schulder, sheepside out (35: 13)." The cad seems to be a pretender, like HCE, whose innocent exterior masks a goatish nature, full of guilt (*Schuld*) for past misdeeds—he is, we might think, a sham. Further, the presentation of sheepskin alludes to one of the archetypal myths that swirl through the *Wake*, the story of the deception of Isaac. Indeed, on the very first page of the book, we read:

> not yet, though venissoon after, had a kidscad buttended a bland old isaac. (3: 10–11)

—not an altogether inappropriate description of what is done to HCE in the encounter in the park (he is, after all, buttonholed and all but ended). Finally, as we shall be told at the very beginning of the indictment of Shem, "Shem is as Short for Shemus as Jem is joky for Jacob" (169: 1). On this reading, HCE would be threatened, exposed, and betrayed by his son.[8]

We have, then, three versions: Gill-the-stranger, Gill-as-HCE, Gill-as-Shem. Which is correct? As I have emphasized in previous chapters, that is a bad question. Each of the lines of connection is available to the dreamer; each can serve to link and develop the underlying anxieties. Identifying Bareniece Maxwelton with ALP, the vignette exposes the unresolved tensions of the marriage, HCE's need to accuse himself in the interests of trying to make himself whole, the postponement of full forgiveness. If the cad is Shem, then the conflicts within the father are an occasion for the rebellion of the son; the view of intrafamilial relations is very far from the comforting view of HCE, seated in state, surrounded by his house, the view with which we began. If the cad is a stranger, then the anxieties shift away from the family, into the broader world and HCE's place in it.

Since all these concerns are present within the dreamer, there is no need for us to decide on one version. All can coexist, coming into prominence or receding as the vignette develops. For the end of the chapter, it seems to me, the focus is very much on the fear of rejection by society.

The gossiping priest at the racetrack is overheard by two more dubious characters, Treacle Tom ("just out of pop" [39: 16]) and Frisky Shorty ("come off the hulks" [39: 20]). Treacle Tom, who "was, in fact, in the habit of frequenting common lodginghouses, where he slept in a nude state, hailfellow with meth, in strange men's cots" (39: 30–3), has more than a few drinks and, in his stupor, tells some version of the story. His drunken performance catches the ear of three others:

> a small and stonybroke cashdraper's executive, Peter Cloran (discharged), O'Mara an exprivate secretary of no fixed abode (locally known as Mildew Lisa), who had passed several nights funnish enough, in a doorway under the blankets of homelessness on the bunk of iceland,

pillowed upon the stone of destiny colder than man's knee or woman's breast, and Hosty, (no slouch of a name), an illstarred beachbusker . . . (40: 15–21)

The vignette has pitched us into a dream caricature of the world of *Dubliners* and of many of the minor characters in *Ulysses*, a world of scraping along, of looking for a good tip on a horse, of cadging drinks and hoping for too many of them, of menial employment and dreary domestic settings. In the vignette, all this is thrown into high relief: the ordinary people become ex-convicts, the homeless, the unemployed, huddled together (at best) in dosshouses.[9] The course of their lives, their "stone of destiny," is hard, dark, cold, and inhospitable. They can neither hope, nor offer, much in the way of human sympathy; there is no knee on which to sit, no breast against which to lean. Out of this cheerless world will erupt a denunciation of HCE in a spirit of momentary exultation, a spirit of carnival.

Hosty, whose previous aspirations seem to have centered on finding his way to a hospital bed or obtaining the means for a relatively easy suicide, uses the story as material for a ballad, and, in the morning, the trio sets out across Dublin

to the thrummings of a crewth fiddle which, cremoaning and cronauning, levey grevey, witty and wevey, appy, leppy and playable, caressed the ears of the subjects of King Saint Finnerty the Festive . . . (41: 21–4)

The desperate inhabitants of the dosshouse have been transformed into the entertainers for a great Dublin festival, and Hosty's violin arouses an appreciative audience for "this longawaited Messiagh of roaratorioes" (41: 28). A brief interlude reminds us of their seedy origins; they stop to reclaim Hosty's false teeth from the pawn shop and to have a drink or two. On the way, they start to pick up a following, first the clientele of the pub, but then a larger cross-section of Dublin life. Their song proves immensely popular—"to the balledder of which the world of cumannity singing owes a tribute" (42: 13–14)—and the exuberant celebration takes in not only the Dublin drunks but working people, schoolboys, and even "the better sort":

not forgetting a deuce of dianas ridy for the hunt, a particularist prebendary pondering on the roman easter, the tonsure question and greek uniates, plunk em, a lace lappet head or two or three or four from a window . . . (43: 11–14)

Carnival has broken out, and all sorts of Dubliners are ready to join the fun.

The ballad needs a name, and what more suitable than to associate it with its central figure, HCE. But how is he to be named?

Some vote him Vike, some mote him Mike, some dub him Llyn and Phin while others hail him Lug Bug Dan Lop, Lex, Lax, Gunne or

Guinn. Some apt him Arth, some bapt him Barth, Coll, Noll, Soll, Will, Weel, Wall, but I parse him Persse O'Reilly else he's called no name at all. (44: 10–14)

In this rousing wind-up to the closing ballad—and we can surely hear the skilled leader of "cumannity singing" exhorting his choristers—we are given one of those rival accounts of how Mr. Earwicker was given his name; Hosty gave it to him, in French ("*perce-oreille*" means "earwig").

Before we take a look at the contents of this ballad, this "king of all ranns" (44: 16–17), compared (as we have seen) to *Messiah* and the Eddas, it is worth pausing to reflect on the way in which the vignette has developed. The story about HCE does not simply become public. Rather it is transformed in ways least likely to prove reliable, from snatches of whispered conversation through the repetition in alcoholic stupor to the deliberate recreation in popular verse and song. The criterion for success is arriving not at an accurate view of HCE, but what will make for a good laugh, what will provide a moment of relief for people whose lives are sad and dreary. These people do not simply include the derelicts who lead the carnival but many others who join the fun. Happiness for them is brief and is only obtained at someone else's expense. The carnival needs a scapegoat, and the story about HCE has provided one. If he has to be destroyed in the process, that is no great loss; he can be burned up to provide a moment of warmth on "the bunk of iceland." As with *Messiah*, another work first performed in Dublin, Hosty's ballad has at its center a man who is "despised and rejected," one who is wounded not for others' transgressions, but for their momentary amusement.

The vignette began, we recall, with the question of HCE's identity, of his name and his acquisition of it. We were offered a reassuring account. The name was given in response to his virtues, and it expresses the regard in which he is held by those around him. From the beginning, we knew that there were alternative versions, versions that the dream voice wished to keep at bay. We have witnessed the unraveling of the preferred story and have been led back to one of those alternative versions, one in which the name is given by a baying mob, as an insult, as a sign of the contempt, derision, and hatred in which HCE is held by his fellows. Moreover, this expression of their vituperation is not a transient blotch on otherwise happy and worthwhile lives, but one of the rare moments in which the utter bleakness of those lives is temporarily relieved.

There is plenty here for the dreamer to be concerned about. If the initial anxiety seemed to center on a sense of sexual decline and the implications of that for ideals of love and marriage, the elaboration of the vignette touches on a far broader collection of fears. It suggests that any notion of community, of public accomplishment, is a farce. Perhaps, then, ALP is right: to live wisely is to retreat from the world and its unreasoning hatreds, hatreds fueled by the prospect of a little relief from misery or boredom. Yet, as the passage describing Hosty's seductive violin unnervingly intimates, ALP is involved in the fun—the sound is "witty and wevey, appy, leppy and playable." Her reaction, of course, was never clearly defined, and the dreamer must reckon with the possibility that the destruction extends into the private sphere.

All these anxieties are reinforced by the actual text of the ballad.[10] It is not just a burlesque of HCE's allegedly disreputable behavior in the park. Instead, it covers a wide variety of complaint and mockery. The balladeer rejoices in HCE's fall because he was once high and mighty. HCE has gone against traditions, trying to "improve" things with schemes of reform ("[h]ideous in form" [45: 20]). He is now (sexually) impotent. What business success he has had depends on dishonesty. He is an outsider, whose arrival in Dublin should be cursed. He has been brought down by his bestial behavior:

> Begob, he's the crux of the catalogue
> Of our antediluvial zoo . . . (47: 3–4)

What he did was both ludicrous and disgusting, the sort of behavior that will provoke the righteous wrath of his wife and embarrassment for his unfortunate children. If ALP acts properly, it will mean the end of HCE. He can be buried with the most hateful specimens of humanity, and the people can have a great celebration.

In this ballad, HCE's life is literally torn to shreds. Every aspect of it that might matter to him, to which he might point with pride, is vilified and mocked. He, who has tried to fit in, but also tried to improve, is derided as a meddling outsider. His honesty and industry are impugned. The decline of his sexual powers is trumpeted with glee. His marriage and family life are wrecked. He is, under it all, an ugly animal, so repulsive as to be comical.

The dreamer is troubled by doubts on all these scores. He will try to conquer them.

9

THE UNFACTS, DID WE POSSESS THEM, ARE TOO IMPRECISELY FEW TO WARRANT OUR CERTITUDE

The *Wake*'s second chapter has a clear structure, for we are given a continuous flow of dream figures and scenes, so that it is reasonable to speak of a single vignette, one that meanders from the fairy tale of HCE and his sovereign to the vitriolic ballad of the end. This single vignette, concerned with HCE's flaws and their impact on his life as family man and as member of a community, serves as a focus for many of the dreamer's anxieties. Disturbing questions about the value of his life are partially swathed in its eccentric fantasy.

Most of the *Wake* is not like that. Often, there are abrupt shifts of topic and of mood, and the dream material is structured quite differently. The differences adapt to the ways in which the dreamer is responding to his predicament. When he is searching blindly, and unsuccessfully, for ways of resolving his uncertainties, the dream scenes displace one another in helter-skelter confusion. The material immediately following the ballad is a case in point.

We begin with an echo of the song—"Chest Cee" is a note produced by a tenor (singing C in chest voice)—but also, of course, with a command to see, to sort out the confusion thrown up by the hostile judgments of the ballad. But the reader, like the dreamer, is in a dense fog, where nothing, not even the sex of the characters, can be surely identified. How, then, is it possible to respond to the worry that the vision of the ballad is correct? One way to proceed is to contemplate the character of those who have brought the charges. Who are they, and are their judgments to be trusted? Finding them proves impossible, for they have vanished from the scene.

Of Hosty, now "poor Osti-Fosti," it seems that "no one end is known" (48: 19, 24). For others, there are stories of their subsequent exploits (often humdrum or squalid—almost always reported with a comic twist) culminating in their deaths—some "propelled from Behind into the great Beyond," others "disappeared . . . from the sourface of this earth" (49: 25; 50: 8, 10). There are many ways to describe the inevitable end, but none of them provides much import to what led up to it. Of course, the lives of Hosty and his band of followers are not a matter of central concern for the dreamer; we drift into this vignette because he wants to know whether these people can be trusted to render a competent verdict; are they the sorts of judges whose assessment of HCE genuinely undermines his conception of who he is and what his life is worth; or are their denunciations products of cruelty and spleen, of which the world—their world—is full? The dreamer can find no answers, because the potential witnesses cannot be brought to the bar, much less interrogated.

There follow a series of cloudy vignettes, which I read as the dreamer's increasingly desperate search for an illuminating reconstruction of the events of the long tale of the previous chapter. Characters from the story of HCE in the park, from the report of the meeting with the cad, and from the account of the spread of the rumor emerge briefly and indefinitely, in unanticipated combinations. A brief mention of someone who may be the priest's confidant ("Phishlin Phil" [50: 33; compare 38: 35]) gives way to the expressed sense that the fog is too thick for identification:

> it is a slopperish matter, given the wet and low visibility (since in this scherzarade of one's thousand one nightinesses that sword of certainty which would indentifide the body never falls) to idendefine the individuoune in scratch wig, squarecuts, stock lavaleer, regattable oxeter, baggy pants and shufflers . . . (51: 3–8)

Just when we, and the dreamer, are beginning to despair of the possibility of achieving a just resolution—the sword of certainty is the sword that delivers justice, the sword that may "indent" (execute), "indemnify" (excuse by cutting free), identify and define—the mists clear for a moment and we can discover a familiar figure. The combination of clothes reveals that we are dealing with HCE, and there is an allusion to the possibility of exposure ("an incipience (lust!) in the direction of area baldness" [51: 9]); but now the vignette takes a new direction; there are three young men in "drenched coats overall" (51: 12), yet these are not soldiers but truant schoolboys (recalling the story "An Encounter" from *Dubliners* and thus casting HCE in a very negative light); unlike the soldiers, but like the cad, they ask HCE a question; it is not, however, the cad's question, but a direct request to relate the "haardly creditable edventyres of the Haberdasher, the two Curchies and the three Enkelchums in their Bearskin ghoats" (51: 14–15). We might now expect a new version of the story, perhaps another attempt by HCE to redeem himself; but once more the vignette turns away, ending with a surprised description of the ways in which time has changed him (and not for the better).

The dreamer is worrying the material of the previous chapter, combining its elements in novel ways in a search for some form of consolation. It is not to be found. There are all kinds of ways of trying to find out who HCE is, what he has done, and what his life means. One can try to track HCE himself, or follow the cad, or begin with those involved in the genesis of the story and the ballad; individual scenes—the Park, the racetrack, Dublin—can serve as starting points for the anxious exploration. Nothing works. When the cad emerges, smoking an evening pipe, he becomes associated with two young women; he now has both a gun and a watch, it seems, but metamorphoses into a priest; the priest echoes the mode of address of the sermon on hell that terrified the young Stephen Dedalus ("my dearbraithers, my most dearbrathairs" [52: 11–12]), but then unaccountably speaks of "the One" and tells of "the Compassionate, called up before the triad of precoxious scaremakers" (52: 12–14).[1] Once again there is the possibility of absolution for HCE, but it is not clearly given—compassion is on trial, not in the seat of judgment.

Again and again, the quest proves elusive. The dreamer can try to focus on HCE and his accomplishments in Dublin (52: 23ff.), on later assessments of the encounter between HCE and the cad (53: 7ff.), on the debate among the partisans in the "house of concord" (a debate that dissolves into banal exchanges in a public convenience) (54: 7ff.), on an overly effusive declaration by a sweating figure who may be HCE (54: 20), on attempts to review the larger place of HCE and his family from a historical distance (55: 3ff). None leads to any definite conclusion. Perhaps the dreamer can find rest in turning HCE into the hero of a romantic fantasy. There is a brief attempt to settle uncertainty by covering the thought of past life in a warm glow, conjuring a pastoral vision of HCE's inn, in which the "lazy skald or maundering pote" (56: 21–2) may find simple comforts (and escape "from van Demon's land" [56: 21]). Yet the dreamer cannot be satisfied with this as a resolution, for it depends on the suppression of serious thought.

> Nonsense! There was not very much windy Nous blowing at the given moment through the hat of Mr Melancholy Slow! (56: 29–30)

Nor are the four canonical historians, the evangelists who represent the four parts of Ireland, of any assistance. Their utterances are cryptic and apparently irrelevant. Only the ass who accompanies them delivers a comprehensible assessment, telling us that HCE was once great, once married to ALP, and that he fell; and that, of course, we already knew.

All this uncomfortable striving and straining leads toward a summation of the dreamer's predicament, one that arrives with the weight of crushing obviousness.

Thus the unfacts, did we possess them, are too imprecisely few to warrant our certitude, the evidencegivers by legpoll too untrustworthily irreperible where his adjugers are semmingly freak threes but his judicandees plainly minus twos. (57: 16–19)

We have been, for ten pages, in the grip of doubt, real doubt, not the kind of philosophical pretense that can be left behind when you move from the study to the gaming room, from abstract speculation to everyday life.[2] Identifying with HCE, the dreamer wants to be convinced that the verdict of the mob is wrong, that what HCE did (whatever it was) did not disrupt his family life and should not have made him the target of such corrosive vilification. The dreamer needs a way to show that the initial circumstances are not as they have been described, or that they should not be evaluated as they have been, or that the chain of transmission has somehow distorted the truth, or that the accusations are founded on envy, or spite, or desperation. The vignettes of these pages explore all the usual ways of trying to establish these things, and they are often extremely funny in the details of how knowledge proves elusive. For the dreamer, though, it is perfectly serious; we cannot miss the anxiety behind this manic series of false starts.

Nor can matters be left with the confession of indecision. Our "notional gullery" needs a fitting monument to HCE (57: 21)—we would, of course, not like to "gull" (delude) ourselves in the manner of the lazy romantic poet, but, in the absence of firm evidence, our notions are likely to be under pressure from our hopes and desires. In any event, "Madam's Toshowus" (57: 20)[3] stands equipped with the appropriate waxwork:

> that exposure of him by old Tom Quad, a flashback in which he sits sated, gowndabout, in clericalease habit, watching bland sol slithe dodgsomely into the nethermore, a globule of maugdleness about to corrugitate his mild dewed cheek and the tata of a tiny victorienne, Alys, pressed by his limper looser. (57: 23–9)

Almost every word in this extraordinary characterization can be nudged toward a positive evaluation of HCE/Dodgson/Carroll or to a negative assessment: what kind of exposure (or flash) is in question? why is he sated? is the gown a mark of distinction or a concealment? is the magdalen sinning or penitent (or just an Oxford college)? is his cheek corrupted? is it mildewed? is the "tata" her farewell gift? is she the victor and he the loser? and why is part of him "limper"? Answers to these questions and many more can come in shades of innocence or guilt. The memorial turns out to be no more definite than the evidence.

The dreamer must take some stand. If his own investigations have broken down, he can perform a census of the opinions of others. So there arises a new vignette, one in which the characters are as concerned with the evaluation of

HCE as he is—he conjures a world in which the HCE affair is on everyone's lips. It

> bulk[s] at the bar of a rota of tribunals in manor hall as in thieves' kitchen, mid pillow talk and chithouse chat . . . (57: 33–5)

Sometimes HCE is summarily convicted[4]; on other occasions he is acquitted. Unsurprisingly, those who feel that they are his beneficiaries incline to a positive view and mourn his loss; others take delight in his downfall, seeing it as cause for festivity. Both groups merge in the celebrants at a wake, where rowdy singing and dancing mix with sighs and mourning. Once more, the dreamer is left with "jostling judgments" (58: 21).

This is not an immediate dead end, however. The dreamer can canvass a wider sample, seeing how HCE lives on in the recollections of all sorts of Dubliners. Indeed, it may be that the enduring imprint of a life in the lives of others is not so much a measure of its intrinsic value as constitutive of that value. So, thick and fast, comes a torrent of vignettes, character sketches of an assortment of Dublin characters who give their own impressionistic assessments. Joyce offers us a wonderfully whimsical census, full of brilliant comic touches (58: 23–61: 27). But it concludes, as we ought to have known it would, with a wide gamut of responses and plenty of informants hedging their bets. The dreamer knows that these may be mere "fablings" (61: 28), cobbled together with no knowledge. Indeed, the whole record is riddled with deception:

> for many, we trow, beyessed to and denayed of, are given to us by some who use the truth but sparingly and we, on this side ought to sorrow for their pricking pens on that account. (61: 33–6)

The thought that denigrators have spoken and written falsely (and that their falsehoods "prick"—wound) prompts the opening of a new series of vignettes, as the dreamer comes to view what has happened as a violation of sanctuary and a kind of betrayal.

For the first time, we pick up an important aspect of the ballad, the depiction of HCE as an outsider, one who has come to Dublin from across the sea, seeking a home and finding a bride. It was full of promise, lush and fruitful:

> The wastobe land, a lottuse land, a luctuous land, Emeraldilluim, the peasant pastured . . . (62: 11–12)

But the local inhabitants rose against him, making him their scapegoat, and subjecting him to

> the horrors of the premier terror of Errorland. (perorhaps!) (62: 24–5)

What is the "premier terror"? The rejection and humiliation of HCE, of course; but also the struggle to find one's way in "Errorland," the awful uncertainty the dreamer has felt, the terrible difficulty of moving beyond "perhaps."

Interestingly, in attempting to resolve the issue of the value of HCE's life by stepping back from the precipitating cause of the public humiliation, the dreamer seems to have found a key to open up new possibilities. For there now emerge some different versions of an encounter with a menacing stranger. The voice acquires new confidence and new excitement:

> We seem to us (the real Us!) to be reading our Amenti in the sixth sealed chapter of the going forth by black. (62: 26)

The dreamer hopes to discover who he is by opening a previously sealed chapter of the Book of the Dead, one that will explain how the confusion of conflicting voices is to be resolved.

The vignette begins with a figure whose identity is far from clear—"one tall man, humping a suspicious parcel" (62: 28–9)—although the hump suggests HCE (one of whose possible first names is "Humphrey," and who will be associated with a hump or a bulge in [II-3] and in ALP's description of his suit [620: 5]). Returning home one evening, he is accosted by a stranger, who places a revolver against his face and threatens to shoot. The assailant appears to have other weapons and to be bent on violence; he appears to harbor a grievance, asking

> with gaeilish gall wodkar blizzard's business Thornton had with that Kane's fender only to be answered by the aggravated assaulted that that that was the snaps for him, Midweeks, to sultry well go and find out if he was showery well able. (63: 6–9)

One of the suggestions of "gaeilish gall" is to connect the menacing figure with "Gaping Gill," the cad in the Park, but the circumstances of the original vignette are almost directly inverted: instead of a dim menace, an apparently trivial question, and a confessional outpouring out of all proportion to the situation, here under conditions of the most direct threat, an inquiry that seems to demand an answer is met with a brusque, dismissive response. The dreamer—"gentlewriter" (63: 10)—is revising the story of HCE so that he will emerge as heroic, rather than guilty; that would continue the perspective constructed in the immediately preceding material, where HCE was seen as an outsider, bent on doing great things, betrayed by the envious mob. Yet at this point, the vignette turns away. This version is "transparently nontrue" (63: 9–10):

> His feet one is not a tall man, not at all, man. No such parson. No such fender. No such lumber. No such race. (63: 10–12)

There is an immediate suggestion that the cause of whatever trouble there was might have involved two girls—and that, presumably, would pitch the dreamer back into the old confusion about HCE's behavior in the Park and its aftermath. But this too is rejected in favor of an alternative vignette involving an aggressive stranger carrying a bottle.

It is worth pausing over the interchange between the assailant and his intended victim, for, although apparently senseless, it contains clues to where the dreamer is headed. First, the introduction of inconsistent meteorological vocabulary is no accident, but one of Joyce's ways of emphasizing the ambiguity of any descriptions or characterizations that might be provided; not even the most mundane details of scene-setting can be taken for granted; the same device recurs in the "star-chamber quiry" of (III-3), where the questioners, baffled in their first attempts at reconstruction, begin again with immense care to pin down the mundane details of a context, offering accounts of the weather that are flatly inconsistent—as one of them realizes (501: 17–503: 2; 519: 16–25). Second, the context of enduring rivalry is reinforced by the allusions to Cain and Abel. Third, the use of "wodkar" for "what" points to the way in which this vignette will eventually be developed, in terms of a late-night attempt to obtain drink. Fourth, "fender" can easily be connected to "offender" and "defender," or simply stand for a metal plate, the sort of thing against which a drunken man, wanting more to drink, might hammer open a bottle.

Most important of all, however, are the names "Thornton" and "Kane," the actual names of Dubliners whom Joyce transformed into the characters Tom Kernan and Martin Cunningham of *Ulysses*.[5] In that novel, Cunningham wins our sympathy (as I have suggested) because of his friendly attitude toward Bloom, while, on the same grounds, Kernan appears as a more neutral figure. Much more significant, however, is their prior appearance in the story "Grace" in *Dubliners*, which opens with Tom Kernan, drunk, having fallen in his attempt to descend the stairs that lead down from the bar of a pub to its toilet; Kernan has bitten through his tongue, and he is in danger of being taken into custody, when he is rescued by a passing medical student and, subsequently, by his friend Jack Power. The main action of the story consists in the development of a plot, hatched by Power and Kernan's wife, to help Kernan change his ways. Power does not think he can manage this by himself but must bring in an older colleague and mutual friend of Tom Kernan.

> —O, now, Mrs Kernan, said Mr Power, we'll make him turn over a new leaf. I'll talk to Martin. He's the man. (*Dubliners*, 155)

So indeed it proves. With Martin Cunningham playing a leading persuasive role, Kernan is induced to attend a Jesuit retreat.

From the perspective of this earlier story, then, Kane (Cunningham) serves as Thornton's (Kernan's) defender—or perhaps it would be more accurate to say "as the defender of his better self." Yet, of course, the whole point of the dreamer's inquiries throughout this chapter is to find a self, to find what parts of himself are "better." Like the dreamer, Kernan is divided, one part of him wanting to conform to an ideal of himself as sober husband and father, another delighting in the free-and-easy camaraderie of the pub (his appearances in *Ulysses* testify to the psychological division—he figures first as one of the mourners at Dignam's funeral ["Hades," *Ulysses*, 100–6 *passim*], and later, in the "Wandering Rocks" episode, reflects on the quality of the gin he has just drunk [*Ulysses*, 239–41]). Kane is the defender of one part of Kernan and an offender (assailant) against another. Of course, another person whom Kane (Cunningham) defends is Bloom, helping him away from the physical menace of the Citizen (*Ulysses*, 335–6); the immediate cause of the trouble is that Bloom is an outsider.

HCE and Bloom are both attacked because members of the Dublin community regard them as not belonging; that is the point from which the dreamer's attempt to reconstruct the vignette has begun, with the voyager from overseas who comes to make a home and to improve what he finds; others resent what he does, and what he dreams, and vilify him on that account. Hosty's ballad derided his attempts at reform. What exactly were these? One item that figures on the list is:

seven dry Sundays a week . . . (45: 17)

Since HCE is identified in the ballad as an hotelier and publican, this is hardly likely as a literal description of what he does. Behind it, however, may lurk a difference of opinion about just what level of carousing and conviviality is appropriate, a difference of opinion that might divide (say) Mrs. Kernan, Jack Power, Martin Cunningham, Bloom, and HCE from Tom Kernan and the Citizen; indeed, the same difference might be present *within* some of these characters. One way to bring out the disagreement would be to present an argument between a drunken man, taking steps to obtain more, and someone or something that provides resistance.

At this point, we can take up again the mysterious encounter between the "tall man" and his revolver-toting assailant. The vignette starts to question itself as soon as the heroic victim has made his dismissive reply. Then, steering by the dangerous suggestion of the involvement of two girls, it transforms the attacker into

the heavybuilt Abelbody in a butcherblue blouse . . . with a most decisive bottle of single in his possession, seized after dark by the town guard at Haveyoucaught-emerod's temperance gateway was there in a gate's way. (63: 15–16, 17–19)

This characterization of HCE hearkens back to the vision of him as presiding ruler and judge ("Humpheres Cheops Exarchas" [62: 21]) in the initial effort to tell a new, and more reassuring, version of his life; here he is the provider of discipline—one who catches offenders and applies the rod—for the emerald isle.

At the heart of this revisionary account, then, is the thought of HCE as arousing hostility, not because he is ludicrous or disgusting, but because of his attempts at discipline (and self-discipline). The vignette continues with the apparent testimony of the sot, into whom the threatening figure has metamorphosed, and his own version of the cause of his trouble with the law. He starts with a confession that parallels the beginning of Tom Kernan's misadventure: he has drunk far too much, and he falls (possibly in an attempt to urinate against a pillar). This confession is rejected in favor of something slightly different: trying to open the bottle he was carrying, he banged it against a gate; the noise aroused "the boots about the swan,"[6] who descends to find out what is happening; the noise is ferocious, and, as reported

> was not in the very remotest like the belzey babble of a bottle of boose which would not rouse him out o' slumber deep but reminded him loads more of the martiallawsey marses of foreign musikants' instrumongs . . . (64: 10–14)

It is, in fact, such an extraordinary disturbance, as if an angry army were beginning an attack on whatever center of order HCE has created, that it awakens others, and

> after this most nooningless knockturn the young reine came down desperate and the old liffopotamus started ploring all over the plains, as mud as she cud be, ruinating all the bouchers' schurts and the backers' wischandtugs so that be the chandelure of the Rejaneyjailey they were all night wasching the walters of, the weltering walters off. Whyte. (64: 15–21)

Plainly, the vignette has gone in an unexpected direction. From the dreamer's concern to depict HCE as the guardian of discipline, order, and enlightened reform, we have been led to the most explicit presentation of an angry ALP we have yet encountered. How has this occurred?

There are two main versions of this ambiguous ending. In one, the original assailant has become a figure who bangs at the door of HCE's inn, and eventually a chorus of carousing voices, perhaps singing Hosty's ballad. This version continues the dreamer's project of viewing the law-abiding HCE as the target of hostile voices who see him as an outsider, meddling with reforms. In it, HCE is placed inside the inn, perhaps in his older guise as the boots (a Sackerson figure), perhaps as the "old liffopotamus."[7] He and his family are under attack from a hostile world, but they remain united. This is the resolution at which the dreamer has been aiming; attaining it has been the point of the retelling that began two pages back.

Unfortunately, the resolution is threatened by a different version in which the figure at the door has become HCE himself, attempting to return home after an evening's carousal. He makes noise—a great deal of noise. Unlike Mrs. Kernan, ALP greets him with anger and recrimination, using the occasion as an extensive exploration of all his lapses; she spreads the dirt over the household linens, so that they will need a great deal of cleansing (plainly the passage points forward to the discussion of the washerwomen [216: 4–5]); in this version, she stands as the representative of rectitude, both queen— even queen of heaven—and jailkeeper ("Rejaneyjailey"). The vignette is not so much about the threats posed to an intact private sphere by hostility from the outside as the strains brought about within that sphere by behavior that expresses a particular part of HCE. The extensive spilling of mud, the soiling of the laundry, represents ALP's use of the occasion to air grievances; it is not simply a matter of HCE's excessive conviviality; if we have read the conversation of the washerwomen (I–8) before we come to this vignette, we know the sorts of stains that have to be washed away (196: 15–19). They involve just the kind of material the dreamer has been avoiding.

At this point, however, a new voice breaks in, as a part of HCE that has hitherto hidden in silence is brought vividly into the sequence of vignettes. The accusatory soldiers are dismissed, and we are promised a film version of "a strawberry frolic" (64: 28). The call—"*Cherchons la flamme!*"—embodies the dreamer's wish to revive the dying flame of sexual interest, as well as to seek out a woman. The worries, and the guilt, are to be laughed away; HCE needs to abandon his sober Puritanism; he has tried to think too hard, and needs to take life more lightly:

> Come on, ordinary man with that large big nonobli head, and that blanko berbecked fischial eksprezzion. . . . Your machelar's mutton leg's getting musclebound from being too pulled. (64: 30–1, 32–3)

There follows the synopsis of a movie, whose plot is loosely based on a scandal of the 1920s. An old man takes up with a much younger woman, and the first thought is that this is absurd, that she is simply exploiting him for the material comforts he can provide and deceiving him on the side. "Old grum," however, has the last laugh, for he has a second sweet young thing, and the vignette builds to a jazz-age dance for three "in his tippy, upindown dippy, tiptoptippy canoodle, can you" (65: 32–3).

It is all momentarily bracing, as though the fogs have cleared, and a new energy pulses through the description; the dreamer is momentarily caught up in the beat of the music. Yet it is forced, artificial, and it cannot last. The movie ends, and we hear the whir of the projector—"Ack, ack, ack" (65: 34)—which is also an expression of regret and sadness—"Ach, ach, ach." The dreamer can neither fully identify with the happy story of the film, nor silence the voice that has found expression in it. There is a moment of intense frustration (66: 8–9)—and then the dreamer is back to the enterprise of the entire chapter, the attempt to arrive at a clear understanding of the conflicts he feels.

As with the earliest parts of the chapter, the dreamer is wandering in fog and darkness. He hopes for the possibility of settling matters by finding a record of ALP's perspective: perhaps the morning will bring a letter from "A Laughable Party" (66: 16–17) to HCE. That letter would, perhaps, enclose her attitude to life in the way that a coffin encloses a dead body. The letter is needed so that we can know what ALP has thought; the coffin is needed for the wake; and it is at the wake that we sum up a life and what it has meant. The letter has not yet arrived, and the coffin has disappeared.

So the dreamer returns to alternative versions of the vignettes that have already appeared. There is a new version of the story of the assailant in "the butcher of the blues" (67: 15; compare 63: 16; and also 64: 18), who now turns into a deliveryman, kicking at a door; but, as so often, those witness proves unreliable. An attempt to trace the young women in the park—"those rushy hollow heroines in their skirtsleeves" (67: 31)—reveals that one has committed suicide, while the other has gone on to more extensive forms of sexual activity:

> selling her spare favours in the haymow or in lumber closets . . . serving whom in fine that same hot coney *a la Zingara* which our own little Graunya of the chilired cheeks dished up to the greatsire of Oscar, that son of a Coole. Houri of the coast of emerald, arrah of the lacessive poghue . . . (68: 5, 9–12)

From the career of a prostitute, we have been led back to HCE and ALP, and to a vision of ALP that is enormously different from any that has figured in previous vignettes ("lacessive" is plainly a cross between "lascivious" and "excessive" and "poghue" is one of Joyce's routine amendments of an Anglo-Irish word for "kiss"). For a moment, the vignette paints their marriage by assigning HCE the role of his wife's pimp. There is an attempt to restore HCE to regal form, but it founders on a new anxiety:

> He thought he want. Whath? Hear, O hear, living of the land! Hungreb, dead era, hark! He hea, eyes ravenous on her lippling lills. He hear her voi of days gon by. He hears! Zay, zay, zay! But, by the beer of his profit, he cannot answer. (68: 24–8)[8]

It is a sad depiction of the decline of sexual response—and of the humiliation of its public exposure.

By an odd twist, however, the vignette returns to its original direction, ending with the question of whether HCE has been the victim of blackmail. Dark possibilities have been explored, but no sure verdict has emerged. Once again, the dreamer strikes out in new directions, eventually settling on a new version of the vignette of the menacing figure at the door. The place is plainly HCE's inn, where he is disturbed by a "hikely excellent crude man about road" (70: 15), who issues familiar threats of physical violence. The visitor's apparent aim is to obtain "more wood alcohol" (70: 27), and he issues a stream of insults, calling on

> House, son of Clod, to come out, you jewbeggar, to be Executed Amen. (70: 34–5)

HCE does not rise to the bait but writes down, instead, a long list "of all abusive names he was called" (71: 5–6). In response to his silence, the visitor throws a few stones, and,

> after exhorting Earwicker, or, in slightly modified phraseology, Messrs or Missrs Earwicker, Seir, his feminisible name of multitude, to cocoa come outside to Mockerloo out of that for the honour of Crumlin, . . . so as he could brianslog him and burst him all dizzy, you go bail, like Potts Fracture did with Keddle Flatnose and nobodyatall with Whollyphamous . . . (73: 3–6, 7–9)

he departs. Quite plainly, the hostility of the visitor to the pub recalls the abuse of the Citizen in the "Cyclops" chapter of *Ulysses:* the connection is made both in the anti-Semitic slur ("jewbeggar") and in the reference to the encounter between Odysseus ("no-man") with Polyphemus. HCE, the outsider, cannot be accepted into the community and is effectively besieged in his private domain. Nor does he have any device for resisting the hatred of the community he hopes to join but can only write down a list of the epithets in which his faults are recorded.

Yet in this final vignette, the transformation of the encounter with a menacing stranger, there are deeper undercurrents. HCE may be secure, but he is alone. Does the private sphere to which he is confined contain a family life? Does he have the consolation and comfort of ALP's presence? That is left quite undecided. She, too, may be outside, with the hostile community. Further, the report of the assailant's threats assign to him what can easily be interpreted as HCE's distinctive stammer ("cocoa come outside"). The potential kinship of the abusive stranger and HCE himself is also suggested by the allusion to a familiar adage—the conflict may be "like the pot calling the kettle black." The dreamer can take no comfort in this final vision. HCE's status is left unresolved; as always, the "unfacts" are unknown and too scanty.

This entire chapter, then, records an earnest effort to tackle the confusions generated from the material of the long vignette of Chapter I-2. The dreamer would like to understand whether he should conceive himself as a bold free spirit, defying a corrupt and repressive society, or whether he ought to conform his standards and conduct to the judgments of those around him, or whether he should engage in certain kinds of self-discipline, even when they are regarded as wrong-headed and restrictive by impulses within himself, or whether a commitment to love and marriage can survive the ravages of time, or whether any such commitment can be insulated against intrusions from a broader community. He tackles these questions from a large number of perspectives, trying to exemplify the possibilities by varying and recombining the material of the original vignette, sometimes introducing further characters whose judgments on the situations can be assessed—different recipes for the "mutthering pot" (20: 7). Nothing works. The attempt to satisfy some of the voices within him provokes a reaction from others, so that a vignette initially suggesting one solution is redirected and becomes confused. It is as if that parliament that argues its way into the "Casaconcordia" were to arrive at a preliminary judgment, and that that, in itself, were immediately to add extra strength to the opposition forces so that they were able to pass a contrary motion. That reversal would itself be unstable, so that there must be constant oscillation until the only possible resting point would be a completely ambiguous judgment.

Because the dreamer is pressed to find a resolution of these internal conflicts, ambiguity can only be a temporary respite. The struggle starts again. How, then, can the chapter end? Only, I think, in a combination of uncertainty and exhaustion. By the end, just as the reader may well be exhausted by the density and confusion of the material (already announced in the third word [48: 1]), so, too, is the dreamer. The fog condenses in clouds and the clouds bring rain. The dreamer's quest temporarily ends in the sleep of HCE, a sleep that bears the obvious markings of defeat. After the harsh end of the closing vignette, where HCE sits besieged, compiling the catalogue of his apparent failings, his energy dissipates; he is old and tired.

> Humph is in his doge. Words weigh no more to him than raindrips to Rethfernhim. Which we all like. Rain. When we sleep. Drops. But wait until our sleeping. Drain. Sdops. (74: 16–19)

Why do we all like the rain? Because, as ALP will eventually tell us, clouds and rain are the source from which she comes, and, in these closing lines, there is a hint of her benign presence and the consolation it will eventually bring.

Between the final vignette and the close of the chapter comes a moment of promise: we are not yet at the end; the dreamer does not have to stop with this exhausted uncertainty. The renewal of HCE is announced as the rebirth of a hero—first as Arthur, or Finn, or Roland, and then as the recipient of a great promise:

> For in those deyes his Deyus shall ask of Allprohome and call to himm: Allprohome! And he make answer: Add some. Nor wink nor wunk. *Animadiabolum, mene credidisti mortuum?* Silence was in thy faustive halls, O Truiga, when thy green woods went dry . . . (74: 6–10)

The promise to Abraham, of course, was that his successors should cover the earth. Perhaps, then, we may think of the elements that have figured within HCE as the sources for better ideals and identities that can respond to the dreamer's concerns about the form of a successful life. A central part of HCE's identity in the vignettes that have figured so far is his role as a family man; "Allprohome" is a very good name for this part of him. Yet this is not the whole. In response to the call from on high, HCE will answer with the traditional "Here" (*ad sum*), but he will also need to "add some," to extend himself, honoring those aspects that have been slighted in the concentration on domesticity. Like the corpse in the ballad of Finnegan's Wake, HCE will ask, "soul of the devil, did ye think me dead?" The line also points in a different direction, first to a familiar folk prayer—"May you be in heaven an hour before the devil knows you're dead"—a message of hope for hopeless sinners. Through this it leads to the conclusion of Goethe's version of the *Faust* story (echoed, obviously, in the transformation of "festive" into "faustive"), where vigilance on the part of the angel cheats the devil of his due (the watching angel does not "wink"). Salvation is brought about, as the last couplet of *Faust* makes evident, by the female voice, the voice of forgiveness; and ALP, the *Wake*'s principal embodiment of that voice, is here too; she can renew the dry woods, falling as rain.

Out of the fog of uncertainty comes a dim promise. We do not yet know what it is or how to solve the dreamer's problems. But there are hints that we should not dismiss them as insoluble.

How can the dream go forward from here? As I have already suggested, the temporary identification of HCE with Abraham can be viewed as promising that elements within him might be recombined into more satisfactory identities. Perhaps the problems that have dogged the dreamer in this chapter stem from the attempt to reconcile incompatible facets of himself, aspirations that cannot consistently be pursued. Perhaps the individual elements should be distinguished and separately appraised. One way to explore that would be to let the irreconcilable aspects of human life that serve as foci of the dreamer's concerns find their own vivid presentation in new vignettes, without any attempt to integrate or control them. Eventually we might come to see these as successors of HCE, his seed, his sons.

Those aspects have already been indicated in the list compiled by the besieged publican. Many of them are familiar, and point to HCE's status as an outsider (for example, "*Barebarean*" [71: 30]), repressor of ordinary pleasures ("*Tummer the Lame the Tyrranous*" [71: 16–17]), a failure in his marriage ("*I Divorce Thee Husband*" [71: 28]), and so forth. One, however, should come as a surprise. This label, reiterated in the list of insults hurled as the customers depart the bar after HCE's long humiliation (374: 27), points to an aspect of HCE we have not yet seen: *Artist* (71: 21).

10

EVERYBODY HEARD
THEIR PLAINT

The main issue that arises with I-2 centers on understanding the significance of what appears to be a grotesque and senseless story; I-3 poses the challenge of discerning some order in a sequence of rapidly shifting scenarios where there is constant confusion of identity. I have tried to respond to the first interpretative problem by showing how the apparently trifling anecdotes of I-2 serve as foci for the dreamer's anxieties, and to the second by exploring how the initially mystifying shifts and jumps reflect the dreamer's attempts to rework the material in light of the concerns that underlie it. The next chapter, I-4, introduces a new collection of difficulties. Its individual episodes are less dense than those of its predecessor, but the order and connection of them is, at first sight, baffling.

As I read it, the chapter is divided into eight main parts, and it is helpful to begin with a conception of this anatomy. We open with an elegiac paragraph in which mourning for the suffering of HCE gives way to the thought that his passing leads to renewal, specifically in the thriving of a city (Dublin, clearly identified by one of Joyce's variations on the city motto [76: 8–9]). Even though the burial of HCE is supposed to issue in regeneration, what speedily emerges in the second part (76: 33–81: 8) is conflict and violence, license and infidelity; the great new city is squalid, a rubbish dump, fit only for scavengers. In the third episode (81: 8–85: 19), we revisit the past, as the violence that follows the fall of HCE seems to crystallize in yet another version of the story of an encounter in which one man meets a single assailant. This gives way to the explicit presentation of a trial (a mad trial in the style of *Alice*), in which the two parties present and argue out their rival versions of the encounter (85: 20–93: 21). Although no definite verdict is reached, one of the contestants is fêted, while the other is derided. In the fifth part, a brief interlude (93: 22–94: 22), we return to the rubbish dump and to the possibility of a letter that will provide a reassuring resolution. The sixth episode (94: 23–96: 25) follows the rambling conversation of four old men, who are supposed to be sorting out the issues— and it is not clear whether their official topic is the recent trial or the career of HCE; they wander in ever more drunken reminiscence. The seventh part (96: 26–100: 8) follows the course of a foxhunt, in which a figure—possibly HCE, possibly the derided participant in the trial—is pursued and hounded into exile. This concludes with a summary, in newspaper headlines, of the original tale of HCE in the Park. The last segment (from 100: 9 to the end) returns us to the original fall of HCE, offering a different story of continuation in which ALP becomes increasingly prominent, until, at the very end, we achieve the peace that was dimly hinted in the closing paragraphs of (I-3). The major task for any reading of this chapter is to determine how this odd, seemingly disconnected, sequence of vignettes hangs together.

I suggest that the chapter traces the dreamer's development of characters and scenes that will serve for the further exploration of his underlying anxieties. HCE is temporarily laid to rest, and the first pages center on his suffering and burial. Yet neither the dreamer nor the reader begins completely afresh. The different aspects of the dreamer are to be isolated and held up for inspection, but they are different aspects of *him,* and it should be no surprise that their generation from HCE affects the way in which the new vignettes are elaborated. HCE's passing initially removes the identity that has mediated conflicting voices, and the result is the eruption of conflict. The ferocity of that conflict means that the resultant setting will be mean and squalid (a dungheap, not a shining city). If anything worthwhile is to result, these voices have to be made audible and their claims assessed. We return, then, to consider the opposition between two principal tendencies within HCE, one devoted to public order, willing to acquiesce in community values, and one rebellious and bent on self-creation. At first, these identities are not clearly formed. The characters who figure in the recapitulations of the violent encounters of I-2 and I-3 are not fully individuated. They develop into two demarcated figures toward the end of the mad trial, where they are officially named and when they receive very different rewards. The harsh judgment directed against one—Shem— gives rise to a reaction, the promise of a merciful re-evaluation of the tendencies Shem represents. Before that becomes fully elaborated, in the emergence of ALP, two further themes need to be sounded. First, the standard ways of trying to resolve the disagreement between the visions of life associated with Shem and his opponent (or counterpart), Shaun, are not resoluble by any simple review; the inconclusive verdict of the trial is echoed in the inconsequential discussion of the four old men. Second, we must become vividly aware of the consequences of Shem's way; he must face repudiation, persecution, and exile. It is important, however, that in this chapter, as in so many, the voice of ALP should speak last: for, as we shall see, the creation and refinement of that voice is the key to the dreamer's resolution of his perplexities.

In effect, then, the chapter grows out of the dead HCE three major characters, whom we come to know as Shem, Shaun, and ALP, characters who both represent tendencies within him and who sometimes serve as foils for other parts of him. Once they have been established for the dreamer, the rest of Part I can find different ways of returning to the fundamental conflicts, and Parts II and III can probe them even more deeply.[1] So, for example, the clash between the visions of Shem and Shaun will unfold from the mad trial of I-4, through the denunciation of I-7, into the contests of II-1 and II-2, and the erosion of Shaun's tidy world in III-1 and III-2. Some of the props introduced here in the presentation of new vignettes will be laid before us more systematically by the orderly Shaun in I-6. Finally, the possibilities of resolution and absolution, implicit in ALP's letter and her final appearance, will be the starting points for further growth in I-5 and I-8, respectively; the last will only come to its complete fulfillment in the *Wake*'s closing pages.

So much for a bald outline. It is time to take a closer view.

We begin with an old man, full of ambiguous memories. The prevailing mood is of loss, of past betrayal, as HCE recalls "those lililiths undeveiled which had undone him" (75: 5-6). He is conscious of enmity; and he has

> prayed, as he sat on anxious seat, . . . , during that three and a hellof hours' agony of silence, *ex profundis malorum,* and bred with unfeigned charity that his wordwounder . . . might, mercy to providential benevolence's who hates prudencies' astuteness, unfold into the first of a distinguished dynasty of his posteriors, . . . his most besetting of ideas . . . being the formation . . . of a truly criminal stratum . . . thereby at last eliminating from all classes and masses with directly derivative decasualisation: *sigarius* (sic!) *vindicat urbes terrorum* (sicker!): and so . . . the obedience of the citizens elp the ealth of the ole. (75: 16–76: 9; parenthetical remarks and digressive characterizations omitted)

The odd twists of this sentence are easily missed because Joyce inserts into it some asides that make the overall structure sufficiently murky to blind the reader to the bizarre sequence of thoughts. We open with HCE in agony. The situation seems to be that in which we left him; he is seated inside his pub with an enemy hurling insults—word wounds—through the door. We might imagine him praying for deliverance, for exoneration from the charges that have been leveled against him, for the defeat of this enemy. That is not, however, the content of his prayer. Instead, he hopes, in a spirit of mercy, contrary to that of prudence, that his assailant might be the beneficiary of the promise to Abraham—that he might found a distinguished dynasty. Then, as we turn the page, we receive a second surprise. HCE wants this dynasty to realize one of his favorite ideas, that of a "truly criminal stratum." His aim, we learn, is to undermine a version of St. Augustine's dictum—"The verdict of the world is secure"—or perhaps to undercut the idea of a completely stable community (city). Finally, the thought of a criminal class contesting agreed notions is immediately conjoined with just the opposite vision, of obedient citizens following the law and producing a healthy community; of course, it is interesting that the aitches are dropped in this clause, suggesting that the speaker may be a member of the less polished classes, even one of the "wordwounder's" dynasty.

I proposed above that the vituperative assailant is another version of HCE, and, in light of that proposal, we can recognize that he is willing into existence heirs who inherit different aspects of himself, some who are law abiding and prepared to accept the judgments of society and tradition and others who rebel against it. These are two of the important characters who will emerge in this chapter, and HCE tells us clearly in advance that the verdict of the world, the dismissal of one as criminal, should not be regarded as secure. The dreamer has already discovered how difficult any stable judgment on such issues will be, and that is where we now begin.

HCE is to be superseded. But, if we are to look to a posterity of different parts of him, we need first to bury him. The coffin, elusive in the previous chapter, is found, and HCE is consigned to his grave. It lies in a place

> enriched with ancient woods and dear dutchy deeplinns mid which were an old knoll and a troutbeck . . . (76: 25–6)

HCE is here in two guises—as corpse and as the "old knoll" (as noted, he often plays mountain or hill to ALP's river; he also figures periodically as "old Noll," Oliver Cromwell). ALP is also present; she is the troutbeck. The sentence continues:

> vainyvain of her osiery and a chatty sally with any Wilt or Walt who would ongle her as Izaak did to the tickle of his rod and watch her waters of her sillying waters of and there now brown peater aripple (may their quilt gild lightly over his somnolulutent form!) Whoforyou lies his last, by the wrath of Bog, like the erst curst Hun in the bed of his treubleu Donawhu. (76: 26–32)

The close gives the expected resolution, as HCE's grave can be envisaged as lapped by the waters of the "Blue Danube"—although even here, there is a disturbing hint in the alternative reading, "don't know who," as if ALP were, as she says bitterly in her final monologue, uncomprehended, unknown. What precedes it is surprising and disconcerting.

In setting out the issue of fidelity within marriage, the dominant focus of the *Wake* is the possibility that the *husband* will be tempted, especially in the decline of his physical powers. Although one of the vignettes of I-3 briefly cast ALP as a prostitute, it quickly rejected the idea (68: 9–23). Here, however, there emerges a doubt, the dreamer's doubt, about female fidelity. Like Gerty

MacDowell, and like the two half-dressed women in the park perhaps, ALP is vain about her hose (the "osiery" is not just the willows on the banks), and she is willing to respond to the advances of those who ogle her. We are left wondering whether her waters are muddy—brown with peat and lutent—or whether she is "true blue." As we shall see, this uncertainty is a periodic concern of the dreamer's, accompanying his more obvious anxieties about his own faithfulness.

Within these first pages, the enterprise of laying HCE to rest has already given signs of the three main characters who are to succeed him, indicating how they connect to the worries that have underlain previous chapters. We begin the second part with a reiteration that the dead HCE is to nourish the world he has left. Yet, as before, the twists of the following sentences are surprising. We are quickly plunged into a world of explosives, of bombs and fuseboxes, of the Tower of London with its associations with political controversy and bloodletting, of funerary urns and memorials, all bringing in a "grand age, rich in death anticipated" (78: 6). Why does war break out in the wake—or at the wake—of HCE?

This turn, from a great fall to ensuing violence, was already presented to us in the *Wake*'s overture, its opening statement of main themes. After the fall of the giant on the first page, we are immediately immersed in senseless battle.

> What clashes here of wills gen wonts, oystrygods gaggin fishygods! Brékkek Kékkek Kékkek Kékkek! Kóax Kóax Kóax! (4: 1–2)

Joyce plainly loathed the dogmatic fanaticisms that have led people to slaughter one another by the thousands and millions, and the *Wake* is full of passages that denounce, or as here deride (with the croak of Aristophanic frogs), the passionate devotion to dubious gods that leads some to view others as beyond the limits of toleration. With the fall of a giant, the imposed order of the world collapses, and his successors are left prey to their vehement delusions. But why should anything similar happen with the demise of HCE?

Most obviously because the figure of HCE embodies an attempt to reconcile conflicts. He does not succeed in fitting together all the different impulses that quarrel within him, but his significance, for the dreamer, consists in the project of integrating them as far as possible. Without that mediating presence, the vignettes must disclose a world divided, initially one of struggle and battle. In terms of the biblical story that Joyce loves to deploy in this context, rival descendants from HCE, different aspects of him, must struggle for the legacy of Abraham, just as Jacob and Esau did. The same ferocity and confidence of righteousness arises in the new context as in the response to the fall of the giant in Chapter 1:

> each, of course, on the purely doffensive since the eternals were owlwise on their side every time . . . (78: 29–30)

"Doffensive" captures adroitly the rhetoric of warmongers who initiate aggression on grounds that they are defending something of transcendental significance. The challenge for us, individually and collectively, is to advance beyond this, to tame our impulses, to integrate, mediate, and tolerate, moving beyond dogma and superstition[2] so that we can hasten the time when "the pharce for the nunce come[s] to a setdown secular phoenish" (4: 17)

Removing HCE from the scene does not only unleash violent impulses but also allows for unbridled sexual activity.

> Fact, any human inyon you liked any erenoon or efter would take her bare godkin out, or an even pair of hem, (lugod! lugodoo!) and prettily pray with him (or with em even) everyhe to her taste, long for luck . . . (79: 19–23)[3]

The result is uncertainty, as what starts in ardent celebration may all too easily end in the dungcart (79: 26).

Indeed, the typical outcome of this world of elemental passions is squalid and uninviting, and the giggling temptresses are replaced by the slatternly figure of withered Kate, who presides over a rubbish dump. The raw impulses that figure as elements of HCE—and as elements of the dreamer—give rise to a sour, noisome, collection of garbage. They apparently produce nothing that can stand as a worthy record of human life. If they are to do so, they must be refined into figures who can channel them in a more constructive fashion; some kind of order and discipline is necessary. The seeds of the new characters are present, but they need to be nourished, developed, and trained. That is to be the dreamwork of the chapter.

We start again with a new version of the familiar vignette of the menacing encounter. The participants are not clearly defined at first; they are individualized versions of the faceless warriors who have fought and died in the carnage of the previous material. Their meeting takes place far from civilization (for there is none yet) under conditions of heavy rain (so there is a serious chance that the hostility is all a mistake). It is marked by the familiar threats of physical violence from earlier versions, but it seems that these threats might be issued by either party; we have an apparent symmetry in the struggle: "the cradle rocking equally to one and oppositely from the other on its law of capture and recapture" (81: 36–82: 2). Yet there are already indications of the grounds for future controversy, for we are given a characterization of "the attackler" as "a cropatkin" (81: 18). The reference is to the Russian Prince Kropotkin, an early twentieth-century advocate of anarchism—and also a defender of the idea that animals (including human beings) are capable of genuinely altruistic acts. So, as these early opponents develop—and the reference to the cradle suggests they are yet only infant manifestations of themselves—we may expect that one of them will turn out to be a rebel, possibly one who protests the oppressiveness and inhumanity of conventional values: Shem, perhaps.

The equality of the struggle becomes evident to the contending parties, and their mutual animosity apparently subsides, and they reach a reconciliation. Indeed, the vignette turns away from the violent assaults of I–3 toward the original encounter of HCE with the cad. Weapons are no longer brandished, but there is a simple request for change. The person asked confesses, with HCE's stammer, that he is unable to oblige but offers a small sum so that the other can buy whiskey. Initial violence seems to have given way to friendship and cooperation, and the incident concludes with a fraternal embrace[4]; the recipient of the small change takes an energetic leave; the donor remains behind.

Now, however, the perspective shifts abruptly. We have been following a tale of reconciliation and friendly exchange among former enemies. As one of the parties departs, we learn that

> this poor delaney, who they left along with the confederate fender be-
> hind and who albeit ballsbluffed, bore up wonderfully wunder all of it
> with a whole number of plumsized contusiums . . . (84: 8–11)

There follows a catalogue of his wounds and woes, which he reports to the authorities; despite the vivid evidence of a physical assault, "it proved most fortunate that not one of the two hundred and six bones and five hundred and one muscles in his corso was a whit the whorse for her whacking" (84: 25–7).

To add to the confusion, we are next informed that the alleged assailant has a respectable history and a different version of the events:

> to the question of boney's unlawfully obtaining a pierced paraflamme
> and claptrap fireguard there crops out the still more salient point of
> the politish leanings and town pursuits of our forebeer, El Don De
> Dunelli . . . (84: 33–6)

I link "El Don De Dunelli" to "the cad with a pipe"; an obvious association for "El Don" is Don Juan, a rake or cad; and "Dunelli" connects easily with Dunhill, manufacturer of pipes and tobacco. As in the description of "poor delaney," the fender turns up here, too, as the "paraflamme" or fireguard. Apparently, the vignette is synthesizing the ingredients of the previous versions of the encounter: HCE meets a cad with a pipe, who asks an apparently innocuous question; a "tall man" is accosted at gunpoint by an assailant, apparently angry about "Kane's fender"; a drunk bangs a bottle against something, possibly a fender. Those ingredients figure now in a story of initial opposition between two new characters, whose identities are not yet clearly defined, a story with incompatible endings; either one batters the other and makes off with some money, or an initial struggle gives way to peace and amity; or, as the "Don's" own story goes, he simply went for a walk.

It is wrong, I think, to suppose that this is a struggle between Shem and Shaun. They are not yet before us. The flickering characters in this ambiguous episode are precursors of them, but their principal traits can flow from one party to another. To create them, it is necessary to impose some order on the flux of this vignette. One device for doing that is to have a trial.

That trial, explicitly dedicated to "solving the wasnottobe crime cunundrum" (85: 22) involves more shadowy figures. The accused, initially known as "Festy King" (85: 23) makes an opening statement. A policeman, speaking for the prosecution, then alleges that King, operating under an assumed name, attended a fair in the company of a "pedigree pig (unlicensed) and a hyacinth" (86: 14). We are off on an extremely comic shaggy dog story, an insanely distorted trial worthy of *Alice's* Queen of Hearts, in which very little bears on the ostensible purpose.

We seem, however, to be promised a moment of sanity: "[r]emarkable evidence was given, anon, by an eye, ear, nose and throat witness. . ." (86: 32–3).[5] Initially, this witness seems to offer something that bears on the alleged encounter between the accused and his supposed victim:

> he was patrified to see, hear, taste and smell . . . how Hyacinth O'Donnell, B.A. . . . on the fair green at the hour of twenty-four o'clock sought . . . to sack, sock, stab, and slaughter singlehanded another two of the old kings, Gush Mac Gale and Roaring O'Crian, Jr., . . . between him and whom . . . bad blood existed on the ground of the boer's trespass on the bull or because he first parted his polarbeeber hair in twoways, or because they were creepfoxed andt grousuppers over a nippy in a noveletta, or because they could not say meace, (mute and daft) meathe. (87: 11–24; digressions and fuller characterizations omitted)

The hyacinth that allegedly accompanied the accused has turned into a man (an educated man) who is at odds with two others, possibly for relatively trivial reasons, possibly because they are contenders for the love of a girl (Issy will turn up as "nuvoletta" in the first of the fables alluded to here, that of the Mookse and the Gripes [157: 8]), possibly because they are deeply incompatible and unable to speak "peace, peace" (see 16: 10ff.). Yet why are there *two* opponents here? I think because the antipathy can extend across the generations. Kings do not reign in the same place simultaneously, and one of the two is marked as "Junior." If the contending parties of the encounter that supposedly gave rise to this trial are brothers, then the opposition is of one brother to the other brother and to their father—or possibly of any of the males to the others. As before, I do not want to identify any of the characters with HCE, with Shaun, or with Shem. We are still in a process through which traits are distributed among different figures and not yet at the moment where they coalesce on the new personae.

The evaluation of this testimony focuses on the reliability of the witness, first in the most abstract terms. He is asked

> whether he was one of those lucky cocks for whom the audible-visible-gnosible-edible world existed. That he was only too cognitively conatively cogitabundantly sure of it because, living, loving, breathing and sleeping morphomelosophopancreates, as he most significantly did, whenever he thought he heard he saw he felt he made a bell clipper-clipperclipperclipper. (88: 5–11)

The witness is "lucky" because he is able to settle matters by appeal to his senses. For him there is no doubt, because the judgment to which he comes on the receipt of sensory information is not in question. This is not the dreamer's predicament. He, by contrast, is quite unsure how to describe things or how to sort out what is real from what is apparent. Whereas the witness is unaffected, the dreamer is gnawed by Socratic doubt—he cannot decide on the right names to apply to things nor can he determine how he should best live. When we ask, however, for the sources of the witness's confidence, we are told of a test that he applies, the verification of his judgment by the ringing of a bell—as though the witness had been the subject of an experiment in Pavlovian conditioning, trained to respond to the world in the manner approved by those around him. Indeed, that is, I believe, his stance: he speaks with the voice of sturdy common sense, or at least what is usually taken for that. Under circumstances where the justifiability of conformity, of adherence to the patterns of conditioning that a community imposes on its young, is at issue, this plain attitude can easily be undermined, and the strange cross-examination that follows, which demands the witness's judgment on a wide range of apparently extraneous questions, does precisely that, leading us far away from his initial narrative and his confident explanation of his cognitive powers.

The testimony is countered by a vehement denial from the accused—now known as "Pegger Festy" (91: 1) —who renounces his hopes for life in "this world or the other world or any either world" (91: 25) if

> ever in all his exchequered career he up or lave a chancery hand to take or throw the sign of a mortal stick or stone at man, yoelamb or salvation army either before or after being puptised down to that most holy and every blessed hour. (91: 30–3)

The confrontation of the accused with the witness brings into being more sharply defined versions of the characters who have been emerging from HCE. The man in the dock may have a past (an "exchequered career") as a "wordwounder" ("sticks and stones may break my bones, but words will never hurt me"), directing his barbs at the conventional pieties he renounces, the innocent practice of approved religion. He is the counterpart to the witness, who is not just "puptised" but fully conditioned like one of Pavlov's dogs to repeat the lore of his society. As we might expect from the first description of their struggle—the equal and opposite wrestling in the cradle—they are conceived as deeply connected, as opposite aspects of a more fundamental nature. That, of course, is their point for the dreamer, who is giving voice to the rival elements within HCE. Their claims are in balance, for they are "equals of opposites, evolved by a onesame power of nature or of spirit" (92: 8–9). There can be no decisive grounds for a judgment between them (as the coming verdict will make clear).

Nevertheless, they are distinct characters who will receive very different reactions and suffer different fates:

> Distinctly different were their duasdestinies. Whereas the maidies of the bar, (a pairless trentene, a lunarised score) when the eranthus myrrmyrred: Show'm the Posed: fluttered and flattered around the willingly pressed, nominating him for the swiney prize, complimenting him, the captivating youth, on his having all his senses about him . . . (92: 12–16)

The suffering figure of the encounter vignette has evolved into the confident witness at the trial and eventually emerged as Shaun. He is the voice of sense and conformity, the champion of the existing order, and it is only appropriate that the community's most attractive representatives, the twenty-eight beautiful—and beautifully brought up—young girls, *jeune filles en fleur,* should cluster around him as his reward. The girls are to serve as props in the dreamer's subsequent vignettes, often figuring as they do here in the celebration of Shaun (see also II-1 and III-2).

A twenty-ninth girl stands apart. Her response is far more ambiguous. Her love is more ardent, certainly more sexual, and its object may be Shaun or Shem—or perhaps both of them. Someone, possibly Shem, possibly Shaun, probably both, looks on at her

> blindly, mutely, tastelessly, tactlessly, innamorate with heruponhim in shining aminglement, the shaym of his hisu shifting into the shimmering of her hers . . . till the wild wishwish of her sheeshea melted most musically mid the dark deepdeep of his shayshaun. (92: 27–32; parenthesis omitted)

Even while Shaun enjoys the public triumph, it is evident that the gifts for which he is celebrated are inadequate to the outcomes that matter most, both to him and to the defeated Shem. The dreamer has constructed a character who will develop those tendencies within HCE that crave the respect of the community, a son who will play the conformist role with far more success. Already at the moment of his definition, however, we know that there are ways in which Shaun will have to be extended if his life is not to prove hollow.

What of his counterpart, Shem? Although the four judges (four old men who serve as the evangelists for HCE—although what they do can hardly be called *gospel* writing[6]) reach a mixed verdict,[7] allowing the accused ("King") to leave freely, the public response to him is quite different from that accorded to Shaun. The girls represent the public view:

> all the twofromthirty advocatesses within echo, pulling up their briefs at the krigkry: Shun the Punman!: safely and soundly soccered that fenemine Parish Poser . . . umprumptu rightoway hames . . . (93: 11–15; parenthesis omitted)

What apparently stands behind the rejection of Shem is his questioning of tradition and his dedication to literature: the "chassetitties belles" denounce "You and your gift of your gaft of your garbage abaht our Farvver" (93: 19–20). Shem has claimed the gift of the gab, the gift of language—he has aspired to be an artist; he has also put forward garbage, dirty trash, about past authority and tradition, personified here by the father; Shem, then, is the artist-rebel, outside decent society.[8] (The adorable maidens who represent that society "pull up their briefs"—perhaps, like Gerty MacDowell, revealing their shapely legs—and use their feet to expel this repulsive excresence.)

The next shift is sudden, and appears quite unmotivated, for we are returned to the topic of the letter that figured briefly in I-3. This letter, eagerly awaited, will settle everything, yielding a new perspective on the life of HCE, as well as on Shem and Shaun. But why does any concern with it arise at precisely this point?

I think this question is best approached by reflecting on the significance of what has just occurred. The dreamer has envisaged a mad trial, one in which nothing is settled but a public judgment is rendered: the fêting of Shaun and the shaming of Shem. We could describe that by supposing that Shaun is rewarded for his conformity to a pre-existent order that Shem has challenged. An alternative would be to conceive the order, the law, the norms of society, as brought into being through the trial itself, arbitrarily, almost nonsensically, in ways that embrace Shaun and reject Shem. The dreamer is aware of both conceptions and of the need to vindicate what has occurred. If this is to count as justice, we need to know why. But where is there a higher authority to which we could appeal?

Perhaps in some record of tradition, capable of defusing the thought that what is picked out as worthy (or contemptible) is more than a matter of caprice. Two significant questions raised about the letter indicate that these thoughts might be troubling the dreamer:

> It was life but was it fair? It was free but was it art? (94: 9)

Behind the letter, too, stands its supposed authoress, ALP, and her voice may be needed to counter the taunts of the twenty-eight girls; the voice of mercy can respond to the voice of "justice" here, as it does at the end of I-7.

We do not yet have the letter; in fact, we do not yet have a well-defined ALP. All we have are the four old judges, the repositories of tradition, from whose memories a more firmly grounded assessment might proceed. All they can manage, however, are disjointed recollections of the trivia of Dublin life, blended together in increasing incoherence as they apply themselves to the bottle.[9]

We are left, then, with the official standoff and the public judgment in favor of Shaun. He may be left, for the moment, to the tender attentions of the flower girls. The dreamer turns next to the consequences of rejection, where the victim is both Shem and HCE. Transformed first into fox, the despised outsider is hunted by the respectable citizenry.[10] The tactics for the fox must be those of Stephen Dedalus: silence, exile, cunning (*Portrait*, 247). In this vignette, the cunning of the fox originally enables him to elude his pursuers. It is difficult, however, to remain silent, and the telltale stammer alerts those who would destroy him. In the end, Shem/HCE must leave his home; exile is the only solution.

So, like Hosty and his followers, Shem/HCE suffers an uncertain fate. Rumors abound. The exile seems endlessly fascinating to those who have driven him out, as if he were a sore on their social body, one needing constant probing. Nothing can be firmly established.[11] In the end, the exile vanishes, leaving only a newspaper digest of his fall.

That headline report repeats, once again, the suggestion that ALP berates—possibly even banishes—her husband (100: 7–8). Yet this is almost immediately reversed in the closing segment of the chapter. She is left, after the fall, apparently to prepare a memorial. The dreamer needs her in sharper focus. We hear voices eager for gossip, anticipating the questions of one of the washerwomen (I-8):

> Do tell us all about. As we want to hear allabout. So tellus tellas allabouter. (101: 2–3)

She emerges slowly, for the description must first present a world in transition, rehearsing the questions that have been raised and the answers that have been recognized. "The loungelizards of the pumproom had their nine days' jeer" (101: 25–6), but ALP rises to refute them, "to crush the slander's head" (102: 17).

She has been a participant in a devoted marriage, one that has involved mutual sacrifice: "she who had given his eye for her bed and a tooth for a child till one one and one ten and one hundred again" (101: 33–5). Worn out in his service, she is a curious, old-fashioned figure, but her life now is, as it was before, centered in her marriage and family. Behind the strains and tensions that have troubled the dreamer, we sense a vast number of minutes, hours, days, weeks, and years, of joint striving, shared successes, mutual consolation in defeat, intimacy, and laughter. Suddenly all that, a history not easily reviewable in a vignette or a sequence of vignettes, looms in the background, and the vision of HCE's flaws is foreshortened. This woman who has lived through so much with him must balance the swirling doubts by seeing the whole—and she, we (reader and dreamer) may reasonably think, has an ability to see the whole that we lack.

The voice of a dream narrator urges her to construct a fitting memorial to HCE:

> Wery weeny wight, plead for Morandmor! . . . And let him rest, thou wayfarre, and take no gravespoil from him! (102: 18, 20–21)

There is a mood of confidence that she will concur. Even if HCE "spenth his strength amok haremscarems"—gave himself to hare-brained schemes (compare 624: 12–13) or ran after other women—he has tried to make amends ("[coin] a cure" [102: 27–8]). The course of their marriage has been uneven:

> Tifftiff today, kissykissy tonay and agelong pine tomauranna. Then who but Crippled-with-Children would speak up for Dropping-with-Sweat? (102: 28–30)

She has given him everything—and she will continue to give after his death. She recalls that here in the verses of a song, and she remembers also the youthful passion that drew them together.[12] That is all gone, but she can offer the words of consolation and peace for which the dreamer has been yearning.

> Nomad may roam with Nabuch but let naaman laugh at Jordan! For we, we have taken our sheet upon her stones where we have hanged our hearts in her trees; and we list, as she bibs us, by the waters of babalong. (103: 9–12)

How much is this consolation worth? It would be quite legitimate to wonder whether anything has been resolved, whether the dreamer has fallen into the trap of sentimentalizing the situation, adopting, perhaps in weariness, the roseate vision of the lazy romantic poet (56: 20–30). At this stage we cannot, and should not, suppress those questions, but neither ought we to view them as intractable. For, in creating three new characters, Shaun, Shem, and ALP, to serve both as voices within HCE and as figures in relation to him, we (and the dreamer) have new resources for tackling the questions that have generated the anxieties.

Although the exile of HCE/Shem is bitter, we can do as ALP bids—we can sit down by the waters of "babalong," hang our hearts in her trees and "list." To do that is to commit ourselves and to remember, to view joint lives for what they are, to reflect on them, acknowledge their deficiencies, work to amend them, be mindful of their ordinary pleasures; to "list" is not simply to listen, but also to review, and, in that review, to incline one's heart in sympathy.[13] ALP represents both a potential object for HCE's devotion and an embodiment of an attitude that he can bring to her and to their marriage. A major work of this chapter has been to bring her persona and her voice clearly into the dream sequence of the *Wake*[14]; much of the rest of the book will be devoted to making it stronger, clearer, and firmer. At this stage, however, we can only guess at how this forgiveness is to be understood as justified. The dreamer must learn what I shall call the *Joycean virtues* and how to exemplify them.

11

CELL ME MORE

Central among the Joycean virtues are those of kindness, understanding, tolerance, acceptance, and forgiveness. Embodied in, and voiced by, ALP—most evidently in her closing monologue, but also at the very end of I-4—all are conceived in a distinctive way. They cannot be easily won, cannot be the warmth induced by an excursion on a fine day or a good meal with entertaining companions. Part of Joyce's conception of them involves a sense of struggle, of prior honesty in facing the realities of situations, of determination to explore those realities no matter how sordid or repulsive they may seem to be. Although Joyce's vision is one of the great versions of humanism, it would be hard to overlook the religious backdrop to his sense of human virtue. The traits he prizes obtain their worth from the omnipresent temptations to deviate from them, either by lapsing into harshness and intolerance, or by settling for a mere semblance, closing one's eyes to the facts or leaving reality unprobed.[1]

The stance exhibited to the dreamer at the end of I-4 hints at these virtues because it portrays ALP as living through the vicissitudes of her marriage, and yet, finally, rendering a judgment of peace and forgiveness.[2] Equally, the dreamer has had to work to explore the realities behind the questions that trouble him, so that his own reaction—and the reader's reaction—is itself hard won. But, as I suggested, we ought to wonder if we have consoled ourselves too quickly. Has the investigation been sufficiently deep? At this stage, ALP is still a shadowy figure. What do we know of her or of her marriage? Should we be convinced that she has faced its realities without blinking, and that her affirmative response has the value we want to attribute to it? We need to rule out the possibility that "there is another cant to the questy" (109: 1)—or several. We need to know more.

Moreover, it appears that the next stage of the dream will deliver just what we need, for at last we are to discover ALP's letter, her "mamafesta memorializing the Mosthighest" (104: 4). This, we might naively expect, will provide just the information we need, acquainting us further with ALP, resolving any doubts we might have to the effect that she has left crucial facts in soft focus, and showing us the details of her married life. We cannot be satisfied this easily (and this early). If the dreamer's worries are genuinely to be settled, he must continue to explore, to come to terms with the ambiguities and uncertainties, and winning anew the right to affirm. Going round and round, in the way the *Wake* does, is crucial to resolving the dreamer's predicament.

What we are given in the mamafesta is an apparently trivial text, a lengthy list of potential titles, most of which yield a sense of ALP's evaluation of her marriage without providing any insight into their basis, and a hilarious disquisition on the problems and possibilities of interpretation. The principal import of the latter is, as I have already claimed, to expose the permanent possibility of alternative perspectives; in effect, I-5 reinforces in a discursive—and entertaining—fashion, the points about uncertainty that emerged from the struggles of I-3. To make up one's mind about the record of a life—or about a life itself—is not a matter of simply looking and seeing; it is not the sort of thing that an "eye, ear, nose and throat witness" can automatically do.

Joyce's treatment of this theme is a bravura performance. Near the beginning of his commentary on how to interpret the letter, he imagines the judgment of an investigator in the style of Sherlock Holmes, who concludes that it is

> the tracing of a purely deliquescent recidivist, possibly ambidextrous, snubnosed probably and presenting a strangely profound rainbowl in his (or her) occiput. (107: 10–12)

That, however, would be the assessment of a "naïf alphabetter" (107: 9). Matters are much more complicated because we approach the record with so many preconceptions, as well as urgent desires that move us in particular directions, and any attempt at objectivity must recognize this and try to compensate for it. We are reduced to blind groping and realize that there will be immense numbers of questions we can never settle. In the face of these difficulties we may be tempted to give up. The right response is to cultivate a Joycean virtue:

> Now, patience; and remember patience is the great thing, and above all things else we must avoid anything like being or becoming out of patience. (108: 8–10)

So, Joyce insists, we must keep before our minds models of patience and commit ourselves to lengthy explorations and investigations of all kinds, so that we avoid the traps and pitfalls of misinterpretation and consider as many perspectives as possible.[3]

The enormous fun of this chapter (I-5) may easily lead us to write it off as a huge spoof—yet we ought to attend to Joyce's advice in reading the *Wake* in general and this part of it in particular. He is not simply concerned to poke fun at ambitious theories of interpretation or to satirize the activities of literary scholars, archeologists, and historians of culture. Instead of chuckling at the absurdity of lavishing years of effort on the hermeneutics of the banal letter whose text we are given, we might be patient and consider the possibility that it is worth the trouble. Perhaps the exploration of the letter is continuous with the struggles of the dreamer, trying to make sense of the conflicting voices within him.

We learn of the finding of the letter, of its retrieval from a mound of rubbish (and there is surely a link here to the tip over which Kate presided [79: 27ff.]), of the text we have, of the forensic possibilities of analyzing the stains and the alterations produced by the years of burial. One obvious question is to authenticate the manuscript—and here, it turns out, we are in luck; we have a letter that can be ascribed to ALP.

> We have a cop of her fist right against our nosibos. We note the paper with her jotty young watermark: *Notre Dame du Bon Marché*. (112: 30–2)

"Our Lady" is, of course, a figure who holds the promise of mercy, and it is appropriate to think of ALP as Our Lady on the cheap. Moreover, what she brings in this letter—apparently not the same one as the banal text largely devoted to greetings and thanks (111: 10–20)—is forgiveness and understanding, in a document far more easily connected with the titles conjectured for the "mamafesta" (especially the last [107: 1–7]). We are offered a redaction:

> All schwants (schwrites) ischt tell the cock's trootabout him. Kapak kapuk. No minzies matter. He had to see life foully the plak and the smut, (schwrites). There were three men in him (schwrites). Dancings (schwrites) was his only ttoo feebles. With apple harlottes. And a little mollvogels. Spissially (schwrites) when they peaches. Honeys wore camelia paints. Yours very truthful. Add dapple inn. (113: 11–18)

This is surely the consoling judgment that the close of I-4 led the dreamer to expect from ALP, but, frustratingly, this text provides no account of how she might have arrived at it, or how it could be justified (or whether it is even sober).

Yet the words ascribed to ALP are full of insight. HCE, she tells us, was a reflective man, a man with the preconditions for the Joycean virtues: he had to see life fully, to see its foulness, to recognize what is mean, filthy, and sordid in it, what is old and diseased ("plak" and "smut" are also Albanian words with these connotations). So, we may suspect, does ALP, and, if that is the case, her judgment here is worth having, for it is not simply a sloppy avoidance of the issues. Indeed, she recognizes that HCE has two weaknesses (although apparently only one type of weakness). She also sees that he is many sided—and, at this stage of the *Wake*, it is appropriate to pick out the two figures who have emerged from him as well as the original persona that attempted to integrate them (thus making three in all). Pinpointing the causes of his temptation—the "honeys" decorated themselves to arouse his desire—she simultaneously absolves (*Honi soit qui mal y pense; evil be to him who evil thinks).

Why, then, given that the redaction seems to bear so closely on the earlier vignettes and the questions that provoke them, is the focus on the more mundane letter obtained from the dump? For it is evident from the pastiches of styles of interpretation that Joyce goes on to give us that the project is to interpret the banal[4] report about Maggy, Father Michael, and the cakes (115–6). The puzzle dissolves if we take the central question for the dreamer to be not *whether* ALP accepts and forgives, but the *character* of that acceptance and forgiveness, how it is generated and sustained. Has she seen life, her life with HCE, "foully,"[5] not blinking the facts about him, and still found a basis for affirming it? The answer to that must lie in the mundane details of their shared existence. Those, I have suggested, cannot easily be brought before the dreamer's consciousness, for the point is the accumulation of years' and years' worth of trivial forms of togetherness—like the mass of falling leaves of the final monologue. The letter, rightly conceived, is a representation of that, a testimony to the ordinary things that ordinary people do and plan and fret about and take pleasure in. If we think of ALP's absolution as proceeding from a clear sense of the value of the everyday ways of living together, then the letter is transfigured. It becomes worthy of interpretative struggle and of extended celebration.

The celebration consists in treating the manuscript of the letter as a work of art, comparable to the illuminated gospel pages of *The Book of Kells*. Plainly, Joyce is enjoying himself, but, as before, I want to suggest that more is going on. We can think of the monks who produced *The Book of Kells* as turning a fragmentary record of what they took to be a highly significant life into an object as beautiful as they could make it. Behind their activity is the life of Jesus, for them a world-changing life, described by the evangelist, who reported its most important moments. The sentences of the evangelist's description are then treated as objects in their own right, worthy of being placed on the page so as to inspire the reader with a vision of holiness and beauty. Similarly, behind the apparently mundane text stands the life of ALP, a life that may exemplify the Joycean virtues. The letter captures the basis of those virtues, the ordinary sharing of everyday moments, whose value ALP has seen clearly—and it is that clear vision that has prompted her acceptance and forgiveness. Just as the "*Tunc*" page embodies an important moment in the world's history for the copyist, so, too, does the letter for the dreamer.[6] It is worth approaching it as art, worth turning it into art.

The comparison seems to me to work at two different levels, only one of which I have traced. Besides the idea of highlighting the significance of an episode by treating the record of it as a work of art, Joyce also brings before us the possibility of the artistic vision as a way of coming to terms with a human life. If ALP has done what we and the dreamer hope, she has viewed the whole of her life, recognizing its dark and squalid corners, and yet seen it as making sense, as having a coherence and integrity that allow her to affirm it. One might think of that as an artistic transformation,[7] something that goes beyond the moment-by-moment factual reports of the "eye, ear, nose and throat witness." The artistic transformation is implicit. ALP does not write her own history, making vivid the structure she discerns. Joyce does that—or rather, according to the view I have developed, he provides materials for the dreamer, and for the reader of the *Wake*, to do that.

Joyce does this for a few of his other characters, primarily for Bloom, and, to a lesser extent, for Molly and Stephen. *Ulysses* gives us a day in an ordinary life, a day in which Bloom suffers a number of defeats and manages some small victories. His final rewards are mundane: a shared cup of cocoa with Stephen, a moment of rapprochement with Molly, perhaps some satisfaction in having helped the Dignams, in having stood up to the Citizen, and in having proved attractive to Gerty. These everyday achievements are transformed in Joyce's narrative, woven into a pattern that gives us a sense of a life as a whole. Molly's evaluation of her husband, her appraisal of his foibles, her appreciation of his good qualities, and her closing affirmation is one we can imagine her making from the perspective of the end of life, from the "awebrume hour"—and one we can envisage Bloom making too. That is not inevitable, but there is hope for Bloom (and for Molly and Stephen, as well), hope that their lives will have an integrity and embody an order that makes them works of art, suited for recording in novels that are also works of art.

The *Wake* contains a character, Shem, who exemplifies this side of Joyce, one who self-consciously sees his life in these terms and attempts to turn it into a work of art. It is no accident that the hi-jinks of the study of the orthography of the letter lead us to Shem. After Joyce has given us his pastiche of an aesthetic study of the manuscript, we come finally to the identity of the scribe for a particular copy (the "Tiberiast duplex" [123: 30–1][8]). A wonderfully inconsequential series of clues lead to an attribution that is made in full confidence—given the data, the question cannot even serve as an exercise for part-time students. The hand is that of "that odious and still today insufficiently malestimated notesnatcher . . . Shem the Penman" (125: 21–3). Shem appears here because he is the vehicle for turning implicit artistic visions into explicit ones—the recorder of the ways in which ordinary people have transformed the mundane and made it valuable.

The characterization of Shem anticipates the tone of the introduction of him in the next chapter (questions 11 and 12 of the quiz show) and of the prosecution of I-7. The prosecutor, "eye, ear, nose and throat" man that he is, cannot see Shem's activities this way; for him, *Ulysses*, the "Blue Book of Eccles," is useless and unreadable (179: 26–7). The objects with which Shem surrounds himself, serving as the material for his art, are taken to be the sordid detritus from which we should want to turn away (183: 11–184: 2). The transformation of his waste products into ink and his skin into foolscap are counted as obscene acts. If we adopt the reading of the "mamafesta" I have recommended, matters look very different: Shem is engaged in the ordering of his life, the explicit rendering of it as a work of art, not in a spirit of narcissism, but as a self-conscious counterpoint to the reflective engagement with all sides of his existence—seeing life "foully." We can believe that this is a matter of great cost for him, that his heart is indeed "attrite" (194: 3).

We should not conclude that Joyce aims to vindicate the explicit rendition of one's life as art as the *sole* way of making human existence worthwhile. Far from it. His is no elitist vision of how the lucky few can find significance in their lives, but an attempt to vindicate, and to celebrate, the ordinary. To find value in life, from the retrospective view of its ending, one need not have written one's own versions of *Portrait, Ulysses,* and the *Wake.* Joyce would surely defend it as *a* way, so that, despite the thundering of the prosecutor, there is hope for Shem. His creation of Bloom and Molly, of ALP and HCE, denies that it is the only way. Moreover, he would view their achievements as implicit constructions parallel to the overt art of Shem; they too are artists, making something of their lives; "artist," we should recall, was one of the charges hurled at HCE (71: 21).

Shem is the refinement of one voice within HCE, a voice that expresses a reflective commitment to making sense of his life and what he is, one that emerges from the character of HCE most clearly in those passages where he is concerned to create, to build, and to reform. The charges against Shem are so severe that they provoke a reaction on his behalf, a reaction that can easily modulate into a critical attitude toward Shaun. Yet we should recall that Shaun also emerges from HCE and that HCE's difficulties of integrating the ill-fitting parts of himself cannot be solved simply through the excision of the impulses from which Shaun springs. The criticisms of Shem that run through I-6 and I-7 need not be heard as emanating from Shaun—and I have deliberately referred to the dominant voice of I-7 as "the prosecutor." Nonetheless, Shaun, the favorite of the "maidies at the bar," is the darling of the existing order, the counterpoise to Shem the artist-rebel, and his adoption of established values could easily lead him into a passive conformism. His life might turn out as one of those on which Joyce had commented sadly ever since *Dubliners,* one judged from the retrospective view as empty and disjointed. We should be aware of this as a possibility but should not assume that it is inevitable.

Shaun is supposed to be the star contestant in the quiz show of I-6, although it is evident that not all of the responses can be his—the answer to number 10 is dominated by Issy, although there are interpolations that suggest Shaun. The style of the chapter is well suited to orderly Shaun.

The dreamer is to be given a table of the *dramatis personae* and the scenic settings for the vignettes: in sequence, they are HCE, ALP, Dublin, the evangelists, Sackerson, Kate, HCE's customers (seen as twelve apostles), the flower girls, the *Wake*—or life itself (an easy equilibration since we know that "[l]ife . . . is a wake, livit or krikit" [55: 7][9]), Issy, Shem, and the ambiguous final response in which we may all be identified with Shem. The procedure is unusually clearly structured, and we might hope it will advance the dreamer's exploration of the figures and situations of the vignettes, an exploration that can teach him more about each of them.

It does not work that way. We open with an extraordinarily long list of characterizations of HCE, some that link him to historical and mythical heroes and episodes, others that revert to the material of earlier vignettes, and many more that form part of an appropriately gargantuan Rabelaisian catalogue. Its function, I think, is to remind us of the *untidiness* of HCE, of the irreconcilable impulses within him (corresponding to the oddly mismatched clothing he typically wears), and thus to underscore the plausibility of the dreamer's strategy of dissolving him into elements that can be separately appraised. The quiz show itself might even be conceived as a table of these elements.

Other answers are pithy and suggestive (as, for example, in the image of the *Wake* as a collideorscape), but, in general, they work obliquely rather than directly. Issy's stream of seductive invitations yields more insight into the anxieties behind HCE than the long opening list. As I shall suggest later in this chapter, the characterization of ALP bears on questions about wifely fidelity. The most revealing of the answers is the penultimate one, not so much for the light it casts on the character and problems of Shem, but because of its wonderful depiction of the perils of living by a triumphant social order.

The voice of this answer need not be taken as that of Shaun. It is pompous and professorial, much concerned with the life of academic debate and the credentials of rival theories. The answer itself offers an initial exploration of the possibilities of a life centered on conformity to order and tradition. This short investigation presents the champion of conformity as unattractive from the very beginning, and that, we might think, is to take an overly narrow view of the available options. Indeed, the more sustained examination of III-1 and III-2 will show us that there is much more to Shaun and the possibilities he represents.

The professor delivers a series of lectures, apparently intended to show the superiority of his preferred perspectives on a variety of topics. With an unusual awareness of the needs of his audience, belied by his torrential outpouring of the rhetoric of scholarly contest, he becomes aware that he needs to present his views more simply:

As my explanations here are probably above your understandings, lattlebrattons, though as augmentatively uncomparisoned as Cadwan,

Cadwallon and Cadwalloner, I shall revert to a more expletive method which I frequently use when I have to sermo with muddlecrass pupils. (152: 4–8)

He will offer a parable—one of the *Wake*'s great set pieces—the Mookse and the Gripes.

The tale is a very simple one. An imposing character, the Mookse, eminently respectable and authoritative, goes forth in full splendor for an evening walk. By the side of a little brown river, he spots a poor, disheveled creature, the Gripes, on a branch of an elm tree. The Mookse sits down on a stone and is addressed, respectfully, by the Gripes. According to the narrating professor, however, this must be viewed as a form of impudence, and the Mookse becomes grandly angry. Still appearing humble, the Gripes asks for the time. The Mookse magnanimously responds but seems to demand the Gripes's explicit submission. When the whimpering Gripes withholds this, the Mookse pronounces excommunication, using all the trappings of his magnificence. The Gripes protests, and a full-scale battle of words breaks out.

Looking on is a girl, Nuvoletta, who tries to attract the attention (and the attentions) of both Mookse and Gripes; but they are oblivious. Twilight descends, and still they continue to argue. Eventually, two women come to the bank and carry both Mookse and Gripes away; the narrator interpolates the judgments that the Mookse had reasons and that the Gripes was wrong. There are left only a tree and a stone, and Nuvoletta, looking on. She leaps into the river and is gone.

Joyce tells this tale in musical prose that captures the mood of a fable, contains passages of great lyrical beauty, is pregnant with associations, and yet remains clear and straightforward; no doubt it is this combination of characteristics that makes it a favorite passage for introducing readers to the *Wake*. It is very easy to advance hypotheses about the principal characters: the Mookse is Shaun, the Gripes Shem, the river ALP, Nuvoletta Issy, and the two women the washerwomen of I-8 or, perhaps, manifestations of ALP as mother, bringing her squabbling children home. Furthermore, the whole tale can be read as an historical allegory on the actions of the English Pope Adrian IV (Nicholas Breakspear), who granted Ireland to Henry II.[10] Yet we can, and should, ask what it is doing here.

I read it as a depiction of the dangers for Shaun and of the kind of course to which he is committed. The Mookse comes before us, in the beginning, with the marks of conventional piety and authority; well fed, clean, well dressed, he emerges from his comfortable house to look at the rest of the world—"to see how badness was badness in the weirdest of pensible ways" (152: 29–30). The Mookse clearly knows what is right and what is not, and what is right belongs to home and what is foreign is bad, bad in ways that challenge the Mookse's thought. We already know that his vision of the world is completely secure, and that it is limited.

He reaches a stream, perhaps the margin of the territory he understands, and across the stream is the pathetic Gripes. The Gripes's first greetings are eminently respectful—"I am rarumonimum blessed to see you, my dear mouster" (154: 2–3). Whether or not this is understood, the very act of speaking provokes the Mookse to stand on wrathful dignity:

> Blast yourself and your anathomy infairioriboos! No, hang you for an animal rurale! I am superbly in my supremest poncif! Abase you baldy-queens! (154: 10–12)

The Gripes's apologetic response, ending with the request for the time (an obvious link to the cad's question to HCE), prompts a more gracious, albeit still magisterial, Mookse to unfold his plan of imposing a uniform temporal order on the world.

> That is quite about what I came on *my* missions with *my* intentions *laudibiliter* to settle with *you*, barbarousse. Let thor be orlog. Let Pauline be Irene. Let you be Beeton. And let me be Los Angeles. Now measure your length. Now estimate my capacity. Well, sour? Is this space of our couple of hours too dimensional for you, temporiser? Will you give you up? (154: 21–7)

Plainly there are numerous allusions, and layers of allusions, here, centering on the use, defense, and extension of papal power. Joyce intends not only these concrete instances, but also to see the Mookse as a general representative of the imposition of order. The world must have uniform standards—of time, of religion, of morality—and those who have knowledge of the pertinent phenomena, those who know the true religion, the right moral principles, how to measure time, have the authority and the responsibility to put those standards in place. Since the Mookse is confident that he knows the right answers, he is prepared to do this—benevolently, as he would no doubt conceive it—bringing illumination to the benighted.

The Gripes, however, does not accede to the Mookse's full authority. He wants to continue in his own way, in his own place—"My tumble, loudy bullocker, is my own" (154: 33–4)—even if this means that there are things he will not be able to do, questions he will be unable to answer (154: 35–155: 2), even if it means that he will go wrong and fall (tumble). For the defender of order, there is only one way to deal with such recalcitrance. Rebels must be cast out, crushed, or exiled. Yet, for all his pomp and the vehemence of his declarations, the Mookse cannot silence the voice of the Gripes. As the dialogue degenerates into a sequence of insults, the narrator (whose official perspective is always that of the Mookse) comments sadly, "It might have been a happy evening but . . . " (156: 36).

The Mookse set out for an evening walk; indeed, he set out to a variation on "A Frog he would A-Wooing go"; and this is an evening on which either

Mookse or Gripes might want to woo. "Nuvoletta in her lightdress, spun of sisteen shimmers" tries to make the Mookse look and the Gripes hear (157: 8, 20–22). Seductive though she is, they pay no attention:

—I see, she sighed. There are menner. (158: 5)

Lost in their quarrel, a quarrel she sees as pointless, they—and she—lose much more. Both Mookse and Gripes become narrowed and sterile; and here we should surely recall the portraits of fanatical battles in I-1 and I-4 with their desolate consequences.

There are dangers for both conformist and rebel—both can be diverted from what is genuinely valuable in their lives by their preoccupation with the other. Yet, for all the narrator's defense of the Mookse, it is plain that he is the chief offender against the Joycean virtues. The Gripes, we recall, asked only for the right to practice in his own place, demanded only tolerance, not conformity. He did not claim to have discovered a universal order, and in that, Joyce leads us to think, he is right. Yet, like his imperialist opponent, he, too, is diminished.

We should read the fable not as a castigation of Shaun, but as a cautionary tale for him. It would be wrong for us, or the dreamer, to conclude that he, a respecter of established customs and prescriptions, must inevitably be led into the excesses of the Mookse. As Part III will reveal, there is a genuine danger here, for Shaun will sometimes veer in the direction of a dogmatic defense of the *status quo;* but we shall also come to see that he is more complex— conformism has more possibilities than are on display here.[11] Better, then, to think of the Mookse as a tendency within Shaun, just as we view Shaun as the development of an aspect of HCE.

The fable can also be seen, I believe, as a commentary on the chapter in which it is embedded. Coming to a quiz show, we naturally expect answers, and we, like the dreamer, are full of questions about the scenes and characters of the vignettes. Everything is laid out in unprecedentedly orderly fashion; there is an official map we can use to locate ourselves. The insights we obtain, however, slide obliquely out of the corners of the questions and of their answers, often from a place where we would not have expected to find them. There are limits, then, to the order, shortcomings of the map. The world of the vignettes turns out to be far messier than tidy minds with general principles might have suspected.

I have suggested that the fable is a cautionary tale for Shaun, but, since both Mookse and Gripes are diverted and distorted by the angry confrontation, we can also think of it as having implications for Shem. The rebel who begins by working for an ideal under the aegis of the Joycean virtue of tolerance, who only wishes for a space in which he can pursue "his own good in his own way,"[12] may be drawn into confrontations with those who lack that virtue, with the result that the battle, not the pursuit of the envisaged good, comes to dominate his life. How is this to be avoided?

Joyce's answer was already given in *Portrait*, when, in dialogue with Cranly, Stephen announces his tactics:

I will not serve that in which I no longer believe, whether it call itself my home, my fatherland, or my church; and I will try to express myself in some mode of life or art as freely as I can and as wholly as I can, using for my defence the only arms I allow myself to use—silence, exile, and cunning. (*Portrait*, 247)

Many of the themes I have been tracing are cryptically present here, most notably the conception of both life and art as modes of free expression and the commitment to the "wholeness" of the act of expression, to "living foully" as ALP's second document puts it. The fable of I-6 shows Stephen's weapons at work and draws attention to the importance of one of them—the primacy of exile.

The Gripes is plainly cunning. Even in the face of intense provocation from the would-be world-ordering Mookse, he evades conflict as long as he can, speaking in the voice of deference and acquiescence of which the prosecutor of I-7 is so scornful (174: 5–21). In the end, however, he is compelled to respond in a way that initiates the quarrel, to take a stand on behalf of his intention to proceed differently, not to serve that in which he does not believe, to express himself freely, within the confines of his own "tumble." The Gripes breaks silence. Indeed, how can he not, when his principal goal is threatened? Silence becomes impossible, once the rebel attracts the attention of the official voices of order. Like the Gripes, the artist—the one who makes his life into an *explicit* work of art—risks attracting attention and, consequently, censure, punishment, and defeat. For Bloom, perhaps, the implicit artist, silence can be a potent weapon, even though there may still be occasions (as in "Cyclops") when speech is forced from him. There remains only one means of defense: removal beyond the sphere in which the order one refuses to serve exercises its power. Exile becomes an essential weapon for the rebel.

So, much to the disgust of the prosecutor of I-7, Shem is constantly hiding and running away. He "sank alowing till he stank out of sight," "kusky-korked himself up tight in his inkbattle house," hides in a house "with his penname SHUT sepiascraped on the doorplate and a blind of black sailcloth over its wan phwinshogue" (175: 3–4; 176: 30–1; 182: 32–4). He is "toed out," "excommunicated," "self exiled in upon his ego" (181: 3; 181: 35; 184: 6). Moreover, as the prosecutor's description makes clear, this exile has enormous costs. Shem is alone (one of the allusions of "alowing"), thrown back on himself (his own ego). For him there is no community, no family—he is "a self valeter by choice of need" (184: 11). His sexual relations are devoid of genuine love, casual encounters with "protoprostitutes" (186: 26–31). For Shem, as for the Stephen of *Ulysses*, there is no counterpart of Molly, of ALP, or of Nora; at least not yet.

The fable of I-6 thus serves to intensify one of the dreamer's questions, revealing not only the ugly face of intolerant conformism but also the necessity of exile for the rebel. The next chapter, I-7, makes plain just how high the costs of exile can be.[13]

The material of the later chapters of Part I develops further many of the themes and anxieties that have emerged from the dreamer's struggles in I-2, I-3, and I-4. So far, I have been examining the ways in which that material elaborates the inevitability of uncertainty, the importance of artistic transformation (whether implicit or explicit), the conflict between conformity and rebellion, and the costs of both. While these ideas and concerns are clearly present in the earlier chapters, it might seem as if the central ingredient in the dreamer's troubles—sexual decline, temptation to infidelity, and the destructive consequences of unfaithfulness—has been slighted. It is, I think, quite evident, that the sequence of vignettes that embody these worries, emanating from the supposed seamy incident in the park, retreats into the background in the last four chapters of Part I. As I shall now try to explain, there is a reason for this but also for the persistence of the old anxieties in novel forms.

These last four chapters begin from the point of resolution attained at the end of I-4. At least temporarily, the dreamer has been offered an attitude, a way of living and conceiving one's life that offers the hope of integrating the ill-fitting parts of himself, of a vindication and acceptance of the imperfect. To adopt and maintain that attitude is to exemplify the Joycean virtues, and that, we have seen, requires avoiding traps that arise for the various personae whom the dreamer has constructed. The focus has thus shifted from a first-level preoccupation with propensities that affect the health of love and marriage or that undermine integration within a community to the second-level enterprise of exploring the threats to what has appeared as a successful way of coping with those propensities. To put this simply and crudely: HCE is a focus for the dreamer's problems because he embodies tendencies whose expression might make a mockery of his (or the dreamer's) life; ALP and the attitude she brings is the promised solution for addressing these problems; the dreamer's new question might be formulated as an echo of Kant—"How is ALP possible?"

The possibility of ALP's forbearance as a genuinely Joycean virtue rests, I have claimed, on her full confrontation with the aspects of a life; part of that life—but only part of it—involves the decline of the sexual ardor of their young love and the temptations that arouse HCE in his age. ALP needs to see him whole, so that these parts of him have to be included, but they must be given their *exact* due. Perhaps that is why, in the long catalogue of characterizations of HCE in I-6, a few, but only a few, recapitulate the incident in the park.

We confront HCE's sexual temptations most clearly in two places in the later chapters of Part I. The first is in the breathless voice of Issy, teasing, coaxing, and urging, as if she could restore the sexual interest of almost any man.[14] Evidently obsessed with her own attractiveness, she is, equally evidently, taboo—off limits for HCE and for the dreamer. Her response is there to arouse, to remind of what is fading, perhaps to indicate what is now a part of life *past*— but also to bring home the grotesquerie of the aging man enflamed by the young temptress. Like ALP, Issy laughs (146: 2–7; 148: 31–2; compare 583: 26). It is clear, however, that their laughter is very different, the one mocking, the other sympathetic and accepting. I shall eventually want to claim that this difference in style of laughter matters, and, indeed, that it is part of the resolution of the dreamer's concern that the love he prizes is no more than bestial impulse.[15]

The second occurs in I-8, the dialogue of the gossiping washerwomen, another of Joyce's beautiful prose poems, that closes Part I of the *Wake*. The chapter begins with an invocation:

> O
> tell me all about
> Anna Livia! I want to hear all
> about Anna Livia. Well, you know Anna Livia? Yes, of course, we all
> know Anna Livia. Tell me all. Tell me now. (196: 1–5)

Surely, after her emergence at the end of I-4, we all (readers, dreamers) *do* want to know all about Anna Livia; how does she fulfill the promise we have been offered? Eventually we shall learn more about her—but not immediately. For we start with HCE, as if he cannot be avoided.

> He's an awful old reppe. Look at the shirt of him! Look at the dirt of it! He has all my water black on me. And it steeping and stuping since this time last wik. How many goes is it I wonder I washed it? I know by heart the places he likes to saale, duddurty devil. (196: 11–15)

This passage, occurring in the context of an allusion to the incident in the park, surely recalls Bloom's response to Gerty MacDowell's "wondrous re-vealment"—"Mr Bloom with careful hand recomposed his wet shirt" (*Ulysses*, 360, 363); it also looks forward to Shaun's advice ("Mades of ashens when you flirt spoil the lad but spare his shirt" [436: 32–3]); like many passages in the *Wake*, it also echoes Lady Macbeth's appreciation of the difficulty of washing away the stains of sin. Yet although the washerwoman starts here, with the sexual unfaithfulness of HCE, she immediately sets it in the context of his early love for ALP, of the dashing young man who came as an outsider (from across the sea), and lit up their lives with youthful ardor.[16]

After this rapturous beginning, the course of their marriage was inevitably a waning of sexual heat. They become caught up in everyday tasks, in the rearing of children, the maintenance and management of the household. It is hard work:

> And there she was, Anna Livia, she darent catch a winkle of sleep, purling around like a chit of a child. . . . And an odd time she'd cook

him up blooms of fisk and lay to his heartsfoot her meddery eygs, yayis, and staynish beacons on toasc and a cupenhave so weeshywashy of Greenland's tay . . . (199: 11–12, 15–18)

The washerwoman emphasizes her constant giving, her love and generosity, even when her husband is dour and disgruntled. Indeed, she suggests that ALP's forbearance goes to inordinate limits, that she is prepared to accept and forgive even to the point of conniving in his own unfaithfulness to her. She was willing to procure for him, trying to persuade "every shirvant siligirl or wensum farmerette" who passes to provide sexual solace for HCE, giving them detailed instructions on "the way of a maid with a man" (200: 18–19, 26).[17]

We are, of course, in a vignette, a dream dramatization of the dreamer's concerns. The anxiety here is evident. HCE's tendencies to wander are more systematic sources of marital corruption, infecting a relationship that declines from initial mutual delight to a life of humdrum drabness, punctuated by episodes that make a mockery of their love, their relationship, their marriage, in which ALP serves as an exploited drudge whose forbearance is pathological, not benign. Yet this is not the last word on ALP, nor even the last picture the gossiping washerwoman will give us.

For the discussion now changes direction, focusing not on HCE and his infidelities (real or imagined) but on ALP herself. Invoked at the beginning, but then apparently demoted to a supporting role, she now steps into the limelight. We start with a poem (or a song) in which she expresses her wish for a new life, a new love. She is tired of waiting for her husband, her "life in death companion" to rouse himself and "bore me down like he used to" (201: 8, 11–12). Her words anticipate the attempt to wake her husband and the wish for a resurgence of that youthful ardor and energy she will express at the very end of her closing monologue (see 619: 25; 628: 8–10). Here, too, her disaffection is linked to an urge to rejoin the sea (compare 201: 19–20 and 626: 4–6; 628: 3–4). Instead of continuing with the affirmation of her life—her life with HCE—that we hear at the close, the washerwomen's dialogue pursues the thought of ALP's longing for a new love.

She has aged, of course, and has children—"three figures to fill," which amount, according to the gossip, to one hundred and eleven (201: 28–9).[18] She is not as attractive as she used to be. In her youth, however, it was a different story. ALP attracted plenty of admirers. So we come to the tale of her past, to the catalogue of her first lovers.

Naturally, the first thought centers on HCE—the dreamer would like to think that there is no earlier love that lingers in ALP's memory. Yet to stop there would be wrong, "anacheronistic" (202: 35). Long before that, in "county Wickenlow" (202: 36; 203: 1), there was another love. It takes a few exchanges to set the scene, but then, we learn, in "the dinkel dale of Luggelaw," there once dwelt a local heremite, Michael Arklow was his riverend name, . . . and one venersderg in junojuly, . . . he plunged both of his newly anointed hands . . . in her singimari saffron strumans of hair, parting them and soothing her and mingling it, that was deepdark and ample like this red bog at sundown. (203: 18–26; parentheses omitted)

After telling of their lovemaking, the washerwoman explains that even this was not the beginning of ALP's sexual life, for there had been earlier incidents, one with "[t]wo lads in scoutsch breeches" and one with a hound (204: 5–6, 12). Yet the incident with the "bold priest" (Michael) is plainly the most significant, for there are clear suggestions in the gossipy report that in this case her heart was touched.

The dreamer's main anxiety about fidelity focuses on the consequences for a loving relationship of male urges to sexual expression elsewhere. The dominant picture here is a version of the washerwoman's first narrative: the passion of young love declines into everyday dullness and is threatened by the last flickerings of the aging husband's sexual desire. Yet the dreamer also fears that this story is wrong from the beginning, that the opening scene of young love blazing and triumphant does not reveal the whole truth, that the woman still longs, with part of herself, for an earlier love, now lost. That fear was one that Joyce had felt.[19] His writings revert to the theme several times— here in the *Wake* and in Molly's recollections of Lieutenant Mulvey. The most poignant evocation of all is in the greatest of Joyce's short stories, the closing chapter of *Dubliners*, "The Dead."

After the party at his aunts', where his wife, Gretta, has been moved by a song, Gabriel Conroy learns that her emotions have been stirred because the song is one that a boy she had known in Galway had sung. Gabriel divines that she had been in love with this boy, Michael Furey, of whom he had never previously heard. The boy died when he was only seventeen. He had been delicate. Gabriel asks:

—And what did he die of so young, Gretta? Consumption, was it?
—I think he died for me, she answered. (*Dubliners*, 220)

It is a terrible moment, as a new window opens on Gabriel's marriage—and on his life—as the change in light makes familiar things appear very different. For all his limitations, Gabriel has enough courage, and self-awareness, to weather the shock. He lies beside his exhausted wife as she sleeps, watching through the window as the snow falls. It is "general all over Ireland," and he knows that it falls upon the lonely grave of Michael Furey, "upon all the living and the dead" (*Dubliners*, 223, 224).

The figure of Michael—or Father Michael—swirls through the *Wake*. He is there in ALP's letter and in the interpretation of it (111: 15; 115: 16–20, 29), in Issy's prospectus for love, sex, and marriage (279 n.1, 32–4), in the instructions for writing a letter, modeled after ALP's (280: 12–13), as Shaun's confessional advisor (432: 7), as Issy's "pettest parriage priest" (458: 4), and as the model for all sexual partners (461: 21). Throughout, there is a suggestion of a sexual love that is prior to—and maybe greater than—that consummated in marriage. Like Gabriel Conroy, the dreamer has to come to terms with this.

Part I does not, however, end with the disconcerting vision of ALP as a woman with an unexpected past. She does not act on the yearnings expressed in the poem/song of discontent (201: 5–20). Instead, the washerwoman tells us, the public hostility to HCE, the condemnation of him as an outsider, arouses her to campaign on his behalf. Dressing herself up—in the mismatched style we associate with HCE—she comes forth laden with presents for all and sundry. Her children are included, of course, but so are others whom we might not have expected. She carries "a hole in the ballad for Hosty" (211: 19–20), and there are gifts, too, for "Festus King and Roaring Peter and Frisky Shorty and Treacle Tom" (212: 1–2). The image we are given is of a woman who has been able to make her peace with herself and her marriage, who defends her husband with forbearance and generosity, and who is prepared to forgive even those who have attacked him—a counterpart to HCE's expansive invitation to "let them all come" (545: 13). If the gossip is right, she has known an intense love before HCE; she has been carried away by his ardor; she has worked with him and worked for him; she has seen him in decline and sadness; she has recognized his own sexual temptations; despite it all, she is still willing to affirm him, to affirm them.

One of the washerwomen—the insatiable listener—wants to hear more. So, of course, does the dreamer, and so do we. For we still do not have the details of ALP's movement to acceptance; perhaps, after all, it might still be the effusion of an overly warm heart, an odd pathology. Her informant has no more information to provide.

> Well, you know or don't you kennet or haven't I told you every telling has a taling and that's the he and the she of it. (213: 11–12)

Even without an extension of the story, however, we see the movement to acceptance and forgiveness, to the Joycean virtues, in the interchanges between the washerwomen, and in their softening attitudes to HCE and ALP.

The twilight falls. The river widens. The women turn into a tree and a stone (as in the fable of I-6). Before they do so, however, they rehearse the stages of an established marriage—two old women who have done their wash together for many years can spar about the chores as well as any married couple.

> Throw the cobwebs from your eyes, woman, and spread your washing proper! It's well I know your sort of slop. Flap! Ireland sober is

Ireland stiff. Lord help you, Maria, full of grease, the load is with me! Your prayers. I sohnt zo! Madammangut! Were you lifting your elbow, tell us, glazy cheeks, in Conway's Carrigacura canteen? Was I what, hobbledyhips? Flop! (214: 16–21)

They are as disillusioned as we can imagine HCE and ALP to have been. But a momentary glimpse of something hard to identify sparks a shared fear, and they draw closer again. It is nothing, but the momentary spat is over. They are aware that the evening is passing, the light fading, that the current is bearing them apart—just as ALP is aware that she and HCE are parting (626: 35–6). The imminence of the end moves them to reconciliation.

Forgivemequick, I'm going! Bubye! And you, pluck your watch, forget-menot. (215: 7–8)

Instead of *hearing* what might have led ALP to forgive and to affirm, the vignette *shows* us the washerwomen in parallel motion. Moved by the recognition of all their shared work together, they make peace.

As they do, they also make peace with HCE and ALP. The critical tone of the early phases of the discussion has already given way to notes of admiration, but now there is genuine affection.

Ah, but she was the queer old skeowsha anyhow, Anna Livia, trinket-toes! And sure he was the quare old buntz too, Dear Dirty Dumpling, foostherfather of fingalls and dotthergills. Gammer and gaffer we're all their gangsters. (215: 12–15)

Their speech fades with the coming night, and we, dreamer and reader, experience the peace achieved at the close of I-4, the peace of acceptance after struggle, the peace promised by the Joycean virtues.

That peace is constantly in question. We could not rest content at the end of I-4 because we knew that there was more to be discovered, and thus a serious doubt that the realities of life had genuinely been faced, genuinely accepted, genuinely transformed. The little we have learned since about Anna Livia, ALP, leaves us with two major concerns: Has her forgiveness sprung from a genuine understanding of the truth about HCE? And is HCE to her what he takes himself to be—the chief object of her generosity and love? As I have said, the former question is the dominant one for the dreamer, but the worry about ALP's romantic history will continue to bubble up in the explorations to come, often marked by allusions to "Father Michael." So, although this is a moment of repose, there is pressure to go on. The insistent voice of the washerwoman is that of the dreamer, that of the reader: tell me more! Only by following that injunction is it possible to adopt and maintain the Joycean virtues and to respond to those fundamental anxieties that prompt the *Wake* and which it attempts to quieten.

The last four chapters of Part I are a first exercise in telling more, not always in the ways we expect. The motion of Chapters 2–8 of Part I, taken as a whole, is first downward, and then upward toward reconciliation. Doubts about the value of the dreamer's life are raised with the long vignette of I-2; they are deepened in I-3 until there seems to be no possible resolution; even in I-4, we have only the ungrounded promise, the hope, of an answer to them. That promise sets a new task, the task of exploring the elements within HCE to see if there is a way of conceiving his life that will allow an affirmative judgment on it. The review of those tendencies represented by Shaun and Shem ends in failure—there are no grounds here for vindicating HCE. We come back, then, to HCE's life as a messy whole—and the specific worries about betrayal and sexual wandering, which have been suppressed in the preliminary examination of Shaun and Shem, recur again, because marriage is so central to HCE's self-conception. By viewing that marriage, for all its flaws and lapses, as the continuation of a movement begun in their early love, the washerwomen bring the dreamer (and us readers) to a momentary peace.

Yet it is legitimate to wonder if *this* peace has come too easily. Have the facts really been faced fully? Has the consoling, affirming movement been made in appreciation of them? The same question that arose at the end of I-4 recurs here. It can only be answered by pressing on, by undertaking the same exploration on a larger scale, probing ever more deeply. That is the work of Parts II and III—they are to extend the range of perspectives we can take, broadening and deepening our understanding of the possibilities represented by the figures of the vignettes, so that we can make, again and more thoroughly, the movement that ALP so often exemplifies and that is dramatized for us by the washerwomen of I-8. The principal task of my reading of the *Wake* is to understand that movement—to return to ALP's closing monologue, to its earlier anticipations and variations, with fuller appreciation. First, however, we need to listen to the unfolding of problems and possibilities, as the second and third parts of the *Wake* tell us more.

12

LOUD, HEAP MISERIES UPON US

Although much of the detail is dark, with the central chapters containing an extraordinary density of material even for the *Wake,* Part II has a very obvious structure. There are four scenes, the first two of which center on the activities of the children, initially at play and then at their studies. In the third, the densest chapter in the entire book, we descend from the upstairs room in which the boys, Shem and Shaun, have been having their "day at triv and quad" (306: 12–13) to join HCE in the bar of his inn and to witness his collapse. The last scene occurs at sea, as four voices, those of the "evangelists," initially embodied as seabirds, track the progress of the ship bearing Tristan and Isolde to Cornwall.

This sequence of extended vignettes ought to puzzle us. If the removal of HCE from the center of attention in the first two chapters serves the purpose of exploring more thoroughly the possibilities latent in his sons, why does he suddenly return, to struggle and to fall before our eyes, in the third chapter? How do the vignettes continue the dreamer's explorations?

In fact, HCE isn't entirely absent in II-1 and II-2. Whether the children are playing or doing their homework, he is in the background, characterized as one of the cast (although not apparently as a principal) in the melodrama that the young act out in "Feenichts Playhouse" (219: 2), and carrying on his trade while they study:

> The babbers ply the pen. The bibbers drang the den. The papplicom, the pubblicam he's turning tin for ten. (262: 27–9)[1]

Significantly, he appears to be on the verge of making a cameo appearance in the game/play, but there is an apparent change of script and "the producer (Mr John Baptister Vickar) caused a deep abuliousness to descend upon the Father of Truants" (255: 27–8), so that the disciplinary intervention HCE might have intended is carried out by his "cutletsized consort" (255: 29). Yet while he is physically absent from both scenes, the worries that swirl around him bubble up again in the action of the drama and in the text the children read (241: 16–242: 24 and 272: 1–6 for two examples).

The central figures in these opening chapters—Shem, Shaun, and Issy, and, in particular, as we shall see, Shem—represent possibilities for vindicating a life both in terms of the achievements they embody and in terms of a continuation of that life in a new generation. If the artistic impulse has been destructive, if the rebellious urge for freedom has disfigured or even blotted out some of the domestic accomplishments the dreamer values, nevertheless there may be enough in what it has created to silence doubt about the significance of his life. Even if there is nothing to which the dreamer can point as his own creation, he may still find satisfaction in the creative work of the child he has begotten and reared. To have a son like Shem (or Stephen Dedalus, or James Joyce) may be enough for HCE (or Simon Dedalus, or John Joyce).

By this point in the *Wake* we ought to know better, for we have heard the long indictment of Shem (I-7). The charge was met with the response of the Joycean virtues. For the dreamer, the remaining question is not whether some form of forgiveness, of acceptance, can be found, but whether this depends on self-deception, on closing the eyes. So there arises a need to probe more closely the impulses Shem represents and to understand how the rebel/outsider comes to be—by watching Shem grow, the dreamer, and we, may take his measure with more confidence.

As I understand the global structure of the *Wake*, the dreamer begins with an extensive examination of one of the possibilities latent within HCE, the life of the artist-rebel. The vignettes of II-1 and II-2 expose this as a dead end—they culminate in Shem's submission to his brother. Effectively, the attempt to discover Shem's way brings us back to HCE whose disintegration and fall are presented starkly in II-3; the insignificance and worthlessness of his life are made even plainer in II-4. We are left with Shaun, the good conformist, as apparently the only hope.

In the first two chapters of Part III, however, Shaun disintegrates before us—he can find no stable identity. Instead, he becomes an archeological site, a mound in which a jumble of options is buried. The "star-chamber quiry" of III-3 excavates those options, draws out the many voices within Shaun, leaving us finally with HCE again, to be evaluated whole, in full awareness of his flaws and inconsistencies. Out of HCE's own presentation of himself, something that itself requires excavation, there emerges a fuller version of the possibility eventually glimpsed by the washerwomen of I-8. A more complete conception of HCE's marriage provides a way of attempting to vindicate his life, and that conception is put to the test in III-4 and IV. Parts II–IV thus cover familiar ground, often circling through thoughts the dreamer has explored before, although never as thoroughly.

So much for a cursory account of the structure, as I see it. Perhaps even an oversimple plan will help as we confront Joyce's mass of detail.

We start with children at play, with what we might hope will be an innocent world of unclouded joy; we move from there to their immersion in the higher culture, the great lore handed down as a treasury from previous generations. In both cases, there are myths to be debunked. For the opening game is no matter of gaiety and delight—the show at this playhouse is not a blithe fairy-tale ("Feenichts") but a drama from real life, one that will recur, phoenix-like, again and again. Nor is the wisdom of the book the children study what it might pretend to be; instead, the accumulated learning delivers, at the end, a few fragments of sordid advice. Descartes' first principle of certain knowledge is recast as the key to mundane, even sleazy, success.

> For I've flicked up all the crambs as they crumbed from your table um, singing glory allaloserem, cog it out, here goes a sum. So read we in must book. It tells. He prophets most who bilks the best. (304: 29–305: 2)

The sober vision of these chapters discloses no "youth in his florizel," no "boy in innocence" (621: 30). If ALP is to place her hope in a child, and to do so without self-deception, then significant work must be done to modify that vision.

Following Shem at play and Shem at work prepares us to appreciate the strength of the tensions within HCE, to understand how his incoherent visions of himself and his life must pull apart and leave him apparently defeated. The latter chapters of Part II bring his fall, and its finality, vividly before us, presenting them even more starkly than in I-3 and I-4, and ALP's consoling voice gives way to the gleefully derisive cackling of the seabirds. The task for the dreamer is to confront all this and yet to learn to laugh and to accept.

With this brief overture, we can let the curtain rise on the next act.

Joyce provides us with a program for the play we are about to see—"*The Mime of Mick, Nick, and the Maggies.*" The plot is that of a children's game, played on the street, in which one of the participants, in this instance the Shem figure, Glugg, must guess the answer to a riddle posed by the others. The other players include one other boy, the Shaun figure, Chuff, twenty-eight "flower girls," the attendants on the Issy figure, "IZOD (Miss Butys Pott, ask the attendantess for a leaflet)" (220: 7). As we begin, Glugg "has been divorced into disgrace court" (220: 1–2), allegedly because "he knew to mutch" (220: 1), and he is challenged to guess the color of the undergarments worn by the fascinating Issy.

Of course, he fails. Indeed, he is given three trials, on each of which he is allowed three guesses, and, despite the fact that Issy provides a clue for the final round, his answers are invariably wrong. In the humiliation of his defeat, under the teasing of the Floras, he becomes enraged and picks a fight with Chuff. He loses. The fight brings an end to the game. ALP enters to pick up her boys and to carry them inside for the evening meal.

As the program tells us, Chuff is the hero of the drama, Izod his leading lady, and Glugg the villain, and yet Shem (Glugg) is plainly the center of the vignette. Shaun (Chuff) figures principally as the object of others' praise. We meet him at the very beginning, already one of the elect, as the girls dance around him, singing their adoration.

> Chuffy was a nangel then and his soard fleshed light like likening. Fools top! Singty, sangty, meekly loose, defendy nous from prowlabouts. Make a shine on the curst. Emen. (222: 22–4)

He has been chosen, apparently arbitrarily—and may even be the chief of fools. Eventually, he will make a shiner on the accursed one, the one who has been cast out—who is "e-men," outside the ranks of men.

In his role as "evangelion" (223: 19), he confronts his brother, as the riddle challenge is posed. After that, however, we encounter Chuff only as the object of the Floras' worship, until the very end, when he carries out the angelic destiny predicted for him at the beginning: as St. Michael, he chastises the devil (255: 12–13).

The intervening action is dominated by Glugg, introduced to us in sharp contrast to the angelic Chuff: "But the duvlin sulph was in Glugger, that lost-to-lurning" (222: 25). Even before he is cast out, Glugg is cast as the devil himself, in whom the fires of hell burn—or perhaps he is just one who has absorbed the predominant elements, the local poisons, in the Dublin environment; we need not accept the contrast between Mick and Nick (the contrast offered by the Maggies) but may think of Glugg/Shem as an ordinary boy, perhaps a little bookish (fascinated by learning), whose lack of street knowledge makes him a prime source of amusement for others. Perhaps he is not born diabolical but has this status thrust upon him.

Glugg would surely like to be accepted, for he cannot be indifferent to the charms of the Floras: "how pierceful in their sojestiveness were those first girly stirs, with zitterings of flight and twinglings of twitchbells in rondel after, with waverings that made shimmershake rather naightily all the duskcended airs and shylit beaconings from shehind hims back" (222: 32–6). Here, and throughout the chapter, Joyce uses the material of children's social exchanges, the scraps of songs, riddles, games, stories, dances, sayings, and rhymes, with an appreciation of the serious business, the competition for status and the cruel sexual teasing, that lies behind them. The coy Floras know things Glugg cannot yet understand; they can play upon him as on a pipe. So it is no surprise that he is enticed into the riddle game.

> Up he stulpled, glee you gees, with search a fling did die near sea,
> beamy owen and calmy hugh and if you what you my call for me I will
> wishyoumaycull for you. (223: 12–14)

Izod, fairest of the fair, offers herself as prize if the eager Glugg can guess
her color (more exactly the color of her underwear)—the euphemism
"what-you-may-call" gives away the fact that there is something at stake that
can't be named directly, and the play on "cull" (both in reference to plucking
flowers and as alluding to the female genitals) is a word to the wise.

But Glugg isn't street-wise. He struggles to answer the riddle, "buzzling
is brains, the feinder" (223: 25–6); "feinder" links him not only directly
to the devil, but through the "fender" to the incidents of Part I, to HCE's
adversary (and "the adversary" is, once again, the Prince of Darkness). His
strategy is perfectly sensible, despite appearances: to discover the color of a
girl's undergarments you might, after all, look at low objects in which a reflection might appear, or hope for a gust of wind, or lie upon the ground, or
look for reflection in the river (223: 29–32). Glugg takes it all very seriously,
and, precisely because of that, it is easy for the girls to enjoy themselves at
his expense—"Apun which his poohor pricoxity theirs is a little tittertit of
hilarity" (224: 36–225: 1)—and they advise him "with a shrug of their hips
to go to troy and harff a freak at himself by all that story to the ulstrama-
rines" (225: 3–5).

Izod, whose attitudes are more ambiguous, perhaps because she wants to
prolong the tease, to toy with both Glugg and Chuff indefinitely, wishes that
the baffled boy would show more social intelligence; perhaps he should try to
charm the girls into divulging a clue, instead of pursuing his fruitless "buzzling" of his brains. She encourages him to try. He guesses, wrongly, and the
retinue breaks into jeers.

> Off to clutch, Glugg! Forwhat! Shape your reres, Glugg! Foreweal!
> Ring we round, Chuff! Fairwell! Chuffchuff's inners even. All's rice
> with their whorl! (225: 29–31)

"Isa" is disappointed by the outcome; wanting both Glugg and Chuff, she
"sits a glooming so gleaming in the gloaming" (226: 4) and must apparently be
cheered by a dance around the maypole, Chuff, the passive totem whom the
Floras adore.

Humiliated and frustrated, Glugg vents his anger (227: 29–35). Excluded
from the children's circle, he vows to go into exile.

> He would split. He do big squeal like holy Trichepatte. (228: 5–6)

Exile isn't chosen in a calm moment, or as the result of recognizing the emptiness of the rites in which the Floras engage. Glugg becomes an outsider partly
because he is thrust out by others, denied the option of joining a group that
lures him with its attractions—he has felt the "sojestiveness" of the "girly

stirs" (222: 32–3), the appeal of the "youngly delightsome frilles-in-pleyurs" (224: 22). Stephen Dedalus portrays himself as making a calm decision, produced by full recognition of the false loyalties that bind others, a decision to dedicate himself to a nobler ideal: "to express myself in some mode of life or art as freely as I can and as wholly as I can, using for my defence the only arms I allow myself to use—silence, exile, and cunning" (*Portrait*, 247). Glugg, by contrast, squeals, as if his hair were being painfully tugged; his resolution to "split" is taken out of resentful misery, and the resentment will linger. For Glugg's verb, "split," signifies that part of himself will be lost, sacrificed, in this decision—like the shamrock St. Patrick ("Trichepatte") used to illustrate the Trinity (perhaps with a trick—"*triche*"), Glugg can be pulled apart into different, but diminished, partial selves, and the one to live on will be less than the whole and will know itself to be reduced through its exile.

For the dreamer, this initial fragment of the career of Glugg can raise obvious disturbing questions. Instead of viewing the artist-outsider as the clear-eyed critic of what is shallow or false, he must consider the possibility that the ideal of artistic freedom is the expression of the *ressentiment* of those who are thrust out.[2] The indictment of Shem characterized him as using disgusting materials in pursuit of his "art," and a comparable judgment returns here. Glugg will make his former home the subject of his "farced epistol to the hibruws" (228: 33–4), writing *Ulysses* for intellectual snobs (highbrows), resentful outsiders (Jews), as a weapon (pistol) drawn in revenge. He will

> [g]o in for scribenery with the satiety of arthurs in S.P.Q.R.ish and inform to the whole sniggering publicking press and its nation of sheepcopers about the whole plighty troth between them, malady of milady made melodi of malodi . . . (229: 7–10)

Like Arthur, rejected in love, Glugg will find satisfaction in allying himself with the imperium (SPQR, in its local form, England, the "nation of shopkeepers," "blighty"), thus disavowing any loyalty (false or not) to his homeland, by revealing the sordid facts behind the apparent romances of its image. His chapters—including "Loathers' Leave," "Nemo in Patria," and "Mother of Misery" (229: 13, 15)—are outpourings of his bile:

> He would jused sit it all write down just as he would jused set it up all writhefully rate in blotch and void, yielding to no man in hymns ignorance, seeing how heartsilly sorey he was, owning to the condrition of his bikestool.[3] (229: 26–9)

So, portraying himself, like Wagner, a misunderstood outsider and telling the story of his expulsion ("why they provencials drollo eggspilled him out of his homety dometry narrowedknee domum" [230: 4–6]), he will win sympathetic ears for his sufferings. In the end, maybe, "liffe" could become "worth leaving" (230: 25).

Yet any satisfaction the outcast Glugg might find in writing an exposé of his homeland is short lived. Perhaps brought on by tasting the sweets of vengeance, a decaying wisdom tooth ("the errorooth of his wisdom" [231: 11]) leaves him in agony. Once again, any inclination the dreamer might harbor to view the exile as one with a superior, higher perspective on the dull conformism he has relinquished is undercut: "For there was never yet philosopher / Who could endure the toothache patiently" (*Much Ado about Nothing*, V.i.35–6).[4] Glugg's philosophical detachment turns out not only to be shallow but also false. A few breathless blandishments from Issy, ambiguous though they are, can quickly turn his head to new hopes.

> For directly with his whoop, stop and an upalepsy didando a tishy, in appreciable less time than it takes a glaciator to submerger an Atlangthis, was he again, agob, before the trembly ones, a spark's gap off, doubledasguesched, gotten orlop in a simplasailormade and shaking the storm out of his hiccups. (232: 30–5)

He returns, eager as ever, and no wiser than when he left.

He kneels before the girls—an appropriate pose both for a returning seafarer and for one who wants a glimpse of the concealed color. The ploy fails.

> Angelinas, hide from light those hues that your sin beau may bring to light! Though down to your dowerstrip he's bent to knee he maun't know ledgings here. (233: 8–10)

For all the words written in exile, the revelations about "his guffer" and "his gummer" (229: 19, 21–2), Glugg is prepared now to conform, to play by the rules and hope to win the prize.

Yet he still must guess, and the guesses are wrong (just like the "poor Gripes" Glugg "got wrong; for that is always how a Gripes is, always was and always will be" [159: 1–2]). Repudiated again, he can only "slink his hook away" (233: 29). He is a sorry sight.

> He had his sperrits all foulen on him; to vet, most griposly, he was bedazzled and debuzzled; he had his tristiest cabaleer on; and looked like bruddy Hal. (234: 1–4)

There seems to be no future for him, and he sinks from view.

Glugg's departure leaves, in center stage, his triumphant brother, around whom the girls dance with songs of ardent worship, songs not merely of innocence but also of (sexual) experience. Chuff appears only through their yearnings, their schoolgirl dreams of a future with him, their hymns of praise and sexual prayer. In following their adoration, we are shown the shortcomings an artist-outsider might have written to expose. The girls look forward to a future of bourgeois delights, hoping that their darling Chuff may become a "bank midland mansioner" (235: 11–12), providing them with an appropriately impressive address, a house where they may reside with "obeisant servants among Burke's mobility at La Roseraie, Ailesbury Road" (235: 12–13). They are to enjoy all the amenities advertised in the magazines read by young women like Gerty MacDowell, and they will be able to play hostess at a grownup version of a children's party:

> Lady Marmela Shortbred will walk in for supper with her marchpane switch on, her necklace of almonds and her poirette Sundae dress with bracelets of honey and her cochineal hose with the caramel dancings, the briskly best from Bootiestown, and her suckingstaff of ivorymint. (235: 32–236: 1)

Yet the vision of conformity and respectability imperfectly covers yearnings for different kinds of sweets. Although the girls' dance around Chuff starts with religious fervor ("Xanthos! Xanthos! Xanthos!"—the adoration of the *Sanctus* [235: 9]), it isn't long before it assumes another character and a profane purpose. The Floras know how to titillate

> each of all has a lovestalk onto herself and the tot of all the tits of their understamens is as open as he can posably she and is tourensoled straightcut or sidewaist, accourdant to the coursets of things feminite, towooerds him in heliolatry, so they may catchcup in their calyzettes, alls they go troping, those parryshoots from his muscalone pistil, for he can eyespy through them to their selfcolours . . . (236: 34–237: 4)

Their invitations to Chuff, "dear sweet Stainusless"[5] (237: 11), mix the religious adoration with ever more explicit sexual invitations: "Bashfulness be tupped! May he colp, may he colp, may he mixandmass colp her!" (238: 20–1). The climax of their devotional prayer makes the apotheosis of heavenly bliss quite explicit:

> And when all us romance catholeens shall have ones for all amanseprated. And the world is maidfree. Methanks. (239: 21–2)

Behind the tastefully trimmed shrubbery of La Roseraie, the girls will discover "the pleasure each will preen her for, the business each was bred to breed by" (268: 5–6)—so the world will be "maidfree."

Glugg's writing, we might think, could have exposed the gaps among the professions of piety, the dreams of bourgeois respectability, and the underlying itch. Only when he is absent, temporarily lost to our vision, can we, and the dreamer, begin to recognize that there might be serious grounds for critique of the lost homeland, that denunciation of the "dear olt tumtum home" (231: 5) might stem from something other than bilious disloyalty. Shaun has not yet come before us as an active figure, and the possibilities he represents remain unprobed (that will happen in the first two chapters of Part III), but we can already suspect that they won't resolve the dreamer's anxieties. Even at its brightest, the Floras' vision of bliss is unsettling—and the golden light in which they dance has, at least once, been dimmed by passing cloud. For, after the rehearsal of their steps in an earlier celebration, there was a different characterization of their movements—"The many wiles of Winsure" (227: 1–2)—and then, suddenly, a grim foretelling of possible futures:

> The grocer's bawd she slips her hand in the haricot bag, the lady in waiting sips her sup from the paraffin can, . . . and here's the girl who she's kneeled in coldfashion and she's told her priest (spt!) she's pot on a chap (chp!) . . . (227: 3–4, 8–9)

The shadow passes, and the Floras "come back, all the gay pack" (227: 15), but, for a moment, we have seen them in the guise of *Dubliners* or the minor characters of *Ulysses*.

Glugg, however, cannot consistently view them in this way, and Chuff in his heaven is visible from hell, where the torments of the damned are intensified by the thought of the bliss that has been lost. Tertullian was right to hold that, conversely, the infernal agonies would increase the joy of the blest,[6] for, hearing the "oaths and screams and bawley groans with a belchybubhub" (229: 32–3), the girls dance on more merrily (239: 36–240: 3).

As befits a children's story, there must be three chances, and the third and last must be the most dramatically complex. Glugg re-emerges, "he rises, shrivering, with his spittyful eyes and his whoozebecome woice" (240: 5–6), shriven not because he sees the virtue of the bourgeois order that has thrust him out but because the same impulses that have been found in the Floras' song of adoration prick him on to reform.

> Examen of conscience scruples now he to the best of his memory schemado. Nu mere for ever siden on the stolen. With his tumescinquinance in the thight of his tumstull. (240: 6–9)

The first two sentences in this passage offer a rationale for Glugg's change of heart, with their intimations of conscience and of scruples. Has he rejected the life of the outlaw (the side of the stolen)? Perhaps decided to cross the sea (*mer*) and return to the mother (*mère*) country? But it is only a rationalization for baser urges that compel, that urge him out of exile. Abandoning his vitriolic attacks on those who have expelled him, he will knuckle under and play by the rules—in short, he will serve.

Stephen Dedalus will grow, perhaps, into Leopold Bloom, stifling the rebellious urges in favor of patience in the face of hostility, contempt, even infidelity.

> He repeat of him as pious alios cos he ast for shave and haircut people said he'd shape of hegoat where he was just sheep of herrgott with his

tile togged. Top. Not true what chronicles is bringing his portmanteau priamed full potatowards. (240: 33–241: 1)

Pius Aeneas, exiled son, brings the gods and trophies of his fathers (kin of Priam) to a new city, surely Dublin, capital of the land of the potato-eaters. Among those trophies, perhaps, is a potato, the charm carried by Bloom on his own wanderings. Father and son are vividly present here in the echoes of Jacob's deception of Isaac (as well as in the allusions to the fundamental division made by "herrgott" at judgment day). Even more important, however, is an echo of a crucial passage in Part I, the story of the initial encounter of HCE with the cad, who is predicted to be passing himself off as a respectable citizen:

> in the same straw bamer, carryin his overgoat under his schulder, sheepside out, so as to look more like a coumfry gentleman and signing the pledge as gaily as you please . . . (35: 12–15)

Glugg is in the process of abandoning his sinful ways (his *Schulden*), among them abandoning drink (signing the pledge), hoping for comfort in conformity.[7] Shem/Glugg is becoming HCE. Yet we should not forget what has apparently driven this change, the "tumescinquinance in the thight of his tumstull" (240: 8-9).

The insufficiency of the bold artistic *credo*, already seen in the first exile, is deepened here. The costs of exclusion are apparent, making the transition from Shem (or Glugg, or Stephen) to HCE (or Bloom) attractive, even irresistible. So, although we begin with the possibilities represented by Shem, it is already clear that the dreamer will be led back to HCE and to a further, more thorough, confrontation with his fall (in II-3 and II-4).

The fusion of Glugg, returning for a third round of the game, with HCE becomes increasingly evident as the vignette proceeds—we find the familiar device of juxtaposed words with the appropriate letters ("heather cliff emurgency," [241: 6]), the associations with salmon (241: 2), mountains (241: 17-19), burial in Loch Neagh (241: 24), the rumors about the incident in the park (241: 24-32), and, most importantly, the wooing and winning of ALP (241: 13–16; 242: 25 ff.).[8] As we shall discover, this identification, or, more exactly, the transformation of Glugg into a character whose dominant persona may alternate between that of HCE and that of Shem, complicates the story of three guesses and eventual humiliation. It also introduces a new perspective with which the dreamer must reckon.

For the apparent purpose of the *Mime of Mick, Nick, and the Maggies* is to reveal the latent possibilities of one aspect of HCE's character, one strain or persona within him. If he is indeed "more mob than man" (261: 21-2), we (and the dreamer) might hope to assess his many-sided life by evaluating the individual elements within it. Glugg does not undergo a simple metamorphosis, for the urges that prompt his return have been there all along, present in his initial eagerness to join the others and to be accepted by them. When HCE enters the children's play, it is suddenly clear that he has always been there, that we may with equal justice take him to be an element within Glugg as take Glugg to be a part of him. Father and son are indeed of the same substance, and, in the initial expulsion, Glugg was split.

The mime shows us the developmental history of an outsider, an exile, but we cannot make any defensible judgments about the fundamental identity of this person—"that sword of certainty which would indentifide the body never falls" (51: 5–6). We look for the original springs of the personality, the intrinsic features that social interactions will shape, but, at each stage, we find a mob of characters—even when we think we have the native form, "a daarlingt babyboy bucktooth" (242: 8), we confront the complexities of an aging man, and HCE looms again before us. Just as his voice lies deepest within Shaun (as III-3 will reveal), it is present within Shem. The elements we seek are elusive. Internal conflict seems unavoidable.

The reformed Glugg is poised to return for his final guesses, but, at this point, the action of the vignette is suspended. It is evening, and the play must soon close. An outside figure walks through the twilight to light the street lamps— perhaps it is Sackerson in his role of Watchman, figuring as adult authority in relation to the ambiguous character (Shem? HCE?) who is at the center of the drama. There is a moment of seeming peace, as Joyce delivers another of his beautiful prose poems, a Nocturne, a childlike vision of a calm world—"Quiet takes back her folded fields. Tranquille thanks. Adew" (244: 28–9). Yet this is a vision available only to those who can be embraced within the cozy walls of home.

For the outsider, matters are quite different, and it is plain that the night is full of dangers.

> Comehome to roo, wee chickchilds doo, when the wildworewolf's abroad. Ah, let's away and let's gay and let's stay chez where the log foyer's burning. (244: 10–12)

The view from inside is serene and reassuring, for the animals in the park are safely confined in the zoo, friendly and domesticated creatures who pose no threat to the children in their homes.

> As Lord the Laohun is sheutseuyes. The time of lying together will come and the wildering of the nicht till cockeedoodle aubens Aurore. (244: 31–3)

Wrapped in the protection of the community, the children can dream of a peaceable kingdom. Glugg, however, is outside, in the territory of the "wild-worewolf," in a park where one can discover familiar adult allurements—"Soon

tempt-in-twos will stroll at venture and hunt-by-threes strut musketeering"
(245: 19–20).

The warmth of the inn is advertised to travelers (245: 27–36), and its security, peace, and fellowship must call Glugg home from his exile. He has an
ally in Issy ("Icy-la-Belle" [246: 20]), still undecided between her two beaux.
His return is greeted with the Floras' stinging contempt, prompting him to
Christ's despairing question: "Teapotty. Teapotty" (247: 15).[9] Once again, he
feels the pains of exclusion, and, as before, he lacks insight into the riddle. Issy,
however, encourages him, offering him a clue for her color[10] and continuing
with her breathlessly seductive cooing (248: 16ff.). He has a momentary sense
of elation and hope, but it is quickly dashed by the mocking of the Floras.

> —I rose up one maypole morning and saw in my glass how nobody
> loves me but you. Ugh. Ugh.
> All point in the shem direction as if to shun. (249: 26–7)

Issy joins the laughter. Glugg realizes (as does the dreamer) that the game cannot be won (" . . . ith ith noth cricquette"[11] [249: 35]), but perhaps he can earn
acceptance by making a brave try, entering into what he takes to be the spirit of
the festivities and giving answers with a show of burlesque (250: 3–9).

His speech hangs without an immediate verdict—it will be three pages
until the failure is officially certified (253: 19–20). Before judgment is rendered, the vignette explores the significance of what has occurred.

It is a children's game, and we shouldn't—Glugg shouldn't, the dreamer
shouldn't—take it so seriously. Or is it? Should we (they)?

A voice first counsels calm:

> So now be hushy, little pukers! Side here roohish, cleany fuglers![12] (250:
> 11–12)

But this voice is almost immediately opposed by one offering an opposed
perspective:

> For you've jollywelly dawdled all the day. . . . Yet's the time for being
> now, now, now. (250: 12–13, 14–15)

The game, perhaps, isn't some preparation for life, real life, but part of it, and
this particular part has been a waste—or worse.

Joyce continues with what initially appears as a clumsy pastiche of famous
lines from *Macbeth*, an odd eruption in the children's mime.

> For a burning would is come to dance inane. Glamours hath moidered's
> lieb and herefore Coldours must leap no more. Lack breath must leap
> no more. (250: 16–18)

We have been viewing a play which is, in large part, a dance, both in the
"holy trooping" of the Floras and the way in which Glugg has been led a

dance. That dance is rightly characterized as inane, empty, for the object of adoration, Chuff, has given no sign of his worthiness, and the professed interests of the girls are trivialities of social distinction. Glamorous though they may be, the Floras seem to have killed anything we might take to be a love (*Liebe*) of any value; they have sold genuine emotional responses for trash, for golden coins (moidores) and other trinkets. For them, as for the dreamer, life is finite: a burning world, doomsday, will close this dance; their bright colors will flash no more as they leap; cold hours are at hand (here-fore), hours in which they will lack breath and leap no more; as they become aware of the approach of that time, they will see themselves as having "dawdled all the day."

Suddenly, they are children again, playing a rhyming game, and danc-ing in harmless fun (250: 19–22). Is that, after all, how we should see them? Joyce holds out a divining rod—a "fork of hazel o'er the field" (250: 23)—and it seems that the choice is momentous, since "Perdition stinks before us" (250: 26). But we are on a map without coordinates, where "before" and "behind" lack clear senses. Should we laugh with the happy girls or weep with Glugg?

Having offered his answers, Glugg is reduced, shorn of his transitory bravado. Issy regrets his oafish stolidity, continuing to dream of Chuff as husband and Glugg as paramour. That dream is interrupted by Chuff's first decisive inter-vention. His mockery of the dispirited Glugg provokes a fight, to be played by schoolboy rules. Despite the superficial politeness, it is serious business, recalling the brotherly conflict between Cain and Abel—"each was wrought with his other" (252: 14).

Great things hang upon combat, since it determines the patterns along which the conformist life will be lived, separating "who is artthoudux from whose heterotropic" (252: 20–1). Underlying the distinction between ortho-doxy and heresy are the facts that determine who is fit to be leader (*dux*).

> he must be put strait on the spot, no mere waterstichystuff in a self-made world that you can't believe a word he's written in, not for pie, but one's only owned by naturel rejection. Charley, you're my darwing! So sing they sequent the assent of man. Till they go round if they go roundagain before breakparts and all dismissed. They keep. Step keep. Step. Stop. Who is Fleur? Where is Ange? Or Gardoun? (252: 25–32)

Just as the hymn of praise (235–9) turned out to express the "law of the jun-gerl" (268 n.3), the boys' fight is the struggle for existence.

There has been no primeval garden here, in which flowers grow and angels walk, no place in which the fundamental distinction between good and evil has been authoritatively laid down. Orthodoxy is only established by struggle, and a large factor in the "assent of man" is sexual selection, the "naturel rejection" of Glugg that we have witnessed. As we have seen, he has not *chosen* exile but been forced into it, and the writings he produces must be rejected according to the only criterion that matters, the judgment of those who succeed in the Darwinian game of mate selection, the girls who select their darling.

Glugg has already betrayed his exile, panting home under the blandishments of Issy, seeking the warmth of bourgeois security. Now he forswears Stephen Dedalus's self-limitation to the weapons of the artist. He chooses to fight. In electing combat, as in returning from exile, his persona fuses with HCE, who enters the drama both as potential restrainer of the conflict and as potential victim.

Initially, it seems that the fight is to be harmless, a piece of good fun that is just part of the game:

> the shifting about of the lassies, the tug of love of their lads ending with a great deal of merriment, hoots, screams, scarf drill, cap fecking, ejaculations of aurinos, reechoable mirthpeals and general thumbtono-sery . . . (253: 25–8)

That may be as our image of childhood play would have it—and if things spin out of control, there is always the possibility of adult intervention:

> one must reckon with the sudden and gigantesquesque appearance un-withstandable as a general election in Barnado's bearskin amongst the brawlmiddle of this village childergarten of the largely longsuffering laird of Lucanhof. (253: 29–32)

Perhaps there is an outside authority—although we should hear an anticipation of Shaun's grim assessment of the tastes of the "longdistance laird" (457: 24) and wonder whether any *deus ex machina* represents a kindly providence.

If we recall Glugg's humiliation, we might hope that the entrance of HCE might transform the cruel rite into an ordinary game. Perhaps the dreamer hopes for an ending to the mime in which "HUMP," "Mr Makeall Gone," eradicates the savagery of the tormenting of Glugg—as at the end of Peter Brook's movie of William Golding's *Lord of the Flies*, the boy Ralph, fleeing for his life, stumbles into an obstacle, which the camera, with a beautifully paced slowness, reveals to be first the ankles, then the calves, legs, body and head of the naval officer who has arrived to rescue the castaways; and the whooping hunters shrink again to ordinary schoolboys.

It is not to be. We aren't given immediately a "god of all machineries" (253: 33). Instead, the apparent arrival of HCE only serves to re-align his fate with that of Glugg. Both were nomads, who crossed the sea (254: 1–2). But HCE has fallen, and the vignette reminds us why: "The mar of murmury mermers to the mind's ear" (254: 18). Like Glugg, he is repudiated, and, as a result of the repudiation, he is not at hand to resolve the present conflict.

HCE's fall and his resultant absence are interwoven with the defeat of Glugg, thrown down in the fight. Any attempt to raise up—"erewaken"—the victim (Glugg or Earwicker?) is questionable:

> Attach him! Hold!
> Yet stir thee, to clay, Tamor!
> Why wilt thou erewaken him from his earth . . . ? (255: 3–5)

Only ALP can bring an end to the conflict between the boys, working the magic that shrinks it to an everyday game: "Gallus's hen has collared her pullets" (256: 2). They are to go in for wholesome supper and evening study, no longer devils and angels, exiles and darlings, but small boys "teartoretorning" (256: 17).

Issy lingers behind, echoing the disappointment of "nuvoletta" at the end of the fable of the Mookse and the Gripes.

> That little cloud, a nibulissa, still hangs isky. Singabed sulks before slumber. (256: 33–4)

Her presence is a reminder of the serious business behind the drama, so that, even at its end, we aren't allowed to rest in the judgment that it was only a game.

The hymn that accompanies the ringing down of the curtain (257: 31–2) begins a coda, a liturgy for the ceremonial entrance of the children "into their habitations" (258: 29). We end with a prayer that settles some of the questions this drama has provoked, revealing the connection between this vignette and the dreamer's concerns.

> O Loud, hear the wee beseech of thees of each of these thy unlitten ones! Grant sleep in hour's time, O Loud!
> That they take no chill. That they do ming no merder. That they shall not gomeet madhowiatrees.
> Loud, heap miseries upon us yet entwine our arts with laughters low!
> Ha he hi ho hu.
> Mummum. (259: 3–10)

"Loud" is an appropriate name for the Thunderer, a frightening and potentially destructive supervisor for the "unhappitents of the earth" (258: 22).[13] Kneeling by their beds (*lits*) in the darkness ("unlitten"), the children pray for relief from childish worries—that they should be continent ("*mingere*" means "urinate," and "merde" is familiar French), that they shall not meet monsters in their dreams. Yet they are more than children, for they hope to obey the commandments that have been most obviously broken in the mime—there has been idolatry in the worship of Chuff, adultery in the sexual invitations, and potential murder in the concluding violence. They have come in from a

Darwinian world of ruthless competition, and, like the dreamer, they aspire to be more than beasts. They have witnessed—or experienced—"naturel rejection" (252: 28), and they know too much to ask from the supervisor of the world that happiness should flow naturally upon them. If it comes, if they make something worthwhile of their lives, then it must be through their "arts," and the arts must be undertaken with laughter.

Among the dreamer's anxieties is the thought that human life, properly understood, is bleak and bestial, but, with the vignettes of Part I, we have recognized the possibility of a transformation, effected through the Joycean virtues. There is a reminder of that possibility here (as well as in the earlier Nocturne [246: 10–15]), a momentary upturn in the overall descent of this chapter and of Part II generally. The descent is forced by the need to probe, to respond to the insistent doubt, the whispers to the dreamer (and to us) that this transformation is illusory, the product of shutting the eyes to reality. The children's play reveals the misery of exclusion, the emptiness of conformity, the brutish impulses that drive the game—and yet it is a play, a work of art that can inspire us to laugh and to accept. So the chapter can indicate the consoling movement the dreamer (and we) must practice. It can lead us to affirm the children's prayer:

Loud, heap miseries upon us yet entwine our arts with laughters low!

It can lead us to view, alternately, the mime *either* as a serious and cruel business *or* as only a children's game—without selecting one of them as the definitive perspective. Even though the doubts remain, and must still be explored, a momentary reminder of the more hopeful possibility reminds dreamer (and reader) of the possible goal, not yet achieved. Recognizing this as *only* a game can urge us on, to probe further and, perhaps, to see clearly and fully, to accept, and to laugh.

At the end, then, there is quiet (mum)—and there too, predictably, is mother (mum), ALP, with the final word.

13

THE TASKS ABOVE ARE AS THE FLASKS BELOW

Philosophy, queen of the sciences, begins from the question "How to live?" and someone, an aging dreamer perhaps, might look to works of philosophy, or those of the subject domains that serve the queen, for an answer. Children, on the other hand, must absorb the wisdom their forebears have laboriously acquired, both in order to make their way in the ambient world and its culture and so they may, with luck, add something of their own or, more exactly, modify tradition for the better. The game on the street exercised and trained bodies—and, even more, shaped and developed social attitudes. Now, after tea "and goody, hominy bread" (256: 18), young minds will be fed by a book.

We are given a dream text, a book that both presents material and describes the reactions of the children as they study it, together with notes written in the margins by Shem and by Shaun, and footnotes from Issy, who is not supposed to be reading at all, and whose contributions sometimes appear to have little connection with the points in the text to which they attach. One set of comments, presumably Shem's, initially on the left (260–287) and later on the right (293–308), are irreverent and subversive; the annotations in the facing margin, Shaun's, first on the right and then on the left, are dutiful, serious, pompously vacuous, and uncomprehending.

The book itself hints at the arrangement of the children. If we climb the stairs of the inn, leaving "the murk of the mythelated in the barrabelowther" (266: 9–10), passing the toilet,[1] we shall come to "the clarience of the childlight in the studiorum upsturts" (266: 12–13). That is the official story of scholarship too, an ascent from myth, prejudice, and ignorance, a purgation of the errors of the past and a new illumination. Yet the children cannot start from nothing—the boys, at least, must absorb before they can correct. They pore together over the same book, while Issy sits apart.

Soon jemmijohns will cudgel about some a rhythmatick or other over Browne and Nolan's divisional tables whereas she . . . with her toot-pettypout of jemenfichue will sit and knit on solfa sofa. Stew of the evening, booksyful stew. (268: 7–9, 12–15)

There are already signs that this dream-text will not help much with the official Grand Questions.

Other things are obviously going on. The boys are in competition, and the prize is Issy, set apart, pursuing the traditional occupations of the educated bourgeois girl, music (sol-fa) and needlework. She is prepared to thumb her nose at the dry material the boys must absorb, for she has no need of it—"all is her inbourne" (268: 16), and she has the maxims she requires from "gramma's grammar" (268: 17). The surrounding text and notes display her womanly wisdom. Aside from her dismissive judgment, Joyce gives us clear clues that the material assigned for study is unlikely to be rewarding: it's a muddle, a "booksyful stew"; the allusion to the Mock Turtle (who recalled educational exercises in Uglification and Derision) signals that this is fake wisdom and the invocation of Giordano Bruno (Bruno the Nolan) suggests clashing perspectives with no resolution.

Indeed, we should have been prepared for the reduction of any claims that Shem might have made, even for his eventual subservience. The burlesque scholarship of the Mamafesta and the pretentious professorial introduction to the fable of the Mookse and the Gripes bode badly for the significance of academic learning. Although we are told of "clarience" in the study upstairs, this at first appears to be a mistake. It is tempting to think that "[t]he tasks above are as the flasks below"[2] (263: 21) in the sense that both are dim and dimming. But, I shall suggest, both are alike in their role of devices for getting on with the mundane business of living.

Advertisement first. We are apparently in for an encyclopedic discussion, one that will cover all things, from the most elementary and childish, to the most advanced—covering the traditional divisions of the traditional subjects will help us understand where, and who, we are (260: 1–3, 8–15). Shem, echoing Stephen Dedalus, quickly guesses that this must involve understanding their father.[3] He is right. The classical curriculum dissolves into the major event that directly affects the children, the marriage of the parents. HCE emerges,[4] and the large questions to be answered focus on him.

But, to speak broken heaventalk, is he? Who is he? Whose is he? Why is he? Howmuch is he? Which is he? When is he? Where is he? How is he? And what the decans is there about him anyway, the decemt man? Easy, calm your haste! Approach to lead our passage! (261: 27–262: 2)

The questions must be put in "broken heaventalk," for, after Babel, that is all we can speak, but these are surely questions the dreamer would like to answer.

He would like reassurance that the epithet—"decent man"—already offered at the opening wake (27: 22) can be justified. The schoolbook opens before us the castle of knowledge, inviting us to enter and seek answers. This repository of tradition is characterized with an unnerving juxtaposition of adjectives: "To house as wise fool ages builded" (262: 18).[5]

Of course, there are no answers to be offered, and, though the review of geography, astronomy, classical history, grammar, letter-writing, and mathematics will swirl tantalizingly around the lives of HCE and ALP, it will not tell the dreamer who they are or how they have come to be. There will be all-too-many reminders of the problematic information that has emerged in earlier vignettes, mixed with education in the tactics of sexual competition, information that would have been useful to the players on the street. That, apparently, is what tradition can and should deliver—not the lofty abstractions Shaun aspires to formulate (and perhaps to understand) but the earthy cheekiness periodically expressed by Shem and, especially, by Issy.

The castle of knowledge turns out to be the inn, not a surprise if the transmission of traditional wisdom begins at home; but the source of the insights, HCE the father, initially characterized as "Ainsoph," the "upright one" (261: 23) is quickly viewed in a less flattering light; as "erst crafty hakemouth," he associates with his pub clientele: "under the assumed name of Ignotus Loquor, of foggy old, harangued bellyhooting fishdrunks on their favorite stamping ground" (263: 2–4). To take on a name that suggests an inability to speak portends the fact that, harangue as he may try, HCE is in no position, or in no state, to trace the lineaments of his own life. Even when the text seeks to honor him, the disturbing old stories erupt into view, and we are reminded of "two lunar eclipses" and "three saturnine settings" (264: 4, 5). They recur when we leave zodiacal signs and take up classical history; there we meet

> Sire Jeallyous Seizer, that gamely torskmester, with his duo of druidesses in ready money rompers and the tryonforit of Oxthievious, Lapidous and Malthouse Anthemy. (271: 4–6)

So, too, with mathematics, where the first problem set for the boys is to show that the "median, hce che ech, intererecting at royde angles the parilegs of a given obtuse one biscuts both the arcs that are in curveachord behind" (284: 1–4).[6]

Why must the children's schoolbook contain this worrying information? Partly, of course, as I have suggested repeatedly, because the story about the park condenses the dreamer's anxieties about conflicting impulses. Yet we should also wonder why they appear here—or, to pose the question in a different way, why the depiction of study upstairs is a useful vehicle for the further exploration of those anxieties. I think there are several ways in which the evening homework advances the dreamer's investigations. Most obviously, it scotches any hope he (or we) might have harbored that there is a body of established wisdom for resolving the fundamental issues about assessing the value of lives—it encompasses the *problems* that confront the dreamer but offers no solutions, indeed, nothing beyond the disconcerting information with which the dreamer wrestled throughout Part I. In doing so it silences the thought that the rebel-outsider might achieve, in dedicating himself to some form of learning, a form of life more valuable than that of everyday acknowledgment of bourgeois conventions. Additionally, this vignette presents the accumulated wisdom of tradition as yielding strategies for getting by, sometimes in questionable fashion—it debunks myths that might have protected the dreamer from facing some of his concerns. Finally, in handing on a depiction of the tensions and conflicts within the father, the schoolbook prepares the sons who read it to expose those tensions and thus challenge his authority. As we shall see, the vignette tends to a moment of unity among the three children, certainly transient but a moment in which they can announce the coming disintegration of HCE.

I want to follow these strands more slowly and systematically. Early in the chapter, the inquiries to be undertaken centered explicitly on HCE (261: 17; 262: 2), and it is no surprise when the first geometric problem[7] is to demonstrate something that alludes quite clearly to his sexual functioning and less definitely to the incident in the park (283: 32–284: 15). The alleged answer, a brilliant pastiche of a proof, wanders through references to many apparently irrelevant parts of mathematics—but taking in such revealing hypotheses as "if the two antecedents be bissyclitties and the three comeseekwenchers trundletrikes" (284: 22–4)—to a conclusion utterly unrelated to what was given as the initial problem (285: 22–6). In the style of helpful commentary, the "proof" continues:

> For a surview over all the factionables see Iris in the Evenine's World. Binomeans to be comprendered. Inexcessible as thy by god ways. The aximones. And their prostalutes. For his neuralgiabrown. (285: 26–286: 1)

Was HCE's transgression actionable—perhaps even reported in an evening scandal sheet? At any rate, it is—and he is—beyond comprehension. His ways and his past (bygone days) are inaccessible and excessive, like those of the creator. Apparently, however, they involve dubious sexual liaisons, and they produce enduring headache. Compressed here is the dreamer's recurrent problem, the problem of fitting parts of himself, and his life, together, and the verdict of a treatment from the knowledge and techniques that have been passed down is that the problem, for all the advertisement of an answer, is insoluble.

Other aspects of HCE's life also swirl through the collection of oddments the boys study, pointed reminders of his fall, unaccompanied by any consoling explanation. We hear the rhythms of Hosty's ballad (273: 1–2; 294: 25–6). There are hints of the importance of writing a letter (278: 12–18; 302: 20–9).

Moreover, in the part of the schoolbook devoted to grammar and writing, we are provided with a pattern for a letter:

> Dear (name of desired subject, A.N.), well, and I go on to. Shlick-sher. I and we (tender condolences for happy funeral, one if) so sorry to (mention person suppressed for the moment, F.M.). Well (enquiries after all healths) how are you (question maggy). A lovely (introduce to domestic circles) pershan of cates. Shrubsher. Those pothooks mostly she hawks from Poppa Vere Foster but these curly mequeues are of Mippa's moulding. Shrubsheruthr. (Wave gently in the ere turning ptover.) Well, mabby (consolation of shopes) to soon air. With best from cinder Christinette if prints chumming . . . (280: 9–22)

The discussion of the letter in Part I (I-5) provided us with two texts allegedly traceable to ALP, one, the focal letter (111: 10–20), which is plainly a variation on this pattern for schoolchildren, and the other, allegedly used for authentication (113: 11–18), which echoes the compressions offered here ("shrubs" for "she rubs," "schwants" for "she wants").

The celebrated letter, then, is a set of minor variations on the paradigm provided by an elementary text for children. It would be natural to exclaim that this undercuts the project pursued with official seriousness in Part I (specifically in I-5). How can we vindicate HCE's life by appealing to a letter whose general form could be applied to virtually anyone? Don't the specific details matter? Of course. Yet we can interpret this observation as a commentary on the idea of looking to scholarly tradition for answers to the question of how to understand HCE, or any other individual. Nothing this book, or any book, can teach will enable the children, or the dreamer, to make sense of a life unless it unfolds the rich particularities—unless it penetrates the everyday with the thoroughness of *Ulysses* or the *Wake* itself.

One further aspect of the pattern letter is worth noting. Where the original talked openly of "poor Father Michael" (111: 15) as the central figure in the funeral (or "funferall"), the textbook offers a vaguer reference to "F.M." as "the person suppressed." The initials are ominous, reminding the dreamer of his doubts about the romantic past of the wife whose love he values so much. As so often in this vignette, the problem is posed, but nothing is done to address it.

Doubts about the value of the relation between HCE and ALP are raised from a different direction in a part of the schoolbook whose ostensible purpose is to cover classical history. The text becomes weary of the labors of the "scribbledehobbles," scholars who pretend to capture the meaning of the past, (275: 22). It wants to lay such endeavors to rest:

> Spell me the chimes. They are tales all tolled. (275: 24)

Instead, it presents a picture of a fading marriage:

> what a world's woe is each's other's weariness waiting to beadroll his
> own properer mistakes, the backslapping gladhander, free of his florid
> future and the other singing likeness, dirging a past of bloody altars,
> gale with a blost to him, dove without gall. And she, of the jilldaw's
> nest who tears up lettereens she never apposed a pen upon. Yet sung of
> love and the monster man. What's Hiccupper to hem or her to Hagaba?
> Ough, ough, brieve kindli! (275: 27–276: 10)

Much later, after HCE and ALP have engaged in their clumsy lovemaking, a
voice will echo the weariness expressed here—"Others are as tired of themselves as you are" (585: 35–6). The textbook presents HCE in the guise that
troubles his wife, a man seeking camaraderie who cannot accept their private
relationship as enough, and it hints at unhappiness to come; a "florid future"
awaits those who are bound for hell, rather than those who join the chorus of
singers in heaven. ALP, seen as a scavenging bird, is not the author of the famous letter (and, we might recall, it turned out to be in Shem's hand); *it* may
have sung of love, but *she* did not. Perhaps, however, she might accept the idea
of the "monster man," another reminder of the dreamer's worries that what is
taken as distinctively valuable, distinctively human, is nothing more than bestial. What, after all, is HCE to his queen? What is she to his concubine? Their
lives are murky and dim, and it is time for them to end.

Reading the schoolbook can thus underscore the importance of the questions about identity and about the value of life, the questions that disturb the
dreamer. It can even make those questions seem intractable. It offers nothing
by way of solution.

What, then, is the point of this education? As the period of study draws to an
end, an exuberant voice—probably that of Shem (who figures here as "Dolph,
dean of idlers" [287: 18])—provides his answer:

> For I've flicked up all the crambs as they crumbed from your table
> um, singing glory allaloserem, cog it out, here goes a sum. So read
> we in must book. It tells. He prophets most who bilks the best. (304:
> 29–305: 2)[8]

The juxtaposition of allusions to scripture with Descartes' candidate for
the fundamental piece of human knowledge, and of both with the idea of
sharp practice in mundane affairs, sends a clear message; that message is
reinforced by the allusions to "crumbs" and to "cramming," and to a competition in which there are winners and losers. This book is a must read
because children need to succeed—survive and reproduce—in a competi-
tive world.

Issy didn't read the book. She didn't need it. Her notes reveal that she has mastered the lessons from "gramma's grammar" (268: 17). Whatever the boys think they are doing, they are engaged in competition for her—even before "wranglers for wringwrowdy wready are" (266: 21–2); the text they study points them toward "the maymeaminning of maimoomeining" and to "pretty Proserpronette whose slit satchel spilleth peas" (267: 3, 10–11).[9]

The boys can study the maxims Issy has internalized, pieces of earthy advice for using sexual attraction in the interests of personal and social advancement; they are told explicitly that "so spake gramma on the impetus of her imperative" (268: 23–4)—surely a sly puncturing of philosophical advice about how to live, advice of the type offered by Nietzsche and Kant. To make her way in the world, a girl needs to lead the lads on without allowing them to reach their intended target. She should "[t]ake the dative with his oblative" but "mind [her] genderous towards his reflexives" (268: 22, 25). Gramma sometimes gives more detail about what the point of the game is and how to play it:

For you may be as practical as is predicable but you must have the proper sort of accident to meet that kind of being with a difference. Flame at his fumbles but freeze on his fist. . . . To me or not to me. Satis thy quest on. Werbungsap! Jeg suis, vos wore a gentleman, thou arr, I am a quean. Is a game over? The game goes on. Cookcook! (269: 13–16, 19–22)

Distilled here is the wisdom of the girls on the street, the fluttering Floras who know how to arouse but also how to avoid the consequences that spell social disaster. They want all eyes, all attention, turned to them. They want to achieve their own satisfactions (the desirable residence in the select neighborhood and so forth [235: 13ff.]) without fulfilling the real quest of those who present themselves as gentlemen—for to allow that would be to risk dishonor and a different kind of life on the street (as a "quean," prostitute). Even among the married bourgeoisie, however, the game will go on, just so long as complaisant husbands never know (or are prepared to turn their gaze away).[10]

Issy's firm grasp on all this is expressed in the note she attaches to "Flame at his fumbles": "Improper frictions is maledictions and mens uration makes me mad" (269 n. 3).[11] The boys, however, need the explicit instructions of the text. Shaun earnestly marks the passage with a single comment about "early notions of acquired rights and the influence of collective tradition upon the individual" (268 right margin), appropriate enough, perhaps, for one who sincerely believes that the book will deliver a form of tradition expressive of the human ascent from bestial struggles, but woefully irrelevant to gramma's worldly advice. Although he is not—yet!—clear on the point of these evening studies, Shem is more closely attuned to what is going on. His marginalia include a reference to "Allma Mathers" (perhaps alluding to the siren charms of Alma Mahler, who managed to fascinate three of the most talented men of the early twentieth century [268 left margin]), as well as a tempo marking "Udante umoroso" (which, besides the evocation of Dante, can be read as a slightly botched attempt to recognize the appropriate pace as Andante amoroso [269, left margin]).

But Shem is quite wrong to think that this is all fun ("umoroso"), for, as the advice from gramma proceeds, it becomes abundantly clear that the competition is very serious, with severe penalties for error, multiple temptations for going astray, and rigorous demands on success. The text is full of warnings, of "Wonderlawn" lost (270: 20), of "mistery of pain" (270: 22), of possibilities of ruin (271: 14–17), of seduction by "the glider that gladdened the girl" (271: 25-6), of the "haunted" "chamber" of "errings" (272: 19–20), of the loss of sexual attraction and of power with age (275: 10–13), of the seductions of the word (278: 13–14). Issy's notes again reveal her command of these grim demands on her. As I have already remarked, she adds her own comment—"hell"—to the prediction of "mistery of pain" (270 n. 3). Apropos of the tempting "glider . . . in the garden Gough gave" (271: 26, 28–9), she admits that she would "whollymost applissiate a nice shiny sleekysilk out of that slippering snake charmeuse"[12] (271 n. 5). To the announcement of the rainbow, promise of peace to Noah, she comments drily, "I'm blest if I can see" (273: 4–5 and n. 2). The inevitable decline of sexual charm prompts her to hypothesize "some bugbear in the gender especially when old which they all soon get to look" (275: n. 3). Acknowledging the self-discipline required to play the game as gramma advises, she conjures up a picture of the sacrifices a girl must make to reveal herself to best advantage: "And if they was setting on your stool as hard as my was she could beth her bothom dolours he'd have a culious impressiom on the diminitive that chafes our ends" (278: n. 2); among the many suggestions of this pithy commentary is the thought that human lives are shaped, not by a providential divinity, but by the female genitalia, and that the shaping is painful. Finally, in assessing the letters of which all the world's in want, love letters and love poetry—perhaps like Stephen Dedalus's villanelle (*Portrait*, 223)—she offers her view of their likely impact and of what they are really worth.

> To be slipped on, to be slept by, to be conned to, to be kept up. And when you're done push the chain. (278: n. 5)

Romantic words are like banana skins on which even gramma's apt pupils may slip; the girl who tucks them under her pillow may commit them to memory ("con" them) and so be deceived ("conned") by them. Issy suggests a coarser, but hygienic, use for the paper on which they are inscribed.

If in this chapter, as in its predecessor, the dominant mood is the debunking of myths, of fantasies about innocent childhood, achievements of high culture, the possibility of human love free of dreams of social advancement or the more primitive struggle for biological reproduction, then Issy appears as the clear-eyed cynic who is far ahead of her slower brothers (especially the earnest Shaun). Yet if Issy sees "life foully" (113: 13), her response is not simply to dwell on the bleak realities she discerns. She knows how to laugh at them—and at herself; even the thought that life isn't merely pain but hell is added "in all frivolity" (270 n. 2). That laughter explodes in a surge of energy in her longest piece of commentary, as she uses all her street wisdom as a springboard for declaring that she will play her part for all it's worth. For, she tells us, "I learned all the runes of the gamest game ever from my old nourse Asa" (279: n. 1, 20–1). She continues with brio, and with more detail:

> This isabella I'm on knows the ruelles of the rut and she don't fear andy mandy. So sing loud, sweet cheeriot, like anagreon in heaven! The good fother with the twingling in his eye will always have cakes in his pocket to bethroat us with for our allmichael good. Amum. Amum. And amum again. For tough troth is stronger than fortuitous fiction and it's the surplice money, oh my young friend and ah me sweet creature, what buys the bed while wits borrows the clothes. (279: n. 1, 30–end)

For all the unpleasant realities behind the "rules of the rut," a clever, spirited girl can manage to navigate her way to pleasure—although she may have to know when to keep quiet (mum) about the dispensations of the "good father." Of course, if Issy expresses the sexual gusto of the young ALP, then the affirmation of life in this note is double-edged, for the presence of "Father Michael" serves as another reminder to the dreamer that older and deeper loves may lie behind the apparent commitments on which his life is centered.

Issy's understanding, I've argued, is much greater than that of her brothers. From this point on, however, her notes appear as the whimsical thoughts of a girl who has learned her lessons and is now at play—although they sometimes express a witty response to the plight of the struggling boys. Her brothers continue to work and "tackle their quarrel" in the style of classical rivals (281: 20).[13] As the official topic of the schoolbook shifts, however, leaving grammar, ancient history, and languages for the apparently less promising terrain of mathematics, Shem's comprehension increases. In a passage reminiscent of *Portrait*'s account of the growth of a child's mind, Joyce presents the emergence of mathematical skills, from simple finger play with numbers, through tricks and games to the tedium of correlating systems of measurement,[14] to the difficulties of algebra and geometry (282: 7–283: 32). The boys are first set the problem of the father, which, as I've already noted, turns out to be insoluble. They turn the page and move on to a new geometrical exercise: they are to "construct ann aquilittoral dryankle," or, as it seems to be rephrased, to "[c]oncoct an equiangular trillitter" (286: 19–20, 21–2).

Shaun, or "Kev" as he appears here, is quite baffled, and Issy notes that his "visage" is "disordered" (286: n. 3).[15] Shem (Dolph), by contrast, has ideas about how to solve the problem, and, at the request of his brother, he launches into an explanation. The task begins with "a mugfull of mud" (286: 31), and

Shaun is (perhaps understandably) nonplussed, not quite seeing the point (287: 3–4). Shem explains that "Anny liffle mud which cometh out of Mam will doob" (287: 7–8), and at this stage we see clearly that the geometrical exercise is the counterpart of the unsolved algebra problem. Just as the boys were previously asked to demonstrate the character of the father (specifically, the sexual activities of the father), now their project is to disclose the sexual organs of their mother. We can recall that the chapter began with a promise of knowledge about origins, and recognize that we're now offered a rather literal fulfillment of that promise. Shaun is still very much in the dark, but Shem has grasped the point.

As appropriate for a geometrical construction, the boys take out their compasses, but, as they start to inscribe, the text breaks off in an interlude (to which I shall return below). When they return to their mathematical work, Shem launches into an enthusiastic demonstration (293: 26). Issy's perceptive note reveals her awareness of the fact that the mathematical texts, from "old Sare Isaac" on, provide "secret stripture" (293: 27, n. 2), and it is not long before Shem is exulting over

> Another grand discobely! After Makefearsome's Ocean. You've actuary entducked one! (294: 12–14)

As he uncovers ("*entdecken*" points to "discover" but there are also clear suggestions of an enthusiastic dive in) the female orifices well known to his father, he breaks into a snatch of Hosty's ballad (294: 25–6). Aware that this is forbidden territory, he enlists Shaun in the trespass:

> O, dear me, that was very nesse! Very nace indeed! And makes us a daintical pair of accomplasses! (295: 25–7)

The construction continues with brio, and ultimately with sexual excitement, as Shem makes his brother see "figuratleavely the whome of your eternal geomater" (296: 31–297: 1).[16]

Poor Shaun finds himself out of his depth, alternately confused and excited—perhaps too excited, since Shem takes the opportunity to tease him:

> And you can haul up that languil pennant, mate. I've read your tunc's dismissage. (298: 6–7)[17]

The taunts continue, as Shem eggs his brother on, and then points out, scornfully, that he is "gaping up the wrong palce" (299: 13–14). Small wonder, then, that Shem's exuberance in discovery provokes Shaun to retaliate. As the demonstration concludes, we return to the first of all sibling conflicts—"And Kev was wreathed with his pother" (303: 15; compare 252: 14).

We shall see below that the fight that erupts here has an unexpected outcome, one that is crucial for the close of this scene and the drama of the next chapter. At this point, however, I want to take stock. Not only has the children's curriculum failed to address the dreamer's questions, not only has it derided pretensions to high culture, but it has exposed knowledge as a vehicle for the competition of life. Shem has triumphed over his brother because he has been quicker to see through the pretense, able to discern the importance of having a clear view of animal functions, and attuned to the power of disclosing shameful secrets. It is a nice irony that this voyage of practical discovery, this awakening of sexual awareness, should be undertaken in the context of mathematics, allegedly the purest of human studies.

A brief coda reinforces the point. As the children wait for release from their homework, congratulating themselves on their studious habits, they launch into a list of titles for children's essays (306: 15–308: 1). The subjects reviewed are reduced to handy morals and useful topics. Shaun, writing in the left margin now, dutifully appends a list of names of the figures studied, whose lives can be condensed into the listed themes—as, for example, Aristotle with "A Place for Everything and Everything in its Place" (306: 17–18). From the perspective of the present, these past individuals only matter insofar as their lives lend themselves to distillation in ways that are currently helpful. The rich detail of an individual existence is lost, rendered meaningless by the passage of time. Only a tag remains—so long as it helps today's students as they learn to "profit most."

The passing of individual lives, occasionally frozen into record by way of some pithy moral, is central to the last disturbing theme of the scene, the theme that comes into prominence as the "day at triv and quad" nears its close (306: 12–13). We leave the children united. Their unity, certainly only temporary, will be needed if they are to consign their parents and the other "old folkers" (308: 22) to the detritus of history, not even to figure on the list of moral exemplars, but simply to drop from view. Issy, Shem, and Shaun have acquired, with greater or lesser ease, bewilderment and humiliation, the practical knowledge that lies under the veneer of culture, and they are now ready to begin the game in their own right. They send down a "nightletter," with "youlldied greetings"—and, as the final line of the chapter indicates, they are determined, "the babes that mean too" (308: 19, 21, 29).

How was the rivalry between the brothers resolved? The high spirits of the geometrical exercise culminated not only in forbidden knowledge but, as we saw, in a bravura performance by Shem at the expense of the more befuddled Shaun. We left them on the verge of a fight. Out of the fight, the predictable overthrow of the bumptious Dolph/Shem, comes a truce. How that occurs, and to what purpose, will occupy us shortly. First, however, it is important to pick up some threads from the interlude that breaks the geometrical demonstration (287: 18–292: 32).

This interlude is ostensibly a characterization of Dolph, one that starts with an emphasis on his weakness and immaturity, in sharp contrast to the confidence displayed in the mathematical demonstration just begun. There are immediate associations with the prosecution's case against Shem (in I-7) and with the traits of Glugg (in II-1). Lecherous, but ineffectual, he is an outsider, one who has landed for the "twicedhecame time" (288: 14), apparently able to use his wits to make a place for himself.

As the narrative proceeds, however, there is an eerie change. Dolph dissolves before us, becoming a much more nebulous figure, occasionally condensed in ways that leave his identity uncertain. At the point of his apparent triumph, there are references that call up a different figure: "Gratings, Mr Dane!" (288: 19); "Wickerworks" (288: 28). Yet the principal subject of this cloudy vignette is not stable for "he" is later associated with the "underlacking of her twentynine shifts" (289: 11–12), recalling the hapless quest of Glugg (II-1). Only when whatever power this character has achieved begins to diminish—"his craft ebbing" (290: 27–8)—do we find the usual indication of the presence of HCE. There are disturbing suggestions of sexual irregularity, of a question about "foundling a nelliza the second" (291: 14); perhaps "man, in shirt, is how he is *più la gonna è mobile*" (292: 11–12).[18] The mind of the protagonist has become a repository of litter from the past, filled with useless driftwood (292: 15–17), and the biography concludes with the suggestion that a judgment must be made, that a line has to be drawn (292: 31–2).

Yet that final assessment is at odds with the dominant tone of the passage. Plainly this figure, Dolph, Shem, Stephen, HCE, has not fulfilled the promise of the high point of his life, the moment when, coming as a stranger, he captivated the natives—as Patrick converted the Irish, as Bloom won Molly, as HCE gained the love of ALP.[19] The meanders of the text indicate how he has lost his way, perhaps at times overly fond,[20] perhaps neglectful of the love to which he is committed for "nuncandtunc and for simper" (290: 23).[21] Certainly there is decline, a "lapse or street ondown" (291: 17), as the river of life flows out "chokered by that batch of grim rushers" (292: 3), but the prevailing tone is one of weary acceptance. There is no precise moment at which one can determine that the promise has been broken, that the life has turned out to be lacking in any significance—"no mouth has the might to set a mearbound" (292: 26)—but at the end it is clear that the judgment of failure must be made.

Dolph does not anticipate this career, of course. He looks forward with gusto to using the knowledge gleaned from his studies in establishing himself, in overthrowing the "old folkers" and shining as his father did once before him. Yet, weak as he is, he needs to charm, to gain allies. This is no time, then, for exuberant teasing of his brother. Instead, they should join forces to win their turn at the big games of life. It turns out that they are impatient, resenting the "dawdling" that prevents them from moving beyond their studies (306: 8–9).

Throughout the boisterous demonstration, Dolph thinks he knows what is important and delights in making sport of his brother. Kev's resentment of the "bladdy bragger" (303: 27) leads to physical violence: "by mercystroke he measured his earth anyway" (303: 27–8). The blow is merciful because, Dolph, knocked down, is recalled to the larger purpose. For the past pages he has been drunk with his own cleverness, enthusiastically displaying his mastery of the forbidden secrets of adulthood. Now, in defeat, he recognizes his need for allies:[22]

> Thanks eversore much, Pointcarried! I can't say if it's the weight you strike me to the quick or that red mass I was looking at but at the present momentum, potential as I am, I'm seeing rayingbogeys rings round me. Honours to you and may you be commended for our exhibitiveness! I'd love to take you for a bugaboo ride and play funfer all if you'd only sit and be the ballasted bottle in the porker barrel. (304: 5–14)

The rainbows Dolph sees are a symbol of peace and compact. Kev is not to be despised or mocked but honored for his part in the acquisition of knowledge. The conciliatory words point directly to the father and to the nature of the enterprise on which the boys are to cooperate. It is time for another "funferall," to be achieved by exposing secrets ("bugaboo"), and, so long as Kev will offer support, Dolph pledges to lead the way.

So they join together in the exuberant camaraderie of young men (305: 3; 306: 7).[23] They are ready, as the next chapter will reveal, to bring about a fall. Yet, as the interlude has reminded us, HCE has been there before them, and they (or Dolph/Shem at least) will follow him in their turn.

The tasks above are as the flasks below; both are devices for coping with life. Study of the schoolbook will prepare the young for the raw competition they face, equipping them to work together to overthrow their elders and make their own turn at "Old Vico Roundpoint" (260: 14–15).[24] Tasks and flasks function at different phases of the life cycle. The tasks are needed to provide the young with knowledge, not the official knowledge of high culture, but the worldly advice "inbourne" in Issy and the secrets of adult sexuality. The flasks provide misty comfort later, when life is descending the "street ondown" and the mind has become a "jetsam litterage" (292: 16). So, even though the schoolbook is hardly what it seems, there is, after all, a "clarience" in the study upstairs that is lacking in the bar below.

To watch the children study, as to watch them at play, advances the dreamer's project by shining a fierce light on aspects of life to which he might have turned for comfort. The Joycean virtues depend on a full confrontation with realities—there is no genuine acceptance or forgiveness if the facts are veiled or sentimentalized. Although ALP has been largely absent from these vignettes, the dreamer must discover her perspective and her voice, must make her movement of tolerance, and must do so knowing that no squalid detail has been concealed. Assessment of whether that is possible—and, if so, how it is possible—has to attend continued probing of the trajectory of a life. The light of the upstairs study has been unforgiving, making plain that we are on a long descent in the large movement of Parts II–IV.

We have *heard* plenty about the fall of HCE. The education of his sons has prepared us to *witness* it. So we go down from the "clarience" of the study to the crepuscular atmosphere of the bar.

14

FROM LIFF AWAY

It is late and there has been plenty to drink. Out of the "murk of the mythelated" comes a cacophony of voices. One of the speakers is HCE. Other voices belong to the customers in the bar, or to HCE's ancient counterpart—and nemesis— the Sackerson figure, lurking here as "sutchenson" (315: 30) or "Pukkelsen" (316: 1; 319: 23). Yet others emanate from the radio, apparently one of the up-to-date attractions of HCE's inn (309: 14–15).

Stories are told, old and familiar stories that belong to the standard repertoire of the raconteur. Prominent among them are a tale about a ship's captain and a tailor and the anecdote of how an Irishman, Buckley, shot the Russian General.[1] The first story swirls through the early parts of the scene; the second dominates a subsequent episode; it is told dramatically by a radio comedy team, Butt and Taff, readily identifiable as Shem and Shaun, who work with the harmony achieved at the end of their studies.

Butt and Taff prepare the third phase, the hunting and condemnation of HCE. HCE is forced to defend himself, but angry voices denounce him and vilify him. Their chorus culminates in a new ballad, which, like Hosty's original, celebrates his passing. As the exultant, accusatory voices depart, a brief coda shows us the defeated HCE, having drunk the dregs from the glasses left by his customers, collapsed on a box in the corner of the bar.

So much, but not much more, is clear. Perhaps because we are now in the depths of the dreamer's night, perhaps because the voices are slurred with drink, the details are even hazier than is usual with the *Wake*. To cite just one example, the opening story of the captain and the tailor seems to have no fixed cast of characters and to proceed in incompatible directions—sometimes the commissioned suit doesn't seem to fit, at other times the captain departs without paying, in yet other versions the captain shoots three tailors.[2] More complexities arise because the narration blurs sometimes into the suggestion that the denizens of the bar are in fact a ship's crew, sometimes into the tale of the Flying Dutchman, and sometimes into the account of HCE's arrival in Dublin (and thence to the history of his wooing of ALP). Frequently it is hard to identify the speaker—or even to tell whether the speech emanates from the voices in the bar or if it is from a character (which character?) within the story. To make matters even worse, there's an apparent, almost obsessive, intention to locate the speaker by deploying pronouns, or even descriptive phrases; the narrative is peppered with variants on "he sazd" or "sazd he," but there is no way of relating "he" to any character in the story; and, when we are offered a name, "Kersse," or "his wife's hopesend" (320: 23), it seems that enormous effort will be needed to attach it to any of the characters who have previously been introduced.

So one might think that coming to terms with this chapter will involve just that activity of puzzle-solving I rejected in Chapter 5: surely we need to find out who these characters are, who is speaking when, and just how the dream story goes. Without doing that, how can we—or the dreamer—learn anything more than a bare summary would provide?

I suggest we pose a different question. We have already explored the fall of HCE and have heard him abused at some length (as for example at 70: 27–73: 22). What more can be added to the earlier gossip, to the trials and sentences of Part I? How is the dreamer's attempt to allay anxieties advanced by turning, yet again, to the uncertainties that attend HCE's fall?

My answer comes in two parts. First, and more obviously in light of the chapters that precede it, this version of HCE's passing introduces his sons as principals. Their knockabout comedy version of the anecdote of Buckley and the Russian General begins the hunting down of HCE, and they, of course, specifically Shaun, are to take his place.[3] HCE's demise is thus framed in a standard pattern of history; the young grow in knowledge and power and seize control from their fathers. In particular, as this chapter will demonstrate, HCE was once a wandering outsider, whose youthful vigor won him a fair prize, and he, in his turn, must now watch haplessly as vigorous youth takes from him what he values. The theme of the outsider, the exile, the wanderer, who seeks inclusion permeated the children's game (II-1), and the arrival of the nomad was seen as a triumph in the interlude of the geometrical demonstration (287–92). HCE's fall is a victory, both for those who have resented his early success—as Hosty's ballad already made apparent (46: 13–26)—and for the nomadic son (Shem) whose life may be expected to follow the same trajectory.[4] Taken in this way, the chapter offers a perspective on HCE that can satisfy the dreamer's determination to face reality without blinking, to come to terms with the inevitability that youthful promise will wither and life decompose into a "jetsam litterage" (292: 16).

A second, and more significant, answer can be achieved by formulating the dreamer's problem as one of finding a stable identity, one that will satisfy the demanding impulses within him while also allowing for its evaluation as worthwhile. Can he find, in HCE, a reconciliation of the conflicts of ideals and aspirations he discovers in himself? Read as a response to this question, the chapter is a somber display of impossibility, for it shows HCE falling apart before us. There is no stable self he can present, no consistent version of the story of his life he can offer, no single voice with which he can speak. He is indeed "more mob than man" (261: 21–2), and the mob is divided, fickle, uncertain in its purpose, united only in opposition and in carnival delight at the fall of "Mocked Majesty" (380: 4–5).

Hence, in large measure, the voices we hear have no definite source. They may belong to impulses within HCE—for even hostile raillery can be self-accusation—or to others with whom he seeks, but fails to find, community. Nor can the individual stories, most especially those that would connect with readings of his own life, have any canonical version. They must all be present in irresoluble cacophony.

Part II should have accustomed us to Joyce's multilevel narration. We have seen how Glugg's exclusion can simultaneously be Shem's (and Stephen's) exile (II-1), how the official learning may diverge from the announced curriculum, how knowledge may be the vehicle of competition, and, ultimately, the spur to truce (II-2). In II-3, however, the shifts among levels are far more frequent and more abrupt, the identities far more fluid, and the demands on verbal association more extensive. Our guiding threads must be the dreamer's resolve to confront the realities of human life, his search for an identity worth having, and the internal tensions that leave HCE at the end with the stale dregs and leavings of a hostile community. Part I has acquainted us with HCE's many-sidedness (126: 10–139: 13), but we shall now discover in detail how the discordant elements within him cause his failure and disintegration. That demonstration is appropriate exactly at this point, when the shortcomings of Shem's uncompromised commitment have been exposed and when the muddle of HCE has again emerged as a serious possibility for the dreamer. To rise to the challenge of seeing him "foully," he must be anatomized yet more closely.

As I have already suggested, the chapter opens with a line that alludes to Odysseus's encounter with Polyphemus and thus recalls the "Cyclops" episode of *Ulysses*. Once again, we are in a tavern, and, once again, an outsider will face fury and contempt. The connection is further underscored by the technique of two long paragraphs, offering gigantesque characterizations first of the radio receiver and second of the uncorking of a bottle (309: 11 ff.; 310: 22 ff.).[5] We are then pitched into the sea stories that pervade the first episode.

We begin, apparently, not with a story, but with a piece of stage setting: there's a newly arrived ship with a Norwegian captain ("Norweeger's capstan" [311: 9]), who appears in close association with a "toyler" (311: 6) and *perhaps* with someone named "Kersse." The next paragraph starts with an elusive pronoun: "So he sought with the lobestir claw of his propencil the clue of the wickser in his ear" (311: 10–11); evidently HCE—"Earwicker," "the only man was ever known could eat the crushts of lobsters" (as ALP proudly describes him [624: 35–6])—is before us; but how does he, or "he," connect to the captain and the tailor just introduced? The puzzle deepens when the next paragraph introduces an unexplained plural reference: "they would deal death to a drinking" (311: 15). "They" may easily be HCE's thirsty customers—or possibly the mariners from the recently arrived ship, who hope to celebrate their safe arrival in port.

At this point, the voice of a raconteur begins (or continues) a story. Joyce uses his advertised device for quoted speech (the initial dash)[6]:

> —Then sagd he to the ship's husband. And in his translatentic norjan-keltian. Hwere can a ketch or hook alive a suit and sowterkins? (311: 21–2)

It looks as though we (and the storyteller's audience) are going to hear another favorite anecdote of Joyce's father about a Norwegian captain who comes to Dublin and seeks a suit of clothes.[7] The traditional plot takes the captain to be humpbacked; when the suit fails to fit, the captain berates the tailor for his inability to sew, to which the tailor responds that the misfit is the captain's fault, for his hump makes a good fit impossible.[8]

But the tale immediately deviates quite radically from the folk pattern, introducing a lady who seems to want—or whose master seems to want— a "peer of trouders under the pattern of a cassack" (311: 28). There are new figures—"Mengarments," "neighbour Norreys" (311: 30, 35). The captain supposedly sails off without paying and embarks on a long voyage: "seven sailend sonnenrounders was he breastbare to the brinabath" (312: 6–7). The storyteller concludes with an account of the trials of this seven-year voyage, and the audience seems to offer a comment on the performance:

> And the tides made, veer and haul, and the times marred, rear and fall, and, holey bucket, dinned he raign!
> —Hump! Hump! bassed the broaders-in-laugh with a quick pid-dysnip that wee halfbit a second.
> —I will do that, sazd Kersse, mainingstaying the rigout for her wife's lairdship. Nett sew? they hunched back at the earpicker. (312: 10–16)

At this stage, it should be clear that any consistent set of identifications is hard to find and that the boundaries between scene and story are highly permeable.[9]

In fact, I think that (at least) five stories, or vignettes, are already in play and that their superposition is critical to the dreamwork of the chapter. One of the stories is the traditional folk anecdote; another is the variant in which the outsider exploits the local merchant and sails away without paying. Besides these, the closing words of the narration, "dinned he raign," recall a vignette from I-1, the tale of Jarl van Hoother and the prankquean. Here, the protagonist, Jarl, a prefiguration of HCE with two twin sons and a daughter, is visited three times by the prankquean, who kidnaps one of the twins on each of her first two visits, arousing angry cries from Jarl (cries that are echoed in the calls after the Norwegian captain); after each kidnapping she goes on a "forty years' walk" with "rain, rain, rain" (21–2).[10]

Even more obviously, the tempestuous voyage recalls the story of the Flying Dutchman, condemned to put into port only once every seven years and doomed to continue forever unless he can be saved by the love of a woman. The possibility of female salvation suggests the role ALP has played in the vignettes that have previously traced HCE's life. Like the Norwegian captain he has come from overseas, and, like the Dutchman, he hopes for the possibility that a woman's love will end his troubles. The connection is deepened by the apparently irrelevant reference to a lady, and the allusion to a "cassack," suggesting the background presence of "Father Michael" and the dreamer's concerns about the secrets of his wife's romantic past.[11]

Before we consider what the point of juxtaposing all these stories might be, it is worth pondering the acts of storytelling that occur in the bar. If "Hump! Hump!" is a response to the raconteur's performance, then it's plausible that the story is told by HCE—one of his possible names is "Humphrey" (30: 2), and ALP's accounting of his "buckly shuit" notes the cost of the "bulge" (620: 4, 5). The customers offer appreciation, probably hoping for a new (free?) round of drinks; HCE agrees, and they "[hunch] back at the earpicker" (312: 16). In this case, the "Kersse" whose agreement has prompted the appreciation is HCE, so that HCE is connected not only with the Norwegian captain (as we might have expected) but with the tailor, too.

HCE, a man with a hump who once came from abroad to Dublin, is telling a story about a Norwegian captain, a man with a hump. In previous vignettes, HCE has not been articulate, and we might expect that his stammer would prevent him from being a convincing raconteur. Why, then, would a poor performer venture a story that seems designed to call attention to his own misshapen physique? Perhaps in order to join in the conviviality, to fit in with the society he has joined. Like Bloom in Barney Kiernan's, HCE may have to pick his way carefully, even though this is his inn and his bar.[12]

Bloom is not—or is not regarded as—a gifted raconteur. There is a moment in *Ulysses* where he ventures a story. As the carriage bearing the mourning party for Paddy Dignam rolls toward the cemetery, Martin Cunningham and Jack Power spot an unpopular Jew. It is an embarrassing moment for Bloom, who begins, "with sudden eagerness," to tell a supposedly amusing story about the stinginess of "Reuben J." Unskilled at setting it up, he is first interrupted by the practiced wit of Simon Dedalus, and then, as he tries to continue, "Martin Cunningham thwarted his speech rudely" (*Ulysses*, 92–3). This is uncharacteristic behavior, for Cunningham is generally helpful and tries to steer Bloom out of trouble. Indeed, when the Citizen begins to look menacing, he maneuvers Bloom out of the pub and into a carriage, and when Bloom attempts to answer the insults hurled at him, he takes control by telling Bloom, "That will do," and urging the driver to move away (*Ulysses,* 335, 336). Why, then, does Cunningham interrupt Bloom's effort at a joke?

I think Cunningham intervenes because he understands Bloom as attempting to distance himself from his ethnic heritage and sees this behavior as a clumsy effort at ingratiation. By taking charge, and telling the story better than Bloom could, he avoids a potential embarrassment. Like Bloom, HCE is concerned to join the community to which he has come; unlike Bloom, he has no sympathetic figure to guide him away from troublesome exposure.

Five stories and an act of storytelling—what common features can we find? Setting aside, for the moment, the tale of Jarl van Hoother and the prankquean, each scenario involves an outsider who seeks something. The Dutchman is doomed to endless wandering unless he can find love when he touches shore; HCE has come to Dublin, seeking a new home, and, having won the love of ALP, he tries to fit himself into the local community; his storytelling in the bar seems to be a continued effort to forge bonds with those among whom he lives; in the original version of the story, the Norwegian captain seeks a suit that fits, and, in the tailor's judgment, he fails because it is impossible to fit him; in the variant HCE first tells, he absconds with what he has sought. All these simple plots reinforce one another. HCE, the outsider with the hump, may be impossible to fit—he may be seen as misshapen from the perspective of those he hopes to join. The response to his storytelling—"Hump! Hump!"—may signal his status as an outsider and foreshadow his rejection. In winning ALP, he may be viewed as having stolen something from his newly adopted land. Perhaps, like a thief, he must leave, to wander, unfulfilled, forever.

The tale of Jarl and the prankquean goes differently, for here it seems as though HCE himself is threatened with loss, that a child will be snatched from him. Yet, as I have suggested, HCE can play either main part in the drama— he can be the triumphant newcomer or the tailor. Indeed, we might expect, from the fusion of his life-course with that of Shem (287–92), that, at different stages, he will find himself in each role. So it will prove. For as this story develops, the customers request a sequel:

> —That's all murtagh purtagh but whad ababs his dopter? sissed they
> who were onetime ungkerls themselves . . . (314: 30–1)

As HCE wooed ALP and took her from her father, so now (no longer a "jungkerl"—or young man) he is threatened with the loss of his daughter—and the suitor, apparently, is another returned outsider, a Shem figure, a "butcheler artsed out of Cullege Trainity" (315: 1–2). Much later, after the story has been told in further mutations, the connection will be made by juxtaposing the tailor, the "dotter of his eyes," and the prankquean (372: 3–4).[13] Later still, in the mocking of HCE that culminates in the exit of his customers, he will be baited on the point: "Umpthump, Here Innkeeper, it's the doatereen's wednessmorn!" (376: 10–11); and his attention will be drawn to the sexual fulfillment she will find (376: 19–24).[14]

There are two further facets of these scenarios that bear on their significance for the dreamer. First is the presence of ALP within the versions of the stories, initially fleeting (312: 20–1), later more prominent in a fusion of the canonical version of the captain-tailor anecdote and the Flying Dutchman myth (318: 12–13), eventually central to a full-scale account of the courtship and wedding of HCE with his wife (325–30).[15] Second is the periodic emergence of an apparent traitor, who figures in the bar as Pukkelsen (316: 1; 319: 23). When HCE is temporarily outside (apparently in the outhouse), Pukkelsen offers "in the fornicular" a series of derogatory remarks about the host—"The kersse[16] of Wolafs on him, shitateyar"—inspiring the other customers to laughter (319: 23–36). Pukkelsen also appears within the stories, when, in the context of resentment of the wanderer's pursuit of local girls, the narrator fulminates: "The goragorridggorballyed pushkalsson, he sazd, with his bellows pockets fulled of potchtatos and his fox in a stomach" (323: 16–18); the pocket with potato connects this version of the Pukkelsen figure to Bloom and hence to HCE, and that link is reinforced through the distortion of "gorbellied" to include a Russian word for "hunchback."[17] Even earlier, in the wake of Pukkelsen's first appearance,[18] the animosity against outsiders encompasses an unusual oath—"the other swore his eric"; in Wagner's version of the Dutchman story, Eric is the admirer of Senta, the girl who pledges herself to saving the wanderer; his jealousy drives him to prevent their union.

Central to these swirling stories is the pattern of a life. A young man, like Shem, Stephen Dedalus, the young HCE—or like Joyce himself—leaves his original home, refusing to follow in the traditional paths laid out by his native culture. He woos and wins a wife, and the marriage becomes one of the centers of his identity. There is another, the aspiration to chart his own course that originally drove him from the homeland of his youth. Because of that aspiration, he will live as an outsider in his adopted place. But the marriage he desires is not one cut off from the surrounding community. He also seeks acceptance for himself and his family, integration within a broader home. He needs to fit.

The variant stories dramatize the incoherence of the identity the dreamer yearns for. Sometimes the resolution is simple—the Dutchman and the absconding captain fail because they are doomed to homelessness. Far more interesting are the versions that start with apparent triumph, with the celebration of a wedding. What happens beyond? Perhaps the protagonist—HCE—continues to live as an outsider in his new environment, viewed, like the captain in the canonical story, as a man who can't fit. Or perhaps he achieves what appears to be more successful integration—despite the fact that the superficially pleasant relations with those around him are underlain by resentment and by hopes that he will fail and fall. To the extent that he is successful in fitting in, he may come to be aware that his youthful energy and freedom have been lost, that he is confined in conventions as little of his own devising as those from which he once escaped. Feeling that confinement, he may be driven to express what he takes to be freedom—he may be tempted by the sirens in the park. Or, perhaps, more thoroughly entrenched in adopted customs, he may resist those who challenge him and who threaten to disrupt relationships he values, young men like his younger self who wrest daughters from fathers.

The dreamer seeks a successful resolution, one that integrates the different aspirations expressed within HCE. Because the most promising stories are those that proceed to marriage, and beyond, it is worth exploring a few of these.[19]

Among the advance indicators of HCE's rejection—the hunt that will occur in the third episode of this chapter—is an allusion to a well-known hunting song, "D'ye ken John Peel?" (322: 14–15). Before this, a returning figure—Kersse—is met with insulting commands:

—Take off thatch whitehat . . .
—Tick off that whilehot, you scum of a botch, . . .
—Tape oaf that saw foull and sew wrong, welsher, you suck of a thick, stock and the udder, and confiteor yourself . . . (322: 1, 5, 8–9)

The repetition of a vaudeville punch line, "Take off that white hat!" recalls the initial attempt to portray HCE as a much-loved member of the Dublin community; this was one of the (ambiguous) lines with which "the catholic assemblage" greeted his allegedly magisterial presence (32: 23, 25). The insults offered here are plainly directed at him, partly in his guise as an incompetent tailor, but more significantly as a cheat ("welsher"), an outsider, possibly not even human ("suck . . . of the udder"), and as a member of an alien culture ("confiteor" suggests a need to be brought to the true—catholic—religion).[20] Most obvious and direct, however, is the use of the punch line to insinuate that HCE is a pretender, one who sports a "white hat," symbol of virtue, to which he is not entitled.

Yet his urge to settle and to fit in is evident. Another voice from HCE expresses his hopes for a family:

I wish auspicable thievesdayte for the stork dyrby. It will be a thousand's a won paddies. And soon to bet. On drums of bliss. With hapsalap troth, hipsalewd prudity, hopesalot honnessy, hoopsaloop luck. After when from midnights unwards the fourposter harp quartetto. (325: 6–10)

In fact, the auspices, as just presented by the radio weather forecast and news bulletin, are quite mixed—announcing a "[g]iant crash in Aden," along with the "abbroaching nubtials" and the "[b]urial of Lifetenant-Groevener

Hatchett" (324: 36; 325: 1); the crash and the juxtaposition of wedding and burial do not bode well, but there is a suggestion of suspension of hostilities between the outsider and the local community, a "burying of the hatchet." HCE's voice begins optimistically, predicting that the "stork derby" will bring many sons, genuine Irish boys ("paddies"), begotten in bliss.[21] But the definite prediction ("will be") shifts to something more guarded ("hopesalot") and a closing recognition of the need for good fortune ("hoopsaloop luck"). We shall, of course, eventually hear what transpires in the marriage bed, from the perspective of each member of the "harp quartetto."

Marriage and membership in the community come at a price, for the newcomer must conform to the ideals and standards at the core of local traditions. If the "rude hunnerable Humphrey" (325: 27–8) is to be brought "into the shipfolds of our quadrupede island" (325: 31–2), he must abandon his alien ways and submit to the rites of right religion. A voice addresses him and makes it clear what needs to be done:

> I popetithes thee, Ocean, sayd he, Oscarvaughther, sayd he, Erievik-kingr, sayd he. . . . (326: 6–7)
>
> . . . out of the hellsinky of the howtheners and be danned to ye, sayd he, into our roomyo connellic relation . . . (326: 12–14)

The stranger must be baptized and given his name (thus providing a third version to accompany those of I-2), brought into religious conformity and the social norms of Ireland.[22] Yet there are clear signs of resistance:

> —Nansense, you snorsted? he was haltid considerable agenst all religions overtrow . . . (326: 21–2)

The skeptical voice asks why HCE would be "daadooped by Priest Gudfodren of the sacredhaunt suit" (326: 24). If the outsider is to conform, then it will require him to abandon prior convictions and to sacrifice the desire for freedom that originally drove him from his homeland. Moreover, if he does conform, there are likely always to be doubts about the genuineness of his conversion—so that critical voices may demand that he expose his true colors and make a proper "confiteor."

Whatever the demands, HCE submits. There is a grand celebration, worthy of the "height of his life" (309: 3), with Dublin aglow (329: 14). The voice describing the scene seems exuberant, but hints at trouble. For the local populace may not be rejoicing at the union of HCE and ALP, but rather at the wedding he dreads, that of his daughter; we hear a rumor that "old dummydeaf" has been seen at the festivities, lagging behind (329: 26–8); and the exclamation "Nevertoletta!" conjures Nuvoletta, the Issy figure of the fable of the Mookse and the Gripes (157: 8). Most ominously, the perspective of the local onlookers on the occasion, "when the Cap and Miss Coolie were roped" (330: 18–19), is expressed in a one-word comment: "Rolloraped" (330: 20).

What really concerns the dreamer, of course, is what occurs after this, whether this marriage proves stable and fulfilling, whether HCE can find a way to retain his independence while integrating himself into the community. The urgent question echoes the demand of the inquiring washerwoman (I-8): "But tellusit allasif wellasits end" (331: 6). Familiar worries surface. Quite early in the story of courtship and wedding, it becomes evident that ALP's charms are well appreciated, especially, perhaps, when she is "titting out through her droemer window for the flyend of a touchman" (327: 22–3).[23] Even more disturbing is a foreshadowing of ALP's complaint that she has not been understood (627: 14–15):

> making every Dinny dingle after her down the Dargul dale and (wait awhile, blusterbuss, you're marchadant too forte and don't start furlan your ladins till you've learned the lie of her landuage!) ... (327: 17–20)

Learning the "lie of her landuage" may involve following the course of the river back to the "dinkel dale," home of the "heremite," Michael, ALP's first love (327: 17, 18).

If HCE must fret over his wife's romantic past, wondering whether the marriage is the height of his bride's life, he also has to acknowledge the limitation of his own freedom. With his distinctive stammer, the groom assesses his situation:

> Cawcaught. Coocaged. (329: 13)

The years of marriage will see their decline—"He's herd of hoarding and her faiths is altared" (331: 3). He grows heavy and gross, as well as deaf (332: 19–20), while her eye proves "changeable" (332: 21–2). Perhaps out of disappointment, out of boredom, out of a sense of failing powers, out of a need to break free of convention and assert the independence of his youth, the marriage veers in a dangerous direction:

> there was a little theogamyjig incidence that hoppy-go-jumpy Junuary morn when he colluded with the cad ... (332: 24–5)

The story is interrupted by the visit of the aged maid-of-all-work, Kate, to the bar, with her mistress's request that HCE shut up shop and come to bed.[24] So, at the point when the dreamer is inquiring about the course of this marriage, HCE's continued devotion is put to the test. ALP is "a wanton for De Marera to take her genial glow to bed" (334: 5). He declines, apparently in the interest of continuing to serve his clientele. The need to ingratiate himself, to fit in, proves paramount, although the dreamer already has plenty of clues that the effort will fail.

The dreamer has wanted a happy ending, so much so that traditional fairy-tale formulas are invoked to provide one:

> Noo err historyend goody. .... for he put off the ketyl and they made three (for fie!) and if hec dont love alpy then lad you annoy me. (332: 1, 2–4)

Bare declarations of "happily ever after" will not work, however, and, once the intervention of Kate has displayed the mundane realities of the marriage, the dark allusions become ever more ominous. From the glancing reference to the encounter with the cad, the voices proceed to an account of a family outing in the "right place . . . by peep o'skirt or pipe a skirl" (335: 9–10), and then, more explicitly, to a tale of "twee cweamy wosen," a "stotterer," and "three longly lurking lobstarts" (337: 16, 18, 20–21). In parallel with this the resonances of the hunting theme (and the hunting song) become ever more urgent, as do the references to Buckley and the Russian general. The dreamer's search for a resolution, a happy ending, seems to produce only a "grimm grimm tale" (335: 5).

We are told that the couple have reached "his awebrume hour, her sere Sahara of sad oakleaves" (336: 14–15). It is time for a new start, although whether this is a new start for HCE and ALP, a new start for the dreamer in the quest for resolution, or a new beginning after the passing of the "old folkers" (308: 22) isn't determined. The attempt to probe the marriage is temporarily exhausted, but the customers in the bar need entertainment. They are not shy in their demands:

> We want Bud. We want Bud Budderly. We want Bud Budderly boddily.
> (337: 32)

The radio presents a popular show.[25]

The official story, apparently a favorite of the clientele (338: 2–3), centers on an Irish soldier, Buckley, serving in the Crimean war. He finds himself in a position to observe a Russian general defecating in the field and raises his rifle to shoot. With the general in his sights, he feels compassion and is unable to squeeze the trigger, but, when the general reaches for a clod of turf with which to wipe himself, the feeling evaporates and he shoots, successfully dispatching his victim.

Butt and Taff, smooth crosstalk artists, present this tale with enthusiasm, weaving into it plenty of references to associate the unfortunate general with HCE and to link the story to the alleged misconduct in Phoenix Park. It is not hard to identify Butt and Taff with Shem and Shaun, although the unity that emerged at the end of II-2 and that melded their voices is preserved here—indeed, once the tale has been successfully told, they fuse completely (354: 8). The effect of the story is to provoke the hunting, vilification, and disintegration of HCE, bringing, with a vengeance, the "youlldied" greetings promised by the "nightletter" (308: 19, 21).

The status of HCE, outsider, enemy, perhaps even subhuman ("suck . . . of the udder" [322: 8–9]), is reinforced by the enthusiastic jingoism of the performance. Butt and Taff are good Irish boys, upholders of the proper religion. The target of their story—and of Buckley's rifle—is plainly HCE.

Erminia's capecloaked hoodoodman! First he s s st steppes. Then he st stoo stoopt. (339: 20)

the Riss, the Ross, the sur of all Russers, as my farst is near to hear and my sackend is meet to sedon while my whole's a peer's aureolies. (340: 35–341: 1)[26]

As Buckley watches the general/HCE, he invokes the true (catholic) religion, contrasting it with his target's "lewdbrogue reciping his cheap cheateary gospeds to sintry and santry and sentry and suntry" (343: 31–2).

He doesn't simply see but also smells. The stench appears to move him to some sense of animal community with this gastrically disturbed dignitary (he recognizes "the travailings of his tommuck" [344: 34–5]). Buckley mingles his own prayers with those of the foreigner and loses the will to shoot: "I adn't the arts to" (345: 2–3).

The comedy continues with reminiscences of the camaraderie of "good tomkeys years" (347: 10) spent in military service, which Butt recalls with "platoonic love," raising his glass with, or to, "bycorn spirits fuselaiding" (348: 8, 11). As he proceeds, the soldiers turn into the familiar watchers in the park:

> for we were all under that manner barracksers on Kong Gores Wood together, thurkmen three, with those khakireinettes, our miladies in their toileries, the twum plumyumnietcies . . . (348: 20–3)

The stage has been set for the appearance of HCE within the story of Buckley and the general.

The screen on which the customers watch the unfolding of the drama displays the "jesuneral of the russuates" (349: 20–1), a hybrid figure, part military, part religious. He is accompanied by the resplendent symbols of his high position, including, ominously, "the cross of Michelides Apaleogos" (349: 23), suggesting that he is the successor of a greater precursor (Father?) Michael.[27] Yet instead of engaging in a solemn blessing or a triumphal procession, he breaks down into apology and confession. Mortifying himself because of his flaws and sexual irregularities, apparently performed not only "in the middenst of the garerden" but "jolly well ruttengenerously olyovyover the ole blucky shop" (350: 2, 6), he imposes particular chastisement on his sensory organs.

Butt continues his enthusiastic recollections of the military life, weaving together the account of the incident in the park and the anecdote of Buckley's shot. Butt and Buckley speak with one voice, first suggesting that the "urssian gemenal" arouses ire because of his "brichashert offensive" toward "them scharlot runners" (352: 1, 5, 6). He is maddened by the "fly fly flurtation" and

> my oreland for a rolvever, sord, by the splunthers of colt and bung goes the enemay the Percy rally got me . . . I shuttm, missus, . . . Hump to dump! (352: 9–10, 14, 15)

Under the prodding of Taff, Butt waxes in enthusiasm and brings the story of Buckley to its standard ending. In this version, the general is guilty of an "instullt to Igorladns" (353: 18–19); he has been defacing "ourloud's lande, beheaving up that sob of tunf for to claimhis, for to wolpimsolff."[28] Buckley's shot avenges the insult.

Throughout this exuberant, often overexcited, dialogue, the Shem figure, Butt, has been sharply distanced from the persona of I-7 or the exile, Glugg, of II-1. He continues the trajectory on which he was set in the reconciliation of II-2 (304: 5), joining forces with his brother (here the calmer straight man, Taff) to expose the flaws and weaknesses of age. It is significant that, as they emerge from the shadow of their father, the boys become one (354: 8–10). This moment of union is pivotal in the dreamer's search. For, as the previous vignettes have defined Shem far more clearly than Shaun, exploring the possibilities the artist-critic-outsider presents, from this point on, Shaun will be the dominant presence. He will embody the succession to HCE, and, through him, the dreamer will probe the value of conformity and tradition.

That, as we shall see, is the work of Part III. For now, however, the cross-talk comedy has juxtaposed the alleged dignity of the general with his lapses, his splendor with his most unpleasant animal functions, and, above all, his status as an outsider with the piety and patriotism of Buckley. The white hat has been taken off (or shot off [10: 19–21, 352: 11–12]), the decorations have been removed, so that the figure of these stories stands, or squats, before us as a "naked, bare fork'd animal," guilty and weak. He might pretend to be one of us, but the pretense is now exposed.

The customers appreciate the performance and what has been revealed by it. They comment:

> Shutmup. And bud did down well right. And if he sung dumb in his
> glass darkly speech lit face to face on allaround. (355: 8–9)

HCE, who has previously been suspected, "seen through a glass darkly," has now been presented for what he is, perceived "face to face." So there comes a clear call to the hunt. They are to "harrow the hill for to rout them rollicking rogues from" (355: 16–17), and then, as victors, to take back the prize: "After their battle thy fair bosom" (355: 19–20). Old and disgraced, HCE will lose the love he once won—like the tailor in one of the stories, he will forfeit his daughter.

A voice, marked as that of HCE by the familiar stammer (355: 21), attempts an apologia. He suggests that his faults are those of the human condition:

> We all, for whole men is lepers, have been nobbut wonterers in that
> chill childerness which is our true name after the allfaulters (mug's
> luck to them!) and, bespeaking of love and lie detectors in venuvarities,

whateither the drugs truth of it, was there an iota of from the faust to the lost. (355: 33–356: 1)

Like lepers, we are all doomed to lose feeling, to inhabit a chill world, one in which we wander and want the love that time has eroded. All of us are faulty, all of us continue to yearn for love, for a variety of loves, for something with which we can palliate, or drug, our sense of loss. Yet it must all be illusory, inevitably detected and exposed, for there is no truth to the possibility of re-demption through love.[29]

This plea for understanding, urged on the basis of common humanity, seeks to portray HCE as guilty only of a near-universal failing. It is immedi-ately juxtaposed with a comment about the importance of individuality—not apparently offered by HCE—the "farst wriggle from the ubivence" (356: 12) is to find our own identity, to discover our distinctive way, and not simply to fall into the patterns provided by others. The young HCE left his native place, with its own traditions, to make himself anew. Can he both endorse that individualistic impulse and simultaneously plead for community with those around him?

His speech resumes, starting with a nostalgic recollection of his youth, as if HCE were dimly aware of the conflict among the parts of himself. It then veers abruptly in a different direction, seeming to commend a book he has been reading. The advertisement already suggests that there may be contrary opinions about the legitimacy of its publication, for HCE hopes that it will command "the widest circulation and a reputation coextensive with its merits when inthrusted into safe and pious hands upon so edifying a mission" (356: 28–30). He tells us that this book is "ambullished with expurgative plates" (356: 30–1), nicely ambiguous between describing the offended puritanical response and noting the important presence of illustrations. Illustrations, it appears, are the work of an "early woodcutter" who turns out to be "Mr Aubeyron Bird-slay" (356: 36; 357: 2–3). HCE has been looking at Beardsley's illustrated edi-tion of Wilde's *Salome*, with its infamous woodcuts. But what relevance does this have either to the apologetic pleading he has begun or to the concerns of the hunters who are massed against him?

Beardsley and Wilde are outsiders who challenge the conventional sexual standards of their day, and, in defending them, HCE is responding obliquely to the attacks on his own predilections.[30] Yet the invocation of the particular work, *Salome*, also serves to connect HCE with the aging Herod, in need of sexual arousal through the strip-tease of a younger woman. That connection is underscored with an evocation of the feast at which Herod makes the bargain with his stepdaughter:

Not the king of this age could richlier eyefeast in oreillental longuard-ness with alternate nightjoys of a thousand kinds but one kind. (357: 17–19)

The further allusion to the story of Scheherazade, as well as the pun on "oriental" and "O'Reilly," recalls the gossip of I-2 and the "uncontrollable nighttalkers," one of whom is "Skertsiraizde" (32: 7–8), who will figure as the girls in the park.

HCE began his defense by suggesting that his sins are those to which all flesh is heir. In summoning his youth, he implicitly contrasts the vigorous courtship that won ALP with the decline in his sexual responsiveness. Like Herod—and, he claims, like all men who feel the failing of their powers—he needs arousal by means that the conventional standards forbid. He protests on behalf of the book because he does not want to see it as a crude stimulant but as something that will enable him to recapture feelings that are no longer readily generated. So the attempt to renew his amatory life percolates through this speech with an ever increasing frequency of suggestive vocabulary. His perusal has led to his "warmest venerections" (356: 33); he alludes to dubious forms of sexual contact (357: 10–15); and he has been stimulated by printed images, viewed in the privacy of the privy:

> I have been idylly turmbing over the loose looves leaflefts jaggled casu-
> allty on the lamatory . . . (357: 20–2)

All of this, he insists, is entirely understandable, for the impulses he is confessing are parts of our common humanity, "natural sins" inculcated in us by "the Author of Nature" (357: 28, 29). The only course available to us if we are determined to avoid them is self-mutilation (HCE recalls Origen's extreme measure for avoiding sexual temptation)—we can become "manmade Eonochs Cunstuntonopolies" (357: 30). Nor have his yearnings caused significant harm, whether consisting of exposure "for relieving purposes in our trurally virvir vergitabale (garden)" or brief glimpses through the "shylight window" (357: 33–4; 358: 1). HCE closes his defense with a Whitmanesque protestation: "I, my good grief, I am, I am big altoogooder" (358: 15–16).

Does he persuade? Six voices immediately respond, beginning with one that accepts the plea that this is nature (358: 36). As others succeed, the judgments become harsher. HCE is eventually described as a "totstittywinktosser and bogusbagwindburster," and the sixth voice wants to hear derisive cries "to singaloo sweecheriode and sock him up, the oldcant rogue" (359: 12–13, 19–20).[31]

Despite the resistance to HCE's claim that he has merely expressed a natural desire to retain a capacity for valuable emotions, the radio interlude takes his part. All the resources of music swell the song of temptation, the song he has heard—"so allow the clinkars of our nocturnefield, night's sweetmoztheart" (360: 11–12). The beguiling of HCE is brought before us, as the sirens sing (360: 22–7). Yet it should already be plain that this is a tease, that his yearning for romance will be seen as gross, disgusting, absurd:

> Did you aye, did you eye, did you everysee suchaway, suchawhy,
> eeriewhigg airywhugger? (360: 31–2)

The seductive song ends with childish protestations of innocence:

What a nossowl buzzard! But what a neats ung gels! (361: 16–17)

The only appropriate response to so grotesque an attempt to revive his amatory yearnings is mocking laughter, and HCE, overcome with humiliation, weeps (361: 35). His accusing customers greet his exposure by raising their glasses to his condemnation (362: 3–4). They recall him from the romance of his ludicrous imaginings to the reality of a drab marriage, conjured in a sequence of lodgings that, at their best, attain a dreary respectability (362: 23–35).[32]

HCE can only respond by reiterating his plea that his faults are common ones—"fellows culpows" (363: 20). Indeed, he offers a direct challenge to his accusers, insisting that they, aging men like himself, feel the same impulses and have no greater powers of resistance.

And fare with me to share with me. Hinther and thonther, hant by hont. By where dauvening shedders down whose rovely lanes. As yose were and as yese is. Sure and you would, Mr MacGurk! Be sure and you would, Mr O'Duane! To be sure and you would so, Mr MacElligut! Wod you nods? Mom mom. No mum has the rod to pud a stub to the lurch of amotion. (365: 22–7)

The "lurch of emotion" is what the aging HCE has felt, but it has led him to stagger and fall, to compromise the apparently central commitment to his marriage. His challenge elicits no reply—he is simply linked to the famous exemplars of subhuman depravity, the Jukes and the Kallikaks (367: 11, 17).

Appropriately, the last words of HCE's "grand remonstrance" (367: 3) are "Fall stuff" (366: 30). This material reveals the collapse of his identity, the cause of his fall and his falling apart. He cannot offer any coherent narrative of the value of his life, unable to center it on his youthful freedom, on the marriage he made, on any achievement. He is simply a broken old man in his decline, a patchwork like Falstaff. Yet in the allusion to Shakespeare's sometime lovable rogue, there is also comfort. Falstaff is at odds with the conventions and judgments of respectable society; he, too, feels the loss of his vigor; and, in the end, he is betrayed, left to a squalid and uncomfortable death. Through his uncompromising realism, however, his talent for seeing "life foully," and, above all, through his ability to laugh, Falstaff is undefeated. Perhaps HCE's collapse may point to a similar resolution.

Not yet, however. The voices of the community, increasingly fatigued and thick with drink, can only wander inconclusively. They are brought into agreement and order as the representative of law arises within the bar to declare closing time and to shut up the inn for the night.

It is polisignstunter. The Sockerson boy. (370: 30)

This ancient counterpart of HCE, the dismal sign of the stunted future that awaits him, has been on hand the whole time, apparently washing the glasses, but, as we saw much earlier, in his guise as Pukkelsen, playing Judas at this last supper. He pronounces a Bacchic benediction to the drunken gathering (371: 1) and leads the departing customers in a closing anthem, another ballad that expresses the judgment on HCE.

> Dour douchy was a sieguldson. He cooed that loud nor he was young. He
> cud bad caw nor he was gray Like wather parted from the say. (371: 6–8)

HCE, "dour douchy," is linked to Sackerson (whom he will become), to the sea, and to gulls. He has flown across the sea, achieving youthful triumph. Now he is no longer young, no longer able to serenade; his sexual life is over.[33] In trying to sing a song of love he can only produce a ridiculous noise. And he has been gulled, led on by the siren call of the girls, but duped most deeply by himself and his failure to understand what his life might amount to. Hence, he is cut off from his element, the sea, from his home, from the place of return for ALP. He is stagnant—an unwholesome pool, not a flowing river.

The cry goes up to Hosty—"Ostia"—to sing more strongly. Hosty is surely here, in the treacherous Sockerson, in the hostile customers, and in HCE too, the host of the inn and the sacrificial host for this rite of passage and derision. HCE also listens, recalling the passage of his life:

> all the chubbs, chipps, chaffs, chuckinpucks and chayney chimebells
> That he had mistributed in port, pub, park, pantry and poultryhouse.
> (371: 11–13)

He can find only a collection of fragments, scattered among the contradictory elements that have led him, with a "lurch of amotion," here and there. There is nothing to tie it together, to vindicate it—or him.

The ballad continues, emphasizing the inevitable replacement of the old with the young. They—not the aging HCE—are fit to "charm the night" (371: 19). He can provide them with nothing; like foul water, he is useless for any sort of refreshment (371: 31–2). The songsters burst out of the pub and into the street, in mirth and mortification of HCE, celebrating his demise and the washing away of the defilement he has brought to their community.

> His bludgeon's bruk, his drum is tore. For spuds we'll keep the hat he
> wore And roll in clover on his clay By wather parted from the say. (372:
> 25–7)

They make up an enthusiastic "lyncheon partyng" (372: 30) and toast, in the final verse of the ballad, the sending away of the funeral boat, not across the sea to HCE's home, but over the foul water with which he has been consistently compared—"O'er wather parted from the say" (373: 10–11).

Even now, they cannot leave him alone but follow the ballad with a long denunciation of his sins. All aspects of the interfering outsider, aspiring to high status in the community, are held up to derision. Through this spiteful, drunken rant, sometimes petty, often pointed, swirl themes we have already discerned in the relation of HCE to the community. There is resentment at his pretense to be a genuine Dubliner, a pillar of the community—"You would think him Alddaublin staking his lordsure like a gourd on puncheon" (373: 19–20). We hear a capsule presentation of the trajectory of his life—"First you were Nomad, next you were Namar, now you're Numah and it's soon you'll be Nomon" (374: 22–3); HCE began as a wanderer, became a vigorous beast of prey (a tiger, or leopard), is now friendless and alone, and soon will be no more.[34] A connection with Shem, and with that part of HCE that has sought freedom and the defiance of convention, is conjured in the taunt "An artist, sir!" (374: 27).[35] The coming triumph of the younger generation is jubilantly predicted: "old Hunphydunphyville'll be blasted to bumboards by the youthful herald who would once you were" (375: 5–7). HCE's decay is contrasted with the vigor of the young, as the voices make clear what young women—including his nubile daughter—really want:

> The eitch is in her blood, arrah! For a frecklesome freshcheeky sweet-worded lupsqueezer. (376: 19–20)[36]

The marriage of the daughter is associated with the triumph of the son, and both connect, by way of the story of Buckley (and its variants) with the fall of HCE.

> The groom is in the greenhouse, gattling out his. Gun! (377: 5–6)

Further suggestions that HCE will be lynched (377: 17–18) lead to a confident announcement of the celebration to come:

> Isn't it great he is swaying above us for his good and ours. Fly your balloons, dannies and dennises! He's doorknobs dead! And Annie Delap is free! Ones more. (377: 36–378: 2)

All the prizes HCE once won are taken from him, and his wife is liberated from the burden of their marriage. All that remains to be done is to close up the orifices of his head (379: 14–16) in a recapitulation of the sensory mortification of the Russian general (349: 28–33).

We are not quite finished with HCE. As the cruel voices fall silent, it's left to "Variants' Katey Sherratt's man for the bonnefacies of Blashwhite and Blushred of the Aquasancta Liffey Patrol" to explain what happened "after that to Mocked Majesty in the Malincurred Mansion" (380: 2–4, 5).[37]

HCE is identified as a king, in the waning days of his reign. His age is given as "between fiftyodd and fiftyeven years," and the scene we have witnessed is the "socalled last supper he greatly gave" (380: 14, 15). HCE's response to collapse is described, in the rambling style of the narrative voice, with four distinct repetitions of the same account: he went "heeltapping through the winespilth and weevily popcorks" (381: 9–10); he lowered "his woolly throat with the wonderful midnight thirst was on him" to drink up the leavings (381: 26–7); he sucked up "whatever surplus rotgut" was left behind by the "lazylousers of maltknights and beerchurls" (381: 32–3); he drank it all "no matter whether it was chateaubottled Guiness's or Phoenix brewery stout it was or John Jameson and Sons or Roob Coccola or, for the matter of that, O'Connell's famous old Dublin ale that he wanted like hell" (382: 3–6).[38]

HCE drinks the dregs of defeat. He also imbibes the leavings of his enemies. The bold nomad who presented himself in the opening pages has been replaced by a man whose life is a collection of fragments and who sucks up the bitter remains of a hostile tradition. As HCE collapses on a box in the corner, the projects he has pursued seem to have amounted to nothing.

Part II, I have suggested, advances the dream explorations by responding to the concern that acceptance and affirmation come too easily. The dreamer must be convinced that he has "seen life foully," and, to that end, comforting myths and disguises have to be torn away. It should be no shock, then, that the movement of this chapter is one of relentless descent, or that the closing picture of HCE is thoroughly bleak.

On previous occasions, the defeats HCE has suffered have been mitigated by allusions to the arrival of ALP. Here, however, we are deprived that consolation. ALP's invitation, conveyed by Kate, was rejected, and her later emergence in the welter of accusations is, at best, ambiguous. We might suppose that the function of the "Aquasancta Liffey Patrol" is to dispense cleansing holy water, but the representative of the patrol is the treacherous Sackerson and the fluids that figure in his tale of "Mocked Majesty" are the unsavory mixtures of liquor HCE soaks up. Perhaps the function of the patrol is even to ensure the purity of Dublin's river, to cleanse the Liffey from the taint of HCE; the verdict of the fugitives from the bar, of course, was that "Annie Delap" would be made free by HCE's death. Moreover, the prospects for the morning suggest that ALP's life will go on, "that hen of Kaven's shows her beaconegg" (382: 10–11), associating her with the victorious son (Kevin/Shaun).[39] The new day will bring reassuring normalcy, the practices of well-established tradition, to Dublin, including the celebration of mass by "Father MacMichael" (382: 12).[40]

HCE is to be carried away from all this. The hostile voices have provided a capsule summary of what his life comes to:

> In the buginning is the woid, in the muddle is the sounddance and thereinofter you're in the unbewised again, vund vulsyvolsy. (378: 29–31)

With emptiness and blank unknowing before and after him, HCE's life has been a muddle indeed, a cacophony of contradictory yearnings, a dance of sound that signifies nothing except for a judicial sentence, a condemnation. From the sea he came, and, despite the ballad, to the sea he returns, to voyage into nothingness.

> So sailed the stout ship *Nancy Hans.* From Liff away. For Nattenlaender.
> As who has come returns. Farvel, farerne! Goodbark, goodbye!
> Now follow we out by Starloe! (382: 27–30)

Despite the kindlier tone of this conclusion, it doesn't lighten the mood of HCE's passing. Whether he (the "foreigner") sails into the void, or into night, he sails away from ALP. Their separation carries with it a premonition of the "turning" she senses, as the chill of regret enters her final monologue (627: 2)—and, for the moment, we hear no answering affirmation. The challenge for the dreamer will be to appreciate this moment of abject failure, the starkest and darkest yet, and *in spite of it,* to make that affirmation.

15

⋙⋘

THE FOUR OF US AND
SURE, THANK GOD, THERE
ARE NO MORE OF US

The funeral ship metamorphoses. We find ourselves above—and then on—the vessel bearing Tristan and Isolde to Cornwall. They have drunk the potion and felt its effect. What began as a voyage to bring a bride to the elderly King Mark is now a celebration of the love of the young.

The seabirds, including the gulls with which the hostile ballad identified HCE, offer a gleeful commentary, taunting "Muster Mark" (383: 1). His aspirations for a renewal of sexual love with a young bride are grotesque, and he is rightly displaced by "Tristy . . . the spry young spark" (383: 11). We begin, it seems, with the conjunction of declining age, youthful succession, and the flaunting of sexual vigor that permeated the renunciation of HCE in II-3.

Why do we need more? If HCE has been vilified and lynched, if he has been embalmed and placed aboard a funeral ship, can't the dreamer now let him go? Not quite. That is only one continuation of the vignettes of the previous chapter. Alternatively, we might suppose that HCE is not literally lynched, shot, or pitched across the sea; he has had a very unpleasant evening, one that leaves him in a drunken and dispirited stupor in his own bar. His life, too, will continue in the morning when ALP cooks breakfast for Kevin and Father MacMichael celebrates mass.

Yet, though the next phase of the dreamer's explorations start with more jeers at HCE/Mark, the dismal future that awaits the aging man is presented obliquely. Other figures are attending to the ship on which Tristan is kissing Isolde: "And there they were too, when it was dark, whilest the wildcaps was circling, as slow their ship" (383: 19–20). "They" are four old men, the "evangelists," Matthew, Mark, Luke, and John, whose voices have sounded before in the *Wake* and who will now be heard at length.[1]

Their utterances have a distinctive common tone, marked by a far higher frequency of standard English (or, more exactly, standard *Irish*-English) words and a corresponding relative lack of neologisms and foreign allusions. Yet the speeches are anything but simple, for, although individual clauses are quite straightforward, they are juxtaposed in odd ways, and the sentences run on without any governing direction. The speakers interrupt themselves, and one another, taking up allusions as the momentary fancy moves them, dropping topics without any conclusion, and then, from time to time, picking them up again. They can become obsessed with individual words or with stock phrases. They wander, they complain, they reminisce, and they drivel. Indeed, "drivel" can well appear the aptest characterization for the contents of this chapter.

Who are these maundering old men, and why are they worth hearing? How does their apparently inconsequential twaddle further the dreamer's project? It might be tempting to suppose that this brief chapter intervenes between the collapse of HCE and the presentation of Shaun (awaiting in Part III) only because of Joyce's commitment to a formal structure, one demanding a fourth chapter for Part II. But that is implausible: the extraordinary density of II-3 would surely have allowed for a division, so that Part II could have closed with drunken HCE on his box and the departure of the ship.

Lear's godson, Edgar, reminds us that, when we can say, "We are at the worst," we haven't yet reached the nadir. As I have suggested, the vignettes of II-3 might continue in either of two ways—with HCE's death and passing or with the continuation of a defeated and meaningless life. The second might well be worse.

With a clarity that has not been common in the recent pages of the *Wake*, the four evangelists speak together to introduce themselves:

> They were the big four, the four maaster waves of Erin, all listening, four. There was old Matt Gregory and then besides old Matt there was old Marcus Lyons, the four waves, and oftentimes they used to be saying grace together, right enough, bausnabeatha, in Miracle Squeer: here now we are the four of us: old Matt Gregory and old Marcus and old Luke Tarpey: the four of us and sure, thank God, there are no more of us: and, sure now, you wouldn't go and forget and leave out the other fellow and old Johnny MacDougall: the four of us and no more of us and so now pass the fish for Christ sake. (384: 6–15)

They are senile and prone to forget. Into their disordered minds float scraps of old desires, fragments of memory, to flow out again in their speech.

That speech centers on three main topics. First, already signaled in their "listening," is the scene in which they are set, with the ship bearing Tristan and Isolde. They attend eagerly, with eyes and ears, to the lovemaking of the young pair. Second is the Dublin they have known, with its cast of absent friends, of mundane activities, well-known incidents and recurrent festivals. Third is the history of the world, which they contemplate in a dim and fragmentary way, perhaps because they are vaguely concerned with its progress or mistily puzzled by its significance. It is hard for them to keep these topics entirely separate from one another, so that, for example, the ship they follow may not only remind them of, but actually seem to be, the stage for some episode of world history or for some trivial occurrence in Dublin life.

Rambling through these subjects in their disorganized way, they deepen the bleak picture of the preceding chapters. HCE disintegrated before the dreamer, presenting no worthwhile coherent identity, no stable narrative of his life. The evangelists' fascination with the young lovers will not only underscore the contrast between the vigor of youth and the decline of age but also show how pitiably these old men cling to reminders of what they have lost. Their pointless excursions through Dublin life will expose its barren dreariness, the apparent lack of anything valuable that it can afford. Their history of the world is a muddle, a rigmarole, without discernible point or progress.

Beyond this, in the inconsequential speech itself we can hear the pathos of HCE's future. "Thank God," they say, "there are no more of us." The lucky, or the good perhaps, don't have to linger on as they do—"The good go and the wicked is left over" (390: 29–30). If HCE is unfortunate, then there may be one more of them; although whether he would be allowed the minimal comfort of company is another question.

The confused conversation of the four grows from the scene with which we began, the lovemaking on the voyage whose ostensible purpose is to bring a bride to the aging King Mark. Excitedly, the four old men monitor the activities of the young pair:

> spraining their ears, luistening and listening to the oceans of kissening, with their eyes glistening, all the four, when he was kiddling and cuddling and bunnyhugging scrumptious his colleen bawn and dinkum belle . . . (384: 18–22)

Apparently they vindicate HCE's claim that the desire for a renewal of love is a natural accompaniment of the awareness of the body's decline; their feeble lusts, evident in the strained ears and bright eyes, recall the grotesqueries of HCE's own thirst for sexual renewal. Yet these four old men are voyeurs and auditeurs par excellence, delighted to attend to Tristan's amatory efforts, to "his poghue like Arrah-na-poghue" (384: 34).[2] Intervention is not for them. Any similar behavior belonged to "the good old bygone days" (385: 2–3). They are feeble residues of those days, the few who have lingered on, and "now, thank God, there were no more of them" to observe the "poghuing and poghuing" (385: 31–2).

Exciting though the scene may be, the old men are sufficiently distract-ible to wander away from the young lovers to think of their own past or of the larger history of the world. By the same token, memories can bring them back to the present:

> the hempty times and the dempty times, for a cup of kindness yet, for four farback tumblerfuls of woman squash, with them, all four, listen-ing and spraining their ears for the millennium and all their mouths making water. (386: 8–11)

They drool. No longer able to control their quavering mouths, they are also impotently lecherous. So, for all the meandering of their talk, through a hap-hazard sequence of past events, it is hardly a surprise that they return again and again to attend to the lovemaking that is no longer for them (388: 1–4, 23–6; 389: 21–3; 395: 6–25).

For they have reconciled themselves to passivity, as HCE has not. They can think of themselves as

> four dear old heladies and really they looked awfully pretty and be-spectable and after that they had their fathomglasses to find out all the fathoms . . . (386: 14–17)

They recall that "thank God, they were all summarily divorced" by "their dear poor shehusbands" (390: 18–20).[3] For all the unsavory glistening of the eyes and salivation of the mouths, the old men count as "respectable." If they need glasses to aid their declining vision, those glasses—or other glasses, perhaps—are useful in fathoming the secrets of private embraces. If their leering and peering "through the steamy windows, into the honeymoon cabins" (395: 8–9) seems offensive, it is nothing more than a harmless nuisance. These doddering watchers are sexually neutral, having been separated from their equally neu-tered partners—and they are thankful for it.

HCE is different, and the absurdity of the difference can be emphasized by recalling the tale of Tristan and Isolde. After describing (with unusual gusto) the consummation of the love of the young pair, the most systematic of the evangelists (apparently Matthew) defends Isolde's actions.

> Could you blame her, we're saying, for one psocoldlogical moment? What would Ewe do? With that so tiresome old milkless a ram, with his tiresome duty peck and his bronchial tubes . . . (396: 13–16)

Unlike the old "heladies," HCE protests the decline of the flesh, arousing a feeble moment of mirth at the ungainliness of his behavior.

Yet what is the alternative? To join these passive observers with their weak mouths and glistening eyes? The last version of a refrain that runs through their speech provides a sober picture of what awaits. They sit "in Old Man's House, Millenium Road," with their "cold knees"

> and all dolled up, for their blankets and materny mufflers and plim-
> soles and their bowl of brown shackle and milky and botherham clots,
> a potion a peace, a piece aportion, a lepel alip, alup a lap, for a cup of
> kindest yet, with hold take hand and nurse and only touch of ate, a
> lovely munkybown and for xmell and wait the pinch and prompt poor
> Marcus Lyons to be not beheeding the skillet on for the live of ghosses
> but to pass the teeth for choke sake . . . (397: 14, 15, 16–23)

Auld Lang Syne, the song that traditionally celebrates the passing of the year,
with its evocations of the old days, is an appropriate song for the four old men,
and it recurs through their conversation; here, the cup of kindness—"kindest
yet"—is a palliative, a momentary relief for the condition to which they are reduced. Wrapped in the protective clothes of infants, they feed on a diet of bland
food that they must eat only sparingly, and they must be guided by the hand
of their nurse. Their familiar concluding request—"Pass the . . . for . . . sake"
(94: 32; 384: 15; 393: 2; 395: 23–4; 535: 25)—now signals their decrepitude;
they are sharers of a single set of teeth. They have returned to "second childish-
ness," "sans teeth, sans everything" (*As You Like It*).

Grotesque as his resistance might be, it is not surprising that HCE should
want to resist this ending.

Perhaps the old men have not yet reached so dismal a condition, for they
are still able to converse, in their disjointed way, about the Dublin they have
known. When these "heladies" turn their "fathomglasses" on the scenes of
their past, they discern an assortment of characters, places and events:

> the auctioneer Battersby Sisters, the prumisceous creaters, that sells all
> the emancipated statues and flowersports, James H. Tickell, the jaypee,
> off Hoggin Green, after he made the centuries, going to the tailturn
> horseshow, before the angler nomads flood, along with another fellow,
> active impalsive, and the shoeblacks . . . (386: 23–8)

What is the point of drawing these connections? I think any catalogue of
Joyce's allusions to Dublin characters and institutions, or to Irish history, will
not prove illuminating. The speaker (Johnny) has provided an unintelligible
jumble.

And that is precisely the point. Whether we attribute the disconnection
to the senility of the narrator, what survives in memory is a set of fragments. Like the Dubliners who haunt Joyce's stories and who make their
small appearances in *Ulysses*, James H. Tickell and the other "impalsive"
fellow once lived lives that extended beyond the moments of their fleeting
appearances. They depart, leaving nothing but their names—or not even
that—becoming utterly insignificant. This residue of trivia is what survives
in the old men's memories of their own lives, in the "jetsam litterage of

convolvuli of times lost or strayed, of lands derelict" (292: 16–17) that their minds have become.

In the "Wandering Rocks" section of *Ulysses*, Joyce gives us fragmentary glimpses of an array of characters, as the viceroy's cavalcade makes its way across Dublin. We know how the lives of many of these characters, of Stephen and Simon Dedalus, of Blazes Boylan, of Martin Cunningham, even of the nameless blind piano tuner, extend beyond this brief interval and how what they are described as doing in these pages fits into larger purposes. Even the smaller and more puzzling appearances—like the flushed young man and the girl with a twig on her skirt (*Ulysses*, 221) who receive the blessing of Father Conmee—are made more comprehensible to us: at the Lying-in hospital ("Oxen of the Sun"), the young man, Vincent, recalls the incident (*Ulysses*, 408–9). But, when the evangelists elaborate the Dublin they remember, there is no such sense of broader purpose. All they can provide is a fragmentary reference, evoking lives that had no significance and no point.

Among the Dubliners of these disjointed recollections is a figure familiar to readers of *Ulysses* and "Grace." The old men dwell on floods and drownings, and the victims include Martin Cunningham:

> poor Merkin Cornyngwham, the official out of the castle on pension, when he was completely drowned off Erin Isles, . . . and a lovely mourning paper and thank God, as Saman said, there were no more of him. (387: 28–32)
>
> Poor Andrew Martin Cunningham! Take breath! Ay! Ay! (393: 5–6)[4]

Even though there may have been a fuller obituary, a "lovely mourning paper," no more of Martin Cunningham survives here than his official service, his retirement, and the manner of his death. His service to the people around him—to Tom Kernan, to the Dignam family, to Bloom, and doubtless to others—his "little nameless unremembered acts of kindness and of love" are of so little account that the old man can only utter the standard formula of resignation, the gratitude that "there were no more of him." Cunningham has perished as though he had never been.

Nor are matters any different when the "heladies" reflect more broadly upon history. Although it is claimed that "they all four remembered who made the world" (384: 35–6), this memory has so little importance that it glides quickly by between the kissing of Tristan and Isolde and a vague recollection of their own past. With their interest in floods and drownings, they can connect the watery death of Martin Cunningham with the "drowning of Pharoah and all his pedestrians" (387: 26) supposing both to have occurred in "the red sea" (387: 27, 30). The "Flemish armada" is juxtaposed with "Lapoleon, the equestrian, on his whuite hourse of Hunover, rising Clunkthurf over Cabinhogan," and both incidents merge with the "Frankish floot of Noahsdobahs" (388: 10–11, 16–17, 18–19). Matt's delineation of the contours of history tends to the metaphysical, and he discovers "in the pancosmic urge the allimmanence of that which Itself is Itself Alone" (394: 32–3).[5] Yet whether pursued in the abstractions of philosophy or with the detailed recording of particular events, history is a muddle. The death of Pharoah (and his "pedestrians") has no more importance than the drowning of Martin Cunningham. What happened to the armada, whether it connects to Napoleon, whether Napoleon belongs in Irish history—all this, too, is irrelevant. There is nothing to the "allimmanence" of "Itself," and no other grand structure for the course of history to take. More-over, if the old men do indeed remember who made the world, the identity of the creator isn't worth a mention.

Yet this chapter concludes, as it began, with the announcement of a new stage. Even though the picture of the past offered by the four old men is muddled and senseless, even though they are confused and decrepit, they still hope for the future. They are dimly aware that it will not be different:

> And after that now, in the future, please God, after nonpenal start, all repeating ourselves . . . let us ran on to say oremus prayer and homeysweet homely, after fully realising the gratifying experiences of highly continental evenements . . . [6] (398: 7–8, 12–13)

Repeat themselves they do, just as the dreamer's vignettes run over, again and again, the same themes. In their second childhood, the old men echo the lan-guage of the prayer that ended II-1 and the address to the parents that closed II-2. Yet if they are genuinely thankful that there are no more of them—and, in sometimes leaving one or two out, maybe even hopeful that there should be less of them—how can they look back on "gratifying experience," especially when the experience in question involves HCE? Only, I suggest, when we think of that experience as the celebration of HCE's demise, recorded from the very first words of the chapter, and accompanied here by a sense of new hope.

The expression undercuts the hope. The opening song exulted in a change, the emergence of the "spry young spark," and, insofar as they have taken any definite attitude, the evangelists have celebrated the arrival of Tristan. They end with a four-verse song, translating the new hero into the Irish context: he is hailed as "the mose likable lad" yet to have come his sweetheart's way (399: 29). As the old men's voices blend with the cries of the seabirds, a new (anonymous)[7] narrator announces a new freedom and gives the hero a name:

> So, to john for a john, johnajeams, led it be! (399: 36)

Despite the enthusiasm for the phase to come, there are already signs enough that it will be no different from what has already been, that the muddle of the lives that have been will repeat itself in the career of the new hero.

The figure to whom we are to be led is Shaun ("John"), who is to replace HCE as the focus of the dreamer's explorations. In the official verdict of the old men, Shaun, Tristan to HCE's King Mark, is the bright promise of the future. Yet their presentation of the past, both in the style and content of their ramblings, makes it clear that the promise will be unreal unless the future is *not* a repetition. Moreover, Shaun has come before us so far as the representative of convention and the darling of those who love the established ways. The four old men are of the same party, associated with the regions of Ireland and with its history, purveyors of tradition and ancestral lore. Unlike HCE and Shem, they are insiders, pillars of the community. Their meandering conversation doesn't bode well for the coherence of the settled mores or the significance of lives lived in pious conformity.

Even in the last line, there is a hint of trouble to come. Shaun isn't simply "John" but "Johnajeams." One allusion is to a line from *Hamlet,* and to "John-a-dreams," signifying a person apt to lose himself in reverie. Perhaps that is Shaun's temperament—or perhaps, at this stage, he is simply the boy of our dreams, the "child we all love to place our hope in for ever" (621: 31–2). That seems to be how the evangelists regard him and how the dreamer might like to view him. But "Johnajeams" also suggests both anglicized versions of the brother's names, "James" (Shem) as well as "John" (Shaun), and if he is indeed a composite figure, then he may bear not only the untested traits of the "fine frank fairhaired fellow of the fairytales" (220: 12–13) but the thoroughly exposed deficiencies of "the bold bad bleak boy of the storybooks" (219: 24) as well. As a synthesis of the sons, he may even be the father, reborn.

Exploration of the possibilities represented by Shaun awaits the dreamer in Part III. Before leaving Part II, however, it is worth reflecting on one aspect I have not yet discussed. In suggesting that the material of these chapters advances the dreamer's project by obeying the imperative to "see life foully," I may well appear to have constructed a reading at odds with the mood produced by immersion in Joyce's prose. For I have seen the movement of this part as a descent, a successive debunking of comforting myths, in which an ever bleaker picture of human life, and its possible point, comes into view. In the hands of many authors, this would indeed be a "grimm grimm tale" (335: 5), but Joyce's exposition of it is full of wit, zest, and comedy. The wordplay of the children's game, the bawdy and the brilliance of the mock-text, the whimsy of the old men's conversation, even the many-faceted allusiveness of the scene in the bar, can all provoke laughter.[8] If Joyce's material is so serious and his perspective so chilling, why does his treatment of it sometimes veer so close to farce?

I have already touched on this objection and already promised a full response to it.[9] But some brief further remarks are appropriate here. Unlike Part I, where ALP's periodic entrances served as signals that a despairing conclusion was not inevitable, the chapters of Part II are almost entirely devoid of her consoling presence (or of any other figure who could play the same role).

As I have interpreted the dreamer's project, by the end of Part I it has taken on the form of probing the movement represented by ALP, of understanding that and how a full confrontation with the realities of human life may permit the expression of the Joycean virtues and culminate in a genuine affirmation. The dreamer—and we, the readers—must learn to make that movement. Joyce's humor, his rich vein of comedy, is the central device through which the needed education proceeds.

A comparison with *Ulysses* will clarify the point. It would be easy to provide a banal summary of the underlying material. A talented young man finds himself at odds with his companions and his country; he is aware of the promise he has failed to realize, and he is without any definite direction. An older man has seen his only son die, and the death has caused a sexual estrangement from his wife; his beloved daughter is growing up and has just left home. During a midsummer day, the man's frustrated wife commits adultery with a business associate, and her husband knows that, and when, this will occur. The older and younger man both wander through Dublin, experiencing minor difficulties and defeats. They eventually meet and have a conversation. It is not obvious whether they will ever talk again.

This is the stuff out of which a skilled novelist could write a tragedy. To take just one example, the anticipated jingling of the quoits on Bloom's marital bed could prove a stabbing obsession, and the author could explore the depths of his hero's pain. Joyce chose differently. Although there is no hiding the sad and unpleasant facts that form the background to his characters' thoughts—no denying the jingling of the quoits—his treatment of their inner lives, always humane and frequently comic, enables him to close *Ulysses* on a famous note of affirmation.

I interpret the *Wake* as a deeper and vaster display of the same technique— deeper because the probing of the dreamer's night thoughts reaches into questions and uncertainties that a waking mind works hard to repress, vaster because the range of concerns interrogated is far broader. As the canvas expands, so, too, does the breadth of Joyce's humor. The result is an even more somber picture of the realities of life, colored with a perspective that evokes richer and more frequent laughter.

That laughter is, as I have suggested, crucial to the resolution of the dreamer's predicament, crucial to the enterprise of the *Wake*. This is not a philosophical treatise that will directly and explicitly answer the questions that gnaw at the dreamer—and nag at us, the readers—a treatise that will add to the litany of gloomy facts some new piece of information capable of transforming their character. It is a *novel*, devoted to *showing* us a new way of responding to those facts, and the humor is an essential ingredient of the showing. If we are to affirm, if we are to achieve the Joycean virtues, we must first know how to laugh.

16

A PICTURE PRIMITIVE

So to Part III, to be dominated, at least initially, by the long-promised hero, Shaun.

A brief prelude sets the scene: a bedroom, perhaps viewed from the four posts of the bed, to which we shall eventually return (III-4). The figures in the bed are plainly HCE and ALP, characterized in the unflattering terms that will be elaborated later (559: 20–29). A male intruder looks on (403: 12)—possibly the dreamer, or we readers who probe the lives of this pair. But the attempt to peep is blocked. The lights darken, and the bedroom becomes invisible.[1]

Then we hear a new, and refreshingly simple, narrative voice. It belongs, as we'll discover, to the ass that accompanies the evangelists (405: 6). Self-deprecating—the ass denies having "the concordant wiseheads of Messrs Gregory and Lyons alongside of Dr Tarpey's and I dorsay the reverend Mr MacDougall's" (405: 4–6)[2]—the donkey-narrator is to reveal the content of a dream (404: 3–4). At the center of that dream is Shaun, who will appear and engage in conversation with the ass.[3]

Shaun's entrance recalls the trajectory the dreamer's investigations have been pursuing. Throughout Part II, Shaun has been promised as a shining figure to come, but he has been barely visible in the gloom. Now he emerges from the "allmurk" (404: 10), guessed at with excitement (the onward-straining rhythms of the prose are almost impossible to resist), and then, at last, visible:

> When look, was light and now'twas as flasher, now moren as the glaow.
> Ah, in unlitness 'twas in very similitude, bless me, 'twas his belted lamp! Whom we dreamt was a shaddo, sure, he's lightseyes, the laddo!
> Blessed momence, O romence, he's growing to stay! (404: 11–15)

As with HCE, Shaun's costume is eccentric, but the ass is at pains to point out the cleanliness and elegance of the odd combination of clothes the boy wears. The voice builds to an excited crescendo, announcing

Shaun himself.
What a picture primitive! (405: 2–3)

The dreamer's fresh start conjures a vision of innocence. The wholesome description of Shaun's costume presents a figure out of a child's picturebook, a
suitable hero for a fairy-tale. The old men offered a prayer for the future and
a "homeysweet homely" (398: 12), and the Shaun we meet is a fitting incarna-
tion. The ass delights in his "beamish brow" (405: 16–17), not only advertising
the sunny candor of Shaun's face and disposition but also his role as the young
liberator who is to end the menace of past dreams.[4] Shaun's diet is similarly
wholesome, and he is a hearty eater (although not "guilbey of gulpable glut-
tony," as the ass hastens to reassure us [406: 33]). In short, he is a very good
boy, who dresses neatly and cleans his plate—one who is obedient and respectful of his elders.

Shaun speaks, and his tone, his pure Irish tenor, is ravishing (407: 13–22).
In the ass's identification of Shaun as a son of Ireland, there are suggestions
of comparison with others, of the inferior beauty—perhaps the unnatural
beauty—of the Italian tenor voice.[5] The youth's taste in music is appropriately
pious, for he sings, not opera, but the music of the Catholic rite ("panangeli-
cal" conjures up performances of the much-loved devotional solo "*Panis ange-
licus*"; 407: 14–15). Not only is he a faithful patriot but a worshiper in the true
church as well. He is set before us as the unspoilt champion of tradition and of
conformity to the established ways.

But what does he say? After the enthusiasm of the introduction, the invocation of Shaun as a wonderful new beginning, we are in for disappointment:

—Alo, alas, aladdin, amobus! Does she lag soft fall means rest down?
Shaun yawned, as his general address rehearsal. (407: 27–8)

The greeting ("Hello") turns into a schoolboy's recitation of a Latin gram-
matical paradigm—perhaps this well-brought-up boy has nothing to say to us
except to regurgitate the formulas inculcated in his education. It is followed by
a vocal exercise, appropriate for a singer's rehearsal, a descending scale (Doh,
te, la, . . .). The fact that it is a *descending* scale is worrying, for it may point
to the fact that Shaun begins at the high point of his career. Moreover, the
weary words and the accompanying yawn introduce Shaun's next theme. He
is tired.

The trouble is that he is overworked. The ass describes Shaun's sinking,
exhausted "upon the native heath he loved" (408: 7). His task is to carry letters, but he complains that he is not up to it:

How all too unwordy am I, a mere mailman of peace, a poor loust haste-
hater of the first degree, . . . no legs and a title, . . . to be the bearer of
these postoomany missive on his majesty's service . . . (408: 10–14)

The deliverer of letters, or the transmitter of the culture of the community, doesn't need words of his own, but he does require energy and commitment. Someone who hates haste, who might prefer to ramble and explore at leisure, is unsuitable for the job.

A better candidate, he muses, might have been his brother, whom he recalls fondly, in the spirit of unity that has been present since the end of II-2. Shem (or "Sim" [408: 21]) has apparently pursued a different course, one not involving the work Shaun finds so oppressive, for, unlike his brother, Shem is underfed (408: 24; 409: 1). Under the questioning of the ass, Shaun explains how he came to his present predicament:

> Forgive me, Shaun repeated from his liquid lipes, not what I wants to do a strike of work but it was condemned on me premitially by Hireark Books and Chiefoverseer Cooks in their Eusebian Concordant Homilies and there does be a power coming over me that is put upon me from on high out of the book of breedings . . . (409: 33–410: 2)

Far from being a willing upholder of tradition, a voluntary conscript in the service of church and country, he has been forced into the pattern of the local elders, specifically that of his father and of remoter ancestors. He has had no chance to forge an identity of his own, "to isolate i from my multiple Mes" (410: 12), and the result is a sense of directionlessness. The boy who came before us as the representative of home and family offers a puzzled sense of his place and his future:

> and where on dearth or in the miraculous meddle of this expending umniverse to turn since it came into my hands I am hopeless off course to be doing anything concerning. (410: 16–19)

Powerless Shaun has chosen from the limited range of options his community has provided for him, and, "being too soft for work proper" (410: 33), he has agreed to walk, to carry the mail. There are rules to be followed, and he has tried to obey them, taking satisfaction in honoring the instructions that his parents and his community have provided (411: 6–18).[6] He performs the rites and ceremonies approved by church and country, telling his beads and avowing "Happy Maria and Glorious Patrick" (411: 19–20). Perhaps, the ass suggests, he has even gone further and patriotically painted the town (or the postboxes?) green (411: 24).

Unlike Bloom or Shem or HCE, Shaun would seem to be the sort of man of whom the Citizen would approve.

As we should have anticipated, this is the portrait of the pillar of the community as a young man. Yet we ought also to have been prepared for the probability that there is no real "picture primitive," no "wold made fresh" (336: 17), no "nonpenal start" (398: 7–8).[7] There are already signs that Shaun contains within him impulses that resist the pious conformity the ass ascribes—and the dreamer might like to ascribe—to him. Can this identification with community and tradition survive the feelings of confinement and the absence of direction that have already flickered in Shaun's answers? Will his "i," like HCE's fractured identity, dissolve into "multiple Mes"? These questions are explored in the ass's exchange with Shaun through what initially looks like an odd response to the commendation of his patriotic behavior. The spreading of the green is initially a source of pride for the young man (411: 25–33). Then, there is a moment of doubt, as Shaun appreciates that his local commitments, his pledge to defend one particular tradition, might be viewed from a different perspective:

> Somebody may perhaps hint an aughter impression of I was wrong. No such a thing! You never made a more freudful mistake, excuse yourself! What's pork to you means meat to me . . . (411: 34–412: 1)

The Freudian slip is surely Shaun's, whose awareness of the difference of customs, mores, and standards raises the concern that his patriotic vigor might be misguided. He tries to silence any doubts, but the suave ass, politely inquiring if the success of Shaun's defense of Irish tradition and Irish independence is assured, provokes an irascible reply. The propriety of his causes is beyond question (412: 13–20).

Dismissing any question of justification, he launches into an account of his plans to explain a quite different matter, apparently concerned with the respectability of older Irish ladies and with the punctilious way in which he has discharged his duties. As his anger dissipates, the ass invites him to hold forth in song. Shaun declines, offering instead to "spinooze you one from the grimm gests of Jacko and Esaup" (414: 16–17). It is another of the classic pieces of the *Wake*, the fable of the Ondt and the Gracehoper.

Why does Joyce insert his brilliant reworking of a familiar moral tale at just this moment? It is, I suggest, immediately relevant to the issue that has surfaced in Shaun's defensive outburst. For one whose life is patterned by local standards, the existence of alternative cultures and traditions comes as a threat. The danger was dodged in using the prevailing mores and values to defend the respectability of local people. To face it, a more general discussion of values and of possibilities for living is required. For that one might turn to philosophy, and it is entirely appropriate that Shaun's tale is full of allusions to philosophers (from "spinooze" on).

Fables are humble, but effective, devices for presenting the clash of values and for revealing the consequences of different commitments. The particular fable Shaun chooses is especially suited to the conflict that has emerged in the earlier exchanges with the ass and to the concerns that have worried the dreamer throughout. What is at stake is the possibility of an outside perspective, one that would question the local rules and traditions and that would dispute the legitimacy of conformity. How better to scotch any doubts than to display two characters, a conformist and a rebel, and to show that the latter's career ends in disaster?

The rebel, of course, is the Gracehoper, initially a freethinking hedonist— "always jigging ajog, hoppy on akkant of his joyicity" (414: 22–3).[8] He indulges in sensual pleasures and recognizes no higher source of duty.

> For if sciencium (what's what) can mute uns nought, 'a thought, abought the Great Sommboddy within the Omniboss, perhops an art-saccord (hoot's hoot) might sing ums tumtim about the Little New-buddies that ring his panch. (415: 15–19)

In the absence of strict commandments from the (nonexistent) "Great Sommboddy," singing and dancing can be the way for those who actually exist, the "Little Newbuddies," ordinary people with no high-flown ideas about cosmic significance, to "kick time" (415: 24).

The Ondt, Shaun's figure of the righteous conformist, finds this behavior profoundly offensive. The conventions, he believes, should be observed, and "[w]e shall not come to party" with those "not on our social list" (415: 30, 31). His life is full of prohibitions, and his home is aptly named "Nixnixundnix" (415: 29). He prays dutifully and cultivates a solemn (perhaps sullen) manner—he can be "muravyingly wisechairmanlooking" (416: 5, 7–8).

The plot follows the simple, moralistic line we might expect from a children's book, designed to bring up good little members of the community. Having taken no thought for the morrow, the Gracehoper finds himself sick, cold, and hungry. He sees "His Gross the Ondt, prostrandvorous upon his dhrone" (417: 11), enjoying the pleasures in which he had once indulged. The Gracehoper's first reaction is one of bitter jealousy and anger (417: 21–3). The Ondt's pleasure is immoderate, and, in accordance with Tertullian's prophecy, the miseries of the Gracehoper increase his merriment.[9] Gone is the solemn, "wisechairmanlike" manner, and the Gracehoper begins to worry that the Ondt's mirth will lead to incontinence (418: 11–12).

That worry signals an important change, one that transforms the fable from a trivially shallow response to the great question of the philosophers, "How to live?" Shaun's presentation closes with a poem, dominated by the voice of the Gracehoper, who has moved beyond jealousy and anger to acceptance.

> *I pick up your reproof, the horsegift of a friend,*
> *For the prize of your save is the price of my spend.* (418: 21–2)

So far, the verse endorses the conventional moral, the commendation of Restraint and Industry and the excoriation of Imprudence and Licence. But the Gracehoper is not finished. He offers a larger perspective on the issue of how to live, one that suggests a fundamental equality between himself and the Ondt:

> *A locus to loue, a term it t'embarrass,*
> *These twain are the twins that tick* Homo Vulgaris. (418: 25–6)

The lot of the species, common man, is to be vexed by love and its finitude. We are veering back to the concerns that have worried the dreamer, concerns about the value of a love that has a term, that will change its form and its intensity with time, concerns that were exposed most starkly in II-3, and that will recur again in III-3 and III-4.

Ondt and Gracehoper differ in how they have distributed pleasure and pain across their lives, but it is not clear that this makes any serious distinction between the value of their existences from the perspective of the "awebrume hour."[10] In a line that foreshadows the mood of ALP's closing monologue, the Gracehoper asks, rhetorically:

> *[Has] . . . that Accident Man not beseeked where his story ends*
> *Since longsephyring sighs sought heartseast for their orience?* (418: 29–30)[11]

The Gracehoper sees that, by the conventional standards, the Ondt has succeeded fabulously, but there is a clear suggestion that this may not amount to much:

> *My in risible universe youdly haud find*
> *Sulch oxtrabeeforeness meat soveal behind.*
> *Your feats end enormous, your volumes immense,*
> *(May the Graces I hoped for sing your Ondtship song sense!),*
> *Your genus its worldwide, your spacest sublime!*
> *But, Holy Saltmartin, why can't you beat time?* (419: 3–8)

The material success (emphasized by the puns on sources of meat) will only impress those who fail to see that the whole idea of "winning" at life is a joke. The "Accident Man" may prosper brilliantly in the Darwinian game of covering the earth, but this doesn't really provide "heartsease" for any of us. The Ondt's life of industry and eventual enjoyment is a struggle against the rhythms of the universe, while the graces for which his unfortunate fellow hoped prove illusory. No less than the Gracehoper, the Ondt fails to overcome the problem of finitude. He, too, will have a day, and no more than a day. For all his success, he, too, fails to "beat time."[12]

Shaun, who has been performing this tale, tacks on to the poem a conventionally pious conclusion. Yet the Gracehoper's poetical celebration of the Ondt has subtly undermined the standard moral, and this means that there are strains within Shaun's identification with the traditional lore. His apparently odd confession of a distaste for work, as well as his sudden anger at the possibility of an external, critical perspective on local mores, are of a piece with the unsettling suggestions to which Shaun's initially childish fable tends. The ass skillfully probes further, leading the boy to expose the cracks within his conformist persona.

It all begins innocently enough, with fulsome praise for Shaun's presentation of the fable:

> It falls easily upon the earopen and goes down the friskly shortiest like treacling tumtim . . . (419: 15–16)

The allusion to "Frisky Shorty" is disconcerting, reminding us that the community whose values Shaun is officially devoted to upholding includes a variety of types, among them an unsavory ex-convict who plays a cameo role in the society's excommunication of HCE (39: 18–20). Impressed by Shaun's expository and interpretative skills, the ass asks whether the lad can decipher "the strangewrote anaglyptics of those shemletters patent for His Christian's Em" (419: 19–20). Flattered, Shaun agrees.

Introducing the "shemletters" at this point opens, once again, the possibility of a critical outside perspective, a challenge to the traditional wisdom Shaun is officially dedicated to passing on. It is hardly surprising that his verdict on the document is angrily dismissive:

> It is a pinch of scribble, not wortha bottle of cabbis. Overdrawn! Puffedly offal tosh! Besides its auctionable, all about crime and libel! Nothing beyond clerical horrors *et omnibus* to be entered for the foreign as second-class matter. (419: 32–6)

Joyce is plainly having fun with responses to his own writing, to charges that he maligns his homeland and its pieties, that he grubs in disgusting things (offal), that his vision is bankrupt (overdrawn), and that he lavishes too much time on trivialities—and, above all, that his stylistic experiments are mere scribble. Yet this isn't a mere excursion; it is important to the movement of the chapter that Shaun should be moved to intolerant criticism.

As the diatribe proceeds, it becomes plain that the content of this unwholesome document includes the familiar stories—the encounter with the cad and the incident in the park (420: 6–8). There is, however, a surprising identification:

> Letter, carried of Shaun, son of Hek, written of Shem, brother of Shaun, uttered for Alp, mother of Shem, for Hek, father of Shaun. (420: 17–19)

The letter Shem allegedly wrote out for his mother is, we recall, supposed to be a vindication of HCE, despite the fact that Shaun's account of the content casts it as accusation rather than defense. The alignment of Shaun with "Hek," as well as the irate dismissal of the rumors, makes it appear that Shaun is standing up for his father. Yet HCE is an outsider, at odds with the judgments of the local community, so that Shaun's loyalty to his father would contradict his role as the good conformist. If he were to persevere in that role, then he would have grounds for opposing any "shemletter" of the type originally suggested in I-5, any attempt to *vindicate* HCE. Which side is Shaun on?

Both. Indeed, he is *fervently* on both sides. Hence, the letter turns out to be undeliverable. There is no way for him to express in action both the contradictory impulses that move him strongly.[13] It is becoming clear that Shaun is his father's son, that he too is "more mob than man" (261: 21–2).

The ass offers a mild criticism of Shaun's excessive use of words in responding to the relatively brief document of his "cerebrated brother" (421: 19). That characterization provokes an indictment of Shem far closer to the angry rhetoric of I-7 than to the proclaimed unity that has extended from the end of II-2 to Shaun's initial discussion of his brother here (408: 17 ff.). Shaun disavows kinship with Shem and denies any duty to his brother (422: 17–18, 13–14).[14]

The apparently flattering, but subversive, ass continues to prod Shaun, asking him to offer his own formulation of the meaning of Shem's document. The request prompts a strange confession—or boast?—to the effect that he is involved in the authorship (422: 23–4). Shaun offers a brief review of the content, a concise account of the incident in the park (422: 31–4), before turning to an ever more vehement denunciation of Shem. Under the cajoling of the ass, the criticism culminates with an accusation that Shem is guilty of plagiarism:

> Every dimmed letter in it is a copy and not a few of the silbils and wholly words I can show you in my Kingdom of Heaven. The lowquacity of him! With his threestar monothong! Thaw! The last word in stolentelling! (424: 32–5)

Shem's supposed linguistic innovations (like the interior monologues *Ulysses* supplies for its three major characters), then, are really the invention of Shaun.

The ass has led Shaun into a position where there is an obvious challenge: why is he simply a deliverer of the word rather than also a creative writer? Shaun rises to the bait, declaring that he "can soroquise the Siamanish better than most" (425: 15–16) but insisting that his composition would be very different from that of his brother: it would be "the authordux Book of Lief" (425: 20). He is completely prepared:

> Acomedy of letters! I have them all, tame, deep and harried, in my mine's I. (425: 24–5)

Yet, having made his boast, he excuses himself from proceeding with the execution.[15] That "ultravirulence" would be beneath him (425: 35). He concludes by invoking his mother and swearing himself to pious defense of her.

We have come a long way from the primitive picture of the ass's opening vision. Shaun turns out to be far more complicated, and conflicted, than that cartoon of innocence and wholesomeness. He mixes ardent dedication to the folkways of home with a passionate intolerance of external criticism.[16] Because there is no single group that represents the spirit of the native people, only overlapping circles with differing interests and conceptions of what is proper and to be upheld, Shaun feels contradictory pressures—should he defend his father or the community that has rejected HCE? His presentation of the fable will not be confined to the simple, childish moral but opens up broader questions about the value of living by conventional rules and invites the outside perspectives he attempts to silence. Within him as well is a desire not simply to transmit the culture but also to contribute to it (not, of course, in the shameful way of his brother), to be an innovator, an artist even. Sensing the obvious peril that artistry will slide into unorthodoxy, or even into the subversion of orthodoxy, he draws back from expressing the urge. The sentimental piety of devotion to mother is a blustering conclusion that avoids the implications of his incoherent affirmations.

Shaun doesn't know how to define himself. As the clever ass presses him, the best he can do is to present himself by opposition—he is *not Shem*. But that fails to resolve his fundamental problem, the problem of isolating "i from my multiple Mes" (410: 12).

The conversation has ended. Shaun's emotions run high. He sheds nostalgic tears for his beloved mother—and behind those tears there surely lie anger and frustration. Wiping them away, he prepares to leave.

Despite the fact that his official job is to tramp the paths of Ireland, delivering letters, Shaun is confined to a barrel (414: 10–13).[17] The barrel is ready to continue its journey down the Liffey, and Shaun leans far back to navigate by the stars (426: 22–5). The local lad is exploring a broader perspective, and it comes at a cost. For he loses his balance, topples over, and is swept away by the current. He disappears from the ass's view, and from ours.

Two voices sound in his wake. The first describes the beauty of the night:

> And the stellas were shinings. And the earthnight strewed aromatose. . . . He was ours, all fragrance. And we were his for a lifetime. (427: 10–11, 12–13)

Joyce is loosely translating the libretto of one of the greatest tenor arias of one of his favorite operatic composers, Puccini. In the third act of *Tosca*, the heroine's lover, Cavaradossi, awaiting execution, sings of the beauty of life and of love, more intense for him than ever as he feels himself on the brink of losing them. It is, I suggest, another calling up of the "awebrume hour," another prefiguration of ALP's sense of the beauties that are flowing away from her, an elaboration of her late cry "mememormee!" (628: 14). Despite all Tosca's courage and ingenuity, Cavaradossi is indeed doomed. So, too, though not so immediately, with Shaun.

The mood is set for the final invocation, a benediction for Shaun, hailed, in a spirit of forgiveness, as "mine bruder, able Shaun" (427: 19). As with the end of II-1, there is a momentary upturn, an evanescent consolation, in a movement of long descent. We hear a tone of compassionate lament for Shaun's good qualities and his mild defects, as if his day is already over and the voice (Shem? the ass? both?) can come to terms with him:

> but for all your deeds of goodness you were soo ooft . . . (427: 24)

Shaun has set out on his own muddled journey, the locus of contradictory aspirations and ideals.

> How you would be thinking in your thoughts how the deepings did it all begin and how you would be scrimmaging through your scruples to collar a hold of an imperfection being committled. Sireland calls you. (428: 4–7)

The home of his fathers needs Shaun as a continuer of the traditions, but he is thinking more extensive thoughts. His initial movement to a wider view—the attempt to look at the stars—tipped him off balance, and he was directed by currents he could not control. The compassionate voice, warm with the Joycean virtues, can only wish him luck, can only hope for benign elements and soft pathways:

> may the tussocks grow quickly under your trampthickets and the daisies trip lightly over your battercops. (428: 26–7)

We, and the dreamer, already suspect *that* Shaun will fail to find a coherent identity. We do not yet know *how*.

17

LIGHTBREAKFASTBRINGER

When Shaun reappears, he has acquired a new name. "Jaunty Jaun," as he is now introduced, has had a long and wearing journey—"nine score or so barrel-hours distance" (429: 8–9)—and has come to rest against a curious mooring, "a butterblond warden of the peace, one comestabulish Sigurdsen," buried upright as befits a pile in the river, who has acquired this status as the result of some impressive drinking, a bout of "night duty behind the curing station, equilebriated amid the embracings of a monopolized bottle" (429: 18–19, 23–4). Jaun naturally attracts the attention of twenty-nine girls, the twenty-eight Floras and "his fond sister Izzy" (431: 15). The Floras greet him with the sexually charged adoration of the children's game (430: 19–33; 236: 33–237: 9; 238: 33–5). Less passive now than then, Jaun responds to their advances with well-mannered restraint (430: 33–431: 13).

He turns to Issy, announcing his imminent departure, and then, including all the girls in his address, he begins an oration:

I rise, O fair assemblage! Andcommincio. (432: 4)

He will speak at great length, almost without interruption.[1] His last words are delivered thirty-seven pages later (469: 28). At that point, he fulfills the intention announced to Issy, careening off. The girls weep for his departure, and a gentle narrative voice, perhaps that of the ass or the dreamer, recalls the valedictory tone that closed the previous chapter.

No other figure in the *Wake*'s long sequence of dream vignettes has so much uninterrupted air time.[2] As the beginning makes clear, the speech is to be a homily, a piece of instruction for the frail creatures whom Jaun is to leave behind, and it proves to be a torrential outpouring of advice, commands, threats, blandishments, exhortations, accusations, warnings, predictions, and even insults. Scathing and ribald by turns, it's an occasion for Joyce to offer an exceptional density of witty one-liners, and yet, rather like an overfruited Christmas cake, it can easily seem too rich. Brilliantly funny though this flood of words is, we might wonder if Joyce could have managed—and managed more effectively—with less.

The clue to understanding why Shaun runs on at such length lies in one of the most obvious features of the total oration. At different stages, he offers counsel of very different types, and some of the precepts are plainly contradictory. To cite just one example, although we begin with Victorian rules for (highly restricted) amatory behavior among properly-brought-up bourgeois girls (433: 12 ff.), Jaun later proceeds from sentimental thoughts about the sister he is to leave behind to the expression of a passion that is more than fraternal (445: 33–446: 26). Later still, he encourages the girls to start an orgy with the friend who is to serve as his surrogate (465: 1 ff.).

The various phases in Shaun's oration cannot be fused to provide a coherent vision of how the girls—or he—should live. There are different possibilities, tried out in sequence, as if the speaker—or the dreamer—were exploring their credentials for adoption. As the shortcomings of one become apparent, we lurch to the next, and, when all have been surveyed and found wanting, there is nothing for Shaun to do but offer a rudely dismissive farewell and depart.

The previous chapter prepares the way for the dreamwork we find here. The cracks in Shaun's identity exposed by the ass's questions make it plain that no mode of life can answer to all his impulses. He stands before the girls and before the dreamer to follow out the implications of identifying himself with various *parts* of the personality of III-1. The dreamer tries out these partial visions of what Shaun might become in hopes that one might prove both coherent and satisfying, that it might be a *worthy* "i" among the "multiple Mes." It is significant that Shaun appears with a new name, that the attributes aligned with that name will vary through the speech, and that further variations on the name will appear. The shifting names signal the search for an identity.[3] After the failures of Part II, the manic series of struggles to find some element within Shaun that can underpin the value of a life appears as the dreamer's last, desperate opportunity to resolve his central problem.

The impulse that dominates initially is an urge to conform, to carry on the established traditions. Perhaps the most prominent set of norms is that covering sexual behavior—everyday talk about morality often reduces to commendations of sexual restraint—and Jaun starts as the apostle of propriety, prudence, and even prudishness.[4] As a prelude to giving his "directions to henservants" (432: 5–6), Jaun aligns himself with the authority of the church, explaining that he has sought the advice of

Father Mike, P.P., my orational Dominican and confessor doctor . . . (432: 7)

The foundation of Jaun's doctrine is thus a shadowy reminder of ALP's early love, raising doubts from the very beginning about adherence to the official rules, doubts that will be reinforced by Issy's later reference to the same source ("young Fr Ml, my pettest parriage priest" [458: 3–4]). Even more worryingly, "Father Mike," while expert in the official maxims of the church, apparently feels the chafing of sexual frustration (432: 8–14), and, in a surprising turn, Jaun announces

how, hell in tunnels, he'd marry me any old buckling time as flying quick as he'd look at me . . . (432: 15–16)[5]

Presumably the priest is following the apostle's counsel that it is better to marry than burn. In any event, it is hardly a promising start for justifying the directions Jaun will give; but, undeterred, he proceeds to substance.

The general message is to follow the rules laid down by the traditional authorities, but it comes with a pragmatic twist. Jaun advises the girls to

adhere to as many as probable of the ten commandments touching purgations and indulgences and in the long run they will prove for your better guidance along your path of right of way. (432: 26–9)

Instead of offering a vision of damnation for those who disobey, Jaun starts with this-worldly dangers, as though the moral maxims were counsels of bourgeois prudence. It is all eminently practical:

Never lose your heart away till you win his diamond back. . . . First thou shall not smile. Twice thou shalt not love. Lust, thou shalt not commix idolatry. Hip confiners help compunction. . . . Collide with man, collude with money. . . . Where you truss be circumspicious and look before you leak, dears. (433: 14–15, 22–4, 32–3, 33–4)[6]

Jaun proceeds with increasing enthusiasm, and, as he does so, the doctrines move ever further from the basic commandments or even from the standard advice for a "nice" Dublin girl.

Love through the usual channels, cisternbrothelly, when properly disinfected and taken neat in the generable way upon retiring to roost in the company of a husband-in-law or other respectable relative of an apposite sex, not love that leads by the nose as I foresmellt but canalised love, you understand, does a felon good . . . (436: 14–19)

The contrast now is not with total abstinence, but with sexual activity that runs out of control—Jaun continues with dire warnings of the effects of alcohol. The girls must know how far to go, and how exactly to go that far (436: 32 ff.).

Finding one's way in Irish society isn't a matter of honoring clear prohibitions but of playing a complicated game. Because the sexual urges are so powerful, they can't be denied altogether and must be "canalised," kept within an approved framework—or, in the family, away from the public gaze that might bring public shame. Jaun recommends a safely "disinfected" regime of sex, because he foresees—or, more exactly, "foresmells"—the evil effects (the stench) of damaged reputation. Nor, in the end, can the rules of the game be grounded in standards that are demonstrably nonarbitrary. Behind it all stands the dubious authority of "Father Mike" and the contingent ways in which the locals have agreed to appraise conduct.

Jaun's growing excitement through these pages reflects the power of the impulses he is trying to regulate. As he looks forward to his own future absence, he conjures up visions of other men, similarly driven, and of the vulnerability of the girls to their wily advances. Potential disasters surround them:

> The next fling you'll be squitting on the Tubber Nakel, pouring pitch-ers to the well for old Gloatsdane's glorification . . . (438: 12–14)[7]

In short, they may be headed for a life of prostitution (from which Gladstone notoriously hoped to redeem the "fallen young women" of London), a "whor-able state of affairs altogether" (438: 17–18). Nor can the agitated Jaun simply leave the matter with the dire picture of degradation and dishonor. Obsessed with the idea of omnipresent male sexual cunning, he resorts to threats of physical violence:

> If ever I catch you at it, mind, it's you that will cocottch it! I'll tackle you to feel if you have a few devils in you. Holy gun, I'll give it to you, hot, high and heavy . . . (439: 3–6)[8]

The dreamer has explored one of the possibilities in a life of conformity, centered on enforcing the conventional norms of the community. What began as a calm review of prudential maxims for an untroubled life, maxims that have become part of the lore of the community because they domesticate parts of our animal nature, has turned into an appreciation of the power of the underlying impulses and the disclosure of the norms as arbitrary instruments of violent repression. The game the would-be good bourgeois (or bourgeoise) is scheduled to play appears both arbitrary and cruel. Jaun comes to appreciate this. Initially wound up to high pitch and self-congratulatory about his peroration (439: 15–20), he comes to see himself as the channel through which the authorities have pro-nounced. The suspicion that he hasn't spoken in his own voice, that he has been a mere "medium" (439: 22), momentarily perplexes him. Are these his words? Is this his anger? Or are the impulses he officially condemns part of himself?

> I feel spirts of itchery outching out from all over me and only for the sludgehummer's force in my hand to hold them the darkens alone knows what'll who'll be saying of next. However. Now, before my up-perotic rogister, something nice. Now? Dear Sister, in perfect leave again . . . (439: 22–6)

It is a new beginning. Jaun takes a moment, a word or two of pause, to calm himself, to throw off the discomfiting persona into which he has grown, and to try to approach the same advisory material with greater success.

He starts with more constructive methods for avoiding temptation, methods of sublimation so beloved of Victorian education. A proper course of reading will turn his sister's thoughts (and those of the other maidens) in proper directions.[9] Education will prepare them for marriage, and they should engage in the approved feminine curriculum, ministering to the poor and sick, sewing, and pious study (440: 21–7). As he proceeds, doubts creep in that these devices will prove effective, for the enemy is determined—the "inimitable in pureseut of the inevitable" (441: 14).[10] So the homily returns again to the same bald advice: "Guard that gem, Sissy, rich and rare, ses he" (441: 18).

But does the young girl have the strength to ward off the threats to her honor—and these are threats not simply to her honor but to that of the family? As he loses control, "hardworking Jaun" comes to the conclusion that the only solution is constant male supervision and the expectation of male revenge. A girl must "divulge" what has happened, identifying the strangers who attempt to talk with her (441: 24, 29ff.),[11] and if any of them take advantage of her weakness, the family will be there to exact retribution:

> rest insured that as we value the very name in sister that as soon as we do possibly it will be a poor lookout for that insister. He's a markt man from that hour. . . . Because then probably we'll dumb well soon show him what the Shaun way is like how we'll go a long way towards breaking his outsider's face for him for making up to you . . . (442: 16–18, 21–4)[12]

The affirmation of the local norms is expressed in a virulent detestation of those with contrary standards, and the family is constantly vigilant to protect its own.[13]

Once again, enthusiasm for violent action has taken over. Although it is first directed toward the alleged culprit, described in especially unflattering terms as an oily and unattractive social climber with a menial white-color occupation,[14] the hand of masculine authority is soon turned against the dishonored female. Male power is stark and is justified in simple terms:

> I overstand you, you understand. (444: 30)

> For your own good, you understand, for the man who lifts his pud to a woman is saving the way for kindness. (445: 11–13)

So whether it comes as a "smack" on the "fruitflavored jujube lips" (444: 22) or a blow that "will bring the poppy blush of shame to your peony hindmost" (a part of the body taken by the devil, perhaps, and one in which the devil continues to reign) (445: 16), the bourgeois code must be enforced on the weak young woman who succumbs to temptation.

Jaun's new start has led him to the same destination, an identity as patriarchal enforcer that he cannot endorse. His first worry is that enforcement is impossible in his absence, and he wishes, for a moment, that he might return disguised (like the Duke in *Measure for Measure*) to monitor the conduct of those whom he has supposedly left behind (445: 26–7). Yet the prospect of his departure conjures a gentler thought, the possibility that love may do more than the fear of violence—that, properly "canalised," the impulse these norms are designed to restrain may even prompt compliance. The thunderous Jaun grows soft ("soo ooft" as the valedictory voice of III-1 characterized him [427: 24]) in recalling the happy times they have shared; his sister fills "a big corner . . . in this unadulterated seat of our affections" (445: 35–6). The energy that has flooded his fierce denunciation of sexual lapses and infused his relish at prospective punishments now flows in a very different direction. He expresses his yearning for Issy—"Iy waount yiou!" (446: 2)—and conjures a vision of the blissful union that awaits his return (446: 7–26).

How can this be a version of the conformist identity to which Jaun is supposed to be dedicated? Turning away from the violence into which his previous efforts have degenerated, he strikes off in a new direction, aimed toward a different bourgeois vision—one in which marriage, industry, and the improvement of self and society figure prominently. After the rhapsodic love letter to Issy, sister and bride-to-be, there is a dedication to joint effort, as if their union could be legitimized by engaging in work that the community will value:

> brace to brassiere and shouter to shunter, we'll pull off our working programme. Come into the garden guild and be free of the gape athome! We'll circumcivicise all Dublin country. Let us, the real Us, all ignite in our prepurgatory grade as aposcals and be instrumental to utensilise . . . (446: 33–447: 1)

There is excitement in the thought that, after two false starts, a genuine identity has been forged ("the real Us"). It consists in socially useful labor, undertaken with pain and sacrifice (it is "prepurgatory," after all), carried out together. With its public demonstration of good to the surrounding people, this "programme," and those who devote themselves to it, can become accepted as members of the community ("free of the gape athome").[15] They are also free of any "gap" at home, a void that might grow within a marriage that withdrew from the surrounding community. (As we have seen, the desirability of engagement with or withdrawal from the public is an issue on which HCE and ALP take different stances; Jaun is siding with his father here.)

The project of "circumcivicisation" is proper, even godly work, for it is the promotion of cleanliness.[16] As Jaun comments, "this labour's worthy of my higher" (448: 21). The scale of the task, however, is daunting—it will take enormous effort to cleanse the "face of our sow muckloved d'lin" (his native city and native land, for Ireland has been seen as a "sow"; 448: 11). The tempo of Jaun's prose flags, as he reflects on his calloused feet and the lack of appreciation for his services. For one with no great wish to "do a strike of work," one "too soft for work proper" (409: 34; 410: 33), this ambition will not do. And, perhaps, he has also begun to wonder whether, in the end, this life of loving union expressed in socially productive activity really amounts to anything.

For Jaun's next experiment in identity is prefaced with a world-weary commentary:

> his onsaturncast eyes in stellar attraction followed swift to an imaginary
> swellaw, O, the vanity of Vanissy! All ends vanishing! (449: 2–4)

Swift's mordant vision has entered Jaun's appraisal of the civic life, and, with an echo of Ecclesiastes, he recognizes the ends of the "working programme" as evanescent. Yet the aging dean could turn for comfort to the girls he named "Stella" and "Vanessa," and Jaun comes to envisage romance in the here-and-now. Perhaps, he can abandon menial labor, supported by his wife's earnings,[17] and they can live together happily, enjoying the beauties of the natural world. He conjures a pastoral vision, the afternoon of a faun.

For a moment Jaun is captivated.[18] He imagines himself making sweet music in peaceful surroundings, in harmony with nature. That activity would develop a part of him that has previously been suppressed, his creative artistic yearnings. He declares that he has talent:

> I've a voicical lilt too true. Nomario! And bemolly and jiesis! For I sport
> a whatyoumacormack in the latcher part of my throughers. (450: 24–6)

Yet, at this moment of confidence, Jaun the would-be pastoral artist has already opened the possibility of trouble in his envisaged garden. His assets include not only a pure Irish tenor voice (like that of John McCormack) but also something (named euphemistically, "whatyoumaycallit") encased in his trousers. Why does Issy, or his "lady of Lyons," need reminder or reassurance about that? Because the romantic union, based on a lopsided division of labor, may prove problematic; the couple will fail to be in harmony.

> Naturale you might lower register me as diserecordant, but I'm athlone
> in the lillabilling of killarnies. That's flat. (450: 27–9)

Jaun recognizes that he has been singing a solo, not a duet, and that the partner on whose support his pastoral music-making relies may be tempted to listen to other voices.

> Yet ware the wold, you! What's good for the gorse is a goad for the
> garden. Lethals lurk heimlocked in logans. (450: 29–31)

Poison has entered the envisaged paradise. This vision, too, proves unsustainable.

Abruptly he abandons it in favor of a more conventional version of marriage. They are to return from Arcadia to the real world.

But enough of greenwood's gossip! Birdsnests is birdsnests. Thine to wait but mine to wage. And now play sharp to me. Doublefirst I'll head foremost through all my examhoops. (450: 33–5)

Jaun pledges himself to a more active, and more remunerative, career than his wife; the traditional roles will be restored.[19] He recognizes that there are obstacles to success and arbitrary challenges that have to be overcome, but "business is business," and he is determined to excel (a double first is the highest level of achievement in the British university examination system).

What is it all for? Jaun promises that he will produce something even more impressive than the ideal of bourgeois domesticity that excited the Floras as they sang praises to Chuff (235: 10 ff.). He recognizes the effort that will be involved, but vows that he is

> the gogetter that'd make it pay like cash registers as sure as there's a pot on a pole. (451: 4–5)[20]

Indeed, he is prepared for all sorts of hardships:

> I'd axe the channon and leip a liffey and drink annyblack water that rann onme way. Yip! How's thats for scats, mine shatz, for a lovebird? (451: 14-16)

Jaun sees himself as the contemporary version of the traditional hero who dares anything in the service of his true love. These are not mere sacrifices to prove his worthiness (although they surely do that) but also means of bringing all sorts of modern delights. The champagne corks will pop as they celebrate their successes, and, after all the determined striving they will have

> shot that blissup and swumped each other, manawife, into our sever nevers where I'd plant you, my Gizzygay, on the electric ottoman in the lap of lechery, simpringly stitchless with admiracion, among the most uxuriously furnished compartments, with sybarate chambers . . . (451: 28–32)

Material wealth, it seems, is to be the great aphrodisiac.

Yet, just as it seems that Jaun has found himself as the successful businessman whose home is a temple of prosperity and romantic rapture, his tone falters. Recognizing the precariousness of this life, its vulnerability to accidents, Jaun admits that he'd be "awful anxious" (451: 35). His enthusiasm dwindles into apologetic admission of his limitations (452: 4–7).

The dissolution of what momentarily appeared as a satisfactory identity isn't just the product of Jaun's timidity, of a failure of nerve on his part. As the valedictory voice of III-1 recognized, Shaun has reflected more extensively (428: 4–7), and his broader perspective has already surfaced in the worry that mundane ends are vanity (or vanishing; 449: 4). That concern inspired his commitment to a loving union, first as a pastoral idyll and then in the form of a successful bourgeois marriage. The doubt that supersedes the excited evocation of gold-plated domestic-cum-sexual bliss may rest not simply on Jaun's anxiety about the chances of attaining or sustaining it but also on the sense that this, too, would be vanity.

For, he tells his sister, as he reads and thinks about what the bourgeois life involves, he comes to have an unnerving recognition of its evanescence. He professes his willingness to "go forth," as young men are supposed to do, and to make his way in the world, what convention views as a "benedictine errand" (452: 17). Even though it is "historically the most glorious mission, secret or profund" (452: 17–18), Jaun knows that vast numbers have undertaken it before him:

> through all the annals of our—as you so often term her—efferfresh-painted livy, in beautific repose, upon the silence of the dead, from pharoph the nextfirst to ramescheckles the last bust thing. The Vico road goes round and round to meet where terms begin. Still onappealed to by the cycles and unappalled by the recoursers we feel all serene, never you fret, as regards our dutyful cask. (452: 18–24)

The serenity is at best temporary. For Jaun has seen that the paint fades and needs to be kept up, that the dead are silent and not up to squeals of rapture "on the electric ottoman in the lap of lechery" (451: 30–1). He appreciates that even the most successful, those with the vastest and gaudiest temples, pass into dust, becoming the "last bust thing," and that appreciation does make the *ricorso*, one's own short turn round the Vico road, genuinely appalling. It is always possible to hope, to tell yourself confidently that things will be different the next time:

> We only wish everyone was as sure of anything in this watery world as we are of everything in the newlywet fellow that's bound to follow. (452: 29–31)[21]

For a moment, Jaun summons up confidence, declaring his willingness to bet on the future. But he understands the humor of the moment, a humor that his mother, present here both as river and recorder of history (Liffey and Livy), will understand and appreciate, knowing, as she does, that what is to come will only be another version of what has been (452: 33).

It doesn't last. Jaun's attempt to suppress doubts about the significance of the bourgeois life, to act as if it really were a "glorious mission," is immediately succeeded by an openly cynical embrace of the pointlessness of conventional restraint. He starts with a brusque dismissal:

> Well, to the figends of Annanmeses with the wholeabuelish business! (452: 34–5)

As he prepares to leave them, he urges the girls to moderate their distress over his absence. After all, it doesn't matter much. So, instead of the long catalogue of rules with which he first regaled them, they should do what they can to be happy. The norms they have been brought up to respect have no serious force, and they can disregard the pious rituals of mourning.

> So cut out the lonesome stuff! Drink it up, ladies, please, as smart as you can lower it! Out with lent! Clap hands postilium! Fastintide is by. (453: 34–6)

Jaun, now Jaunathaun, concludes with a laugh, as if he were now convinced of the folly of his earlier exhortations and were now resolved to treat the "problem" of living with the lightness it deserves.

Yet, as the Floras flutter around him, perhaps unconvinced by his commands to festivity in parting, Jaunathaun's mood changes once again:

> when suddenly (how like a woman!),[22] swifter as mercury he wheels right round starnly on the Rizzies suddenly, with his gimlets blazing rather sternish . . . (454: 20–2)

Jaun's previous instructions in conventional morality have been, as we've seen, counsels of prudence; there has been no invocation of religion as a backdrop for morality or of the possibility that the point of mundane existence lies in preparation for a life beyond. Now the cynic of the preceding speech becomes the stern voice of warning.

Instead of dancing and drinking, the girls must follow a very strict regime. Their devotions are directed not toward the worldly successes that have been dismissed as evanescent and valueless, but to obtaining treasure in heaven.

> It's prayers in layers all the thumping time . . . in the suburrs of the heavenly gardens, once we shall have passed . . . to our snug eternal retribution's reward (the scorchhouse). (454: 28–33, with omissions)

In this multilayered sentence, the girls are exhorted to pray on earth, so that they will gain an eternal reward in the heavenly "suburbs" (for presumably the higher circles of paradise are not open to them), where they may continue to pray (all the "thumping time"), perhaps clad in rough clothing ("burrs"); but this is already prefigured as highly unlikely, since earthly conduct typically calls for retribution, and the probable destination is the "scorchhouse." As if this were not a grim enough prospect, Jaun continues with a lackluster advertisement for the joys of heaven.

> No petty family squabbles Up There nor homemade hurricanes in our Cohortyard, no cupahurling nor apuckalips nor no puncheon jodelling nor no nothing. With the Byrns which is far better and eve for ever your idle be. (454: 36–455: 3)[23]

Family life dissolves entirely in heaven, where there is no conflict of wills, no "coupling," no "puckering of lips" in kissing, no drinking and singing—in short "no nothing," a complete absence of all those things that make human life interesting. Jaunathaun, or "Joe Hanny," offers a tip (a Revelation?):

> Postmartem is the goods. With Jollification a tight second. Toborrow and toburrow and tobarrow! That's our crass, hairy and evergrim life, till one finel howdiedow Bouncer Naster raps on the bell with a bone and his stinkers stank behind him with the sceptre and the hourglass. (455: 11–16)

Eternal life is the alleged good, and it is for the godly. But "jollification," possibly achieved through drink (getting "tight") is a close second. The rest is the scraping regime of conventional life, not the hard-won material and sexual pleasures of one of Jaun's earlier visions but the cadging, the hiding from hostile forces, and eventually the burial mound. A sequence of meaningless yesterdays, todays, and tomorrows leaves only a stench behind.

Jollification is surely hard to achieve. But Jaun's vision suggests that observing the rules that have been set for us is even harder. The life we live in our "miseryme heretoday" pales beside the "Hereweareagain Gaieties of the Afterpiece," but the one in charge has constructed a "Harlequinade," one that will turn out to be "Mark Time's Finist Joke" (455: 24, 25, 28, 29). The great director has done it by "Putting Allspace in a Notshall" (455: 29). The thundering list of prohibitions—"Thou shalt not . . . "—virtually ensures that all of us are set for "retribution's reward (the scorchhouse)."

Having conjured this bleak vision, Jaun turns away, reverting to his earlier hedonism.[24] Settling for what jollification he can find, he takes the simple pleasures of the table and endorses his official round as postman (455: 30 ff.; 456: 24 ff.) He has momentary thoughts of finishing off the meal with some sexual pleasure (457: 5–7), but, as the cynical mood deepens, he recognizes the pointlessness of bringing into the world other beings who will live lives of no point, little "jollification," and much pain.

> Ye can stop as ye are, little lay mothers, and wait in wish and wish in vain till the grame reaper draws nigh, with the sickle of the sickles, as a blessing in disguise. Devil a curly hair I care! (457: 8–11)

The "henservants" of Jaun's "introit" (432: 5, 6) have become "little lay mothers," insignificant beings whose function is to produce more creatures like themselves. After a "tear or two in time," they will be at the service of "His Diligence Majesty, our longdistance laird that likes creation" (457: 21, 23–4).[25]

Although she begins with an apparent agreement, Issy opposes this stark farewell message. Breaking into Jaun's homily, with its ever more abrupt recent oscillations between biting skepticism and mindless hedonism, she tries to woo him back to what she perceives as happiness. The breathless gush of her sexually heightened version of Swift's "little language" streams over the small pleasures and small setbacks of a bourgeois girl's existence, bypassing the broader thoughts that have troubled him. She would surely like to return him to the "electric ottoman in the lap of lechery" (451: 30–1), rejected by Jaun partly out of a sense of his own inadequacy, partly out of a sense of its inadequacy as a ground of enduring significance.

Her method is to tease and cajole, to conjure up simple delights, but above all to perform for him the ecstasy he might have enjoyed. So, in the end, she will show him and take herself into the "sever nevers." Although she may have a different partner,

> your name of Shane will come forth between my shamefaced whesen with other lipth I nakest open my thight when just woken by his toccatootletoo my first morning. . . . Coach me how to tumble, Jaime, and listen, with supreme regards, Juan, in haste, warn me which to ah ah ah ah. . . . (461: 25–8, 30–2)

Like Molly Bloom, Issy hopes to rouse the ardor of a lover who touches her more deeply than the man with whom she couples—the cry of the cock recalls Blazes Boylan, and the Spanish versions of the names link Issy to Molly.[26]

Juan neither accepts nor condemns the sexual invitation. His rapid switches of perspective, voice, and plan are now behind him, and he is resolved to be off. The conformist has become the wanderer, bent on self-imposed exile, and his long goodbye is permeated by restlessness, as if he itched to be free. Before he departs, he has two last tasks to perform for the girls he leaves behind.

One is to create a festive mood, to go with gallant *joie-de-vivre*. Again he tells the girls to be cheerful:

> be not on your weeping what though Shaunathan is in his fail! (462: 7–8)

In the terms of the homily, he has indeed failed, for none of the identities he has explored has proved stable. Yet his hedonism can be merrier now, for he has abandoned the old project in favor of one that will suit his uncertainties; he is off to wander freely where the mood will lead him.

The second task is to give his old role to another. Shaun is "not for forgetting me innerman monophone" (462: 15–16)—he will not leave them without a counselor who can speak to them with a single voice (as he has notably failed to do). He will leave behind his "darling proxy," his "dear old man pal," a character named "Dave" (462: 16–18), whose arrival is immediately promised. Sure enough, Dave appears, "coming home to mourn mountains," "after his French evolution" (462: 32, 34). The hints are broad enough: Dave is a version of Shem or Stephen, a native lad returned from France on a mission of mourning. Clues multiply, as Jaun continues his introduction, announcing his kinship with the newcomer:

> Got by the one goat, suckled by the same nanna, one twitch, one nature makes us oldworld kin. (463: 15–17)

But if this sorry figure, "scaly skin and all, with his blackguarded eye" (464: 11–12), is to play the role envisaged for him in the girls' festivities, Jaun has work to do. As Issy's dramatic performance has made clear, they have sexual needs to be satisfied, and Dave requires a lot of encouragement.

Mixing explicit instructions with teasing and jeering, advertising Dave's talents at one moment and apologizing for his performance at another, Jaun pours out a torrent of energetic words in an effort to get the party going (465: 1–468: 19). This great piece of Joycean bawdy can be read for its raucous high spirits, or for what it reveals about Jaun's progress. Jaun has broken completely with the premises and principles from which he began; the conformist has become a determined free spirit. All that he wants to do is to wind things up as quickly as possible, to leave, and make a completely fresh start.

So the pitch of his last speech—"my positively last at any stage" (468: 23)—is wound to a new height. It erupts in restless energy, in sentences that shake off the coils he takes to bind him and succeed one another in panting rhythms.

> This shack's not big enough for me now. I'm dreaming of ye, azores. (468: 33–4)
>
> Daughters of the heavens, be lucks in turnabouts to the wandering sons of red loam! The earth's atrot! The sun's a scream! The air's a jig. The water's great! Seven oldy oldy hills and the one blue beamer. I'm going. I know I am. I could bet I am. Somewhere I must get far away from Banbashore, wherever I am. No saddle, no staffet, but spur on the moment! (469: 2–8)

The only direction for Jaun is away. The only place is somewhere else. The only possibility is something else. What he is to become is quite unknown, but it has to be different from any of the things he has been.

In the end, he chafes at further delay and closes with a coarse dismissal:

> Break ranks! After wage-of-battle bother I am thinking most. Fik yew! I'm through. Won. Toe. Adry. You watch my smoke. (469: 26–8)

Like Glugg, he has been "buzzling is brains" (223: 25–6), but now Jaun says (emphatically) goodbye to all that.

The girls express an elegant distress at Jaun's departure, but their wailing is far less interesting than the manner of his leaving. Just as Joyce captured in the music of his prose the turbulent energy of Jaun's impatience to leave, to be free—*presto, staccato, molto vivace ed agitatissimo*—so now, in a surging, swirling, eddying paragraph, he depicts the clumsy comedy of the launching:

> but when next to nobody expected, their star and gartergazer at the summit of his climax, he toppled a lipple on to the off and, making a brandnew start for himself to run down by his easting, by blessing hes sthers with the sign of the southern cross, his bungaloid borsaline with the hedgygreen bound blew off in a loveblast (award for trover!) and Jawjon Redhead, bucketing after, meccamaniac, (the headless shall have legs!), kingscouriered round with an easy rush and ready relays by the bridge a stadion beyond Ladycastle (and what herm but he narrowly missed fouling her buttress for her but for he acqueducked) . . .
> (471: 8–18)

It is a crazy mixture of motions and directions, showing Jaun at odd postures and angles, as his barrel bobs and tips with the currents and the obstacles. He is quite out of any control, on a voyage that will be set not by him, not by any of the plans he might have made, but by forces beyond him.

We hear a valedictory voice, echoing the close of the previous chapter. It responds to the departure of Jaun—now Haun—with protective well-wishing. There is a firm sense of the finality of this farewell, sadness for the loss, and appreciation of the youth's bright promise.

> Good by nature and natural by design, had you but been spared to us, Hauneen lad, but sure where's the use my talking quicker when I know you'll hear me all astray? . . . Thy now paling light lucerne we ne'er may see again. But could it speak how nicely would it splutter to the four cantons praises be to thee, our pattern sent! For you had—may I, in our, your and their names, dare to say it?—the nucleus of a glow of a zeal of soul of service such as rarely, if ever, have I met with single men.
> (472: 10–13, 22–7)

In recalling the high expectations, this voice recalls all the ways in which Shaun was presented as the envisaged solution to the dreamer's central problem. He was to show how a worthwhile life is to be lived. His own admission, "Shaunathaun is in his fail" (462: 8), has been underscored by the sodden Sickerson,[27] who has recognized Jaun's change of course in bidding him farewell (471: 34), and is now certified by a more authoritative voice. But has the dreamer given up too quickly on the possibilities of conformism?

There are many ways to try to reveal the oppressive effects of accepted schemes of values. One can try to show systematically the crippling consequences of particular precepts, as, in their different ways, Rousseau, Mill, and Dewey all do. Or one can trace a general system of values to some more basic set of social or economic conditions and demonstrate the tendencies of those conditions to produce increasing misery, as Marx and his followers attempt. Or one can undertake a general "revaluation of values" that attempts to probe and question any forfeiture of individual autonomy, as Nietzsche (at least sometimes) seems to envisage it. Joyce has not provided anything like a philosophical demonstration of the impossibility of a worthwhile life centered on acceptance of the norms of a community. There has been no serious canvassing of all the possibilities, and many of Jaun's acts of discarding a possible identity seem to depend on highly particular features of Irish life in the early decades of the twentieth century.

Yet, like Dickens in his more incisive moments as social critic, like Shaw, and, above all, like Ibsen, Joyce has mounted a real challenge to conformism. The Norwegian interiors Ibsen presents to us stifle the lives of his central characters because of very specific features of the social environment in which his protagonists are embedded, but the presentation forces us to reflect how a wide variety of lives in affluent societies are molded and confined. So, too, with the vacillations of Jaun. They ask whether the dreamer—or we who follow the dream—can tell a better story about ourselves. Can we feel the responses that prompt Jaun's erratic transitions and still avoid his mad career, his headlong fall?

By the end, Shaun has effectively changed places with his brother; the pious conformist has become the free-spirited rebel. The movement of Part II, of course, was in the opposite direction, a portrayal of the wretchedness of exclusion that culminated in the union of the brothers to bring about the supposedly bright day of Shaun. It is no accident, I think, that when Shem emerges here, as the forlorn Dave, he is a pathetic substitute for the vigorous Shaun. We are left with a surrogate conformist, an ex-rebel limp and drained, and a newly converted apostle of freedom, a wandering outsider whose graceless exit suggests that he has little talent for the part. Each brother's trajectory leads to a dismal version of the other's starting point, and both consequently are doomed to failure.

Yet in the course Jaun has followed, there must be a moment when he has occupied the muddled position of his father. Somewhere, perhaps, he has tried the experiment of life as HCE. I suggest that appreciating just that possibility is crucial to the next chapter. For although, as I have insisted, Joyce is not writing philosophy, he has presented the dreamer, and us, with a sobering demonstration. Lives can be oriented toward either of two poles or to any intermediate position between them. Widely shared human impulses will prompt us to leave either pole and move toward the other. Neither pole is acceptable and intermediate compromises are unstable—including, it would appear, HCE's own attempt to find a middle way.

This abstract structure underlies Joyce's vivid series of vignettes in the chapters that have led us to this point. The latest, the apparently closing move in his demonstration, shows us the fall of a figure that entered the children's game in the role of an angel (222: 22). Yet, although the valedictory voice is sadly reconciled to the permanent loss of Haun, the farewell concludes on a note of hope.

> Brave footsore Haun! Work your progress! Hold to! Now! Win out, ye divil ye! The silent cock shall crow at last. The west shall shake the east awake. Walk while ye have the night for morn, lightbreakfastbringer, morroweth whereon every past shall full fost sleep. Amain. (473: 20–5)

Is this the familiar self-deceptive hope for a new beginning—seen before in the ungrounded optimism of the four old men (398: 7–28), the excitement of the ass (404: 11–15), and Jaun's expression of the human tendency to suppose that things are bound to get better (452: 29–31)? I think not. Joyce is preparing us for a solution to the problem he has posed, not one that brings into our view any dramatically different possibility but a perception of something (indeed someone) the dreamer has already scrutinized, to be observed now in a new light.

Shaun was first discerned in the gloom by his light, his "belted lamp" (404: 13), and the "paling" of his light (472: 22–3) has evoked his loss. He has been the light-bearer, or light-bringer, Lucifer, most beautiful and most promising among the angels. Like Lucifer, he has rebelled and fallen, and the promise has gone. But now, according to the voice, the morning will play that role, bringing light—and, of course, breakfast.

Appropriately enough, the voice addresses Shaun as "ye divil ye!" Shaun, as well as the morning, is aptly named "lightbreakfastbringer," not only because letters arrive at breakfast time and because he is Lucifer. Shaun is like Joyce's most celebrated breakfastbringer, Leopold Bloom, the husband who delivers the letters (including the ominous letter from Blazes Boylan) along with his wife's breakfast tray (*Ulysses*, 61–3). When we meet him, Bloom is a wanderer, directionless—and that, too, is what Shaun has become. If he is to find his way again, perhaps it will be a version of Bloom's way.

18

ARISE, SIR GHOSTUS!

Conflicted Shaun tried to find an identity, a way of living, that would give enough to each of the incompatible impulses within him. He failed and fell, and, when we meet him again, he is recumbent.

> Lowly, longly, a wail went forth. Pure Yawn lay low. (474: 1)

His cries of distress attract the four old men (and their attendant ass). They climb to the burial mound, the barrow, on which Yawn lies, and begin a lengthy interrogation, their "sworn star-chamber quiry on him" (475: 18–19).

Their motivation is plain. They, the dreamer's surrogates, hope to discover who he is, or who he (and they) should be: "For he was ever their quarrel, the way they would see themselves"[1] (475: 19–20). Their inquisition will have to probe the past—"traversing climes of old times gone by of the days not worth remembering" (474: 22–3), like the meagre Dublin lives they rambled over in II-4. It involves "seeking spoor through the deep timefield" (475: 24), a place in which potentially explosive events and thoughts have been buried (as in the battlefields in which HCE's successors fought in I-4; 77: 4-11). No wonder they approach the figure on the mound with trepidation.[2]

The senile old men we recall from II-4 (and their briefer appearances earlier) hardly look like good candidates for this task. Their ass has already shown more skills as an interviewer than we would expect from them. Nor will this assessment be modified by what follows, for the long inquisition will contain a large proportion of miscommunications, inept questions, and evasive answers. The interrogators are incompetent, and the witness is unwilling.

This should not be surprising, however. All these are night thoughts, veiled in the obscurity of a dream, precisely because the dreamer is so reluctant to face their content directly. Shaun/Yawn, once the apparent hope, is a complex of discordant voices, and it is painful to give them audience. So the process is slow and inefficient, often cacophonous and confused—but, as always with the *Wake*, it constantly flashes with humor.[3]

The interrogation is also a dissection, the "postmartem" Jaun predicted would be "the goods" (455: 11–12). So it proves, for the exposure of the elemental voices within Shaun reveals, behind his fears, uncertainties, and conflicting impulses, the figure of HCE; and the further probing of HCE will eventually lead the dreamer to understand him in a new, and more hopeful, way. The fitful archeology of the chapter unearths a surprising find. Or, to switch metaphors, after the long descent from the beginning of Part II, the movement of the *Wake*'s music finally achieves a more sustained upturn.

The dreamer's problem, as I suggested, has recently taken the form of finding some stable identity that will survive Shaun's internal conflict, and to solve it requires resisting the disintegration of Jaun we've just witnessed. Joyce releases us from his problematic demonstration by disclosing a possibility overlooked in Jaun's hectic sequence of experiments, an unlikely possibility given the bitter failure of II-3. The integration of opposing voices undertaken by HCE, flawed and muddled though it is, turns out to be the best Shaun can do. The orthodox son, the supposed avatar of a better order, resists that possibility, but, as we'll soon learn, "[t]he old order changeth and lasts like the first" (486: 10).[4] Moreover, when these bumbling questioners have dragged from Shaun the sources of his aspirations and anxieties, that old order, HCE's life, will come to look different.

Shem and Shaun originally emerged as elements within HCE, expressions of different aspirations within him. As we followed the possible development of Shem in II-1, we discovered HCE,[5] and so, too, HCE will appear as the deepest stratum in Shaun's many layers. Perhaps he deserves "the nickname Here Comes Everybody" (32: 18–19). But it will take enormous effort to retrieve him and to remove his disguises.

Yawn lies on a "prehistoric barrow" (477: 36), and the past beneath him will have to be excavated. The starting point of the investigation, however, is the present, and the old men[6] begin with his mundane role, inquiring about his letters. Yawn responds with a surprising expression of how he now views himself:

—Throsends. For my darling. Typette.
—So long aforetime? Can you hear better?
—Millions. For godsends. For my darling dearling one. (478: 3–5)

No declaration like this surfaced in Jaun's long oration. When romantic love emerged in his canvass of identities, it was sometimes passed over quickly before describing a life of shared work or a pastoral idyll, was sometimes understood in terms of rhapsodic sexual activity. Jaun's childish cry, "Iy waount yiou!" (446: 2), and the adolescent fantasy of reunion that succeeds it, provides no prospect of a dedication expressed over years ("So long aforetime?"), in thousands and millions of devotional offerings ("godsends"). Yawn's wanderings, and his apparent crash, have brought him to a new ideal, that of a loving union, sustained, with thousands or millions of small efforts, across a long time.[7]

Under further questioning, Yawn adds another dimension to his opening declaration. Asked "Whu's teit dans yur jambs?" (478: 23)—"Whose head is in your legs?" or, more exactly, "What conception of yourself have your wanderings brought you to?"—Yawn responds:

—Trinathan partnick dieudonnay. Have you seen her? Typette, my tactile O!
—Are you in your fatherick, lonely one?
—The same. Three persons. Have you seen my darling only one? I am sohohold! (478: 26–30)

He has discovered the divisions within himself—the lover, the cynic, the dutiful Irish son and defender of the true religion (Tristan, Jonathan Swift ["nathandjoe," 1: 12], and Patrick)—and has also learned that he is corrupt, fallen ("part Nick").[8] Yet over these divisions, he insists on his love. Three persons, Shaun, Shem, and HCE, he may be, but the urge to find his beloved is dominant. This urge has survived time, for, as he declares, he is "sohohold"—so old.

The answer to the inquisitors' primary question, the question of who Yawn is, is here right at the beginning, blurted out in the first phase of the dialogue. Yet there are plenty of voices within Yawn, and within the mound of the past on which he lies, voices that want to issue denials, retractions, and qualifications, to express fears and doubts. Those fears and doubts emerge very quickly in an apparently strange continuation.

In reply to an utterly uncomprehending question, Yawn makes an association with dangerous predators. He cries out in genuine fear: "Do not flingamejig to the twolves!" (479: 14). After one of the inquisitors laughs off the fear, a more organized questioner begins the archeology of the burial mound, suggesting that this "plagueburrow" contains a burial ship (479: 24–31). That ship is associated with Denmark and the raids of the Vikings. Yawn expresses another fear:

A destroyer in our port. . . . Laid bare his breastpaps to give suck, to suckle me. Ecce Hagios Chrisman! (480: 13–15)

To which one of his interlocutors replies, apparently irrelevantly:

—Oh, Jeyses, fluid! says the poisoned well. (480: 16)

Evidently HCE has emerged and is a disturbing prospect, but, at first sight, the associations with wolves, buried burial ships, and household cleaners (Jeyses's fluid) seem hard to fathom.

Yawn has acknowledged three persons within himself, and he is frightened of two of them, viewing them as destructive of the values to which the third aspires. The two, "the twolves," are predatory,[9] like the wolves of the sea (480: 4), the Vikings who came across the sea to ravage Ireland. Both HCE and Shem have made similar journeys, and both may be regarded as similarly destructive when they reach port. HCE, in his failure, was sent out on a burial ship, after the custom of the Vikings, and that ship—and his corpse—lies beneath Yawn, infecting the ground and contaminating the water. HCE, the outsider-father, has also passed on his alien customs and traditions to his sons—symbolized here by the practice of the male suckling the children, a practice condemned by the Irish Saint Patrick. The poisonous fluid is inside them, potentially infecting their ventures and ideals. Yawn fears that the love on which he insists will be tainted by HCE's corruption, that it will fail as HCE failed. He wishes to speak with *some* of the voices within him, those associated with Tristan, with Patrick, with Shaun. The voices of Shem, and especially of HCE, are to be silenced.

Yet, much as Yawn, like Stephen Dedalus, would like to escape from the nightmare of history, he is forced to acknowledge his parentage (482: 3–4). The interrogation again takes what initially appears as an inexplicable turn. Yawn, bearer of letters, is asked about the celebrated letter of the early vignettes (I-3, I-5). The point of the question emerges, as one of the old men interprets the physical evidence:

> I will let me take it upon myself to suggest to twist the penman's tale posterwise. The gist is the gist of Schaum but the hand is the hand of Sameas. (483: 1–4)

Yawn is under pressure to acknowledge one of the voices he hopes to keep silent.[10]

He protests, endeavoring to dissociate himself from the problematic figure of Shem:

> What cans such wretch to say to I or how have My to doom with him? (483: 17–18)

But the protest is inept, for, in the next breath, Yawn must acknowledge the kinship; the twins were "wombful of mischief" (483: 18). Yawn wants to emphasize the pious course he has followed (483: 31ff.), as if to separate two distinct paths from a single beginning, but the voice of Shem won't be silenced, intruding itself into the answer. Eventually Yawn must concede that he is "twosides uppish" (484: 14) and allow his union with Shem:

> I saved you fore of the Hekkites and you loosed me hind bland Harry to the burghmote of Aud Dub. (484: 20–21)

The fall of HCE ("Hek" [420: 17]) was brought about through the union of the brothers, and, in the crosstalk act of II-3, it was Shem/Butt who played the leading role, Moses to Shaun/Taff's Aaron.[11] Now, in injured tones, this voice announces betrayal—the speaker has been turned over to the traditional court of Ireland, taken to be a traitor, a rebel. Through Shaun's urge to conform, Yawn has betrayed the part of him that speaks for Shem.

Yawn continues to insist on his righteousness and devotion to tradition, concluding with a traditional avowal, "Itch dean" (485: 3—"*Ich dien,*'" "I serve," the motto of the Prince of Wales), one that inverts the declaration of Stephen Dedalus (and of Shem).[12] His pugnacious conclusion arouses the anger of one of the inquisitors, who insists that Yawn cannot free himself from his history and his ancestry (485: 17–24). In response, Yawn grovels, prostrating himself before the questioner.[13] Mollified, the voice offers a summary appraisal:

> History as her is harped. . . . Mere man's mime: God has jest. The old order changeth and lasts like the first. (486: 6, 9–10)

Yawn's attempt to deny the historical residues within him has failed. The next stage is to probe him further and determine exactly what these remains are.

The analysis reveals first the love that Yawn originally declared.[14] Behind it, however, is something different, a disturbing presence, waiting outside a door. Yawn plainly senses a threat to the love he has taken as central to himself, and the dim perception of menace is the source of his reluctance to acknowledge some parts of himself. One of his interlocutors feels compelled to ask

> did it ever occur to you, *qua* you, prior to this, . . . that you might, bar accidens, be very largely substituted in potential secession from your next life by a complementary character, voices apart? (486: 35–487: 4)

It is, as the inquisitor recognizes, a disturbing question, one that raises the prospect of something within Yawn that is at odds with his ideal for himself, something sufficiently powerful that it can destroy what he wants to be. The starkest form of the threat is that within Yawn is HCE, HCE as others see him, an outsider, impious, destructive, and, above all, incapable of the enduring love, the commitment, that those thousands (or millions) of letters represent. Yawn has resolutely insisted that this is wrong, that the "Hekkites" have been overthrown, that his father is firmly confined to the burial mound.

Under pressure, he must allow that there are occasions on which other aspects of himself, other potential selves, appear, but his confession is grudging and confused: "a few times" in his "ericulous[15] imaginating" he has a feeling

> that I'm not meself at all, no jolly fear, when I realize bimiselves how becomingly I to be going to become. (487: 13, 15, 18–19)

The questioners insist on a straight and clear answer, and, after offering a general suggestion of the two-sidedness of things and the identity of opposites,[16]

Yawn eventually comes clean—part of him identifies with his brother. It is easier to confess the Shem within than to acknowledge HCE.

Once confessed, Shem must be absolved, or, at very least, partially excused, appreciated for his good qualities, pitied for his bad luck. Yawn begins with a brief characterization of his brother,

> whom 'tis better ne'er to name, my said brother, the skipgod, expulled for looking at churches from behind . . . (488: 22–3)[17]

Plainly, there are suggestions of impiety, of lapses from religion so profound that they demand excommunication and exile. Yet "skipgod" can also be "scapegoat," and Shem can be taken as a sacrificial victim who has taken on the burden of sins for a larger group. So Yawn is prepared to allow that the guilt is not entirely Shem's—"He feels he ought to be as asamed of me as me to be ashunned of him" (489: 18–19). Confessing his love, he declares his brother to be "my shemblable! My freer!" (489: 28).[18]

Yawn has been forced to an admission but not to the confession that would disturb him most. For a few short exchanges, it appears that matters will rest there, that there is no more to discover than that his personality has two sides, one conformist, devout, and steady in its commitment to love, the other restless and nomadic, but exiled, kept at a safe distance.[19] Then, taking up a stray remark of Yawn's, a questioning voice comments: "You told of a tryst too, two a tutu" (491: 12–13). The incident in the park enters the inquiry, and Yawn is invited to sing Hosty's ballad.

He opts instead for the jeering song of the seabirds (491: 17–20; compare 383: 1 ff.). Concerned as he is to distance himself from HCE, and especially from the incident that stands for HCE's lapses in love, Yawn responds with enthusiasm. For a moment, inquisitors and witness are in harmony, and the examination becomes a carnival, the exultant excoriation of HCE that has been heard so often. But then a passing reference, to "Annie Delittle, his daintree diva," (492: 8–9) summons up a new voice within Yawn.

It is ALP. She speaks, as she so often does, in exoneration of her husband. Her (hilarious) defense offers all sorts of reasons for why HCE couldn't have done the things of which he is accused, but the climax of her vindication is to insist on his constant preparedness for his husbandly role:

> he never battered one eagle's before paying me his duty on my annaversary to the parroteyes list in my nil ensemble . . . and, my charmer, whom I dipped my hand in, he simply showed me his propendiculous loadpoker . . . (493: 4–5, 9–10)

The form of the defense is important. HCE's continued sexual attraction to his wife is a counter to the fear of inconstancy, of the inevitability of the fading of love, that so worries the dreamer (and his surrogate, Yawn). Moreover, the stark evocation of the physiological details both recognizes the animal quality of human copulation and allows ALP to introduce her laughter as a solvent for the dreamer's doubts. If ALP is proud that her husband's penis is perpendicular, she also finds it ridiculous.[20]

The eruption of ALP's voice throws the questioners into confusion, and it is hard for them to identify her. When one of them succeeds (493: 32–3), it provokes a cry of acquiescence from Yawn:

> My heart, my mother! My heart, my coming forth of darkness! (493: 34–5)

There should be no mystery in this, since ALP's defense has expressed just that constancy of love that Yawn is concerned to emphasize.

After an angry inquisitorial voice has contradicted ALP's defense, she reappears, to insist in ways we have heard before that the rumors are idle and the witnesses untrustworthy. But there are two moments in her speech that speak to the dreamer's anxieties. Contradicting the thought that age has made HCE gross and repulsive (494: 17–18), she replies:

> What about his age? says you. What about it? says I. (494: 30)

Opposing the thought that these are rumors that will drive them further apart, tarnishing further a relationship that has already become dull and tired, she declares that their response will be to assert both their continued companionship and their mutual attraction:

> How we will make laugh over him together, me and my Riley in the Vickar's bed! (495: 16–18)[21]

If Yawn can trust ALP's account of the matter, then he doesn't need to deny the voice of HCE within him—for HCE is no longer a "destroyer in the port," a threat to the commitment to love with which Yawn began.

But, with unusual lucidity, the inquisitors deny that ALP is reliable. Echoing the worry that has been present ever since the consolations of Part I, they see her as overfond, (self-)deceived: "I am afraid, my poor woman . . . you are misled" (495: 35–6). The inquisitors rehearse the almost-universal repudiation of HCE, and Yawn provides a childish version of the incident that led to his fall (496: 18–21, a mixture of a nursery rhyme and the *Genesis* story)—as if he had learned this as part of the entrenched moral lore of the community. But now comes an obvious challenge, as one of the old men raises the troubling possibility:

> if so be you may identify yourself with the him in you . . . (496: 25–6)

Yawn's response is that HCE and all he stands for is firmly dead, his passing celebrated at a carnival wake. He is

> healed cured and embalsemate, pending a rouseruction of his bogey, most highly astounded, as it turned up, after his life overlasting, at thus being reduced to nothing. (498: 36–499: 3)

With the consoling thought that, reduced to nothing, HCE can hardly be present within Yawn, three of the old men can celebrate the new era, hailing Yawn as the new king, the father-killing king ("adipose rex" [499: 16]).

There is a dissenting voice, an angry voice, perhaps the voice that earlier insisted on the impossibility of evading history. Alleging that this happy conclusion is a lie, the inquisitor challenges Yawn, claiming that he is "repeating [him]self" (499: 22). In response, the youth declares that he is sitting on the mound, as if confining within it

> all that's buried ofsins insince insensed insidesofme. (499: 25–6)

What is supposed to be buried will not, however, stay quiet (nor can noxious gases be entirely concealed by incense). There is a rumbling in the earth, a sound from the past. The old men are confused:

> —Whoishe whoishe whoishe whoishe linking in? Whoishe whoishe whoishe? (499: 35–6)

It is, of course, the big question, the question this chapter, and Part III up to this point, has been all about. Posing it leads to a confusion of tongues.

The source of the rumbling is, in fact, quite clear—it is "[t]he dead giant" (500: 1). The stirring of HCE, present within Yawn and unable to be confined, prompts the release of other voices within him, as well as interjections from the old men.[22] The clearest, most dominant expression from Yawn is the declaration of love with which he began.

Shaun, or Haun, vanished at the end of III-2, becoming a wanderer without an identity or direction. Now, as Yawn—reminding us of the drowsy way in which he first began to speak (407: 28)—he offers a new account of himself, as a man whose life is centered on a love recorded in a thousand (or a million) messages. The dreamer has encountered that conception of life before, in the figure of HCE, but his particular version has been written off as a failure.[23] Hence, it is only with great difficulty that HCE can be exposed within Yawn.

This first stage of the "star-chamber quiry," the anatomical dissection of Yawn, ends in confusion—as if several radio stations were competing for the air—and then a moment of silence. Then the show begins again.

The second phase offers a change of medium (as if the dreamer were attending a theatrical production) and a different line of questioning. With the exposure of HCE, Yawn's sense of himself has been threatened by all the stories that have portrayed HCE as unfaithful in his love. This material is now approached in a new way, through developing an account of origins. Through exposure of the ultimate causes of human tendencies and behavior, the question of corruption is to be settled. In their meandering and indirect way, the inquisitors, and the reluctant Yawn, seem to be tracing human frailty and inconstancy to its root, debunking any idea of the endurance of love, rejecting the consolation ALP has endeavored to bring.

The first task is to set the scene, and the discussion opens with a crazy report of the prevalent weather—Yawn is apparently willing to agree to all the incompatible meteorological conditions suggested by his interlocutors (501: 17; 503: 3).[24] Next, there must be agreement on place, and a questioner asks if it is "Woful Dane Bottom" (503: 21); the Scandinavian associations with HCE (most prominent in II-3), and with Sackerson (evident in III-2), make it clear that we are embarked on an investigation of the fall of the forefathers. That is reinforced by an exchange in which Yawn's replies are relatively direct:

—And what sigeth Woodin Warneung thereof?
—Trickspissers vill be pair secluded.
—There used to be a tree stuck up? An overlisting eshtree?
—There used, sure enough. Beside the Annar. (503: 28–32)

In the version of the Nordic myths Wagner chose for the origins story in the *Ring*, Wotan comes to the world-ash, the tree on which life depends. Sacrificing an eye to obtain wisdom, he breaks from the ash-tree a bough that becomes his rune-engraved spear, symbol of his power. Risking his sole remaining eye, he wins a wife, to whom he will constantly be unfaithful. These initial acts set in motion a course of history that leads to his own decline and the collapse of his world.[25] Wotan's act of trespass is linked to HCE's self-destructive urges in Yawn's account of "Woodin's Warneung."

This tree is easily linked to another, also famously declared to be off-limits, and a different account of the source of sin, that of Eve, tempted by

her downslyder in that snakedst-tu-naughsy whimmering woman't seeleib such a fashionaping sathinous dress out of that exquisitive creation and her leaves, my darling dearest . . . (505: 7–9)[26]

Between the Nordic story and the biblical account, however, Yawn also offers a Darwinian explanation that emphasizes the pressures of sex and of sexual competition (504: 26–9),[27] one that leads to another allusion to the Nordic myth.[28] Just as we were offered many inconsistent accounts of the weather, so, too, there are three—or four if we hear a reference to Vico in the response to the thunder (503: 2–3)—alternative versions of the origins of human nature. What the three main ones share is a depiction of us as essentially corrupt, as beings with uncontrollable sexual impulses that eventually bring about our doom.

The night that descended at the end of Part I, like the tale of the Mookse and the Gripes, left us with "an only elmtree and but a stone" (159: 4; 216: 2–4). Here, too, the tree is paired with a stone to emphasize the moral of these tales:

—A shrub of libertine, indeed! But that steyne of law indead what stiles its neming?
—Tod, tod, too hard parted. (505: 21–3)

The rottenness of human nature confronts the unyielding law (the "stein" or stone), and, since we can never satisfy the requirements of the law, death ("tod") is inevitable for us "[f]inight mens" (505: 24). The allusion to the text of Romans that so troubled Luther[29] translates into the dreamer's secular version as a pronouncement that the source of our corruption, our sexual inconstancy, undermines the only real possibility for valuable lives, lives based on the enduring commitment (the commitment from which Yawn began).

The decay of love is expressed in a sad evocation of the life of the marriage of HCE and ALP. An echo of ALP within Yawn responds to the question of "how near" the witness feels to HCE (identified here with Howth head [506: 19]):

> There do be days of dry coldness between us when he does be like a lidging house far far astray and there do be nights of wet windwhistling when he does be making me onions woup all kinds of ways. (506: 20–3)

There are intimations here of ALP's melancholy mood as she feels her husband parting from her (626: 35 ff.). The sad admission begins a search for the causes of this decay, and the questioners move from the accounts of origins to the ways in which corruption reveals itself in the mundane events of human life.

The initial focus is on a seedy character, first identified as "Thom" (506: 28; perhaps "t' hom[o]" or "the man"?), later as "Shivering William" (507: 35), but evidently HCE. This character, plainly "wandering," let down his trousers, exposing himself (508: 7, 9–11). The act can be taken either as a revelation of the squalid, bestial functions behind the veneer of respectability and cultivation (condensed into the story of Buckley and the General [509: 7–14]) or as the manifestation of HCE's sexual wandering (captured in the tale of an indecent exposure to the girls in the park [508: 21–31]).

Yet as the questioners try to understand the exact form in which HCE has failed and fallen, all the uncertainties of Part I recur. The familiar misty stories are all reviewed—the celebratory wake (510: 14 ff.), the freeing of the widow and the concerns about ALP's sexual past (511: 10–15, 27–31), the exultation of the sons at the overthrow of the father (513: 7–15), the tense encounters between HCE and various strangers (515: 1–25; 516: 3–30; 518: 15–17).[30] All this material is dragged out from Yawn with the tones, and evaluations, of many of the voices that speak within him. The treacherous Sackerson is there (511: 17–19, 20), as well as the cad who encountered HCE (516: 3–30).

The dominant mood, as we should expect, given Yawn's reluctance to acknowledge any kinship with HCE, is negative. The plethora of jumbled stories serve the same purpose as the rival accounts of origins—to suggest that, however it turned out, HCE's nature compelled him to fail, to lapse in his love, and to be repudiated. Yet there are suggestions of an alternative perspective, more understanding and more appreciative. I hear an echo of the washerwoman's appreciation of the role HCE once played:

> Nautaey, nautaey, we're nowhere without ye! . . . So lent she him ear to burrow his manhood (or so it appierce) and borrow his namas? (512: 21, 23–5; compare 215: 14–15)[31]

Here the more positive appraisal comes from one of the old men. Yawn does not assent.[32]

Of course, there is no more chance that the figure of Yawn can resolve the dreamer's doubts so long as the worrying material is pursued in just the same way as it was earlier (for example in I-3 and I-4). The crux of this second phase of the inquiry comes with the re-eruption of the angry voice, who recognizes, after many pages of dialogue, that the voices within Yawn are full of contradictions.

> This is not guid enough, Mr Brasslattin. . . . Didget think I was asleep at the wheel? D'yu mean to tall grand jurors of thathens of tharctic on your oath, me lad, and ask us to believe you, for all you're enduring long terms, with yur last foor foremouthst, that yur moon was shining on the tors and on the cresties and winblowing night after night, for years and years perhaps, after you swearing to it a while back . . . that there was reen in planty all the teem? (519: 16–25, with omissions)

It has taken long enough to acknowledge the initial inconsistencies, and, typically, the inquisitor focuses on the relatively inconsequential, the weather details, rather than on the accounts of the origins of human behavior or the variety of tales about HCE. The point, however, is to appreciate that the star-chamber has so far settled nothing.

Yawn replies with a mad amalgam of all the stories the voices within him have been spinning, a version that seeks to implicate the four old men themselves in the events. The indignant voice remains unsatisfied, accusing the youth of accepting bribes to make things up (520: 35; 521: 2). The charge prompts dissension among the inquisitors, and order is only resumed when the most authoritative among the four intervenes:

> Let me once more. There are sordidly tales within tales, you clearly understand that? (522: 5–6)

Yawn has made the same judgment from different accounts of HCE, the judgment that his behavior was "sordid," but, since not *all* of the accounts can be correct, the reliability of *any* is at issue. And, of course, if all are unreliable, then Yawn's judgment is groundless.

The question is put starkly, in terms of the choice left open at the early stages of Yawn's discussion of HCE's misdemeanors:

> Which moral turpitude would you select of the two, for choice, if you had your way? Playing bull before shebears or the hindlegs off a clotheshorse? (522: 14–16)

Yawn is asked to choose between the story of the incident in the park and the tale of Buckely and the General. He ducks the question and then offers both a protest and a confession:

> Are you to have all the pleasure quizzing on me? I didn't say it aloud, sir. I have something inside of me talking to myself. (522: 25–6)

Indeed he does. Yawn's head, like Prospero's isle, is full of noises. The conflicting voices have thus far been out of control. Now that their existence is recognized, Yawn, like a psychoanalytic patient, can begin to let them sound in a more organized way.

In response to the inquisitorial command, "Get yourself psychoanolised!" (522: 31–2), Yawn is dismissive—he can do the job himself. He demonstrates as much by speaking in the lisping tones of "Sylvia Silence," the "girl detective" who appeared briefly in I-3 (523: 2–4; compare 61: 1, 6–11). Part of the significance of this first example is to underscore the point the inquisitors have stumbled on. Although this voice doesn't exonerate HCE, it offers a more sympathetic perspective on his life than has been sounded in Yawn's earlier responses. Perhaps when all the competing parts of him have been isolated and allowed to express themselves, the confident conclusion that all scenarios lead to rejection of HCE will no longer be sustained.

The inner voices are by no means all sympathetic to HCE, and the very next to emerge, one who claims "Frisky Shorty" as an "inmate friend" (523: 23), probably Treacle Tom (39: 16, 28ff.), uses the style of the pub raconteur to support the reliability of the rumor he originally helped to spread. Even more antagonistic is the voice of Hosty, who adds a derisive and explicit verse to the ballad:

> *There's an old psalmsobbing lax salmoner fogeyboren Herrin Plundehowse.*
> *Who went floundering with his boatloads of spermin spunk about.*
> *Leaping freck after every long tom and wet lissy between Howth and Humbermouth.*
> *Our Human Conger Eel!* (525: 21–6)

HCE is an outsider (foreign born), a hypocrite (psalm sobbing), and a destroyer (plunderer), but his overarching fault is his uncontrolled sexual license. The exaggerations of Hosty within Yawn make it even more evident that the source of the great fear that HCE is part of himself concerns the betrayal of commitment, the replacement of what called itself enduring love with widespread lust.

By the time of Hosty's raucous eruption an important change has occurred. Yawn began by controlling these inner voices, producing Sylvia Silence in response to a request for a sample. She is, of course, a minor figure in his internal cast, whose presence need not involve the fears that trigger resistance. Hosty, however, deeper within Yawn, speaks at the prompting of an inquisitor, signaling their direction of voices. Despite his boast, Yawn will have to suffer the "quizzing" of the four—he will not be allowed to "psoakoonaloose" himself (522: 25, 34).[33]

Typically, ALP emerges to provide an exculpatory account, suggesting that the incident has no significance, that small lapses are to be tolerated rather than vilified (526: 20–33).[34] Her speech provokes a general concern about female narcissism that focuses on whether Issy, too, is similar. The question summons from within Yawn the familiar treacly tones of her "little language," no longer addressed to her brother/lover but to her own reflected image. After a long rant from the angry inquisitor, first Sackerson and then Kate are called to speak. All these voices sound within Yawn, as they do within the dreamer (and "Yawn" is obviously an apt name for the dreamer's surrogate). As we might expect, Sackerson's voice glories in his act of betrayal[35]; Kate's is more tolerant but hardly provides a flattering view of HCE.

The cacophony and confusion have been partially regimented. The accusations of guilt and the excusing defenses can be brought to Yawn's, and the dreamer's, awareness. But simply hearing one voice at a time still leaves the fundamental issue unsettled: if HCE lies deep within Yawn, does that mean that Yawn's love and Yawn's life, like his father's, are fatally flawed? The leading inquisitor calls for a resolution:

> A final ballot, guvnor, to remove all doubt. By sylph and salamander and all the trolls and tritons, I mean to top her drive and to tip the tap of this, at last. His thoughts that wouldbe words, his livings that have-been deeds. (531: 29–32)

It is not to be a genuine ballot, a matter of counting heads (or voices). Instead, the dreamer is finally prepared to listen to the figure whose presence he has feared, the personification of the uncertainties about a particular kind of life, one that involves, in an untidy way, a marriage, an attempt at creativity, and a yearning for inclusion in a community that is sometimes hostile, jealous, and spiteful. Can it be seen as worthwhile, despite its flaws, its squalid details, its reversals and failures? It has been difficult and painful for Yawn—and the dreamer—to reach this point, to allow the inquisitor to summon HCE directly. An exorcism is needed, one that might use the mystical powers of pagan gods and spirits (trolls and tritons), the magic of spells and potions (salamander), as well as incantations:

> The sinder's under shriving sheet. Fa Fe Fi Fo Fum! Ho, croak, evil-doer! Arise, sir ghostus! As long as you've lived there'll be no other. Doff! (532: 2–5)

For all Shaun's, Jaun's, Yawn's efforts to find a different way, there is no other. HCE is unavoidable. The dreamer has to decide what he is worth.

As we have already seen, HCE's apologia starts badly.[36] His opening speech offers the most direct response to the doubts that trouble Yawn and the dreamer: the rumors of his wanderings are laughable because of his devotion to his "ripest littlums wifukie" (532: 30). Yet even while he is trying to shrug off the damaging gossip, the denials are compromised, not only by the allusions to his "serial dreams of faire women, Mannequins Passe" (532: 33), but also by his recognition that he and ALP are no longer young. To speak of "the pu pu pure beauty of hers past" (533: 3) or of his "bestpreserved wholewife" (533: 4) is to acknowledge just the possibility that has been so disturbing, that the initial ardor must inevitably fade. HCE is blustering, attempting to dismiss as unreal the impulses toward younger women that he painfully, and obliquely, confessed in the scene in the bar (356: 16–358: 16).

No amount of invocation of character references (533: 8–33) or of angry denunciations of those who have spread rumors about him (534: 26–31; 535: 13–21) will overcome Yawn's resistance to HCE, or, equivalently, will resolve the dreamer's doubts. These are paths that the *Wake* has already pursued with great thoroughness (most obviously in I-3 and I-4 but also in the immediately preceding pages [508–31]), and we know that they lead nowhere. If HCE is to address the sources of the dreamer's doubts, he must acknowledge his own weaknesses and failings, offering a perspective on them, and on him, that makes acceptance, forgiveness, and even respect possible.

Just as there are layers within Yawn, strata whose exposure is painful, so, too, with HCE. The first peeling away of HCE's superficial denials occurs with the emergence of the pathetic "Old Whitehowth" (535: 26).[37] Pleading for pity, this voice within HCE can only offer the most general grounds for forgiveness:

> I askt you, dear lady, to judge on my tree by our fruits. I gave you of the tree. I gave two smells, three eats. (535: 31–2)

The cryptic reference to their past lovemaking and to the children it produced is hardly enough. To allow the confession at all is to open a wound; to offer so brief a confession is ineffective. No wonder, then, that, after this first foray into exposing a deeper part of his psyche, HCE distances himself from the pleading voice and reverts to the attempt to laugh off his alleged weaknesses.

Yet the eruption of Whitehowth changes HCE's tone in important ways, for it signals that there are layers within him to be probed. HCE, like Yawn earlier, would prefer to leave these buried and asserts that he has exposed everything:

> Well, yeamen, I have bared my whole past, I flatter myself, on both sides. (536: 28–9)[38]

Since it is clear that that is just what he has *not* done, and that it is what *needs* to be done, he must talk on in ways that try to substitute for the agonizing self-revelation. Even painted at their blackest, his weaknesses are minor; he is committed to self-improvement; the stories about him are absurd. As he continues, however, the words of protest run out, and he finds himself drawn into explaining who he is and how he has come to be.

The crucial change occurs when HCE moves away from the attempt either to deny his weaknesses or to beg for mercy, offering instead a broader account of his character and what he takes to be central to his life. The first turning point comes with a last reference to the absurdity of the gossip against him:

> The amusin part is, I will say, hotelmen, that since I, over the deep drowner Athacleeath to seek again Irrlanding . . . (539: 16–18)

So we leave the frailties, the wanderings, henceforth neither confessed nor disavowed, embarking on the baring of his whole past that HCE assured us had already been achieved. We return, as so frequently in the most hopeful parts of the *Wake* to the moment of HCE's arrival in Ireland, and to his wooing of ALP. How beginning here will help with Yawn's, and the dreamer's, worries will become clear when we understand where he is headed.

The first level of HCE's revelation is the tale of the greatly reformed city, rebuilt by his creative energy. He has come as an outsider, changing the environment around him to make what he sees as tremendous improvements and what the local inhabitants may view as the destruction of established values—for, as we read HCE's catalogue of achievements, we should recall the perspective of Hosty's ballad:

> He was fafafather of all schemes for to bother us. (45: 15)

The grandiose list includes schemes aplenty, and there are plain hints of local resistance (542: 18–26). Yet, as I suggested in Chapter 3, HCE's creative reforms are directed by a spirit of openness and generosity. His great invitation, "all, let them all come" (545: 13), expresses his counterpart to the Joycean virtues—sympathy, tolerance, and forgiveness—that we have seen in ALP. So far as the community is concerned, he may be an outsider, even a blundering, interfering outsider, but his efforts at improvement are infused with sympathy for those around him and with a desire that their lives should flourish in peace.[39]

There is, however, a deeper level within HCE, one that explains the ultimate purpose of his creative activity. The second critical turn in his speech echoes the first[40]:

> Annoyin part of it was, had faithful Fulvia, following the wiening courses of this world, turned her back on her ways to gon on uphills upon search of louvers . . . (546: 30–1)

ALP's faithlessness would have rendered everything else pointless. As we have seen, doubts about her romantic past have swirled through the *Wake*. Here, however, they are overcome, first on the explicit testimony of "mmummy goods waif" (547: 4), then in the energy of his lovemaking, the devotion, the protection, and the gifts he showers upon her.

The expression of love for ALP is the source of HCE's striving, his relationship with her the center around which his life is formed. He leaves us in no doubt that this began with passionate courtship, but it did not end there. As he proceeds, HCE recognizes the many facets of their life together in which his love has been expressed, the prosaic as well as the more obviously romantic:

> fortiffed by my right as man of capitol, I did umgyrdle her about, my vermincelly vinagerette, with all loving kindness as far as in man's might it lay and enfranchised her to liberties of fringes. (548: 17–19)

> I sate me and settled with the little crither of my hearth. (549: 29–30)

> I did devise my telltale sports at evenbread to wring her withers limberly, wheatears, slapbang, drapier-cut-dean, bray, nap, spinado and ranter-go round: . . . (550: 25–7)

He buys her clothes, sits and talks with her, plays card games with her in the evenings.[41] At the end of his long list of loving services, HCE recalls how he has taken her riding in a carriage, and her vigorous delight attests to the continued joy of their sexual relationship.[42] So, at the very bottom of Yawn, he offers a fervent declaration of his enduring love in his marriage—the condensation of the thousands, or millions, of love letters Yawn claimed to carry.

It is all overblown, of course. The claim to have founded a city, or even to have laid down the "waggonways" (553: 29–30) along which HCE and ALP ride, is absurd. As I suggested in Chapter 3, HCE's gigantesque description reveals the structure of his activities and the motivations behind them. On a far more limited scale, in his local environment, he has given his creative energy to an attempt to make improvements, and he has welcomed others to share in what he has done. All this has been shaped and developed, in the everyday patterns of their shared life, by a love and solicitude for ALP. No doubt it has lapsed at times; no doubt the deafness so often attributed to HCE signals his failure to recognize his wife's needs, and we have heard her own passing testimony to shortcomings in his attentions (201: 7–12). Yet as ALP's own interventions have made clear, the failures are deviations from the central tendency of their marriage, the tendency that is magnified in HCE's apologia.

The important point is that the surging movement, associated with his arrival and successful courtship, endures. We have had many evocations of the passion of the young HCE:

> *At Island Bridge she met her tide.*
> *Attabom, attabom, attabombomboom!*
> *The Fin had a flux and his Ebba a ride.* (103: 1–3)

When they saw him shoot swift up her sheba sheath, like any gay lord salomon, her bulls they were ruhring, surfed with spree. (198: 3–5)

And Dub did glow that night. In Fingal of victories. (329: 14)

and knew her fleshly when with all my bawdy did I her whorship, min bryllupswibe: Heaven, he hallthundered; Heydays, he flung bliss-forhers. (547: 27–30)

Neither Yawn, nor the dreamer, has had any doubts about the vitality this love *once* had. Their concern has been that this is transient, that it must decay with the mundane life of marriage, with the body's decline, and that the withering away deprives even the ecstatic moments of any genuine significance. Throughout the *Wake* doubts have been reinforced by a portrait of marital tedium, of a disappointed wife and a wandering husband who vainly, and grotesquely, tries to recapture something from his youth.

On this occasion, however, HCE doesn't leave us with the heaven-thundering, earth-moving moment. He goes on to show us how this love has persisted, touching all the corners of his life. The great sweep of his speech is invigorated with the ardent movement of his youth. Imperfect though his love is, it sets the scale on which he is to be judged, and though the flaws, the failures, are to be acknowledged, they are not so heavy as to overwhelm the whole.

That has been ALP's perspective throughout, and her earlier interventions in the "star-chamber quiry" endeavored to introduce it. She has seen him "foully," and she can set his lapses in their proper context, in the context of a love that has endured:

He will kitssle me on melbaw. What about his age? says you. What about it? says I. I will confess to his sins and blush me further. (494: 29–31)

The inquisitors dismissed her, patronizingly suggesting that she is misled. Now HCE's outpouring of his continued dedication to this marriage effectively silences them. Once he has abandoned his pose of protective denial, exposing the ways in which he has come to be what he is, their interjections become progressively more aligned with his own perspective (547: 10–13; 550: 4–7; 552: 31–4). At the close, they are no longer inquisitors with skeptical questions, no longer seabirds with derisive mocking, but horses who draw the carriage in which ALP plies the whip (554: 8–10).[43]

Yawn has vanished—unless, having at last acknowledged the deepest part of himself, he has become HCE. In any event, the dreamer no longer needs him as an independent figure, a focus of further explorations. For, in the revived person of HCE, we can discern behind the contradictions and confusions, behind the lapses and the flaws, a coherent central tendency, one recognized and appreciated by ALP, a counterpart to her version of the Joycean virtues.

Yet, as at the end of Part I, doubts should linger. Does this appraisal come too quickly and easily, depending on a sentimental veiling of the sordid realities of the life that HCE and ALP undertake together? The long unmasking of Part II should not be lightly forgotten. The dreamer must return to the shortcomings we have seen so starkly and extensively in the later chapters of Part II and must ask whether they undermine the case for HCE as true to the original surge to ALP. It is no accident that we find ourselves next in the aftermath of the scene in the bar, where HCE's internal contradictions were exposed. The excavation of Yawn has offered the possibility that a single central movement, a continued turning to ALP, lies behind his conflicting impulses. Before this *possibility* is hailed as more than that, as a genuine *solution*, the dreamer must probe it further. It is time to disclose the realities of this marriage, time to enter the marriage bed.

19

MALE AND FEMALE
UNMASK WE HEM

As at the very beginning of Part III, there is a sleepy stirring, a dim awareness that this is all a dream (555: 1–2). Then, once again, the scene is set
by assembling the characters and by defining time and place. The familiar
figures are present: the four old men and their ass; the two sons, one full
of bright promise and the other troubled and troublesome; the beautiful
daughter for whom there are many (incompatible) futures in which she will
play a starring role; the decrepit figures of Sackerson ("Wachtman Havelook
seequeerscenes" [556: 23–4]) and Kate; the twelve customers, meandering
to yet another confused judgment; and the flower girls who laugh and cry
over the departure (or disintegration) of Shaun. The time, as suits a presentation of the marriage of HCE and ALP, with its mixture of achievement
and failure, is "those good old lousy days gone by" (555: 5–6). The place is
the anatomical theater in which the dreamer can try to dissect that marriage:
HCE and ALP lie

> in their bed of trial, on the bolsters of hardship, by the glimmer of
> memory, under coverlets of cowardice . . . (558: 26–7)

They have emerged, as we have seen, as a possible solution for the dreamer;
but they must be scrutinized, tried; the underlying worry—"has acceptance
come too easily?"—must be addressed; the coverlets must be removed; as we
have already seen in III-3, the exposure is painful and requires courage.

We are offered a kaleidoscope of scenes, some apparently set in this
bedroom and in this bed, some in the rooms above, and some in quite other
locations.[1] The time, too, is variable. HCE and ALP appear as young parents,
calming the night fears of young children, and as much older, "wedded now
evermore" (585: 22), even on "their diamond wedding tour" (578: 32–3). The
dreamer has to see it all, the "good old" and the "lousy days gone by."

The skeptical worry about this married life, the worry to which HCE's ardent apologia responds, is that the trend is steadily downhill. There was the brief moment of youthful passion, the "height of his life from a bride's eye stammpunct" (309: 3–4), followed by a long decline into tedium and disillusion, the failure of the flesh and the withering of love. So, perhaps, we meet the young parents before they have fallen too far, sharing delightful hopes for one of their sons and worrying together about the prospects for the other, dreaming of the alternatives for the lovely daughter. Other figures remind the dreamer of what may lie ahead, the squalid homeless wandering of Sackerson, the slovenly servitude of Kate, the uncomprehending repudiation by those around them, the failure of the promising son.

Indeed, as we saw in Chapter 2, there is a story of decline here, a tale of hopes that are unfulfilled, of reversals, of the erosion of youthful powers. If the sexual expression in which HCE and ALP engage is not their last, it is clearly close enough to the end to confront the dreamer with the passing of this aspect of their marriage. Because the chapter traces a downward movement, showing the replacement of what was once fresh, vigorous, and graceful with substitutes that are tired, grotesque, and even bestial—at least as judged from one perspective—it can appear to reinforce the skeptical worry and to deny HCE's impassioned defense of his life. Will we be returned to the descent, the bleak failure, of Part II?

Because there are clearly losses, tears might be the appropriate response to this anatomy of a marriage—but, as I have suggested, Joyce invited us to appraise it differently, with applause.[2] The vignettes of the chapter constitute a story of decline, of aging, but also a tale of indomitable persistence. HCE insisted that the vigor of his courtship continued in a life dedicated to ALP, and, for all the erosions and reversals disclosed by removing the coverlets, this resolute dissection vindicates him.

For, as I interpret it, the chapter consists of a central line, one that displays the orientation of HCE and ALP to one another, their mutual devotion and support, that continues while their bodies decay and while the disappointments of everyday life beat against their union. The movement that brought them together long ago continues here, just as HCE claimed. Of course, the details are far more messy than his grand rhetoric suggested—we already knew that from ALP's laughter (kindly laughter) at old "Blusterboss" (273: 23). For all the gracelessness of their coupling, it can still celebrate the joy they find together:

> the queenbee he staggerhorned blesses her bliss for to feel her funny-man's functions . . . (590: 28–9)

ALP predicted that they would "make laugh" (495: 17) over the suggestions of their marital failure—and that is exactly what they do. Although the "stagger" and the "funnyman" indicate the loss of grace, a loss that ALP recognizes, she can still "bless her bliss."

I suggest that the interruptions of this central line, the apparently strange vignettes that take the dreamer to different settings, should be understood as cross-examinations, efforts to turn the vindication in a different direction. They introduce just the sort of material that has previously served to condense the dreamer's doubts—HCE's waning attraction to his wife, his yearning for newer, and younger, loves, his wish to win acceptance in the community around him and his failure to do so. Yet the central line persists, despite these efforts at deflection. They dissolve inconclusively, leaving us again and again with HCE and ALP, persevering through age and failure. The preponderance of lousy days may increase as they go on, but they continue to love, and laugh, together.

The first attempted disruption of the idea of a genuine, persisting union between HCE and ALP occurs when their visit to the bedroom of their son, the Shem figure, Jerry, has led to an attempt to calm him. The scene dissolves into an image of the quiet and restfulness of the inn (565: 33–566: 6). There is then a sudden transition:

> In the sleepingchambers. The court to go into half morning. (566: 7)

We are at a court ceremony, and the full cast of characters is present, assigned various roles. Three are particularly important. ALP, the "dame dowager," is to stay "kneeled how she is, as first mutherer with cord in coil" (566: 18, 19).

> The dame dowager's duffgerent to present wappon, blade drawn to the full and about wheel without to be seen of them. The infant Isabella from her coign to do obeisance toward the duffgerent, as first futherer with drawn brand. Then the court to come in to full morning. (566: 21–25)

Removing a cover from the marriage bed, the vignette challenges the dreamer to see the facts, what the light of morning discloses; and it should produce mourning for the decline of mutual love.

ALP, subservient and complaisant, kneels, HCE turns away from her, exposing himself to a young woman. She, it appears, is to gratify him. The familiar suspicion of HCE's fidelity is presented in a new guise, with the inquisitors' verdict that ALP is "misled" (495: 36). The sight inspires a cry of disgust at the ugliness, the brutishness, behind the court ceremonial. The voice of the disruptive narrative delights in giving the squalid details:

> At that do you leer, a setting up? With a such unfettered belly? . . .
> I leer . . . because I must see a buntingcap of so a pinky on the point. It
> is for a true glover's greetings . . . (567: 5–8)

This image of a gross man, aroused by a young girl, with the telling detail of the absurdly placed condom, is to serve as the proper symbol for HCE, his "effigy of standard royal" (567: 9–12).

The vignette uses that thought to attack from another direction, to tell of a court progress that culminates in HCE's receipt of his name (568: 25–6). He appears as a ridiculous figure, whose apparent dignity masks the bodily decay and grotesque sexual impulses that have been disclosed. A change of voice comments on HCE's increasing girth and places the scene late in his marriage (570: 17–21).[3] Then, to close the scene, there is a vision of Issy, initially described, as her mother was earlier (564–5), as a landscape. She rises from bed, needing to urinate, and, as she finds relief, speaks in the tempting tones that have so often marked her.[4]

This is all familiar material. We have heard many times that HCE's love for ALP is dead, that his sexual interest needs to be aroused by younger women, that his bodily decline reveals the gross animal appetites behind the decorative dress of civilization, that his desire for acceptance and honor in the community leads him to neglect his marriage. On this occasion, there are no stammering denials, no elaborate excuses, simply a turning away. Issy-the-temptress concludes: "Listen, listen! I am doing it" (571: 24). The dreamer is not to be drawn:

> Hear more to those voices! Always I am hearing them. Horsehem coughs enough. Annshee lispes privily. (571: 24–6)

We return to HCE and ALP, waiting to see if their son's night fears are calmed.

There are voices that tempt this aging man, that might lead him to deviate from the course he has taken as his own. Here, they fall silent at his cough; he has listened enough. The cough is deprecating and disapproving, a rejection of the silken whispers. He clears his throat—and his mind—of unhealthy matter.

HCE and ALP resume their shared project, and any sexual stimulation is redirected:

> Legalentitled. Accesstopartnuzz. Notwildebeestsch. Byrightofoaptz. Twainbeonerflsh. Haveandholdpp. (571: 28–9)

They pause for a moment, seeing that their daughter's door is open, and there is a brief uncertainty about whether the pressure to deviate will be felt again.

> For our netherworld's bosomfoes are working tooth and nail overtime: in earthveins, toadcavites . . . (571: 35–6)

The "bosomfoes" are the impulses that would prompt HCE to wander from his course, to deviate from the steady movement, the continuation of his courtship surge, with which he has identified. They speak of his waning years, of the coming triumph of youth (572: 2–6). He ignores them, resuming the whispered exchanges with ALP.

A consoling voice celebrates the successful passage of the trial: "Live well! Iniivdluaritzas!" (572: 15). I hear in it the hope that this pair are making their own way, that they seem to be discovering the identity for which Part III of the *Wake* has been searching. It is echoed by a brief fragment of the washerwomen's final exchange, as if we were returning to the vindication of HCE and ALP that emerged at the end of I–8. Yet, just as that couldn't end the dreamer's quest, so, too, on this occasion. A new accuser intervenes.

It is "Interrogarius Mealterum" (572: 19)—the questioner of the alternative ego, the scrutinizer of whether HCE is who he takes himself to be, the advocate of doubts about affirming the value of this marriage. He brings a case for legal resolution, one whose tangle of sexual liaisons, of bribes and threats, exceeds in complexity the most elaborate paradigm of Roman debauchery and decadence. At its center are all the familiar figures, beginning with "Honuphrius . . . a concupiscent exservicemajor who makes dishonest propositions to all" (572: 21–2) and his wife "Anita" (572: 26–7). Although her liaisons are less extensive and less varied in terms of sex, age, and kinship relations than those of Honuphrius, there is a figure in her past, a "perpetual curate" (573: 4),

Michael, who has formerly debauched Anita (573: 18)

and who continues to play the major role in directing her conduct.

As with the first challenge, the vignette begins with the wandering of HCE and his desire for a young woman to whom he is related. This time, however, ALP is not merely a bystander but an active participant, one whose relationship with HCE is subordinate to an earlier love. The eventual question posed about the case is far from straightforward: the pronouns it contains are multiply ambiguous. The resolution, however, veers off in a completely new direction, without reference to any of the parties mentioned in the initial statement of the case. Honophrius and Anita vanish, giving way to a commercial dispute between "rival concern[s]"—"Tangos" and "Pangos"—ultimately involving many characters named "Doyle," including "Ann Doyle" and a "Monsignore Pepigi" (573: 5, 9, 28, 30–2; 574: 6, 29).

A little Latin helps decipher the relationship between this strange pair of vignettes. "Tango" can mean "I touch," or "I cheat"—and, perhaps, the "star-chamber quiry" reference to "Toucher 'Thom'" (506: 28) exploits the ambiguity; "pango" can mean "I fasten" or "I promise," and "pepigi" is its past perfect. I suggest that the contrast between cheating and promising is dominant here, so that the issue of keeping or breaking faith is the principal concern. The concluding judgment, "Pepigi's pact was pure piffle," returns us to the initial indictment of Honophrius as dishonest. More significantly, in the context of the dreamer's investigations, the alleged "enduring commitments" of this marriage have been broken. HCE's promise to devote himself to ALP has lapsed into a voracious lechery, while, to the extent that ALP has kept faith, it is with her earlier and more significant love.

Again, there is no attempt to answer, explain, or excuse. The celebration of the promise-breaker's downfall, of the loss of ALP ("Nancy"), of her alignment with the local people (all the Doyles) who are arrayed against him builds to a carnival challenge:

> Will you, won't you, pango with Pepigi? Not for Nancy, how dare you do! (576: 7–8)

It is succeeded by the murmuring of the disturbed child. We return to HCE and ALP, the comforting parents, at the top of the stair—and, as before, they turn to one another. This has been a nightmare, a distortion in sleep of the impulses within the dreamer.

> And whew whewwhew whew.[5]
>   —He sighed in sleep.
>   —Let us go back.
>   —Lest he forewaken.
>   —Hide ourselves. (576: 9–13)

Once again, HCE and ALP have not been deflected from their central course, their mutual commitment.

In acknowledgement, a steadier and more sympathetic voice describes the many sides of this marriage. They have come through dangers, avoiding the self-betrayal that would abandon their central commitment to one another, negotiating "the labyrinth of their samilikes and the alteregoases of their pseudoselves" (576: 32–3). They descend the stair, taking at the same time their "diamond wedding tour" (578: 32–3), heading for the bed in which they will recelebrate their original union. It is a decline. Their fall, their death, is inevitable. Yet, in another sense, they have not fallen, for they have steered between the lures and threats that would have sent them off course. In turning to one another and descending the stair, they reply to "Interrogarius Mealterum," they find their joint way through the labyrinth, they avoid lapsing into pseudoselves. Following their own decisions, the laws on which they have agreed, they have overcome obstacles and endured reversals—together.

> Now their laws assist them and ease their fall!
>   For they met and mated and bedded and buckled and got and gave and reared and raised and brought Thawland within Har danger, and turned them, tarrying to the sea and planted and plundered and pawned our souls and pillaged the pounds of the extramurals and fought and feigned with strained relations . . . (579: 26)

This is not, evidently, the glorious creative accomplishment of which HCE boasted in his apologia, but it contains within it the same important elements— the construction of a shared way of life whose central tendency, however perturbed by lapses and reversals, is one of mutual support and dedication. Against the decline and failure of Part II, against Shaun's disintegration and collapse, it sets the message of HCE's apologia, the persistence of the motion begun in his wooing of ALP and its pervasive shaping of their married lives.

Now their aging bodies will put to the test the survival of their sexual love. The lamp that ALP carries in her hand, as they descend the stair, will throw their shadows on the blind for the outer world to see. That outer world has been hostile to HCE "inwader and uitlander" (581: 3), and, as ALP unites with him, she is included in the scorn:

> he never was worth a cornerwall fark, and his banishee's bedpan she's a
> quareold bite of a tark: . . . (581: 8–10)

At first sight, the perspective from within the bedroom supports the jeers from without, from the absurd strain visible on HCE's face (582: 28–9), to ALP's chattering teeth and disjointed motions (583: 3, 5–7), to her laughter at the way "he was slogging his paunch about" (583: 27), and the ambiguous consummation.[6] Small wonder that this final trial of the marriage encourages a last attempt to deny the central tendency HCE has claimed for it. It comes, as we might have expected, from the representative of HCE's alternative future, the loveless, rootless, vengeful Sackerson. He is a witness to the clumsy performance in shadowshow upon the blind. His observation gives way to the voice of pub gossip:

> Hiss! Which we had only our hazelight to see with, cert, in our point of
> view, me and my auxy, Jimmy d'Arcy, hadn't we Jimmy? (587: 3–5)

The raconteur is one of "three jolly postboys" (587: 6).[7] What he claims to have seen is an incident involving two girls, "Elsies from Chelsies, the two-legglegels in bloom" (587: 26–7). HCE is held up to ridicule:

> his old face's hardalone wiv his defences down during his wappin still-
> stand . . . (588: 4–5)

The story blends into a different vignette, in which the central figure, the temptress, is Issy:

> Izzy's busy down the dell! Mizpah low, youyou, number one, in deep
> humidity! (588: 24–5)

The aging voyeur is very different from the proper expression of sexual attraction, among the young (589: 1–2), but the children need the resources their parents have acquired. The tale switches to a broader denunciation of HCE, an answer to his vision of himself as one whose creative energies were directed at general good, whose urge was to improve life for all.

> So childish pence took care of parents' pounds and many made money
> the way in the world where rushroads to riches crossed slums of lice

and, the cause of it all, he forged himself ahead like a blazing urbanorb, brewing treble to drown grief, giving and taking mayom and tuam, playing milliards with his three golden balls, . . . our hugest commercial emporialist . . . (589: 3–10, with omissions)[8]

HCE's effect on those around him is seen as destructive—he is, once again, the "destroyer in our port" (480: 13), taking advantage of the locals.[9] The jeering interruption ends with the account of the collapse of HCE's business, leaving him (in an echo of the way he was left at the end of II-3) "weeping worrybound on his bankrump" (590: 3).

The financial collapse will be mirrored in the definitive end of his sexual life, a verdict we considered in Chapter 2:

That's his last Tryon to march through the grand tryomphal arch. His reignbolt's shot. Never again! (590: 9–10)

All the accusations have been heard before: in his old age HCE has lost his love for ALP; he can only be aroused by unseemly spying on younger women; he is at odds with the surrounding community; his marriage is a failure both outside the bedroom and within—if it isn't completely dead already, the end is very near.

HCE and ALP have responded to previous efforts at derailing them from their course by turning to one another. This time, however, there is no conversational reply. They are lying together in bed, and the last perspective[10] discloses them:

Tableau final. Two me see. Male and female unmask we hem. (590: 23–4)

HCE is surely asleep, "[a]fter having drummed all he dun" (590: 26). ALP's status is uncertain—perhaps she lies awake, perhaps she too sleeps, or perhaps she drowses. But her feelings are clear, "bliss" at her "funnyman's functions" (590: 28–9).

Is she self-deceived? Has the clumsy lovemaking succeeded, to the extent that it has, because HCE has ignored the woman beneath him and been momentarily aroused by some other, younger vision? The worry, as always, is that all the facts have not been faced and that acceptance has come too easily. Yet all we have learned in the long journey through the vignettes of the *Wake* tells us, and the dreamer, that the facts cannot be completely fathomed, that motivations are always opaque, and that this dream has no bottom. Despite all the doubts, however, the movement of HCE's life, begun in the youthful wooing of ALP, has continued its arc through this chapter. In response to the deviations of the dream, he has turned to her and she to him, and their shared work, their shared journey, have culminated in the embraces we have witnessed. However this lovemaking may have been initially inspired, it has been directed toward her, as her responses have been to him. Having worn himself out in her service, "drummed all he dun," he sleeps, and, sleeping, drowsing, or waking, she smiles at the comedy they have enacted together.

HCE testified to the trajectory of his life in a gigantic boast, a huge amplification of the course he regards as central to it. Just as he is not the founder and builder of a magnificent city, he is not a royal figure who exposes himself to a young girl, or a corrupt Roman with extraordinary tastes, or a grasping swindler whose finances come to ruin. Just as the image of the city serves to delineate the mundane ways in which his loving union with ALP has transformed the local sphere around them, the images of him as royal aspirant, elderly lecher, and ruthless exploiter are exaggerations of impulses within him—he does yearn for acceptance and honor, his waning sexual ardor is stirred by young women who recall to him what his wife once was, and he is concerned to change accepted forms in creating his own way. These characteristics do threaten the central trajectory on which he has set himself, but the dissection of the marriage shows them in their place. The central line persists, despite the perturbations of the nightmare challenges. The impulses those challenges represent are parts of HCE, imperfections in his love and life, but they neither defeat his marriage nor compromise its value.

Recognizing the line that has run through this marriage, with the mutual turning at moments of attempted deflection, responds to both the concerns that arose for the dreamer at the end of Part I. Not only does it reveal that the acceptances, the acts of forgiveness, are made in full acknowledgement of the realities, including the reality of physical decline, but also that *whatever* preceded the courtship of the pair, their youthful ardor for one another has set the trajectory of their marriage. However many Michaels lurk in ALP's past, they are present only as reinforcements of her love for HCE. Even in this strained coupling, she turns to her "funnyman," just as he "drummed all he dun" for her.

The drawing back of the covers, the unmasking of the marriage bed, reveals the course of the lives of HCE and ALP. Those lives do descend, and we see them "near the base of the chill stair" (580: 23). They encounter obstacles and have to steer through difficulties (579: 2–4; 579: 27–580: 12). Although they fall in one sense, declining toward death, in another they do not. For they are not driven off course; their "[t]ableau final" (590: 23) is a recognizable development of how they began. In this sequence of scenes, the basic structure of these shared lives is visible—the persistent line that resists the forces that would deflect it.[11]

So, at the end, we can shed sympathetic tears for the decline of these people, as they approach their deaths. But we can also applaud, laughing with them in celebration of their power to endure, to continue to delight in their ordinary lives together.

20

THE KEYS TO. GIVEN!

We are ready, it would seem, for the affirmation of ALP's closing monologue. Her elegy for the life she has shared with HCE promises to develop the resolution to which the dreamer has come. She records the mundane ways in which they have found joy, she recognizes the flaws that have threatened them, she is momentarily swayed by a bleak vision of her own that would see her time as wasted, and yet, holding true to their shared course, she overcomes her doubt and affirms their lives. Set in context,[1] her monologue would seem to make more explicit what I have teased out of the chapters that precede it.

But not yet. Joyce interposes more than twenty pages before giving us first another letter from ALP and then, finally, allowing her the *Wake*'s last words. This intervening material involves short vignettes that recall other parts of the long dream, vignettes that often seem to have little relation to the worries that have been dominant since the end of Part I. Why do we need this disjointed series of reprises?[2]

Throughout the long initial section of this final chapter, from 593 to 615: 10, there is a new energy, new enthusiasm, even hilarity. Day is dawning, and the voices are full of exhortations. The world is to waken to a new order of things.

A hand from the cloud emerges, holding a chart expanded (593: 19).

The proclamation that follows is full of renewal and of cleansing—there are witty references to bars of soap (594: 11–13)—announcements that the old, tired arrangements of the past are done with (595: 31–2), and predictions of the arising of a son, who will succeed HCE (595: 34–596: 34). Yet HCE is already there in the cloud and the chart, and, as the description of his replacement unfolds, his continued presence becomes plain—the new hope is "hailed chimers' ersekind," he is "one of the two or three forefivest fellows a bloke could in holiday crowd encounter," he "stoatters some" but is "quite a big bug after the dahlias" (596: 5, 15–16, 27–8). So, as the indignant inquisitor explained a long while back:

God has jest. The old order changeth and lasts like the first. (486: 10)

That prediction was borne out by the excavation of HCE from the depths of Shaun.

Exactly the same assessment will be made about the exultant celebrations of this bright morning. Although the voices that sound in these vignettes may express their excitement in the new, the verdict is the same.

> Yet is no body present here which was not there before. Only is order othered. Nought is nulled. *Fuitfiat!* (613: 13–14)

The creator's declaration "Let it be!" is coupled with the invocation of the past, "It was." So nothing is annulled, nothing changed.[3] For, it turns out, the "wholemole millwheelilng vicociclometer" (614: 27) will reveal to us "the sameold gamebold adomic structure of our Finnius the old One" (615: 6–7).

The excitement, then, is unfounded, just as it was when the ass greeted Shaun (404: 11–15) or when the four old men anticipated a new beginning (398: 7 ff.). Yet the dreamer hasn't only seen this repetition in the dark swirls of the night, most recently in the disintegration of Shaun and the reappearance of HCE, but has also been told of the human tendency to yearn for a different and improved future. As the reflective Jaun explained:

> We only wish everyone was as sure of anything in this watery world as we are of everything in the newlywet fellow that's bound to follow. (452: 29–31)

I suggest that the self-deceptive faith in a new beginning is the real subject of the vignettes that succeed one another in rapid succession through the opening section of Part IV, the *ricorso,* or return, of the *Wake.* Having found a better way—the acceptance of flawed lives centered on ordinary things—we (and the dreamer) have to repudiate the yearning for new starts and grander ventures.

The tempting promise of the morning is completely clear—"It is perfect degrees excelsius" (597: 31)—as clear as the contrast with what has preceded:

> It was a long, very long, dark, very dark, an allburt unend, scarce endurable, and we could add mostly quite various and somewhat stumbletumbling night. (598: 6–9)

The sense of relief may inspire rededication to projects previously abandoned as unlikely to succeed—and, as we shall see, ALP will feel the tug to try again.[4] In the preliminary section, however, two bright hopes are most prominent—one that involves the arising or return of a pure young hero (a Shaun figure) and one that centers on the arrival of an outsider, a great innovator.

Once again, the rainbow girls, the Floras, are a-flutter:

A dweam of dose innocent dirly dirls. Keavn! Keavn! And they all setton voicies about singsing music was Keavn! He. Only he. Ittle he. (601: 17–19)[5]

As he appeared out of the gloom in III-1, so now, the "lightbreakfastbringer" (473: 23), with "that smeoil like a grace of backoning over his egglips of the sunsoonshine" (603: 1–2), comes back, to great acclaim, better than ever. Once he is fully established, an even more auspicious future is predicted for him. A crier's voice proclaims the sanctity of Kevin.

It is another of Joyce's great spoofs, an account of the pious practices of Kevin, centered on rites of cleansing that he performs with his altar-cum-bath (his "portable *altare cum balneo*" [605: 8]), and reveals him whisked up through the hierarchy of holiness to become "Saint Kevin, Hydrophilos," who, after girding "his sable *cappa magna* as high as his cherubical loins, at solemn compline sat in his sate of wisdom, that handbathtub" (606: 4–7). The final promise is that this new high doctor of the church will offer "the regeneration of all man by affusion of water" (606: 11–12).

Once the ceremony is over, however, it's clear that no regeneration has occurred. We're back in an earlier era (a "purvious century" [606: 16–17]), plainly the age of HCE and ALP, returned to the park, the fall, and the celebrations at Finnegan's Wake (607: 16). Nor should we have expected anything different. Shaun, after all, disintegrated in the dream vignettes of Part III, giving way to HCE, and, for all the holy water and pious washing, that flawed and unregenerate figure lies behind Kevin too. He also will dissolve—or "disselve" (608: 5).

The second announcement of new hope begins in another reprise, this time of the crosstalk act between Shem and Shaun figures (here "Muta" and "Juva").[6] They set up a tale of conflict between a representative of local mores, the archdruid, associated here with names that suggest "Buckley" and an outsider, St. Patrick, introduced as "the Eurasian Generalissimo" (610: 12–13). The theological disputation is interwoven with a horserace (610: 34–611: 2). Even if Patrick, the representative of innovation, should win (which is entirely unclear), it can only be a temporary victory. For, as the names assigned by Muta and Juva indicate, and as the many references to the story of Buckley and the General (which figured in their previous performance) make clear, the reforming outsider will be vilified and defeated (612: 24–5, 32–5; 613: 1). There is no genuinely new option here, a fact recognized in the most lucid exchange of the crosstalk act:

Muta: So that when we shall have acquired unification we shall pass on to diversity and when we have passed on to diversity we shall have acquired the instinct of combat and when we shall have acquired the instinct of combat we shall pass back to the spirit of appeasement?

Juva: By the light of the bright reason which daysends to us from the high. (610: 23–9)

Human beings are compelled to retrace old patterns, to take their turn round the Vico road, and if the day brings them the hope that "bright reason" may find them a different way, that is a mistake—a natural illusion, perhaps, but an illusion nonetheless.

There has been no advance. The dreamer is left with the possible solution that emerged from HCE's apologia and that survived the trial by dissection in the marriage bed. False leads and absurd hopes need to be exposed, if only because the desire for more, for improvement, is so natural. After the vital bursts of the opening exhortations, the voice has become tired:

What has gone? How it ends?
   Begin to forget it. It will remember itself from every sides, with all gestures, in each our word. Today's truth, tomorrow's trend.
   Forget, remember!
   Have we cherished expectations? (614: 19–23)

We cherish expectations, hopes for a genuinely new and better beginning, because we forget the lessons that the past has taught us. Those lessons will come back to us as, once again, the options that have failed before break down. So it is entirely natural to want to do better than HCE, to believe that Shaun— or "Saint Kevin, Hydrophilos"—will transcend his flawed life. In the end, though, we must continue, follow the trajectory—the trend—that HCE and ALP have set for themselves.

Part of that trajectory, as we have seen so often before, consists in ALP's loyal defense of her husband; so as morning comes, and the round continues, it's no surprise that there should be a last letter:

Cockalooralooraloomenos, when cup, platter and pot come piping hot, as sure as herself pits hen to paper and there's scribings scrawled on eggs. (615: 8–10)

She begins with polite thanks for the dreamwork of the *Wake,* these "secret workings of nature" (615: 14), which she takes to have absolved HCE.

Mucksrats which bring up about uhrweckers they will come to know good. (615: 16–17)

Perhaps this is another instance of the faith in the cleansing power of the new day. But in the sleepy muddle of her longest letter, ALP returns to the dominant theme of her defense, HCE's continued turn to her and their shared laughter.
   Their lovemaking, clumsy as it may have been, has quelled her doubts and brought her to peaceful sleep.

That was the prick of the spindle to me that gave me the keys to dreamland. (615: 27–8)

She returns to the theme indirectly as she proceeds (616: 24-5), before responding to the charge that he is old and tired.

One must simply laugh. Fing him aging! Good licks! Well, this ought to weke him to make up. (617: 16–18)

The years cannot simply be denied, however. As ALP ponders what he might awaken for, she envisages an imminent "fooneral" (617: 20). Despite his strenuous efforts in the marriage bed, despite the laughter that accompanied them, HCE's time, their time, is nearly over. Yet she resists to the end. Her husband is not to be consigned to the past, to be buried.

He is another he what stays under the himp of holth. The herewaker of our hamefame is his real namesame who will get himself up and erect, confident and heroic when but, young as of old, for my daily comfreshenall, a wee one woos. (619: 12–15)

In part, she is right: HCE has maintained his course, turning to her, his "wee one," for shared intimacies (confessions) and renewal (refreshment). But this is also her version of the natural illusion, the thought that the new day can revive what they have been, that decline can be reversed, growth can be continued, and their world, their marriage, be cleansed of its flaws and constantly improved.[7]

The drowsy tone of the letter, between sleep and wake, gives way to the clearest of all the voices we've heard. ALP is beguiled by the promise of the morning and its new possibilities. They are glimpsed through the leaves that have fallen, all her memories, most importantly the expression of their young love:

I am leafy, your goolden, so you called me, may me life, yea your goolden, silve me solve, exsogerraider! You did so drool. I was so sharm. But there's a great poet in you too. (619: 29–32)

She condenses much that we have seen in HCE, the grandiosity of his vision (the exaggerations[8] on display in his apologia), but also the creative energy within him, energy he has directed toward their life together. There is indeed a poet in him, for he contains Shem (Stephen Dedalus—and Joyce), but the poetry has been expressed in the conduct of his marriage, recognized only by her.

She wants him to awaken, to put on the freshly cleaned clothes, to look fine for her (620: 1–2). They are to walk out together, to undertake one of the shared projects, the thousands (or millions) of ordinary experiences—the active expressions of Yawn's letters—that have made up their marriage. They will do something new, something long planned but put off.

Come and let us! We always said we'd. And go abroad. (620: 10)

It is her version of the natural illusion, the hope that this new day will show HCE in his finery (with the special suit perhaps disguising his hump) and will allow them the chance to do what they have previously been prevented from doing. She, too, hopes for difference, growth, improvement.

Yet the leaves, the memories, are still there, and they are golden. ALP recalls the events of their marriage, the obvious large ones, the birth and care of the children, and the everyday details of work and conversation, of evenings in the pub and shared walks (620: 23–4, 35–6; 621: 5–12). As she gradually awakens, however, the memories are interrupted by a more sober appraisal of her husband and of their life.

> All men has done something. Be the time they've come to the weight of old fletch. We'll lave it. So. We will take our walk before in the timpul they ring the earthly bells. (621: 32–4)

The dreamer has worried that ALP closes her eyes, accepts too easily, but here she acknowledges her husband's flaws. He has come to "the weight of old fletch," and she recognizes the imperfections. But her response is ambiguous. Are they to be left, accepted, seen within the context of his entire life? Or are they to be cleansed away? Is this envisaged walk together, now understood to be one of their last, seen as a change of direction or a continuation of what they have been?

ALP wants a change but also a return. She hopes to recapture an intimacy she fears they have lost, associated with a place where they were together, apart from the world.

> You know where I am bringing you? You remember? When I ran berrying after hucks and haws. With you drawing out great aims to hazel me from the hummock with your sling. Our cries. (622: 17–19)

All deep relationships have such moments (even many of them), occasions that can later inspire one of the parties to ask, "Do you remember when . . . ?" and to summon up for both of them a shared joy. The possibility of return to the closeness, the joy, presents itself to ALP as a remedy:

> It seems so long, ages since. As if you had been long far away. (622: 13–14)

As I suggested in Chapter 1,[9] she takes HCE's involvement in the world to have contributed to their emotional separation. In returning to their special place, they will be alone:

> Not a soul but ourselves. Time? We have loads on our hangs. (622: 21–2)

That is self-deception—ALP knows that the "bells in the timpul" will soon ring. She *hopes* that there is "loads" of time, because she hopes there is enough for renewal.

The form of this renewal gradually becomes more definite. It is to be more than a walk. They are to return to the "heathery benn" (623: 25), overlooking the sea:

> Ourselves, oursouls alone. At the site of salvocean. And watch would the letter you're wanting be coming may be. And cast ashore. That I prays for be mains of me draims. (623: 28–31)

ALP has a dream of renewed love, of vindication for HCE, of the intimacy that makes them complete for one another—a dream of salvation.[10]

That dream includes a new start, a new home for both of them. She appeals to HCE:

> So content me now. Lss. Unbuild and be buildn our bankaloan cottage there and we'll cohabit respectable. (624: 6–8)

For a moment, he is her master builder and she is the young woman who inspires him to new heights.

> Amid the soleness. Tilltop, bigmaster! Scale the summit! You're not so giddy any more. (624: 10–12)

She knows, however, that this is false, that like Tim Finnegan—or Ibsen's master builder (Solness)—HCE can no longer rise to her dream. Indeed, he has failed her before.

> All your graundplotting and the little it brought! (624: 12–13)

That realization brings her an acceptance of what she has had, as she turns away, wearily, from the project of renewal.

> On limpidy marge I've made me hoom. Park and a pub for me. (624: 15–16)

She chides him for his weaknesses, advising him to "redoform again" (624: 20). Then, quite suddenly, the caressing tone of her opening returns: HCE is again her "dowling" (624: 23).

What prompts the reversal? The deepest, fondest memory of all—the memory of how HCE courted her as a young girl, "pressing for his suit" (624: 29). Inspired by that recollection, she can see again the ordinary joys of their marriage, the mundane activities and conversations that have filled the years. As they proceed, however, their steps are no longer attuned (625: 21–2), and that realization prompts her to see the daily round as a matter of trifles, the old inconsequential things (625: 23–5, 27).

Once again, there is great sadness in the memories, and ALP reflects on the losses of the past (625: 28–32). She rouses herself with the vision of renewal, the thought of the morning walk, but it cannot be sustained. They do not have "loads" of time after all, only one another in their waning days, only the memories of their union, and the wind that makes her faint (626: 1) scatters them, blowing away the leaves with which she has been covered. There will be no new future, and the past now appears to her as a steady accumulation of losses, offset only with a scattering of trifles. She can only hold on to one recollection—of their beginning:

> And one time you'd rush upon me, darkly roaring like a great black shadow with a sheeny stare to perce me rawly. (626: 23–5)

She was "the pet of everyone," and he "the pantymammy's Vulking Corsegoth" (626: 27–8). He thrilled her with "the joy of fear" (626: 29)

> Like almost now. How? How you said how you'd give me the keys of me heart. And we'd be married till delth to uspart. And though dev do espart. O mine! Only, no, now it's me who's got to give. . . . And can it be it's nnow fforvell? Illas! I wisht I had better glances to peer to you through this baylight's growing. But you're changing, acoolsha, you're changing from me, I can feel. Or is it me is? I'm getting mixed. (626: 29–32, 33–6)

It is too late for renewal, for some new event or new start to modify what her life has meant or been. Its meaning or insignificance is set by what is past, and she is caught between two views of it. Perhaps that initial surge, that rush upon her, carries into the present; perhaps through the many days of their life together there is a single trajectory, one that involves the turning to one another we witnessed in the bedroom. Or perhaps it is not like that at all; perhaps they are parting from one another, and that thrill of joy and fear is simply an isolated occurrence, carried in memory like a single leaf.

It seems that the more bitter judgment will be sustained. As the end approaches, ALP sees her life as a decline from her youth, a frittering away of her days on small things—sees her acceptance as self-deception.

> How small it's all! And me letting on to meself always. And lilting on all the time. . . . I thought you the great in all things, in guilt and in glory. You're but a puny. (627: 20–1, 23–4)

The supposed Joycean virtues have turned out to be sentimental credulity, the forgiveness of laziness. ALP, the judge who has so often spoken with the accents of mercy, delivers a guilty verdict.

> But I'm loothing them that's here and all I lothe. Loonely in me loneness. For all their faults. I am passing out. O bitter ending! (627: 33–5)

It is not, however, the ending.

For ALP reverses herself. There is a last memory, a last leaf remaining. As she is about to say farewell to life, to plunge into the cold emptiness of death, there comes a new recognition.

> Avelaval. My leaves have drifted from me. All. But one clings still.
> I'll bear it on me. To remind me of. Lff! So soft this morning, ours.
> (628: 6–8)

That memory, the last leaf, conjures up the mood of her opening, her turn to HCE, the joy in waking beside him. Then it was a mingled celebration of the past of their marriage and a hope for renewal in the future, the natural illusion that has hung over this *ricorso*. Now, however, she understands completely that there will be no renewal, and she has anatomized her past. Yet that one memory, the memory of life and love, condensed into the image of the vigorous suitor, rushing upon her to "perce her rawly" (626: 25), cannot be shaken. She responds still to the same movement.

> Yes. Carry me along, taddy, like you done through the toy fair! If I seen
> him bearing down on me now under whitespread wings like he'd come
> from Arkangels, I sink I'd die down over his feet, humbly dumbly, only
> to washup. (628: 8–11)

The movement so often associated with the arrival of HCE, the great surge of the sea, runs through her still. The love he inspired in her cannot be shaken, and the course on which they set out together persists, despite the deviations and perturbations. She can utter Molly Bloom's word of affirmation, accepting her life, after all.

So, as the Liffey comes into view of Howth head, ALP recalls the days of their young love and the gulls who celebrated it (like those that accompanied Tristan and Isolde [II-4]). She can turn, one last time, to HCE:

> Us then. Finn, again! Take. Bussoftlhee, mememormee! Till thousend-
> sthee. Lps. The keys to. Given! (628: 13–15)

She is momentarily back at the scene of her original acceptance of HCE but knowing this time what will come after, how it will end. Even with that knowledge, even after the scrutiny of their lives in which she has engaged, she can ask for it again, ask him to take her, and open her lips for his kiss.

For what she knows is that the promise he made will be kept. His romantic boast that he would give her the keys to her heart was not empty.[11] She feels the motion of that early courtship still, and, feeling it, can trace it through her marriage and her life. Because of that, she can accept the history of their union, without minimizing the losses or overlooking the imperfections, without hoping for improvement or renewal. So, for her, and in her, the Joycean virtues—kindness, understanding, tolerance, acceptance, and forgiveness—can be realized.

21

AISY NOW, YOU DECENT MAN

Music runs through Joyce's prose, and through *Finnegans Wake,* in particular. It is not simply a matter of the constant eruption of the songs Joyce had heard his father sing, or had sung himself, but the use of rhythm to set the mood and of tonal coloring to evoke reactions in his readers. Even more significant, however, is the large-scale musical structure of the *Wake.*

According to critical consensus, the pattern of the book is set by Vico's account of human history, a cycle of three great ages, in which similar sequences of events repeat, followed by a *ricorso,* or return, to the beginning. That pattern can easily be discerned in the division into four parts, but it is quite superficial. Attempts to find parallels in the internal developments of the first three parts seem to me doomed either to pointing out the obvious—"in each case there is a fall"—or to slighting the important differences in mood: the consolation of the end of Part I, the bitterness, mixed with hope for the new, in Part II, and the hard-won endurance of Part III. I want to suggest a different way to think about the organization of the whole.

Joyce begins with an overture, an opening chapter in which important themes are sounded, relatively briefly. Yet, in something like the way in which the opening pages of the "Sirens" episode of *Ulysses* embody the complete chapter, the entire *Wake* is already present in miniature. The rest of Part I, culminating in the gossip of the washerwomen and their acceptance of HCE and ALP, constitutes a larger presentation of the same themes. Although they are not as compressed and fragmentary as the vignettes of the opening chapter, the dramatic incidents here remain relatively concise. Then, from the opening of Part II to the close of Part IV, Joyce develops his material far more expansively. Only at the beginning of the *ricorso* (Part IV) do we return to the more disjointed treatment of Chapter 1.[1] In effect, he offers us an orchestral prelude, a symphony of Mozartean dimensions, and, finally, something on a Mahlerian scale.

Viewed, or heard, in this way, the *Wake* comes to three major endings, one in the scene where the celebrants at the wake address the corpse, one when night descends on the washerwomen, and one at ALP's moment of final affirmation. Joyce's text can be closed at any one of these points, the great cadences in his music. As I shall propose below, one valuable reading is to make the return that ALP's unfinished sentence invites and to take the opening chapter for the last, as a retrospective restatement of her acceptance. One view of the *Wake* is a view from the wake.

Each of the three sections I have discerned shares a similar movement. In each case, the project for the dreamer—and for the reader—is to make sense of a life. Difficulties, failures, frustrations, lapses must be faced and recognized for what they are; the apparent triviality of most of what we do has to be appreciated. Through all of this, however bleak, unrewarding, insignificant, even disgusting it may initially seem, the text works its way to the Joycean virtues, to sympathy and acceptance. When the opening chapter is read for the first time (not as the continuation of Part IV), the themes are stated abruptly, and the comfort of the conclusion comes quite unprepared—it may even be overlooked. The end of Part I is more convincing, for we have heard those same themes at sufficient length, and with enough transitions among them, to respond to the movement that brings consolation out of defeat. Yet, as I have repeatedly suggested, the suspicion that acquiescence comes too easily needs to be allayed. Hence, Joyce leads us through the sweeping presentation of Parts II–IV, with the long descent of Part II, the false upturn with the new beginning and the emergence of Shaun, another fall, and then the salvage that leads from the wreckage of Yawn, through the re-emergence of HCE and the trial of the marriage, to ALP's elegy. Like a skilled musician, Joyce interpolates passages that hint at future development of his themes. Not only does the movement to acceptance in I-8 point to the full exposition in the *Wake*'s last pages, but it also fulfills the promise we have heard at the ends of I-4 and I-7. So, too, there are gestures of consolation, moments of upturn, even when the trend is downward. The image of ALP cooking the evening meal (246: 10–15) anticipates the bittersweet prayer that closes the chapter (258: 25–259: 10); the valedictions of III-1 and III-2 prepare the way for the revival in the last pages of III-3 and for the appreciative close of III-4. There are deceptive cadences as well, most notably in the hopes for renewal expressed at the end of II-4, in the opening pages of III-1, and at the beginning of Part IV.[2]

To understand Joyce's debt to Vico, we need to understand the large movement of his music and how that movement is echoed and re-echoed through the *Wake*. Always there are the same anxieties about the significance of what we do and about the worth of the ideals we so often fail to realize. The dreamer must search, again and again, for a response to this predicament, first by confronting the limitations and the lapses and then by coming to accept and to forgive. It can be done quickly and abruptly, with a bald statement, but that will only produce a temporary relief before the concerns break out anew. Even a relatively extensive exploration of the type undertaken in I-2 to I-8 can leave room for serious doubt that weariness, or sentimental self-deception, has substituted for a genuine solution. What Joyce's dreamer—and surely Joyce, too!—seeks is a presentation sufficiently extensive to carry conviction, and that is supposed to be provided by the great sweep that leads from Part II to the close, or even better, by the three elaborations taken together, the *Wake* as a whole.

As Jaun explains, "The Vico road goes round and round to meet where terms begin" (452: 21–2). Joyce writes with the conviction that few people will fail to understand the dreamer's predicament, that the project of making sense of a life arises for the ordinary and the great alike, for the ancients and the moderns, for those who seem to succeed most of the time and for those who usually fail. We may begin, like Stephen Dedalus, with a serious reflection on ideals and a bold delineation of who we aspire to be—or we may tacitly fall into a pattern for our existence. Either way, most of us will come to a time, the "awebrume hour" (336: 15), when we are prompted to ask, "What has gone? How it ends?" (614: 19), and, like the dreamer, we shall observe a decline, recognize opportunities lost and ideals compromised. Each particular tour around the Vico road has the same large features.

In responding to this predicament, Joyce thinks, with some plausibility, that there is nothing much to do except to go round and round. Hence, the dreamer explores, time and again, the same lapses and shortcomings, changing the elements in the kaleidoscope until they can fall into a satisfying arrangement. The movement to acceptance has to be repeated until its real possibility is no longer in question. Because of this, the *Wake* needs the threefold repetition of that consolatory movement; and, in the midst of the painful explorations, at moments when the failures loom large, the minor versions of that movement echo the success of previous efforts and point toward the possibility of resolution.

Imagine a fantastic alternative to the *Wake*, an attempt to respond to the same predicament by calmly evaluating each aspect of a life and integrating the results to form an assessment of the whole. A philosopher of extraordinary lucidity sets out to assign objective measures of value to the component pieces and tallies them to yield the correct score. The fantasy is absurd not only because the existence of the objective measure of value is highly dubious, but also because the exercise fails to take into account just that difficulty in facing the issues that made Joyce write the "book of the night." The explicit sum would carry no conviction, precisely because the serious anxieties that prompt anyone to compute it come with the recognition of our powers of avoidance—like Bloom, turning his thoughts away from the assignation in Eccles Street, we have ways of not seeing our lives "foully."

There are occasions on which intelligent people try to bring the precise tools of the day to difficult evaluations. In his *Autobiography,* Darwin describes his decision to marry his cousin, Emma Wedgwood. He tells us that he drew up a list of the advantages and disadvantages of marriage—female society in the credit column, loss of time for scientific pursuits among the debits. But Darwin's decision did not proceed by adding up and comparing the items in his ledger. After entering a number of pros and cons, he drew a line across the page and scribbled "Marry! Marry! Marry!"[3]

Joyce's dreamer doesn't proceed with the orderliness of Darwin's original plan. The night thoughts, distorted representations of what is too painful to acknowledge directly, do not come in tidy units, and they must be appraised on many occasions. Yet, there is a real kinship between the two endeavors. For in both instances, the final response comes because the review that precedes has prepared a new emotional state, a moment of release where something can be whole-heartedly affirmed. Neither Darwin nor the dreamer adds up measures of value to determine the balance. Both explore and survey, until a new attitude has crystallized and a judgment can no longer be resisted.

I have frequently hinted that the *Wake* is concerned with philosophical material, with the question, old as philosophy itself, "How is one to live?" The history of philosophy shows sporadic attempts to tackle that question directly, mixed with sustained attacks on issues that begin as ancillaries and then take on lives of their own. If philosophers often turn away from the issues that are the ultimate sources of significance for their pet projects, other intellectuals and artists do not. So, in great dramas, great poetry, great operas, and great novels, there is sometimes a different style of engagement with the central concerns of philosophy, one that deserves the attention of philosophers.

Joyce read widely in philosophy, but he did not attempt to write philosophical treatises. Instead, he deployed his enormous intellectual and literary gifts to address central philosophical questions.[4] The movement I take to dominate each of the three structural units of the *Wake* does not proceed by assigning measures of value or by developing chains of reasoning. Instead, it explores the night thoughts that trouble those who ask how it has been and how it will end, showing the facets of a life from different perspectives, turning the kaleidoscope again and again, until, as with Darwin's marriage decision, the pattern evokes acceptance and assent. The dreamer is not argued into submission but *shown,* and the many-sided showing eventually produces conviction.

Opera and drama, poetry and fiction can aid us in our thinking about what is valuable by bringing before us, in rich detail, possibilities that condense our dilemmas. Philosophical discussions of values (or value) frequently soar into the abstract, seeking principles of high generality that will legislate for all people and for all occasions. As with the flight of Icarus, the journey often does not end well. Yet there is an alternative approach, a minority position that tries to avoid the disaster of Grand Theory. It takes the project of working out our values in historical terms: we begin within a tradition, cope with the conflicts it bequeaths to us, and try to find our way to something better. This position supposes that illumination about how to live our lives—more exactly, how to live them a bit better than we might otherwise have done—is unlikely to come from the ambitious systems. Instead, we should find inspiration elsewhere:

> the arts, those of converse and the literary arts which are the enhanced continuations of social converse, have been the means by which goods are brought home to human perception. The writings of moralists have been efficacious in this direction upon the whole not in their professed intent as theoretical doctrines, but in as far as they have genially participated in the arts of poetry, fiction, parable, and drama.[5]

So, by providing us with new perspectives on an issue of value that matters to us, a great novel might bring more "home to human perception" than a systematic treatise whose connection with the "general theory of value" is more immediately apparent.

The method of refining views about values through imaginative presentation and emotional response should not be beyond criticism. It is reasonable to wonder whether we should trust the reactions that are wrung from us. Although skepticism is in place here, I envisage a double response to it. First, we can pursue the imaginative experiment more thoroughly, confronting ourselves with different perspectives on the same possibilities, constantly probing to see if the emotional conviction can be undermined; we can go round and round, in the way the *Wake* does. Second, we can ask what alternative can be provided, what other ways are open to us, other than attempting to rehearse the envisaged drama with as much detail and repetition as we can manage and then to carry out "experiments of living."[6] In the end, like Darwin, we find that there is no systematic procedure but simply the production of a decision.

These brief reflections may earn some credibility for the general idea of the exploration of values through fiction, but Joyce may seem initially to be a poor candidate for exemplifying the theme. Other novelists present themselves as more likely exemplars: George Eliot perhaps, or Henry James—for we might focus on the aspirations and conflicts of Dorothea Brooke in *Middlemarch,* or of Strether in *The Ambassadors.* Alternatively, to come closer to the issue I have seen at the heart of the *Wake,* the question of understanding how a life can be worthwhile, we might turn to Thomas Mann, considering Hans Castorp in *The Magic Mountain,* or the unfortunate Buddenbrooks, or Adrian Leverkühn of *Doctor Faustus,* or Aschenbach's death in Venice. How can a novel whose figures are as fluid as those of the *Wake* bring any clarity, or concreteness, to judgments about the potential value of various ways of living?

To answer this question, it helps, as so often, to start with *Ulysses.* Precisely because Joyce takes us deeply into the mundane details of Bloom's day, revealing what is trivial and squalid in it as well as the persistence and humanity that guide Bloom in his wanderings, he brings home to us the worth, even the worthiness, of an ordinary life. Our reaction is the stronger for the awareness that it is made "despite all": Bloom demands our sympathy and respect despite our having seen aspects of him that literature (and "social converse") typically keep hidden. In the *Wake,* Joyce hopes to excavate even more deeply, confronting the dreamer (and us) with thoughts from which Bloom's waking consciousness turned away. Stable characters aren't needed for this dramatic exposure. The only props Joyce requires are the common features of ordinary lives, the physical decline of aging, the possible continuations of love in marriage, the surrounding presence of established practices. These can be rendered concrete, in dream distortion or with greater realism, in vignettes that involve *personae* that are allowed to shift and blur. The foci of the quest are the possibilities of love, lapse, betrayal, repudiation, and fulfillment, as the particular elements of ordinary life are made vivid in new combinations. The kaleidoscope—or "collideorscape" (143: 28)—provides a sequence of images through which the most central issues about values can be explored.

Joyce's distinctive brand of humanism, centered on what I have called the "Joycean virtues," can be viewed as a particular development of that tradition in approaching questions of value through understanding our sentiments.[7] He takes the refinement of our attitudes to consist in extending and enlarging our sympathetic appreciation of others.[8] In both the *Wake* and *Ulysses,* this emphasis on sympathy is important in two ways; as I have just noted, it is the source of his ability to address issues of value, through the delineation of possibilities that eventually generate our affirmative judgment; but the characters, and possibilities, we affirm are themselves remarkable for the sympathy, tolerance, kindness, and forgiveness they express. Joyce expects us to feel sympathy for sympathy, specifically for that sympathy that endures "despite all," that can withstand the sight of details that are trivial or sordid or both.

The central movement of the *Wake* is the dreamer's sympathetic acceptance of a life that is full of flaws, that aspires to nothing extraordinary, that fails in many ways, and that recognizes its own physical decline. That sympathetic acceptance is won through the persistence and enlargement of sympathy in the characters who are central, ALP and HCE. To trace a simple line through the complex details that have occupied us in previous chapters, the chapters of Part II show us the hostile forces that tend to narrow sympathy, Parts II and III together show us the failure of all kinds of central values, and the great climaxes of III-3, III-4, and IV reveal a capacity for sympathy to persist, even grow, despite all. That is a radical oversimplification, of course, but, if the dreamer can quiet his anxieties at the end—as, I have claimed, he can—it is through his appreciation of the power of this simple line.

As a guide to resolving the puzzles and conflicts about value that arise for us, the exercise of sympathetic enlargement and exploration can easily seem an unreliable tool, one that will inevitably inherit the prejudices we absorb in early social training and that will leave us prey to the vicissitudes of mood and situation. These are real dangers, and they should induce doubt that the process of refining our value judgments can ever be finished. They do not, however, eliminate the possibility of improvement: although we never free ourselves entirely from bias, we may escape some of the distortions from which we began; although we are always vulnerable to an emotional tug that is too great in one direction or too feeble in another, we may gain a greater ability to broaden our perspectives and to achieve more constancy.[9]

In reading Joyce as a great humanist, I may seem to miss what is most important about his two major novels. Isn't Joyce the high priest of modernism, whose conception of fiction repudiates the entanglement with ethical questions found in the writings of George Eliot and Henry James? In taking the psychological lives of Bloom, Stephen, and Molly, and of the dream figures of the *Wake* as seriously as I have done, in supposing that the dreamer uses HCE and company as props in an exploratory drama, and that readers can mirror the dreamer's struggles in a sympathetic identification with these fluid characters, don't I fail to see what is truly revolutionary about Joyce?

As I have already suggested, I do not see how to account for the power of the *Wake*, its impact *as a whole*, in terms of a collection of amusing puzzles or a cacophony of unrelated voices. One might maintain, however, that the fragmentation of language and culture is a central modernist theme, found in *Ulysses*, in *The Waste Land*, and, above all, in the *Wake*. That idea stands in need of qualification. For Joyce, and I think for T. S. Eliot too, the ruins, the chaos, are not simply to be recorded or expressed; they serve as occasions for deciding how to go on. The question of how to live against the background of a "dividual chaos" (186: 4–5) becomes *the* question of values.

We might read *The Waste Land* as the interplay of the many voices that were once explicitly referred to in the title ("He Do the Police in Different Voices")—and we surely do not find ourselves in sympathetic engagement with the characters whose voices we hear. That is not, however, because T. S. Eliot fails to pose the issue I have taken as fundamental. For, in the second part ("A Game of Chess"), we hear the question directly:

What shall we do tomorrow?
What shall we ever do?

Eliot cannot find the answer in the game of chess, in the "closed car at four," in the incidents that surface in the pub conversation, in the seduction of the typist—indeed, in any of the mundane proceedings about which his voices speak. If the poem itself indicates an answer, it can only be through the invocation of something very different from the ordinary, in the silence in the garden or in the Hindu benediction. In his later poetry, in *Ash Wednesday*, and especially in *Four Quartets*, that invocation is more explicit.

Modernism might be seen as breaking with earlier ethical explorations in fiction in light of a perception that there are no longer *any* values that can be uncontroversially invoked. The novel leaves the world of George Eliot and Henry James, in which received values conflict and in which the protagonists struggle to reconcile them, as best as they can. It becomes centered on finding *something* valuable in human life, when all transcendental foundations for that value have been abandoned. This is, I believe, the shift that Joyce makes, a shift *within* the domain of posing and addressing issues of value—and it runs in parallel to the modernist themes in T. S. Eliot's poetry. Because Eliot's own response to the question of finding value—"What shall we ever do?"—consists in *returning* to the transcendent, the voices of his people sound hopelessly, echoing the bleak world in which those who find only the ordinary must live. Joyce, more thoroughly shaped by Nietzsche and Ibsen, and by the nineteenth-century skeptical tradition that stands behind them, will have none of this conservative retreat to transcendent illusions.[10] For him, the question must be answered within the ordinary—the mundane must be conceived as worthwhile, so that life "seen foully" remains valuable. The detachment of the reader from the protagonists we find in T. S. Eliot is not, then, essential to modernism. Rather, it results either from leaving the fundamental question hanging (and how can it be left hanging?) or from an answer that finds value in something external to individual people and their everyday doings.

Joyce's break with the ethical traditions of the novel consists, I believe, in recognizing that the explorations of his great predecessors—George Eliot and Henry James, for two examples—depended on confidence about particular human values. He was not alone in posing a different (and deeper) ethical issue, the issue of how to find value in any form of human life; both Thomas Mann and Franz Kafka can be seen as wrestling with kindred worries. Yet because of the intensity of his dedication to the value of the mundane, to the thought that ordinary human lives can be fully worth living, he was, I believe, compelled to bring his readers deeply and sympathetically into the psychological lives of his characters. Thence comes his extraordinary humanity, his distinctive humanism.[11]

I have addressed, probably too briefly, a literary concern about my reading. There is also an obvious philosophical challenge. Joyce's humanism, and the Joycean virtues, can easily seem to inflate the claims of mercy at the expense of those of justice, to slight courage and overemphasize passive acceptance. It would be hard to deny that this impression captures Joyce's priorities (as the closing pages of I-7 make plain), but it is equally important to resist the suggestion that his ideal favors the spineless or those who are so moved by each person's difficulties that they override considerations of fairness. To be genuinely sympathetic to *all* the parties involved in a situation where interests conflict requires appreciating when reparations are due; real sympathy with those whose concerns are threatened, or violated, entails a resolve to resist the sources of the menace. It is no accident that Bloom stands up to the Citizen and that intolerance of intolerance pervades the *Wake* (for just two examples, 76–80; 371–80), no surprise that Bloom's extensive sympathy draws him to the Lying-in Hospital, then to Nighttown, and, finally, as he understands even more, to home and bed, no surprise that the culmination of the *Wake* reveals HCE and ALP turning to one another, again and again (546–54; 619–28).

As I have suggested, the *Wake* must continue beyond Part I because the dreamer cannot be satisfied with an acceptance that comes too easily. The long probing of Parts II and III is required to allay the anxiety that Joyce's moral perspective, his humanism, substitutes self-deception for harsh judgment. Few serious readers of *Ulysses* can have failed to worry that Joyce is too lax and complacent, too apt to forgive the prickly arrogance, even egoism, of Stephen, to condone the infidelity of Molly and the wandering passivity of Bloom. To gaze intently on his brilliant portraits of these characters, with their open presentation of grubby details, leads the sympathetic reader to Joyce's human conclusion—to acceptance, forgiveness, even admiration. But have we been beguiled?

That question hangs over the *Wake*, too, and it is addressed with even deeper penetration. The flawed figures who swim before the dreamer are interrogated again and again, until they secure a sympathetic response, a response based on appreciation of the enlargement of sympathy in their lives. Joyce wants to take us beyond the lure of standard moral rules—and, of course, he makes brilliant fun of conventional maxims (e.g. 268–72; 433–8; compare also 579: 8–25). Despite the apparent laxity of his moral vision, there is, I think, not only a certain kind of strenuousness in matters of value that he wants to escape but also another that he commends.

A contrast with William James can help focus these reservations about Joyce's humanism. One of James's several interesting attempts to defend the importance of religious belief argues that the attitude of the faithful is particularly conducive to the moral life.

> The deepest difference, practically, in the moral life of man is the difference between the easy-going and the strenuous mood.[12]

James asserts that the "strenuous mood" manifests itself in the ability to make sacrifices in the cause of an ideal and that this commendable mood is difficult to arouse. The importance of prodding ourselves in this way is sufficiently great to justify the best means of accomplishing it:

> The capacity of the strenuous mood lies so deep down among our natural human possibilities that even if there were no metaphysical or traditional grounds for believing in a God, men would postulate

one simply as a pretext for living hard, and getting out of the game of existence its keenest possibilities of zest.[13]

Nothing could be more directly antithetic to Joyce's version of humanism. For it is not just that Joyce would object to the famous Jamesian move of leaping beyond the evidence when the consequences are "good for life" but that he would deny the values James takes for granted. To see human life "foully," acknowledging all our impulses, is to recognize that the hardness that comes from religion has little to do with "zest" and far more with the spirit that pervaded the chapel where young Stephen Dedalus was shocked into terrified acknowledgment of his sinful state. As Jaunathaun points out, the creator's finest joke is to put "Allspace in a Notshall" (455: 29), to provide us with means for inculcating absolute prohibitions that warp and cripple us. Nor would Joyce accept the idea that religions are the only means of arousing the "strenuous mood." Catalogues of norms figure in the *Wake*'s many condemnations, secular versions of religious commandments, appealed to by members of communities that prosecute deviations with "zest," and whose virulence is untouched by any sympathy.

Nevertheless, if he opposes all the particular rules that override the nuances of human lives, the simple abstract ideals James thinks are needed for us to move on to a higher moral plane, Joyce offers his own kind of strenuousness, his own central commandment (or imperative). That directive is to enlarge our sympathies and to direct our conduct by the broadest and deepest engagement with the predicaments of those who will be affected by what we do. To attain the Joycean virtues is difficult. To be easy-going in the right way requires hard work.

Joyce's longer fiction, from *Portrait* through *Ulysses* to the *Wake*, shows the trajectory of a life that responds to this imperative. We are given portraits of the artist at many stages of his career, portraits that embody Joyce's distinctive humanism. In giving us those portraits, Joyce helps us to an appreciation of that humanism, by using his prose to foster the process of enlargement of sympathy.

It is right to think of all of these as portraits of the *artist*, and not only because the central figures are surrogates for Joyce. Bloom and Molly, HCE and ALP are *primary* artists, pouring creative energy into their lives together, extending the single, individually drawn line of mutually directed sympathy that makes their shared ordinary experiences worthwhile. They make the ordinary pieces form an original whole, harmonized by the pervading sympathy. The more obvious artists, Shem, the young Stephen Dedalus—and Joyce-apart-from-Nora—record this primary creative effort, using their skills at depicting the enlargement of sympathy in the lives of their protagonists to expand the sympathy of their readers. If Shem fails to find his own way of enlarging sympathy, if Stephen does not learn from Bloom—and if Joyce does not discover Nora—then the resulting art will be secondary and the fierce denunciations of I-7 may have a point. The literary accomplishment depends on the sympathetic movement lived by the artist.

Without that movement, the art, as well as the life, will be truncated and stunted.

An important part of the explicit artistic process, through which the sympathies of the reader are enlarged and the Joycean virtues revealed, involves teaching us to laugh. There are two kinds of laughter *in* the *Wake*, one unsympathetic, hostile, and derisive, that erupts in the carnival celebration of I-2—although even here, Joyce can point the way to sympathy with those celebrants who have found themselves "under the blankets of homelessness on the bunk of iceland" (40: 18–19)—and in the customers' exodus from the bar (371:6–379: 31); the other heard most loudly in the voice of ALP (273: 23–4; 495: 16–18; 583: 26). Far more pervasive is the laughter produced *by* the *Wake*, even if it is not openly expressed in guffaws (although it is sometimes hard to keep it muffled inside). As I have already admitted, the thesis that so constantly funny a book is concerned with serious issues, with the perspective of the "awebrume hour," needs some explanation. In baldest terms my defense is that the wit and humor are deployed to bring us to that form of laughter expressed by ALP and that the enlargement of our sympathy is a concomitant of the process.

The thought that laughter and sadness are so interconnected that deep forms of one involve similarly deep forms of the other is a familiar one. Keats, a writer whose idiom is quite remote from that of Joyce, voiced it at the end of his "Ode on Melancholy," insisting that the "shrine" of melancholy cannot be entered by everyone:

> Though seen of none save him whose strenuous tongue
> Can burst joy's grape against his palate fine.

Joyce's one-time amanuensis, Samuel Beckett, offers a different expression of linkage between laughter and tears. Toward the close of *Endgame*, Hamm reflects:

> You weep, and weep, for nothing, so as not to laugh, and little by little . . . you begin to grieve.[14]

The *Wake*, as I read it, combines elements of Keats's conception with an inversion of Hamm's reflection: the awareness of deep sadness that comes at the "awebrume hour" is only complete when we are also moved to laughter by it, and the laughter is what enables each of us to go on, to smile so as not to weep, until, little by little, we begin to laugh.

Joyce's sense of how laughter and tears are woven together is condensed into a moving line of the secular prayer that closes the children's game (II-1).

> Loud, heap miseries upon us yet entwine our arts with laughters low!
> (259: 7–8)

The episode in the street has left no doubt about the heaping of miseries, not only for the rejected Glugg but also for the yearning, dissatisfied Issy, for the Floras who are as likely as not to become "the grocer's bawd" with "hand in the haricot bag" (227: 3), even for the enigmatic Chuff. These are to be borne with laughter that comes from the heart, laughter like ALP's; that is what the arts of living amount to. Such laughter can soften the grimness of the miseries, the squalor, the triviality, expressing and augmenting a sense of the absurdity of it all, of the silliness of pretending that it will amount to anything timeless or transcendent. As Jaun reminds the girls, several episodes later:

> A tear or two in time is all there's toot. And then in a click of the clock, toot toot, and doff doff we pop with sinnerettes in silkettes lining lon-groutes for His Diligence Majesty, our longdistance laird that likes cre-ation. To whoosh! (457: 21–4)

Reflection on our finitude, our pettiness, our disappointments, and anguish can be met by treating it all as farce. It is no accident that the laughters are low—earthy, ribald, and deep, like the *Wake* itself.

So, at the bleakest moment of Part II, when HCE has been left as "Mocked Majesty" (380: 4–5), we aren't treated to the catharsis of tragedy. He has disintegrated into a collection of incompatible impulses, all unsatisfied, his life apparently amounting to nothing. No agonizing climax follows; there is no self-blinding, no immolation, not even a wretched death. Instead, HCE wanders around the bar, drinking the odd residues of stale drinks that his scornful customers haven't bothered to finish. He is described in the rambling tones, bordering on senility, of the old men, and the deep sadness of the moment fuses with the comic. Misery is treated with an art entwined with laughters low.

The irrepressible humor of the *Wake* carries us through the wretchedness, the squalor, and the apparent insignificance of the lives it displays, bathing them in a different light until we can recognize their sad failures and still appreciate, with sympathy, their everyday qualities. We can both feel the "chill" at the base of the stair, the stair that ALP and HCE descend in their decline, while simultaneously laughing sympathetically with the "large incorporate licensed vintner" who presides over the "hydrocomic establishment" (580: 23–5). Laughter enables us to trace the line that leads through these lives and finally to treat that dreary scene in the bar as a mere incident.

Yet there is, I think, a danger of overemphasizing Joyce's capacity for laughter. If, indeed, "God has jest" (486: 10), then why not reply by treating it all—everything—as a joke? I don't think Joyce's complex humanism can be reduced to the thought that, in the face of the absurdity of human life, our best response is laughter—he is not the class clown for whom nothing, absolutely nothing, is to be treated with a straight face.[15] There are moments in the *Wake* at which the laughter ceases, at which there are no more jokes. Most notable is the wave of bitterness, of repudiation, that sweeps over ALP (627: 14–628: 5). Indeed, the reconciliatory movement, the closing affirmation that succeeds her anguished regret, is also beyond laughter.

I want to generalize further, to suggest that there are definite moments when the *Wake*'s flood of humor is halted and that many of these are at the places where the dreamer has won through, if only temporarily, to a condition of sympathy and acceptance. In ALP's closing elegy as a whole, the laughter subsides—and so, too, with her response to the coupling of the previous scene (590: 27–30), with the valedictions to Shaun (427: 17–428: 27; 471: 35–473: 25), with the descent of night on the washerwomen (215: 12–216: 5), with the earlier consolatory portents of ALP (102: 18–103: 12; 194: 21–195: 6), even in the secular prayer that enjoins us to laughter (258: 25–259: 10). On all of these occasions, the fund of humor has already done its work. By bringing us, and the dreamer, through to a moment of sympathy, it is no longer needed, or even appropriate. The relief, the appreciation, the delight we feel for these ordinary people and their ordinary lives, although *attained* by laughters low should not be *expressed* in them. They should be honored with a sympathetic smile.

How, then, *does* it end? Perhaps with ALP's unfinished sentence, affirming her life—an untidy life but a life distinguished by a central course that we, readers and dreamer, can endorse as valuable. Or we can go one stage further, continuing "along the riverrun" (628: 15–16; 3: 1). That will bring us to a wake, an occasion for much singing and drinking. We return to a world of large figures, giants and patriarchs and generals and more. There are brief flashes of landscapes and incidents that have been dreamed in later sections of the *Wake*, whose import we can discern, as we read for a second (or third, or fourth . . .) time. But these are fragmentary vignettes that break up a central scene, one that presents a corpse, that of "Bygmester Finnegan, of the Stuttering Hand" (4: 18), laid out on his bier (and, very probably, on his beer).

Whoishe? (499: 35–6). The answer now is as it was in the later part of the dream, signaled by the stutter, by the fact that Finnegan is a "man of hod, cement and edifices" (4: 26), by the fact that he "addle liddle phifie Annie ugged the little craythur" (4: 28–9) and by a host of other clues. HCE is here again, as he will be in Finnegan's successor (29: 30–6) and as he will be in Shem and Shaun. He is, as I have said, inescapable.

The dreamer can move with ease among his various manifestations. It makes no difference whether he appears as a legendary giant, a great religious leader, a king, a general, a builder, or an innkeeper. Having dreamed the whole dream, the dreamer knows that scale is irrelevant, that the problem of understanding and vindicating a life arises for the large figures of history (or myth) as it does for those whose names vanish from the record. To be remembered is to become a one-liner, a moral for the children's study-book (306: 15–308: 1). If this was a life worth living, its value resided in a central course that can only be understood in terms of mundane details. Whether Finnegan swells to giant proportions, whether he's a builder with a hangover who fell off a ladder, or whether he's the "incorporated licensed vintner" of the later vignettes, his success, or failure, will depend on the same things.

So how do they view him, those who attend the wake? They laugh and they dance and they drink (6: 18–19, 28). They also bemoan the loss (6: 13–15, 21). They dissect him, treating him as potential material for their own renewal—and the dissection reveals that not everything within is wholesome (7: 17–19). The verdict, however, is by no means as negative as those we have heard from the community in the later dreams:

'Twas he was the dacent gaylabouring youth. (6: 23)

So, as we should have expected, mourning and laughter mingle, the recognition of faults is mixed with sympathetic understanding.

In this initial phase of the dream, the verdict about Finnegan/HCE is quite inconclusive, the tensions unresolved. The dreamer's explorations continue with brief vignettes, rapid changes of the kaleidoscope, that confront us with patterns we have seen in the longer episodes of the later chapters. We seem to have lost our central figure, the corpse of Tim Finnegan whose wake this ostensibly is—until Joyce picks up a line from the song that gives his book its title. Splashed by drink, the corpse revives and asks, "Did ye think me dead?"—or, in the *Wake*'s words, "Did ye drink me doornail?" (24: 15).

Finnegan/HCE cannot die, I think, until he knows what he has meant and how it has ended. In response to his question comes a voice, apparently that of an ordinary Dubliner, one of those who have been acquainted with the dead man. That voice is unlike those of the jeering locals heard in the later dreams; although it is not that of ALP, it is tinged with the sympathy of which she is the emblem.

Now be aisy, good Mr Finnimore, sir. And take your laysure like a god on pension and don't be walking abroad. (24: 16–17)

The ghosts that haunt the dreamer can only be laid by resolving doubts about the life that has finished. The first consolation is that Finnegan/HCE has passed into the stuff of legend (25: 9–31). But this, as we who have followed all the dreams know, is an illusion.

The tone changes. From the grandiose predictions of lasting fame—the same inflated style that pervaded HCE's great apologia (III-3)—the voice descends to the continuities that really matter. It abandons the yearning for the (impossible) transcendent, in favor of the ordinary.

Everything's going on the same or so it appeals to all of us, in the old
holmsted here. (26: 25–6)

The boys (Kevin and Jerry in this account) continue in the familiar patterns;
the daughter's beauty distinguishes her. And there is ALP, finding her way,
regretfully, uncertainly, without him. If he were only there, to help her (28:
10–11), her "lips would moisten once again" (28: 11–12), as long ago, on a
drive they took together:

> What with reins here and ribbons there all your hands were employed
> so she never knew she was on land or at sea or swooped through the
> blue like Airwinger's bride. She was flirtsome then and she's flutter-
> some yet. (28: 13–16)

We are back at the close of III-3, back with the joyful ride that HCE and ALP
take together—back, too, with the movement begun in their courtship that
has continued through their lives, the movement that defines them both.

So this sympathetic voice, plain, uncomplicated, beyond laughter, sounds
Joyce's dominant musical theme for the first, or the last, time. In the great
central course of their lives together, in the mutual turning to one another, the
other mundane details, the ordinary events they have shared and whose patterns continue beyond HCE's death take on the value for which the dreamer
has been searching. This life has been, as the opening presentation of the wake
made clear, a mixture. It can now close:

> Repose you now! Finn no more! (28: 34)

> Aisy now, you decent man, with your knees and lie quiet and repose
> your honour's lordship! (27: 22–3)

Both the dreamer's main anxieties are addressed. There is no slighting of the
difficulties, the reversals, the betrayals, the squalid aspects of this life, but
rather a new understanding of them in light of the persisting direction of its
central relationship. Nor is the value of that relationship to be compromised
by the uncertainties about the distant past, by the shadows of some menacing "Michael," for, whatever the sources of ALP's great capacity to love,
the trajectory of their lives shows that love to have been directed toward her
"funnyman."

The epithet, "decent," echoes the tipsy lament expressed in the conviviality of the wake, regret for the "dacent gaylabouring youth" (6: 23).[16] HCE
is hardly "best of men" (28: 11), or even "good Mr Finnimore" (24: 16). The
figure on the bier is not the Buddha, not Christ, not Caesar or Wellington,
not Oscar Wilde or Dean Swift or Charles Dodgson. He is a decent man,
who has lived an ordinary life, within a community to which he has been
sympathetic, and about whose continuing career the voice offers reassurance.

Even more crucially, that life has centered on his family and on a wife whose heart he has opened. The movement begun in his young love persists, despite his decline, despite her doubts in the face of imminent death, despite the perturbations and the failures. Knowing that, he, and the dreamer, may rest. It is enough.

NOTES

Awakening

1. An epigraph might well be drawn from a writer whom Joyce regarded as close to the pinnacle of literary achievement: Dante's *Commedia* begins, *"Nel mezzo del cammin di nostra vita/ Mi ritrovai per una selv' oscura/ Che la diritta via era smarrita* [In the middle of this earthly life, I found myself in a dark wood, where the straight way was lost]."

2. So, although I divide the text of the *Wake* into three main parts (Chapter 1 of Part I, the rest of part I, Parts II–IV), we can think of a four-part structure if we count the opening chapter twice: Prelude (Part I, Chapter 1), Exposition (Part I, Chapters 2–8), Development (Parts II–IV), Coda (Part I, Chapter 1, again).

Chapter 1

1. Hugh Kenner rightly draws attention to this as a "nodal" passage (*Dublin's Joyce* [revised edition, New York: Columbia University Press, 1987], p. 315). He understands the kaleidoscope image in terms of limitations on perception; as will become apparent, I shall develop that image differently.

2. The suit would be appropriate for the special occasion ALP envisages; but his best clothes would also be required for the corpse of HCE, to adorn him at his wake.

3. As William York Tindall notes, "sama sitta" not only connotes "same city," but also, for those who know Esthonian, "same shit" (*A Reader's Guide to "Finnegans Wake"* [Syracuse: Syracuse University Press, 1969], p. 331).

4. I shall return to the significance of this in Chapters 20 and 21.

5. In his wide-ranging and illuminating study of the myth of Lot and his daughters (*Lot's Daughters*, Stanford University Press), Robert Polhemus interprets this passage as suggesting that ALP resigns her husband to their daughter. As will become very clear below, I agree with him that HCE's attraction to younger women is *an* important aspect of the *Wake*, but I think that much more is involved in this part of ALP's monologue; there's both a recollection of her own youth and the dawning love for the young HCE and the appreciation that younger versions of themselves will feel the old ardor (and eventually follow the same trajectory). The difference in emphasis is readily explicable in terms of our

respective goals: Polhemus wants to reveal the complexities of a single myth in a wide variety of texts and cultural episodes; I hope to explore the many aspects of a single work.

Chapter 2

1. I shall offer an expurgated version of the chapter, not in the sense that I slight the sexual detail, but in the sense that I concentrate on a central line and theme and omit what I take to be digressions from them. Those digressions are, nevertheless, important, and I shall return to them in Chapter 19 when we have a richer perspective on the *Wake*.

2. The descriptions offered in the chapter are given from the perspective of one of the four bedposts, each identified with one of the four "evangelists" who represent the different quadrants of Ireland. I shall not discuss this aspect of the chapter here.

3. The highly idealized descriptions of the daughter, here and elsewhere in the *Wake*, are probably prompted by Joyce's recollections of earlier years in his own marriage before his daughter, Lucia, began to show the disturbing behavior that eventually led to her confinement in an asylum.

4. The view is diagrammed earlier in the *Wake* (II-2; 293), where HCE's two sons construct it in response to a "geometrical problem."

5. In citing these passages, I gloss over, for the moment, the fact that they occur in one of the chapter's several digressions. Although they do not figure in the central narrative of the lovemaking between HCE and ALP, they continue the realistic depiction of their decaying bodies.

6. For sensitive discussion of this aspect of HCE's emotional life, see Polhemus, *Lot's Daughters*. As already noted, I am concerned to embed this complex relationship within the broader constellation of doubts and failures, lapses and transgressions that HCE embodies (see Chapter 1 n. 5).

7. The characterization here evokes Havelock Ellis, conceiving him as a sexual snoop in the service of community norms, rather than as a liberatory figure.

8. One way of responding to this scene is to suppose that the onlookers who announce their regret are HCE's sons, peeping through the doorway to their parents' room. I can accept that idea as providing additional layers of meaning, but following out the thought of wide-eyed children at the primal scene will not be central to the main themes of the reading I develop.

9. Many pages of the book are devoted to a set of overlayered stories about HCE's behavior in Phoenix Park. I am deliberately attempting to introduce the main lines of my reading without taking up this complex of material. But its turn will come.

Chapter 3

1. His longest previous account of himself comes in II-3 (355: 21–356: 4; 356: 16–358: 16). The early phases of the long speech that closes III-3 are similar, in their inept apologies, to this previous material.

2. This is the most condensed version of the story, which has many variations, with differing accounts of HCE's own state of dress or undress. We shall explore the significance of all this in later chapters. For the moment, a bare account of the accusation will suffice.

3. This isn't the only occasion on which Joyce suggests that the disturbing elements of the dream stories are the results of unhappiness of the stomach rather than the psyche; see 599: 19–20.

4. Besides the obvious fun in renaming three great European writers, Joyce's choices are suggestive, inviting us to think of Dante as austere and forbidding, Goethe as elderly and stiff, and Shakespeare as licensed supplier of culture to the bourgeoisie.

5. Interestingly, the first on the list is "Tamlane the Cusacke," surely an allusion to Michael Cusack, the Citizen of the "Cyclops" section of *Ulysses,* whose hostility toward the outsider (Bloom) is so vehement. As we shall see, there are many resonances of this part of *Ulysses* in the dream stories around HCE.

6. B. S. Rowntree, *Poverty: A Study of Town Life* (3rd edition, 1902).

7. Martin Cunningham commands our sympathy for several reasons, but one is that he is a well-regarded Dubliner who shows concern and respect for Bloom.

8. As we shall discover, HCE, like Bloom, channels his creative energy into his family life.

Chapter 4

1. For a prime example, see the fable of "The Mookse and the Gripes" (152–9), to be discussed in Chapter 11 below.

2. As I have already noted, and as I shall explore further below, there are many connections between the *Wake* and *Ulysses.* There is an obvious signal here in "greekenhearted yude," which links Shem to Bloom. Even without that, however, the sentence conveys the same revulsion Bloom feels observing the eaters in the "Lestrygonians" episode of *Ulysses.*

3. *Ulysses,* 34. I read Stephen's remark about history as a nightmare as a development of the commitment (from the end of *Portrait*) to his forging of "the uncreated conscience" of his race. He responds to Mr. Deasy's vision of history with a detheologized version of Hegel: history culminates with the state, the community, the shout in the street; but this is not the fulfillment of human freedom, but the oppression of the individual. In hearing the boys outside playing, we should remember the pupils at Clongowes and look forward to the children's game of II-1 of the *Wake.*

4. This is the new nickname Stephen predicts that Mulligan will assign him (*Ulysses,* 36).

5. *Ulysses,* 212. John Eglinton attributes the line to "Dumas *fils* (or is it Dumas *père*)."

6. This passage occurs in an interruption of the main flow of the prosecutor's charges, the second of a pair of newspaper advertisements (or "personals"). The first, for Johns the Butcher, is a celebration of the healthy pleasures of

meat, with threatening overtones of violence and slaughter. The second is labeled "ABORTISEMENT" (181: 33).

7. This is a vivid expression of Joyce's own dilemma, the gnawing thought that his own art was achieved through the sacrifice of his beloved family, the doubt that one can be both a committed artist and a spouse (or parent).

8. The allusion to Wilde's famous story is as open and direct as anything in the *Wake;* less familiar is Balzac's *Le Peau de Chagrin,* which inspired Wilde's story. Of course, the prosecutor may be suggesting that this particular artist is deceived and that his work of art, too, is doomed to decay.

9. Here I connect Shem's response to the fable of the Ondt and the Grace-hoper, told later by Shaun. I shall be concerned with the significance of this concluding line in Chapter 16 below.

10. Joyce became deeply interested in Ibsen in his teens, studying Norwegian so that he could have access to the original text of the plays. Ibsen crops up frequently in the *Wake,* and *The Master Builder* (and the Master Builder) is particularly relevant.

11. I also take the preceding lines to contain veiled allusions to Stephen's voyage home to his dying mother.

12. I read the opening word of this paragraph as an evocation of Stephen's response to the ghost of his mother in the "Circe" scene of *Ulysses.*

13. I take the second part of this to be deliberately ambiguous between betrayal of mother and betrayal of father. The idea of the child suckling the father becomes explicit in the "star-chamber quiry" (480: 14).

14. It is also a technical term of theology, signifying an intermediate state of reconciliation to the church.

Chapter 5

1. I write as an aficionado of the (London) *Times* crossword. Those who doubt that crossword puzzles can aspire to genuine (Joycean) wit should consult Brian Greer, *How to Do the Times Crossword* (London: Timesbooks, 2001).

2. It is also an open question among those who ponder Joyce's life as to how much his immersion in the *Wake* interfered with his recognition of the needs of his beloved—but schizophrenic—daughter, Lucia.

3. Here I agree with Kenner's judgment that reading should not begin with a "lexicon" for the "jabberwocked materials" (*Dublin's Joyce,* p. 311).

4. It's correct to protest, here, that newsreels aren't as transparent as they seem. Often, significant work must be done to expose and challenge the background assumptions—the ideology—behind the celebratory, or condemnatory, presentations. As I'll suggest, excavation of this sort is central to the *Wake.*

5. In particular, there is the well-known occasion on which Joyce asked Gilbert whether the text was complicated enough yet.

6. As I shall eventually suggest, what we should aim for is an understanding of the *musical structure* of the *Wake,* an understanding that discloses its grand form, the

ways in which various sections and chapters contribute, the ways that the parts of the chapters fit together, the interlocking of the paragraphs. The words come last.

7. Much as I admire the work of many Joyce scholars—John Bishop, Richard Ellmann, Hugh Kenner, Roland McHugh, Robert Polhemus, and William Tindall, in particular—the best source for this orientation seems to me to be the work of a novelist: Anthony Burgess's *Re Joyce*.

8. There is an available recording of the whole *Wake*, read by Patrick Healey. Although it has some fine moments, it is marred by a tendency to gabble and displays far too little vocal, rhythmic, and dynamic variation. In my judgment, it misses the musical structure of the *Wake* at all levels. No listening can substitute for reading the text out loud oneself—although combining one's own overt reading with those of others is best of all. (Joyce's own reading of the end of I-8 is also not to be missed.)

The teacher who offered the wise advice was Olive Peto, who occasionally taught small groups of relatively advanced students at Christ's Hospital in the 1960s. I am extremely grateful to her. (As I later discovered, many other readers of the *Wake* have also arrived at the conviction that it should be read aloud: see, for example, Kenner, *Dublin's Joyce*, p. 309.)

9. In characterizing Joyce's mind as broad but shallow, I draw on a standard used by Pierre Duhem for assessing scientists. There are two kinds of minds, Duhem tells us in *The Aim and Structure of Physical Theory* (Princeton: Princeton University Press, 1951), the English mind, broad but shallow, good at surveying a wide range of things and seeing connections, and the French mind, narrow but deep, following out the consequences of precise ideas in rigorous detail. Unfortunately, the geographical/political thesis is a little spoiled by Duhem's main examples: Napoleon is his prime instance of the broad-but-shallow (English) mind, and Newton is the paradigm for the narrow-but-deep (French) mind.

In identifying Joyce as broad but shallow, I intend no criticism. (I share the same temperament, although (alas) not the same range.) Michael Seidel tells me that Joyce is supposed to have stopped a friend from going into detail about Montesquieu's *Spirit of the Laws* on the grounds that he already had what he needed from one or two simple ideas.

10. *Letters* (letter of 24 May 1924).

11. Some Joyceans are less enthusiastic. Kenner, for example, views Gilbert's *Jame's Joyce's "Ulysses"* as having gained an unwarranted authority because of Gilbert's close association with Joyce. I agree with Kenner's skepticism about the value of Gilbert's formal schemata, but I'm inclined to give more weight to the thought that Gilbert helped "thousands to persevere past the opening pages" (Kenner, *Ulysses* [revised edition, Johns Hopkins University Press, 1987], pp. 169–70). See also Richard Ellmann, *Ulysses on the Liffey* (Oxford University Press, 1972).

12. I am not alone in defending something like this view. See Robert Sage's essay "Before *Ulysses*—and after," in *Our Exagmination Round His Factification for Incamination of Work in Progress*, particularly p. 169.

13. Many commentators tend to see the *Wake* as extending the "Circe" section of *Ulysses*. I agree that there are important connections, both in the interweaving

of voices and in the reconstruction of sound. Another important precursor is the opening of the "Sirens" chapter, partly because of its anticipations of the musical allusions of the *Wake*, but even more because of the compressed presentation of the themes of the chapter in its first two pages (*Ulysses*, 256–7). Once we have read the whole chapter, we can recognize what is going on in that introduction (overture? statement of themes?). If you imagine a version of *Ulysses* with "Sirens" reduced to its first two pages, printed without any paragraph breaks, then the *Wake* would seem less of a radical departure. Yet another portent of the later work is the close of "Oxen of the Sun," *Ulysses*, 425–8.

14. Eugene Jolas is inclined to the "language for language's sake" view; both Stuart Gilbert and Robert Sage emphasize the attunement of language to material. See their respective contributions to *Our Exagmination*. . . .

15. Madison: University of Wisconsin Press, 1986.

16. Bishop's discussions of the apprehensions of the ear, with reference to II-3, and of the significance of the catalogue of river-names in I-8, are particularly illuminating. See Chapters 9 and 12 of *James Joyce's Book of the Dark*.

17. Second only, I believe, to the *Wake* itself.

18. See Kenner, *Dublin's Joyce*, p. 9, and Chapter 15.

Chapter 6

1. The titles of the short stories in *Dubliners* show up in the prosecutor's wind-up for his summation as "Justius" (186–7). The standard designations of the stages of Bloom's voyage in the central part of *Ulysses* are wittily parodied in the account of Glugg's wanderings in the "Children's game" chapter of the *Wake* (229: 13–16). "Bullyfamous" and "Naughtyscalves" seem to me particularly brilliant names for "Cyclops" and "Nausicaa."

2. This isn't simply a matter of indifference. Joyce supposes that there is an important asymmetry between male and female attitudes to romantic love and sexuality. His female characters are often able to infuse the dominant relationship of their lives with the energy of earlier loves; for them, the existence of a first—lost—love poses no threat to the love that is expressed in a long marriage and may even enhance it. Joyce's male characters, like the Joyce who discovered unsuspected parts of Nora Barnacle's past, find this much more worrisome and problematic. I am indebted to Michael Seidel for convincing me of the importance of this asymmetry; I shall be periodically concerned with it below.

3. Issy is also linked to the young Molly. A revealing footnote—"One must sell it to some one, the sacred name of love" (268 n.1)—recalls Molly's recollection of her thought before yielding to her first lover: "I thought well as well him as another" (*Ulysses*, 783).

4. To find what Shaun will later call "me innerman monophone" (462: 15–16); it is an amusing irony that this occurs at a stage when it has become abundantly clear that he, like HCE, has no such thing.

5. In presenting the issue in this way, I reply on a particular understanding of Nietzsche's idea of the "eternal recurrence," one that I take to be especially

illuminating. See Alexander Nehamas, *Nietzsche: Life as Literature* (Cambridge, Mass.: Harvard University Press, 1985).

6. I parse this odd sentence by inserting a comma after "Dear" and another after "trespassing."

7. I am not sure if Robert Polhemus would articulate his treatment in *Lot's Daughters* to defend an affirmative answer to the question. As I shall eventually suggest, the dreamer subdues this particular doubt by probing the state of HCE's and ALP's marriage, as their bodies decay. See Chapters 19–20 below.

8. In the "Cyclops" episode, the Citizen is minding Giltrap's dog, Garryowen, of whom Gerty says that it "almost talked, it was so human" (*Ulysses*, 352). This near-humanity isn't much on display in Barney Kiernan's, or outside, when Garryowen chases after the carriage carrying Bloom.

9. It seems to me that there are obvious allusions here to Molly's descriptions of her initiation of sex "under the Moorish wall"; see the last two pages of *Ulysses*.

10. As we shall see below, the casting of the lecher as a cleric is also significant. It plays a role in the dreamer's worries about the fidelity and sexual past of his spouse. Joyce fuses the figure of the young lover in the past of his central female characters—Michael Furey in Greta Conroy's past, "Michael Arklow" in ALP's (203: 18), and Michael Bodkin in Nora's—with the figure of Father Moran, who fondled Nora when she tried to tell him of Michael Bodkin's death. So, as we shall see, there are recurrent, disturbing, references to "Father Michael."

11. I shall have more to say about the relation of Joyce's laughter to his serious concerns in Chapters 15 and 21 below.

Chapter 7

1. The last two words point forward to the more detailed exploration of the theme that will occur in I-5. See, for example, 112: 23–7.

2. "At sixes and sevens" connotes a state of disorder; I take the "seventies" to be there because the topic is a life, and Joyce is reminding us both of the "three score and ten" readings and the biblical span.

3. Indeed, Joyce makes plenty of use of Milton's *Paradise Lost* to reinforce the theme.

4. The good that comes may come from Wicklow—pointing to the salvific role of ALP. But the allusion to "Nick"—and his counterpart "Mick"—suggests that the effect may be more complicated. ALP, we should remember, has a past in Wicklow.

5. We can also read a third reference to a deity: "haloed be her eve" suggests Venus, the evening star—and also, of course, the goddess of love.

6. *The Book of Kells*, one of the great Irish texts, is an illuminated manuscript of parts of the Gospels. "*Tunc*," "then," is the first word of the page on which the act of crucifying Christ is described. Joyce parodies Sir Edward Sullivan's introduction to the *Book of Kells* (119 ff.).

Chapter 8

1. Interestingly, one might think that self-identity is not a very wonderful recommendation to be noted in this context. Yet if the dreamer's central anxiety is one of finding an identity, then it would be very important to have a constant self-conception that guides one's actions. Whether HCE actually lives up to this billing is another matter.

2. The first of these will recur in the hounding of HCE in II-3. It also connects to the vignette of the Willingdone Museyroom of I-1. In *Ulysses,* this popular punchline forms part of Bloom's meditation on the coarseness of Irish popular culture (*Ulysses,* 167).

3. The offense was to the male watchers and was thus freed from certain sexual overtones.

4. The persecuted HCE is often compared to the derided Christ. See, for example, 24: 19 and 75: 17–18. In this chapter, as we shall see, the idea is developed through a comparison of the hostile ballad about HCE with Handel's *Messiah.*

5. Just as the young Stephen Dedalus's sense of sin gave rise both to shame and to feelings of confinement (*Portrait,* Chapters 3 and 4).

6. The idea of pieces of vegetation as incriminating evidence is suggested by the encounter between Father Conmee and a young man and a young woman in the "Wandering Rocks" section of *Ulysses:* the couple emerge from a gap in a hedge and the woman bends to detach "with slow care . . . from her light skirt a clinging twig" (*Ulysses,* 224).

7. The opening verse of "Annie Laurie" runs: "Maxwelton's braes are bonny / Where early falls the dew. / And 'twas there that Annie Laurie / Gave me her promise true. / Gave me her promise true / Which ne'er forgot should be / And for bonnie Annie Laurie / I'd lay me doon and dee."

8. This reading would condense one of Joyce's own anxieties—that as an artist he had betrayed, and was continuing to betray in the *Wake,* his much-loved father.

9. I link these unfortunates to the seedier members of the population whom HCE will embrace as his "villeins" at the end of III-3 (544: 7–545: 8). If those who contribute to his fall are welcomed into his city (or kingdom), then his willingness to forgive his enemies gives substance to the commendation of him as "Christlike" (33: 28–32; see p. 76 and n. 3 above).

10. Joyce supplies a tune, so that the reader can sing along with the crowd. It is simple and straightforward, good for lots of people to sing in the street; and I assume that Joyce wrote it himself. The pitch at which it is set reflects Joyce's past as a serious singer (a tenor). Tenors (or contraltos) could sing it at pitch; sopranos would find it more comfortable an octave up; basses an octave down. Most men and women do not fall into these categories and are likely to find any of these options difficult.

Chapter 9

1. Throughout this entire section, Joyce's principal device is to juxtapose contradictory attributes for the indefinite figures who appear. Like the gender reversals,

the alternation of viewing the priest as sternly unforgiving and as compassionate underscores the uncertainty of any assessment of HCE.

2. In the sentence just cited, the doubt should extend to how exactly we read it. It says, quite clearly, that we lack sufficient information to judge HCE, that the shortcomings of the testimony cannot be repaired, that the whole thing may be a joke (the witnesses may be pulling our legs). But, quite deliberately, it remains ambiguous as to which sides which witnesses are on: "adjugers" and "judicandees" can be taken in different ways.

3. To which there is an entrance fee, "one kudos," although the exit is free. One has to give up something, part of one's integrity, I think, in adopting an answer; one can leave gratis because nothing has really been gained.

4. Joyce writes, "sentenced pro tried with Jedburgh justice," alluding to the system of the Scottish border town in which accused were sometimes hanged before a verdict was rendered. In the light of the monument to Dodgson, there is clearly an allusion to the dream trial in *Alice* and the Queen's demand for "Sentence first, verdict afterwards."

5. This is one place where the scholarly activity of tracing Joyce's allusions proves extremely helpful. Roland McHugh makes the connection to *Ulysses* (see *Annotations to "Finnegans Wake"* [Baltimore: Johns Hopkins, 1991]; the pagination and layout of this book is exactly that of the standard editions of the *Wake*, so that my references to it are always given by citing the passage in Joyce's text to which McHugh's explications correspond).

6. Here again McHugh is helpful. *The Boots at the Swan* is a novel in which the title character is named "Jacob Earwig."

7. HCE is represented as a hippopotamus (a gross beast that wallows in rivers) on several occasions. Most pertinent for now is the use of the characterization in Hosty's ballad (47: 9). It is worth noting that the fact that the female pronoun in "as mud as she cud be" refers back to the "liffopotamus" does not tell against this identification, since gendered pronouns are in constant flux throughout this chapter. In any event, the female pronoun is clearly needed for the second version of the ending, to be considered shortly.

8. I don't think it is far-fetched to hear in the last sentence an echo of the porter's speech in *Macbeth*.

Chapter 10

1. As I suggested above ("Awakening," pp. xxi–xxii) and will explore more concretely in Chapter 21, the same movement is repeated, on different scales, in Chapters 2–8 of Part I, and in the whole of Parts II–IV. The appraisal of Shem and of Shaun, offered more briefly in I-7 and I-6, is carried out more thoroughly in II-1, II-2, and III-1, III-2. As we shall discover, the counterpart to I-4 with its development of the characters out of HCE is III-3, which excavates HCE (and others) from the depths of Shaun.

2. "Owlwise" conjures up the obvious "always," and also a sense of self-certainty that is myopic and parochial.

3. Again, this aspect of the world after the fall of the pre-existent order is presented in the opening material; see 4: 9–12.

4. There may be an echo here of a scene in the "Eumaeus" episode of *Ulysses*, where Stephen Dedalus is accosted by his father's acquaintance, Corley (who, along with Lenehan, is one of the two unsympathetic "gallants" of the *Dubliners* story). Corley points to Bloom, who is standing aside, and claims to have seen him "in the Bleeding Horse in Camden street with Boylan" (*Ulysses*, 618). It is an implausible account of antagonists as drinking companions.

5. Some commentators take this to be a personification of Oliver St. John Gogarty, Joyce's original for Buck Mulligan. If the witness is viewed as Shaun (or a precursor of Shaun), one might try to extrapolate Joyce's attitude to Shaun from his dislike for Gogarty. I shall not rely on, or be further concerned with, any of this.

6. Both because it is so uncertain and because it is in no sense good news.

7. It is "Nolans Brumans" (93: 1). As on so many occasions throughout the *Wake*, Joyce exploits the central idea of Giordano Bruno (Bruno the Nolan) of the identity of opposites to emphasize the two-sidedness of something.

It is interesting that the four judges seem to be distracted by the lovemaking between (among?) the young. As in II-4, the old men are observers of youthful sexual fulfillment.

8. Here, as in I-7, the vituperative accusations express Joyce's own dilemma. Writing, his gift to his family, ruins his family relationships, exposes some that he loves (his father, John Joyce, and his brother, Stanislaus), and causes him to neglect those dearest to him (Nora, Lucia, possibly even his son, Giorgio). The *Wake* acknowledges this—and continues the work of exposure.

9. We are treated to their reminiscences at greater length in II-4, where, however, I shall suggest that their ramblings serve a different purpose; see Chapter 15 below.

10. "Mr. Fox" is Parnell's alias in the Kitty O'Shea affair.

11. The list of rumors contains some interesting vignettes and allusions. The double identity of the victim, as HCE and as Shem, is clear in many places, as for example, in the suggestion that he has become "beetly dead" (100: 1). Here, the victim is linked to HCE through the use of language pertaining to insects, a common Joycean device for indicating the presence of HCE, or "Earwicker"; but, quite evidently, the phrase echoes Buck Mulligan's comment to his mother that Stephen's own mother is "beastly dead" (*Ulysses*, 10), connecting the victim with Stephen, and with Shem, his counterpart in the *Wake*.

12. As we'll see in Chapters 19–21, this prefigures the resolution of the dreamer's doubts.

13. "Bibs" and "babalong" also suggest ALP's maternal care and consolation.

14. As I shall suggest in Chapter 21, a voice with the qualities ALP exemplifies does make an appearance in the first chapter, although it is not associated with her.

Chapter 11

1. Joyce's moral vision thus shares something important with the religious attitude against which his humanism rebels: the virtues he commends are not easily won. He rejects completely a different kind of "strenuousness" that is most clearly exemplified by religious morality, the insistence on absolute rules. See Chapter 21.

2. That judgment can easily seem to come far too quickly, as if ALP simply overlooked everything with which the dreamer has been struggling. As I'll argue below, a central issue for the *Wake*, from this point on, is to recognize the forgiveness as a genuine virtue, to provide it with a basis—and that is why the dreams go round and round, working over the same anxieties at ever greater depth.

I see this point as a generalization of an issue that has often troubled Joyce's readers. Joyce has been held to construct women who enable the lapses of his male protagonists. Drawn in the image of male fantasy, they acquiesce too readily. Although I shall not tackle the problem in this form, I view it as one part of the question of establishing the Joycean virtues as genuine. The gestures of kindness, generosity, reconciliation, and so forth cannot have the status Joyce assigns to them unless they are rooted in full awareness of the blemishes, the weaknesses, the betrayals, and the other moral lapses. On my reading of the *Wake*, Joyce takes this concern extremely seriously. The dreamer cannot rest content with the promise of forgiveness at the end of I-4, or even with the more extended version offered at the end of I-8. Whether the even deeper exploration begun in Part II and culminating at the close of Part IV resolves the doubt is a matter for further debate. I think Joyce believed that it did, and I shall try to defend him on this score—but I can imagine readers who would dispute the point. Perhaps they would need an even longer version of the *Wake*.

3. This serves as the occasion for an elegant piece of Joycean humor: the tongue-in-cheek reprimand to those who think that the failure to use inverted commas implies that the "author was always constitutionally incapable of misappropriating the spoken words of others" (108: 35–6)—a sly allusion to his own style of reporting indirect discourse from *Portrait* on.

4. Banal *as a whole*—but, as we shall see shortly, it contains one very disturbing element, the reference to "Father Michael." That reference is a pointer to the dreamer's anxiety about his beloved's past love, and it may be that the letter takes the gnomic form it does because its real content cannot be presented. I shall explore this possibility later in the present chapter, when we take up the life story of ALP as it is presented by the washerwomen.

The letter might be interpreted as announcing the *death* of an old love. That would be reassuring if the love in question is ALP's passion for her young "Michael"; it would be quite another matter if it were her love for HCE. I am very grateful to Michael Seidel for making me more sensitive to this aspect of the *Wake*.

5. That, of course, would be an entirely natural stance for a hen, with whom she is here associated.

6. One significant point is that the "*Tunc*" page is concerned with the betrayal of Jesus.

7. This might be viewed in terms of Nietzsche's famous slogan in *The Birth of Tragedy* to the effect that the world is to be justified as an aesthetic phenomenon, a slogan apparently repudiated in the discussion of the asceticism of the artist in Part III of *The Genealogy of Morals*. The general attitude of that later text, however, emphasizes the kind of artistic transformation of life with which I'm concerned here. Once again, I am indebted to Alexander Nehamas, *Nietzsche: Life as Literature*.

8. It seems to me unnecessary to settle whether this is supposed to be the original, dug up in the mound; if the original were not in ALP's writing, there would, of course, be little sense in introducing a genuine specimen of her hand in the process of authentication; but this is a dream, and there is no reason to expect consistency even in this apparently more straightforward part of the *Wake*.

9. This pregnant phrase also suggests that life can be viewed as a cricket match, a connection which, as we saw in Chapter 2, is made vivid in the coupling of the aging HCE and ALP.

10. The tale also allows Joyce to present his case in a debate he engaged in with Wyndham Lewis on the character of modern art and literature. I shall not be concerned with this.

11. See Chapters 16 and 17 below.

12. I deliberately use the Millian phrase from *On Liberty*. But both the Millian and the Nietzschean notions of individualism are important to the *Wake*. Mill's version offers the ideal of a free choice among an ever-widening menu of possibilities—the recorded "experiments of living"—with the *possibility*, but not the *necessity*, of idiosyncratic mixing or modifying of elements. Nietzsche, as I read him, suspects that any such engagement with the practices of the past will fail to be a true expression of the individual, so that his ideal always involves a confrontation with traditions, a revaluation of values. Yet, as he also sees very clearly (for example in Part II of *Genealogy of Morals*), being in community with others matters to us. These two strains within HCE, even more evident in Shem, are obviously bound to give trouble. Indeed, one way to formulate the dreamer's ultimate assessment of HCE would be to understand him as realizing, for all his flaws, Mill's individualistic ideal, suffused with Nietzsche's emphasis on the creative artistry of life.

13. A point that will be reinforced in II-1—see Chapter 12.

14. Burgess (*Re Joyce*) describes her as irresistible. I think this is far too simple an evaluation. Polhemus (*Lot's Daughters*) shows very clearly how complex the attitudes involved can be. He and I offer different versions of the dynamics of the HCE-Issy relationship but would agree in opposing Burgess's assessment.

15. See Chapter 21.

16. The rapid move to this moment in their lives is significant. It prefigures the approach most thoroughly developed at the end of III-3, in III-4, and in the closing monologue, where the lives of HCE and ALP are conceived in terms of the line begun in their youthful wooing. That conception is the center of the dreamer's eventual resolution of his doubts.

17. This is one place in which the general problem I have taken to be central—that of showing that the Joycean virtues are hard won—is formulated as the more specific issue (raised in n. 2 above) of ALP's complaisance in HCE's infidelities.

18. Once again, we get the answer that corresponds to many of the vignettes—three, the "three figures" of Shaun, Shem, and Issy—and also the Arabic reading of the Roman numeral "III."

19. During a visit to Ireland in August 1909, one of Joyce's old acquaintances temporarily convinced him that Nora had been unfaithful to him at the time of their courtship. Joyce wrote her anguished letters (see the letters of August 6 1909, and August 7 1909 in Richard Ellmann's edition of Joyce's *Letters*). Despite learning that the reports were lies, Joyce's uncertainties continued (see letter of December 3 1909), and the painful possibilities seem never to have left him. Richard Ellmann's *James Joyce* (Oxford University Press, 1959) provides a poignant account (see Chapter XVII).

Chapter 12

1. Here again there is a link between HCE and Bloom, who is addressed by his daughter Milly as "Papli."

2. Nietzsche, of course, views the "slave morality" of the Judeo-Christian tradition as the outgrowth of *ressentiment,* to which he contrasts the aspirations of the "free spirits" (*Genealogy of Morals,* I). Joyce seems to give the screw a further turn.

3. "Blotch and void" is not, I think, simply "black and white" but also, in accordance with the prosecutorial accusations of I-7, the vomiting forth and excretion of matter from Glugg himself. His "bikestool" is both a confessional chair (*Beichtstuhl*) and also the privy.

4. Toothache also featured in Stephen Dedalus's exile in Paris; see *Ulysses,* 42.

5. "Stainusless" also points to Joyce's brother Stanislaus, as a potential counterpart to Shaun. This has already been foreshadowed in I-7; the telegram (172: 24–6) recalls the entreaties Joyce sent to his brother from Trieste.

6. In a famous passage quoted by both Gibbon and Nietzsche, Tertullian suggests that those who are saved will take great delight in viewing the torments of their enemies on earth.

7. Besides the obvious similarities in clothing suggested, I take one of the associations of "tile" to be "hat," recalling the cad's "straw bamer."

8. There are also anticipations of HCE's great welcome to the respectable (543–5) at (242: 3–5).

9. "*Tipote, Kyrie, tipote?*"—"Why, Lord, why?" The next line is: "Kod knows. Anything ruind. Meetingless" (247: 16).

10. Heliotrope—the word has figured in earlier characterizations of the Floras ("holytroopers"—[223: 11]) and their adoration of Chuff ("heliolatry"—[237: 1]).

11. "Not cricket" is an (old-fashioned) English phrase for unfair practices.

12. "*Seid ihr ruhig kleine Vögel!*"—"Be calm, little birds."

13. As is well known, Joyce was terrified of thunder. The thunder words that punctuate the *Wake,* one of which ends the mime (257: 27–8), are one of the most substantial signs of Vico's influence. According to *The New Science,* thunder plays a constructive role in human history by prompting people to take shelter in caves and thus to associate with one another. The thunder word here (composed

of expressions for "shut the door") recalls this idea, as the children enter their homes.

Chapter 13

1. It is small wonder that the toilet deserves a mention, since, according to Professor MacHugh (in the "Aeolus" section of *Ulysses*), the Roman Empire and the British Empire are both dedicated to the pious construction of waterclosets (*Ulysses*, 130, 132). Thus, as a principal achievement of civilization, it rates a mention in a chapter devoted to reviewing the cultural accomplishments of human history.

2. This piece of wisdom is due to HCE, stemming from "the emerald canticle of Hermes" (263: 22).

3. His first note, "With his broad and hairy face, to Ireland a disgrace," recalls Stephen's childish vision: "His father told him that story: his father looked at him through a glass: he had a hairy face" (*Portrait*, 7).

4. As he does so, there is another allusion to *Portrait;* a note of Issy's locates HCE by his address, "Kellywick, Longfellow's Lodgings, House of Comments III, Cake Walk, Amusing Avenue, Salt Hill, Co. Mahogany, Izalond, Terra Firma" (261 n. 2), echoing Stephen's self-identification in his school geography book (*Portrait*, 15–16). At Clongowes, and in the "studiorum," the children identify themselves locally and work outward.

5. The next line, "Sow byg eat," is also disconcerting. For it isn't just an invitation to begin, but both a wry suggestion that pigs might be the begetters of knowledge (an anticipation, as we shall see, that the wisdom to be garnered is much earthier than might have been expected) and a reminder of the lurking presence of HCE (the begetter). I also hear the echo of Stephen's remark, "Ireland is the old sow that eats her farrow" (*Portrait*, 203).

6. The attempt to solve the problem contains a clear allusion to the incident in the park—284: 22–4.

7. In fact, the problem wanders from geometry to algebra, taking in material about permutations and combinations—a fact that allows Joyce to allude again to the underwear of the girls in the park ("minney combinaisies" [284: 12]).

8. Shem's enthusiastic jingle follows a brief fight in which his brother hits him in the eye. Shem isn't dispirited by the outcome, which, as we'll see, is an important stage in the movement to fraternal unity. The rhythm of the final line echoes Coleridge's pious moral in the "Rhyme of the Ancient Mariner": "He prayeth best who loveth best."

9. As so often in this chapter, there is a connection to HCE and the scandal that swirls around him, here in the suggestion that the goddess has parted her clothes to urinate. Issy's note 2 has already seen the point.

10. "Cookcook!" not only continues the advice to "flame" at sexual advances, as well as suggesting cuckoldry, but also recalls Bloom's observation of Gerty MacDowell, accompanied by the sound of the rectory clock (*Ulysses*, 375–6), his attraction to the well-dressed ladies of Dublin, and Molly's infidelity with Boylan (the brothel clock also sounds "Cuckoo" as these events emerge in the night world of "Circe" [*Ulysses*, 461]).

11. I link "improper frictions" to the sexual mathematics that dominates the latter part of the chapter (284–7, 293–303) and to the "rubbing" and "licking" alluded to in the pattern letter (280: 10, 16, 19, 27); "mens uration" connects (via "menstruation") to the discomforts that Issy often sees as part of the female conditions, as well as to the incident in the park ("urination").

12. It's an intriguing thought to envisage the tempter in the Garden giving his life, or at least his skin, for what the daughter of Eve really wants—a tempting way to cover her nakedness.

13. In this passage, Joyce alludes to *Othello* to introduce the serious implications of the competition and the jealous rivalry between the boys. Neither Shem nor Shaun seems to see what is going on—but, as usual, Issy picks up the underlying scenario (281: n. 4).

14. Joyce's references here (283: 12–20) are likely to resonate most with those who grew up, as I did, using exercise books whose rear covers were stuffed with information about the relations of bushels and pecks, gills and pints, links and chains, stones and hundredweights, and all the other residues of British measures.

15. Although the boys are named "Kev" and "Dolph," there is little problem in deciding how to identify them. First, Kev appeals to "Sem" for help (286: 30); second, Issy characterizes Dolph as "the trouveller" (286: n. 2); third, Dolph is characterized as "dean of idlers" (287: 18), and the subsequent account of his education and behavior connects him directly to Stephen Dedalus and to Shem.

16. The growing excitement of the boys is plain in the rhythms of their duet (296: 13–18), although they are only incompletely aware of what they are discovering ("the muddest thick that was ever heard dump" [296: 20–21]). The verbal connections here are extremely rich: "compleat anglers" (296: 23) points back to "Izaak" and the troutbeck, and the doubts about ALP's past (76: 28); the sermonizing address, "beloved bironthiarn" (296: 23), recalls the sermon of *Portrait*, with its denunciation of adolescent "uncleanness"; "Like pah, I peh" (296: 28) puts Shem in his father's place and also reminds us of the incident in the park—a point underscored by Issy (296: n.4); Shem's excitement takes the form of an erection, "a poke stiff" (296: 29–30), and again, Issy's comment (296: n. 5) leaves no doubt about what is going on; that same comment also recalls Bloom's interest in cross-dressing and the transformation in the "Circe" episode (*Ulysses*, 523–4); finally, "figuratleavely" reminds us that Shem is removing the fig leaves that "our parents" donned to cover their shame.

17. Again, I take there to be an allusion to the mocking of Bloom in "Circe" (*Ulysses*, 528–9).

18. Joyce's operatic reference here is particularly witty, since the Duke who sings of the fickleness of women ("La donn' è mobile") is, unlike his victim, Rigoletto's daughter, an unprincipled rake; I also detect an allusion to the Catalogue Aria in *Don Giovanni*—"*Pur che porti la gonnella, voi sapete quel che fa*" ("So long as she wears a skirt, you know how he behaves").

19. The opening of the next chapter will identify this moment as "the height of his life from a bride's eye stammpunct" (309: 3–4). I suggest that the passage beginning at 288: 13 should be read with this in mind.

20. The allusion to Dante's *Inferno*, "let drop as a doombody drops" (289: 15), recalls the moment when the pilgrim (Dante) is too susceptible to the illicit love of Paolo and Francesca (Canto V).

21. The neglect is suggested in the passage from 291: 4 and recalls the attentions Bloom's acquaintances lavish on Molly: "so many of the tomthick and tarry members . . . tipped to console with her at her mirrorable gracewindow'd hut" (291: 7–9). Issy's note—"O hce! O hce!"—can be read either as an invitation to look ("h" is silent) or a lament for the folly of her father (291: n.1).

I interpret the absence of notes from the boys throughout this interlude as a sign of their unawareness of the male trajectory that they, like their father, are to follow. Issy understands and continues to comment.

22. Initially Kev, his opponent in the fight. But Issy is quickly recruited to the team (304: 19–26).

23. In tone, this passage recalls the closing paragraphs of "The Oxen of the Sun" (*Ulysses*, 419–21).

24. In invoking Vico, I don't intend to advance any claim about historical epochs but simply to reinforce the idea that individual lives follow the same pattern of promise and failure—as the interlude in the geometrical demonstration suggests with respect to Dolph and HCE.

Chapter 14

1. See Chapter 7 above, pp. 66–7.

2. The shooting serves to link the story to the anecdote about Buckley and the Russian General; the number three connects to the rumor about HCE in the park.

3. The succession of Shaun only becomes clear in II-4, but it will dominate the first two chapters of Part III.

4. Here I rely on my reading of the interlude in the geometrical demonstration.

5. Bishop (*James Joyce's Book of the Dark*) provides a fascinating discussion of the first of these, showing how Joyce draws on the internal anatomy of the ear. While I appreciate the subtlety of his reading, my interpretation will go in a very different direction. Gigantism is a dominant technique in the "Cyclops" episode of *Ulysses*.

6. See Chapter 11 above, n. 3.

7. One of Beckett's literary debts to Joyce is surely his use of a story about a tailor (who makes a pair of trousers that fail to fit) as Nagg's much-told anecdote in *Endgame*.

8. McHugh notes that in the traditional plot, the tailor is J. H. Kerse of Sackville Street in Dublin.

9. For example, the last two pieces of quoted speech are naturally taken as responses to the narration of the story, so that Kersse seems to have moved out of the story and into the bar.

10. There are several further connections between the storytelling in the inn and this vignette: first, the rhythm of the captain's question about buying a suit imitates that of the prankquean's opening question to Jarl; second, "Recknar Jarl"

soon shows up in the storytelling in the bar (313: 15); third, the resolution of the story, which ends with peacemaking and "all drank free," points forward explicitly to "kirssy the tiler" and the "Narwhealian captol" (23: 10–11).

11. This may also be foreshadowed in "sowterkins," which may allude to a priest's soutane.

12. There have already been indications of an apologetic tone; HCE has denied committing various "sins" (311: 12–14).

13. The link to the prankquean is made by introducing a variant of her opening question to Jarl. Interestingly, the variant connects Jarl/HCE with "Moke the Wanst," preparing us for his role as King Mark in the next chapter.

14. Again, the allusions point forward to II-4.

15. As with other parts of the chapter, the material in these pages is very dense, and other versions of the anecdotes intervene. For example, there are passages suggestive of the old HCE and his attraction to his daughter (327: 27–36). But, as we proceed, the focus on young HCE and young ALP is ever more definite (329: 14 ff.).

16. Besides naming a character, "Kersse" can serve Joyce as a verb or common noun ("curse"), as here, or as a name for a type of material.

17. Here I am indebted to McHugh. I take the reference to the fox to signal that HCE will be the victim of the hunt to come.

18. More exactly, the first *identification* of Pukkelsen. He may enter the bar earlier as "a several sort of coyne in livery," perhaps the odd-job man of the inn, and may even offer money (or buy drinks) in the interest of inspiring resentment against HCE (313: 16–17, 22–8); but this is admittedly speculative.

19. I hope it is clear that any exhaustive survey of the material in the early part of II-3 is impossible; by following a few strands, I hope to show how the perspective I have adopted can be developed.

20. There's also an echo here of the prosecution of Shem and the invitation to "have a nightslong homely little confiteor about things" (188: 3–4). That echo will be heard again in a few pages, at a crucial juncture of this scene, when the invitation to "pree" or "pray" (336: 10, 11) recalls the prosecutor's "Let us pry" (188: 8).

21. In a later version of the marriage tale, we hear of the actual progeny born of ALP: out of "hippychip eggs, she will make a suomease pair and singlette" (329: 1–2).

22. I take the social initiation to be a secondary suggestion, implicit in the allusion here to Daniel O'Connell.

23. As I've already remarked, this passage recalls Molly's behavior on the afternoon of her tryst with Blazes Boylan; see Chapter 6 above, p. 53.

24. See Chapter 2 above, pp. 13–14.

25. But, as befitting a dream, the characters of the radio drama become visible within the bar. Detailed stage directions, of the kinds used by Ibsen and Shaw, describe the ways in which the comedians appear at various stages of their act. There are even hints that the customers might be watching a film, or a television (Joyce refers to part of the presentation as "teilweisioned" [345: 36]—and has previously used the familiar name for a then recently introduced piece of technology, with strict attention to the Greek roots [52: 18]). However we envisage the technology, it seems that the call of the clientele—"We want Bud Budderly boddily"—has been answered.

26. There's an obvious echo here of Hosty's ballad (of Persse O'Reilly): "the rann, the rann, the rann, the king of all ranns" (44: 16–17).

27. "Paleo" indicates the precedence of Michelides (Michael), who was there before this embodiment of HCE in everything that matters.

28. Of course, if we take the canonical version of the story, set in the Crimea, there is no despoiling of the soil—or turf—of Ireland. HCE, however, is seen as an invader, a violator of Ireland.

29. So the reference to Faust here suggests, I believe, a repudiation of its consoling conclusion.

30. Wilde is associated with HCE elsewhere, as for example, in his appearance as "Old Whitehowth," when he asks for pity for "poor O. W. in this profundust snobbing" (535: 26, 29). Interestingly, Wilde appears in a gesture of Butt's in the crosstalk act (350: 11–16). I read this as a reminder that the rebel-outsider remains within Butt/Shem, even as he is allying himself with the slogans of tradition.

31. The last line may allude to the exit of Bloom from Barney Kiernan's, with the citizen in hot pursuit (*Ulysses*, 339).

32. This plainly foreshadows the great sequence of "respectable" dwellings that figure in HCE's welcome (543–5). It may also allude to the wanderings of the Dedalus family.

33. McHugh cites a ballad about a castrato, one using the same refrain that figures here.

34. Here again, I am indebted to McHugh: "namar" is a Hebrew word for "tiger" or "leopard"; "namá" is an Irish word for "alone." The final word "Nomon" naturally points to HCE's approaching death—"no more"—but also to "no man," signifying his exclusion from the human community; it also alludes to the acrostic of the opening line and the connection with Ulysses; in this case, however, the giants have surely won.

35. Compare the much earlier list of names hurled at HCE, which, as we have seen, includes "Artist" (71: 21).

36. This points both backward to Issy's native understanding (268: 4) and forward to the charms of Shaun in Part III.

37. The initial informant is, presumably, Sackerson, associated with washing the bottles, the counterpart of Kate, and often associated with enforcing the laws (and norms) of the community. He tells Kate, who passes the story on to others.

38. The fourfold repetition conforms to other stylistic features of this coda in suggesting that the voices are those of the evangelists. I shall explore this more systematically in the next chapter.

39. As with *Ulysses*, there's a promise of eggs for breakfast in the morning. Here, however, they will not be cooked for HCE/Bloom, but for the triumphant son who has succeeded. This contrasts with ALP's preparation of breakfast for HCE ("meddery eygs, yayis, and staynish beacons on toasc" [199: 16–17]; the menu also includes "blooms of fisk" [199: 15–16]) in the early days of her marriage.

40. If Father Michael is ALP's original love, perhaps Father MacMichael is his—and ALP's?—son. The juxtaposition with the reference to Kevin is disturbing. Perhaps this echoes Joyce's terrible doubt, voiced at a stage when he still believed the

stories about Nora's infidelity, that Giorgio was not his son (letter of August 7, 1909, in Ellmann, *Selected Letters*).

Chapter 15

1. They served as judges in the mad trial of I-4 (see Chapter 10 above, p. 109). They return to play a similar judicial role in the hunting of HCE in II-3 (367: 8–14; 368: 24–369: 5). In the jubilant repudiation of HCE, they dither ineffectually (372: 34–373: 7). And, as I have suggested, their meandering voices present the account of HCE's solitary heeltapping (380: 7–382: 26). They will dominate this chapter and return to prominence in the star chamber "'quiry" of III-3 and in the observation of the couple in bed in III-4.

2. As I've already noted, "poghue" is an Anglo-Irish word for "kiss." "Arrah-na-poghue" is the title of a popular Irish play. Because of its phonic similarity to "poke," the word can suggest further stages of sexual activity (as, for example, words for "kiss" in other European languages). Joyce uses both the word (and its cognates) and the title to highlight the obsessive looking-on of the four men.

3. At this point, the reminiscences (perhaps of Marcus) have referred to four *Welshmen,* so it might be supposed that the divorced "heladies" are not the evangelists but some counterparts of theirs. Interestingly, one of the alleged Welshmen has the same surname—"Tarpey"—as Luke, indicating a closer connection. But, as I have repeatedly emphasized, the principal point is to connect the voices in terms of themes. "Shehusbands" echoes "heladies," and the thankfulness at the cessation of sexual activity is part of the attitude of withdrawal I am tracing in the principal voices of the chapter.

4. Martin Cunningham may figure even more briefly (as "Cominghome") in the speech of Marcus (388: 13).

5. I interpret this as an echo of Mr Deasey's simpler Hegelianism: history moves to the goal of the "manifestation of God" (*Ulysses,* 35). Interestingly, Matt's muddled metaphysics includes a parenthetical remark—"hear, O hear, Caller Errin!" (394: 33–4)—that brings HCE back into the dream speech. This is appropriate enough, since HCE is the central focus of the dreamer's attempt to work out the purpose of his personal history.

6. Here 'ran' connects to Hosty's ballad, the "king of all ranns" (44: 16-17), juxtaposing the pious and patriotic devotions of the old men with the history of the world ("highly continental evenements") and the carnival condemnation of HCE.

7. I read the interpolated "Haw!" (399: 32) as marking a transition to the voice of the ass, who accompanies the four evangelists. As we shall see, the ass serves as Shaun's interlocutor in the next chapter.

8. As Burgess points out, the *Wake* is one of the few books that can make us laugh on every page (This thought is explicitly attributed to Burgess on the back cover of the Penguin edition of the *Wake;* Burgess makes essentially this point on p.188 of *Re Joyce*).

9. Chapter 6, p. 62. My full response will come in Chapter 21.

Chapter 16

1. A cluster of allusions to *Midsummer Night's Dream* closes this prelude and makes a connection to the dream of the ass that follows. Most evident is Bottom's promise to roar "as gentle as any suckling dove" (403: 16–17). But the command, "Come not nere!" (403: 17), echoes the song of the fairies who guard the sleeping Titania—especially if we think of the "aal" (eel; 403: 16) as akin to the "spotted snakes with double tongue" and the other creatures whom the fairies warn off. If Bottom, the ass, is sleeping next to Titania, and she is ALP, then we can connect HCE with the ass. Bottom's famous boast, that his dream has no bottom, can then become an expression for the inexhaustibility of the *Wake.*

2. Joyce nicely divides the three synoptic Gospels from the Gospel of John and also honors the traditional suggestion that the author of Luke was a physician.

3. As we shall discover, the ass is no mean interviewer. In light of the cognitive deficiencies of the four old men, the ass's characterization of them as "wiseheads" prefigures the tact and manipulative skill that will be on display in questioning Shaun.

4. "Beamish boy" is, of course, the epithet bestowed on the lad who slays the Jabberwock.

5. The ass asks, apropos of "Mara O'Mario," an Italian tenor, "what more numerose Italicuss ever rawsucked frish uov in urinal?" (407: 16–17). I take the suggestion to be that the Italian style of tenor is dependent on unnatural, and unpleasant, backstage practices.

6. The rules include "Never back a woman you defend, never get quit of a friend on whom you depend, never make face to a foe till he's rife and never get stuck to another man's pfife" (411: 8–11). The response, "Amen, ptah!," suggests that the rules are handed down by father (and that Shaun agrees). I also hear an echo of Simon Dedalus's counsel to Stephen, "never to peach on a fellow" (*Portrait*, 9), and, in the concluding command—not to march to another's music—a recapitulation of Shem's "first riddle of the universe" (170: 4ff; 356: 12–14). The *command* not to pattern one's life after others is interestingly paradoxical, for to obey it is to disobey and to disobey is to obey.

7. See Chapter 7 above, pp. 68–71.

8. It is a lovely irony to find the dutiful and sober Kant here, especially juxtaposed with Joyce himself.

9. See Chapter 12 above, note 6.

10. This is underscored by the appearance of Joyce's famous device for indicating double-sidedness—the allusion to Bruno the Nolan at 418: 32.

11. I take the "longsephyring sighs" to be those of ALP (102: 29–103: 7; 627: 13–15). As she seeks an end to her story, she turns to the East, flowing into the sea, her original source.

12. As I read the fable, "beating time" has two resonances. One is to suggest that the Ondt, unlike the Gracehoper, is clumsy and ill-attuned to the songs and dances of pleasure. The other, which recalls the Gracehoper's earlier "kick time" (415: 24), takes both of them to fail to overcome time, both to be doomed to insignificance

because of the finitude of their lives and achievements. (The play of space against time also serves as part of Joyce's debate with Wyndham Lewis.)

As usual, Joyce's names are interesting. The Gracehoper hopes for grace, that is, for a relief he knows he doesn't merit; perhaps he even sees that no amount of effort on his own part could make his life have a lasting meaning. The Ondt sees this attitude as a feeble self-deception. He prides himself on a more realistic approach— ontology is the study of being, and the Ondt adapts his desires to the constraints imposed on him by external reality. In light of the last line of the poem, an alternative title for this philosophical fable would be *Being and Time.*

13. Joyce provides a bravura passage indicating the various ways in which the letter fails to reach any addressee (420: 19–421: 14). Along the way he includes the addresses of the places in which he lived in Dublin.

14. The denial echoes Cain's evasive protest: "Am I my brother's keeper?"

15. That Shaun's pretensions are hollow should be clear from the fact that the issue of the "mine's I" is highly problematic for him.

16. I take this already to be suggested in the early contrast between Irish and Italian tenors (407: 16–17). The celebration of homeland culture is fueled by dismissal or derogation of foreign ways.

17. This is surely not the way in which he initially enters the dream, since the opening description of him reviews his clothes from head to toe (404).

Chapter 17

1. The single intervention will come from Issy (457: 25–461: 32). See below, pp. 209–10.

2. ALP's closing monologue is only nine pages. The principal washerwoman of I-8 has twenty pages but is frequently interrupted or prompted by her interlocutor. The prosecutorial voice of I-7 has twenty-four. Even HCE, in the great apologia of III-3, receives only twenty-two, and there are occasional interpolations from the evangelists. Jaun's speech occupies thirty-two. (The only narrative breaks come with a substantial paragraph on 454 and a three-line paragraph on 468.)

3. Shaun begins as "jaunty Jaun" (429: 1). Later he is "hardworking Jaun" (441: 24), "Jaunathaun" (454: 9), "Joe Hanny" (455: 11), "Juan" (461: 33), "Jaun the Boast" (469: 29), and eventually "rural Haun" (471: 35). I don't claim that the name changes are correlated in any systematic way with the possible identities that emerge in the speech—sometimes Joyce simply switches the tone without introducing any phrase to reidentify the orator; rather, they alert us to the general fact of a variety of lives the dreamer can envisage for Shaun.

4. There may be a deeper reason for the salience of sex. If what separates human communities from the social arrangements of our evolutionary relatives is the ability to give ourselves prescriptions, worked out by and enforced within communities, and if the initial function of this rule-giving is to forestall social conflicts, then sexual behavior is one of the prime areas—if not *the* prime area—in need of regulation. It would thus be no surprise that all societies about which we know have systems

of rules licensing and forbidding various types of sexual relations. Shaun's starting point may thus be in harmony with the dreamer's interest in the achievements that separate genuinely human life from the bestial world.

5. The apparently inappropriate gender here is balanced by Juan's first word of response to Issy's interruption—"MEN!" (461: 33). Given that Issy's speech has mounted to sexual climax, "WOMEN!" is what we'd expect from Juan. There is another gender reversal at 454: 20.

6. The last precept I have quoted plainly urges the audience to guard against the fate of the girls whom HCE supposedly observed in the park.

7. The image of the "squitter" on the "Tubber Nakel" recalls Issy's great expression of sexual joie-de-vivre, as she boasts of her understanding of the rules of the game in her longest note of II-2. She recalls herself sitting "astrid uppum their Drewitt's altar, as cooledas as culcumbre" (279 n.1, 29). Issy sees herself as a girl with a bright future; Jaun replies with a prediction of a very different fate.

8. The forbidden practice here is to allow suave young men, scathingly characterized (438: 32–6), to "trespass" on the girls' "danger zone" (439: 2–3). The stammer at "cocottch" may indicate that Jaun is assuming the role of his father, (although there's obviously also an allusion to "cocotte"), and, as we'll find below, the punitive violence of patriarchy will break out again. Jaun follows up his threat of corporal punishment with a crazy curse that brings the first phase of his homily to an end.

9. Two items on the list have real charm—"*Through Hell with the Papes* (mostly boys) by the divine comic Denti Alligator" and "Mary Liddlelambe's flitsy tales especially with the scentaminted sauce" (440: 5–6, 18–19).

10. This section of Jaun's speech is laced with allusions to the excited (and post-excited) states of male and female genitalia. Strictly speaking, neither sex can imitate the anatomy and the physiological responses of the other, but it's important for the girls to appreciate that the enemy (in the form of sexual desire) is within as well as without.

11. It's noteworthy that Jaun's "voixhumanar" swells at this point, as if, once again, he's an instrument (an organ) on which the community's music is sounded. He is also "clenching his manlies," presumably holding his own sexual excitement in check.

12. Shaun's ambivalence about the role he is taking on is already evident in the hedges and qualifications—"possibly," "probably," "a long way."

13. "We are all eyes" (443: 1). The line may also be read ironically—we are all individuals; those who conform to, and enforce, the standards of the community cannot, of course, be "all I's."

14. I take Joyce to be offering an imitation of the city clerk who plays the role of seducer in Part III of *The Waste Land*. The reference to the "angry boils" (444: 1) recalls the description of "the young man, carbuncular."

15. Joyce echoes the lines of a Victorian love song (set to a poem by Tennyson), reinforcing the idea that the love of the married pair is expressed in their joint work, and, perhaps, that this work creates acceptance of their love.

16. In the allusion to "circumcision," it may also suggest a modification of those desires (and organs) that have caused trouble in the previous phases of Jaun's oration.

17. I take this to be the suggestion that Shaun would willingly "turn back" if he could find a teashop waitress to be his true love (a "nippy girl," "my lady of Lyons")—449: 9–12.

18. He seems also to have switched sides in the disagreement about the ideal for marriage. His new position endorses his mother's vision of love in retreat from the world.

19. "Thine to wait" connects to the initial suggestion that Jaun's partner serves in a teashop (see note 17); it also alludes both to the division of sexual roles in *Paradise Lost* (appropriate at a moment when Jaun's vision of paradise has just been lost) and to the last line of Milton's sonnet on his blindness, the credo of waiters and waitresses everywhere: "They also serve who only stand and wait."

20. The closing words "a pot on a pole" recall the story of HCE's moment of alleged great honor, when he is named and commended by the king. As we were told, he was bearing "a high perch atop of which a flowerpot was fixed earthside hoist with care" (31: 2–3); "perch" names an English measure of distance, also called a "rod" or "pole"; so HCE's success comes when he is carrying a pot on a pole. But, as we and the dreamer have painfully learned, the success is dubious and the whole story radically uncertain. Hence "as sure as there's a pot on a pole" already augurs badly.

21. As I'll suggest below (Chapter 20), this insight about irrational optimism plays an important part in Joyce's treatment of the *ricorso* of the *Wake* (Part IV).

22. As I've already noted, we have here another gender reversal. See above, n.5.

23. It's tempting to read this as a condensation of the vision Shaw presents at much greater length in the interlude of *Man and Superman:* Hell (the "Byrns" or burns) is far more interesting than the tedious monotony of heaven.

24. In the recommendation to the girls to drink and dance (453: 35–6).

25. I've discussed this passage in Chapter 6 above; see p. 54.

26. As we have seen in earlier chapters, Issy yearns for both Shem and Shaun. I'll suggest at the very end of this chapter that there is an important link between Shaun and Bloom.

27. This drunken substitute for a mooring post frames the disintegration of the conformist Jaun in an interesting way. He is there at the beginning, I think, to remind us that the community contains—as the enforcer of its norms, no less—this unsavory and decrepit figure. He speaks once at the beginning, in praise of his consolatory bottle (430: 15–16), and once at the end to recognize Haun's desertion (471: 33–4).

Chapter 18

1. I take this to recapitulate the end of II-4, in which Shaun is taken as a new beginning.

2. As they approach, the old men apparently conceive Yawn as a "crossroads puzzler" (475: 3–4). I take this to shed light on the character of the "crossmess parzel" that is the *Wake:* it is not a collection of isolated puzzles but a sustained effort to work out how we should understand ourselves. My interpretation here reinforces the approach developed in Chapter 5 above.

3. The miscommunications give Joyce many wonderful opportunities for engaging in the verbal analogue of slapstick comedy.

4. Joyce inverts and undermines Tennyson's famous lines ("The old order changeth, giving place to new / And God fulfills himself in many ways / Lest one good custom should corrupt the world"). As is abundantly clear by this stage of the *Wake,* there is no benevolent deity with high purposes to fulfill, and also no genuinely new order. The human task is to live with, and acknowledge the value of, what is inevitably corrupted.

5. See Chapter 12 above, pp. 139–40.

6. Commentators on the *Wake* are often concerned to distinguish among the inquisitors, using references to parts of Ireland as clues for deciding which is talking at different moments. I see little point in this exercise. There is a voice (often taken to be that of Matt) that is more focused in questioning and that takes a leading role, another voice that erupts in angry challenges (sometimes interpreted as that of Luke), and a voice that is rather more clueless than the others (often supposed to be that of John). While it may be valuable to distinguish the tone and level of comprehension of the questioner, nothing much hangs on whether a single individual is always relatively organized, or truculent, or wandering in irrelevancies, or whether the traits shift among the participants in the scene.

7. Latent here, I believe, is Joyce's more familiar wanderer, Leopold Bloom, who, like Yawn, appears to be laid low but who sustains, across the years, a love for Molly, a love that she reciprocates; he does so through numerous small acts, a tiny sample of which we observe and a few more about which we hear from Molly herself.

8. The earthier aspects of his tripartite nature may be suggested by his expostulation "my tactile O!", alluding perhaps to the jubilant disclosure of the female genitalia in II-2, and the "geomatrical" diagram of 293.

9. I think there are two other connections, one to the wild beasts that disturb the dreams of Shaun/Kevin, the "phanthares" who are associated with "bad bold faathern" (565: 19–20), and one to the father-son duo of outsiders (*Wolfe* [Wotan] and *Wölfling* [Siegmund]) who are feared and hated by Hunding and his kin in *Die Walküre;* with respect to this latter link, it may be significant that the wolves Yawn fears are associated with a wood.

10. "Schaum" (German for foam or froth) suggests that the idealistic vision Yawn is attempting to preserve is a superficial bubble, that underneath he is the "sameas" the others whom he struggles to reject.

11. The obvious resonance of the sentence I have quoted is with the liberation of the Israelites from Egypt.

12. It also conjures up the sexual urges of the aging Dean Swift.

13. Here clearly identified as Luke—appropriately enough since, among the Gospel writers, Luke is distinguished by his concern for history, and it is the inescapability of history that is at issue.

14. Understood here in terms of his identification with Tristan.

15. Besides the obvious "ridiculous," Joyce's neologism also suggests the figure of Eric, the aggrieved lover who disrupts Senta's love for the Flying Dutchman.

16. Joyce uses his familiar device of alluding to Giordano Bruno (Bruno the Nolan) in constructing Yawn's declaration (488: 4–12). Similar references permeate the next phase of the inquiry.

17. The last phrase recalls Bloom's interest in the anatomy of Greek goddesses and his inspection from behind of the statues outside the National Library.

18. The allusion is to Baudelaire, "mon semblable, mon frère" ("my likeness, my brother"), famously quoted by Eliot at the end of Part 1 of *The Waste Land.* Shem is also the one who has freed Shaun, both through his role in the overthrow of II-3 and through his assumption of the burdens of guilt and exile.

19. It's significant that the brother, the Shem figure, of Yawn's forced confession (488: 19 ff.) is supposed to be in Australia—not only is this an appropriate place for wrongdoers (the place to which the British deported minor criminals), but it is also far enough away to keep the home country secure.

20. This passage looks forward to ALP's later apologia in this chapter (494: 27 ff.) and to her laughter during the copulation of III-4; 583: 26.

21. The reference to the "Vickar" alludes both to the sanctity of their relationship, and of the marriage-bed, and to the producer of the children's mime (255: 27); since the dreamer produces all these vignettes, ALP is promising to respond to the dreamer's worries by "making laugh" in a coming vignette—as indeed she will in the next chapter.

22. I shall not attempt to determine the identities of the speakers who utter the lines in this sequence (500: 1–501: 5). Yawn is clearly there, but there are various possibilities for Issy, Shem, ALP, and HCE, even for Kate and Sackerson, as well as for the four inquisitors. The important point, I believe, is the release of voices within Yawn and the presence of HCE at the most fundamental level.

23. Joyce's readers have also met it before in the journey of Bloom. Although the movement of *Ulysses* is toward increasing success, as I have already noted, the outcomes for its major characters remain uncertain (see Chapter 6 above, p. 56).

24. The only exception is his avoidance of the commitment to thunder—by hiding his head. As we shall see, Joyce interweaves several different types of stories about origins. I take the reference to thunder here to introduce Vico's distinctive idea that human civilization began when men were driven by the thunder to shelter in caves— like Yawn (and Joyce) they hide in terror. The device of the incompatible weather descriptions is taken over by Beckett in his versions of Hamm's story in *Endgame.*

25. The clearest presentation of this story is in the Prelude to *Götterdämmerung.* For discussion of the significance of these events in the four-part *Ring,* see Philip Kitcher and Richard Schacht, *Finding an Ending: Reflections on Wagner's "Ring"* (New York: Oxford University Press, 2004).

26. In Joyce's version, the serpent makes an offer that appeals to woman body-and-soul (*Leib* and *Seele*), and Issy has already expressed how attractive she finds it (271 n. 5).

27. See the discussion in Chapter 7 above, p. 70.

28. Joyce alludes to the world-ash, Yggdrassil, with "eggdrazzles" (III-3; 504: 35).

29. Romans 8: 21–4.

30. So, for example, the "fender" and "delaney" (or "El Don De Dunelli"), originally introduced in the vignette of I-4; 84: 8–36 recur in 518: 15–30. This passage also serves as a reprise of Joyce's denunciation of violence in I-1 and I-4 (see Chapter 10 above, pp. 102–3); in this later presentation it is used to cast doubt on the idea of the Great War (World War I) as "the war to end wars" (e.g. 518: 31–2).

31. There's also an echo here of (101: 33–4): "she who had given his eye for her bed." I suspect that Joyce had made a common misunderstanding of Wagner's origins story in the *Ring*, conflating the incident in which Wotan sacrifices an eye to gain power with the *later* episode in which he is supposed to have risked his sole remaining eye to gain Fricka.

32. There may be a faint suggestion of a more positive tone in one of Shaun's replies, his remark that "there is no hay in Eccles's hostel" (514: 15). If "Eccles's hostel" is read as the Blooms' house in Eccles Street, then Shaun can be taken as denying that there is an "A" in that house—for all her afternoon activity with Boylan, Molly Bloom doesn't deserve the scarlet letter. This is reinforced by Yawn's next response—a vowels-only version of "Finn's Hotel" (514: 18); Finn's hotel is the place at which Nora Barnacle worked as a chambermaid when Joyce met her.

33. In this portmanteau word, I find the suggestion that the style of analysis to which Yawn is being subjected will ultimately "soak loose" the dirt inside him, and leave him "one". In other words, it will be the process through which the dreamer will at last discover the adequate identity for which he has been searching.

34. Besides the forgiving tone, the voice is easily associated with ALP through an allusion to Molly Bloom's final monologue (526: 20; *Ulysses*, 757).

35. Sackerson offers two lines from Ibsen, one of which announces his torpedoing of the Ark (530: 23–4).

36. See Chapter 3 above. The discussion that follows is intended to complement my emphasis there on the outward-directedness of HCE's conception of marriage. Here I am more concerned with the deepest layer within him, the commitment to ALP.

37. See Chapter 3 above, p. 23.

38. "Yeamen" acknowledges that the inquisitors are the peers (yeomen) who should judge him; "flatter" not only has its obvious sense, but also recognize that HCE has flattened himself, compressing layers and smoothing surfaces to present an acceptable image of what he is.

39. All these are attributes HCE shares with Bloom. As so often in the *Wake*, Joyce provides a passing connection: "as you pay in caabman's sheltar" (542: 13–14) recalls Bloom's aid to Stephen in the "Eumaeus" episode of *Ulysses* (and the "tar" alludes to the bragging sailor).

40. "Amusin part" (539: 16) and "Annoyin part" here signal HCE's euphemistic ways of acknowledging that the story he is telling is a mixture of successes and failures, of genuine qualities and flaws. The euphemisms are there because the act of self-revelation continues to be painful.

41. Once again, there is a connection with Bloom. In the catechism of the "Ithaca" section of *Ulysses*, Bloom and Stephen discuss the question, "What to do with our wives." Bloom has thought of a number of solutions, including the parlor games HCE alludes to here; *Ulysses*, 685–6.

42. Not only does the language of the penultimate paragraph point forward to the copulation scene of the next chapter, but Joyce introduces ambiguous language that can connect the carriage to the bed—"poster," "nod," "aroger," "covertly" (III-3; 554: 1, 2, 3, 4).

43. Equally, as I have suggested (n. 33 above), they are the four bedposts who will observe the lovemaking of the next scene. For the moment, however, they are harnessed, caught up in the surging movement of the marriage.

Chapter 19

1. As I noted above (Chapter 2, p. 13 and note 1), the shifts among scenes are often abrupt. My discussion in what follows will aim to discharge my promise to provide a systematic treatment of the chapter, no longer ignoring the apparent digressions I omitted earlier.

2. See Chapter 2 above, p. 21.

3. Here, as in other places in the chapter, HCE and ALP become Mr and Mrs Porter (see, e.g., 560: 22 ff.).

4. It is not hard to see the story of the incident in the park as a dream version of HCE's version of his adolescent daughter urinating; but I don't think anything much is gained by taking this as the "reality" behind this vignette.

5. This line recapitulates an earlier trial, the visit to the "Willingdone Museyroom" in I-1. As they emerge, the visitors appropriately express the fact that they have had a "warm time": "Phew!" (10: 25, 24). On both occasions the warmth derives from the effort expended in responding to a threat.

6. See the discussion in Chapter 2 above, pp. 19–20. I also rely on the interpretation of the descent of the stair and the shadow play on the blind that I presented in Chapter 2 (pp. 16–18).

7. Presumably, the speaker is another version of Shaun, again conspiring with Shem ("Jimmy") to denounce the father. Since he has been dominant in this part of the *Wake*, and since he and Shem reversed roles in III-2, it is appropriate that he leads the way (as Shem/Butt did in II-3). The third member of the trio can be taken to be a version of HCE, whom we have seen to be self-accusing.

8. I interpret this speech as a direct counterblast to HCE's apologia in III-3. It poses this chapter's last major challenge to the affirmation the dreamer seeks.

9. I find the reference to "three golden balls" suggestive. This classic symbol of pawnbrokers' shops associates HCE with the hatred for usury, usurers, and Jews expressed in *Ulysses*, and, once again, links him to Bloom.

10. The marriage bed, and the activities within it, are supposed to be viewed sequentially, from the four bedposts, each identified with an evangelist. The final one, much the shortest, is assigned to "johnny" (590: 23).

11. Of course, the skeptical question—"Has it come too easily?"—can arise again even here. Joyce has one last reply to it, leading us through the bitter turn and overcoming of the final monologue. That, too, could be questioned—one can always question. So the *Wake* goes round and round, giving the dreamer renewed opportunities for raising doubts and allaying them—until, perhaps, we come to feel

the force of the motion that runs through HCE's life and conclude that we have doubted enough.

Chapter 20

1. I began in Chapter 1 with this monologue *out* of context. As with the discussion of III-4, I intend to add a new perspective to my initial reading.

2. I confess that, on my first few readings of the complete *Wake*, I found this section the most puzzling—and frustrating—part of the book. It seemed more of the old material, superseded by the thematic development of Part III, and hence eminently worthy of omission. As I shall suggest in what follows, it is indeed more of the same—that is precisely the point—and, because the dreamer needs more of the same, it cannot be left out.

3. Joyce's influence on Beckett can again be heard in the opening line of *Murphy:* "The sun shone, having no alternative, on the nothing new."

4. The urge to make a new beginning and to try again for a goal previously dismissed as out of reach may be intensified by the thought that time is running out. Joyce already prefigures some of the urgency ALP feels by identifying the time in terms of the span that is left to "Grossguy and Littleylady" (598: 30–4), as if it were a countdown to the end.

5. Kevin was, of course, the "nicechild" in the nursey (555: 16); here he rhymes, appropriately, with "heaven."

6. As we have seen, there is a crosstalk act at the center of the scene in the bar, where HCE is vilified and defeated (II-3). An earlier dialogue occurs in the opening chapter (16–18).

7. There is a hilarious P.S., in which ALP points to particular ways in which she hopes for improvement. She declares herself "fetted up now with nonsery reams. And rigs out in regal rooms with the ritzies." (619: 17–18). These are obviously Nora's complaints about her husband's preoccupation with the *Wake* and their constant living in hotels (without a home of their own).

8. Joyce's "exsogerraider" also alludes to HCE's status as an outsider and to the hostile vision of him as a Viking "raider."

9. See above, p. 9.

10. I take the "heathery benn" to be Howth, where Bloom and Molly first made love; the awaited letter is presumably to play the vindicating role assigned to it throughout the *Wake;* the water of the ocean (as in the vignette of "most holy Kevin") is to cleanse.

11. So she judges, against the attempted deflection of the previous chapter, that "Pepigi's pact" was *not* "pure piffle" (576: 6). ALP's image of the unlocking of her heart has been anticipated earlier in Issy's contribution to the quiz show (148: 32).

Chapter 21

1. As I suggested in the last chapter, this serves his purpose of exposing the yearning for renewal and improvement. Similarly, the interruptions to the

central vignette of III-4 are designed as parts of the trial in which the dreamer is engaged.

2. Also within smaller units of thematic expression—for example, 336: 12–18; 606: 4–12; and 621: 8–17. Joyce presents the same thematic movement at a number of different scales.

3. Charles Darwin, *Autobiography*, edited by Nora Barlow (London: Collins, 1958).

4. Recalling the ferocity of his attack on the deceptions of artists (*Republic*, Books III and X), it is amusing to speculate that Plato might have viewed Joyce, rather than many of the eminences of twentieth-century philosophy, as one of his most dangerous competitors.

5. John Dewey, *Experience and Nature* (New York: Dover, 1958, 432). Similar views occur throughout Dewey's writings (see, for example, *Human Nature and Conduct* [Amherst NY: Prometheus Books, 2002], p. 155), and parts of *Art as Experience* can be read as an attempt to develop an explanation of how the artistic exploration of value works.

6. The phrase is Mill's; see *On Liberty*. It seems to me that the experimental attitude is more thoroughly developed by Dewey.

7. The most prominent founders of the tradition are David Hume (*Enquiry Concerning the Principles of Morals*) and, especially, Adam Smith (*Theory of Moral Sentiments*).

8. In this formulation, I would connect Joyce to a specifically pragmatist version of the tradition, one that has freed itself from the desire for an ultimate overarching principle (like Hume's appeal to utility and agreeableness). I read Joyce as having an inchoate version of a philosophical position that combines elements in Smith with elements in Dewey. For an attempt to develop a position of this type, see my essay "The Hall of Mirrors" (*Proceedings and Addresses of the American Philosophical Association*, November 2005).

9. For more on these potential problems, see "The Hall of Mirrors" (cited in n. 8).

10. The last words of *The Waste Land*—"Shantih. Shantih. Shantih."—are heard several times in the *Wake*, sometimes with simultaneous allusion to the Christian "Sanctus. Sanctus. Sanctus." (See, for example, the adoration of Chuff [235: 9]; Jaun's grimly apocalyptic prediction [454: 33]; and the illusory hope for a new beginning [593: 1]). In each instance, the promise of any transcendent consolation, or any transcendent answer to the question "What shall we ever do?" is firmly denied.

11. Readers who find my humanist readings of "The Dead" and of *Ulysses* old-fashioned and misguided may object in particular to my approach to the *Wake*. I owe to an anonymous reader the intriguing thought that humanism may prove *more* apt for reading the *Wake* than for Joyce's earlier writings. Perhaps, this reader suggests, Joyce had learned more about marriage and had become wiser by the time he finished his last novel. From this point of view, one might combine my reading of the *Wake* with a very different vision of the works that preceded it.

12. "The Moral Philosopher and the Moral Life," in *The Will to Believe* (New York: Dover, 1956), 211.

13. *Ibid.*, 213.

14. *Endgame,* New York: Grove Press, 68.

15. In thinking about this possible interpretation, I am indebted to conversations with David Albert.

16. As is proper, it is also included in the children's schoolbook (261: 31–262: 1).

INDEX OF PASSAGES

Passages from *Finnegans Wake* are cited in standard Roman font to the left of the colon. The pages on which they are discussed are given in italics to the right of the colon. Principal discussions are highlighted in bold.

INDEX OF NAMES

Made in the USA
Middletown, DE
30 January 2017